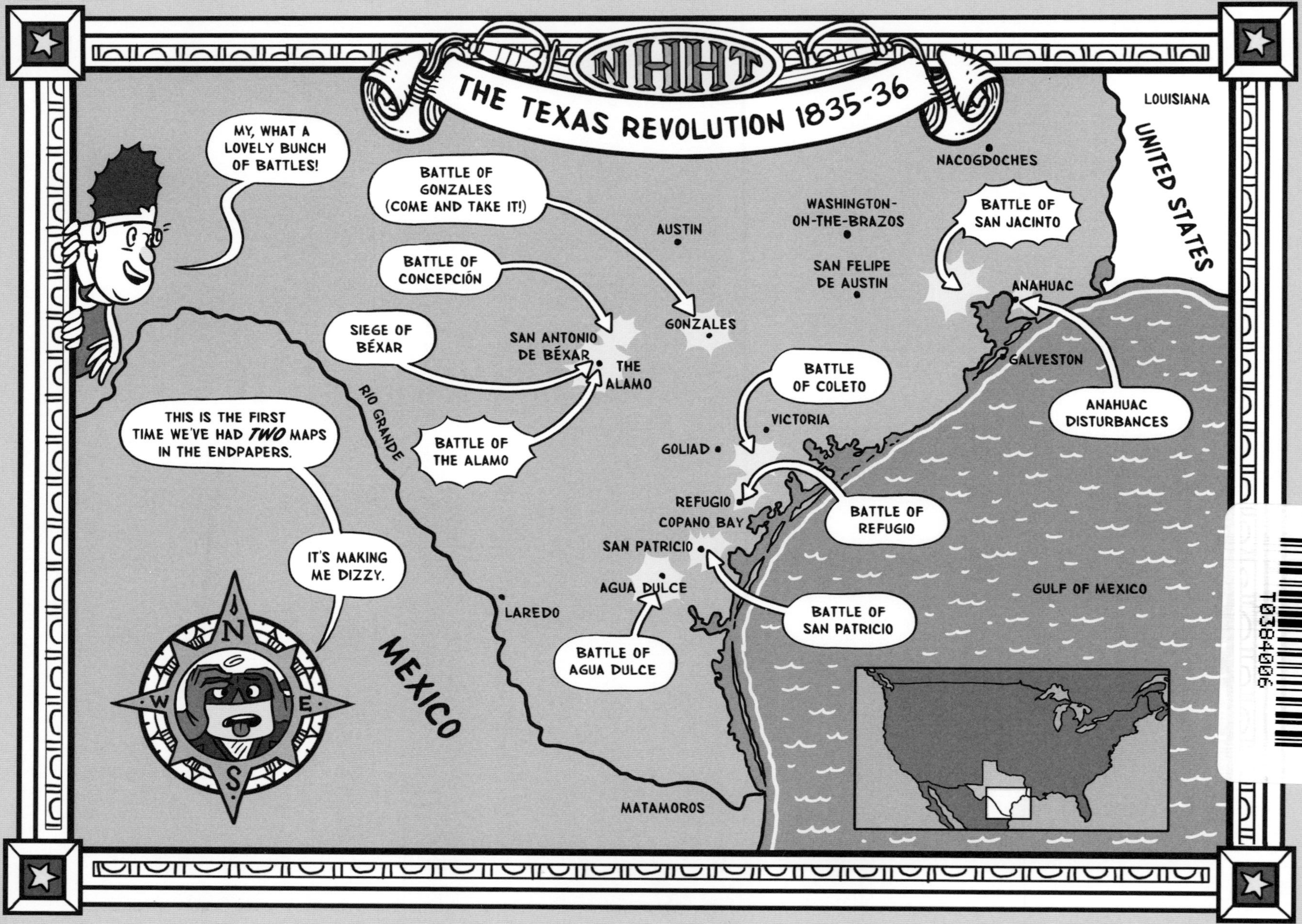
NHHT
THE TEXAS REVOLUTION 1835-36
MY, WHAT A LOVELY BUNCH OF BATTLES!
BATTLE OF GONZALES (COME AND TAKE IT!)
BATTLE OF CONCEPCIÓN
SIEGE OF BÉXAR
BATTLE OF THE ALAMO
THIS IS THE FIRST TIME WE'VE HAD *TWO* MAPS IN THE ENDPAPERS.
IT'S MAKING ME DIZZY.
N
E
S
W
RIO GRANDE
MEXICO
LAREDO
SAN ANTONIO DE BÉXAR
THE ALAMO
AUSTIN
GONZALES
WASHINGTON-ON-THE-BRAZOS
SAN FELIPE DE AUSTIN
NACOGDOCHES
LOUISIANA
UNITED STATES
BATTLE OF SAN JACINTO
ANAHUAC
GALVESTON
ANAHUAC DISTURBANCES
BATTLE OF COLETO
VICTORIA
GOLIAD
REFUGIO
COPANO BAY
BATTLE OF REFUGIO
SAN PATRICIO
AGUA DULCE
BATTLE OF AGUA DULCE
BATTLE OF SAN PATRICIO
GULF OF MEXICO
MATAMOROS

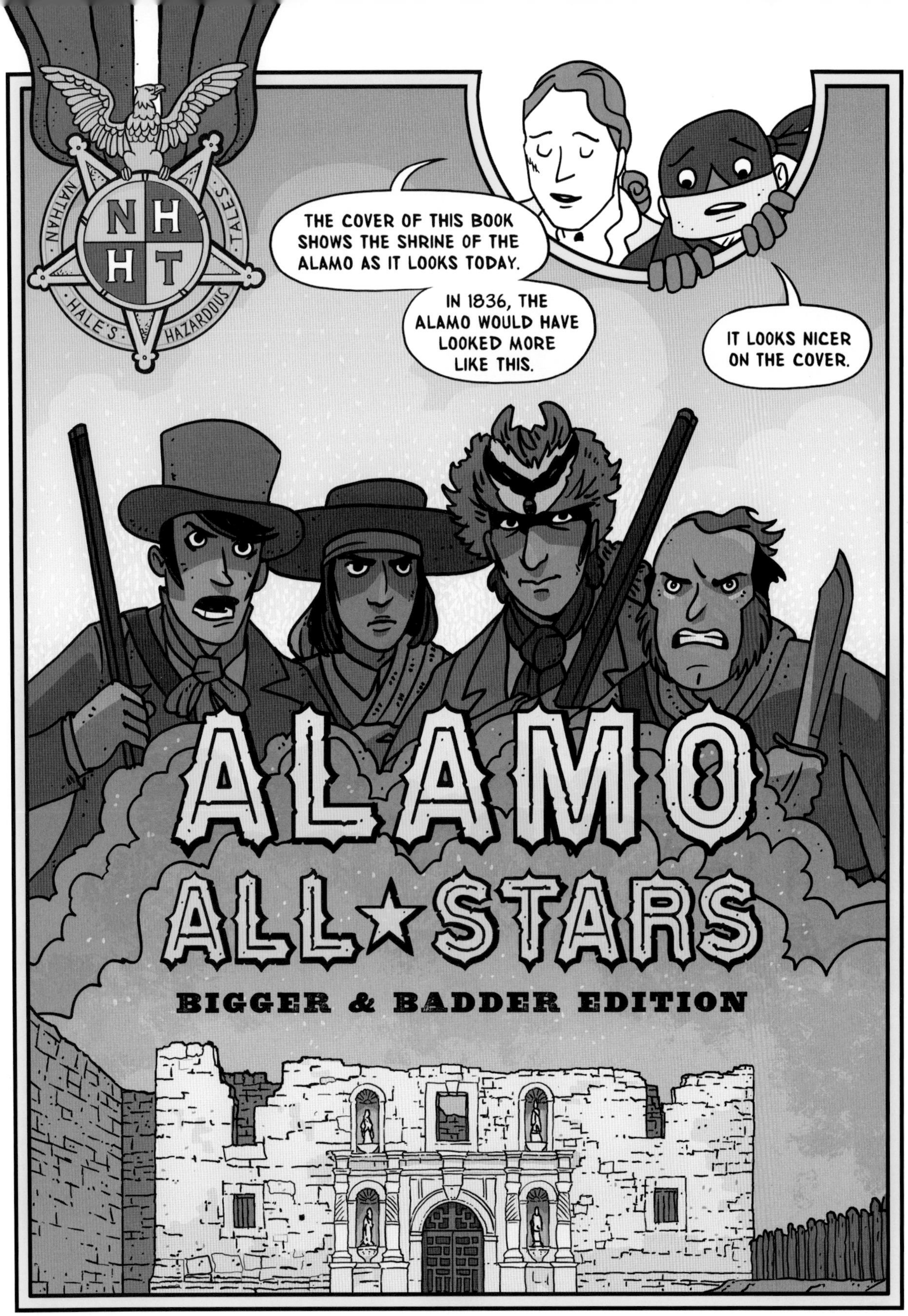
NATHAN HALE'S HAZARDOUS TALES
NH
HT
THE COVER OF THIS BOOK SHOWS THE SHRINE OF THE ALAMO AS IT LOOKS TODAY.
IN 1836, THE ALAMO WOULD HAVE LOOKED MORE LIKE THIS.
IT LOOKS NICER ON THE COVER.
ALAMO ALL★STARS
BIGGER & BADDER EDITION

AMULET BOOKS, NEW YORK

LIBRARY OF CONGRESS CONTROL NUMBER FOR THE 2016 HARDCOVER: 2015916055
ISBN FOR THE 2016 HARDCOVER: 978-1-4197-1902-8
ISBN FOR THE 2019 BIGGER & BADDER EDITION: 978-1-4197-3794-7

TEXT AND ILLUSTRATIONS COPYRIGHT © 2016, 2019 NATHAN HALE
BOOK DESIGN BY NATHAN HALE AND MAX TEMESCU
ORIGINAL BOOK DESIGN BY NATHAN HALE AND CHAD W. BECKERMAN

PRINTED AND BOUND IN CHINA
10 9 8 7 6 5 4

AMULET BOOKS ARE AVAILABLE AT SPECIAL DISCOUNTS WHEN PURCHASED
IN QUANTITY FOR PREMIUMS AND PROMOTIONS AS WELL AS FUNDRAISING OR
EDUCATIONAL USE. SPECIAL EDITIONS CAN ALSO BE CREATED TO SPECIFICATION. FOR
DETAILS, CONTACT SPECIALSALES@ABRAMSBOOKS.COM OR THE ADDRESS BELOW.

AMULET BOOKS® IS A REGISTERED TRADEMARK OF HARRY N. ABRAMS, INC.

ABRAMS The Art of Books
195 Broadway, New York, NY 10007
abramsbooks.com

TO GUS AND CALL,
WHO SPARKED MY INTEREST
IN TEXAS HISTORY

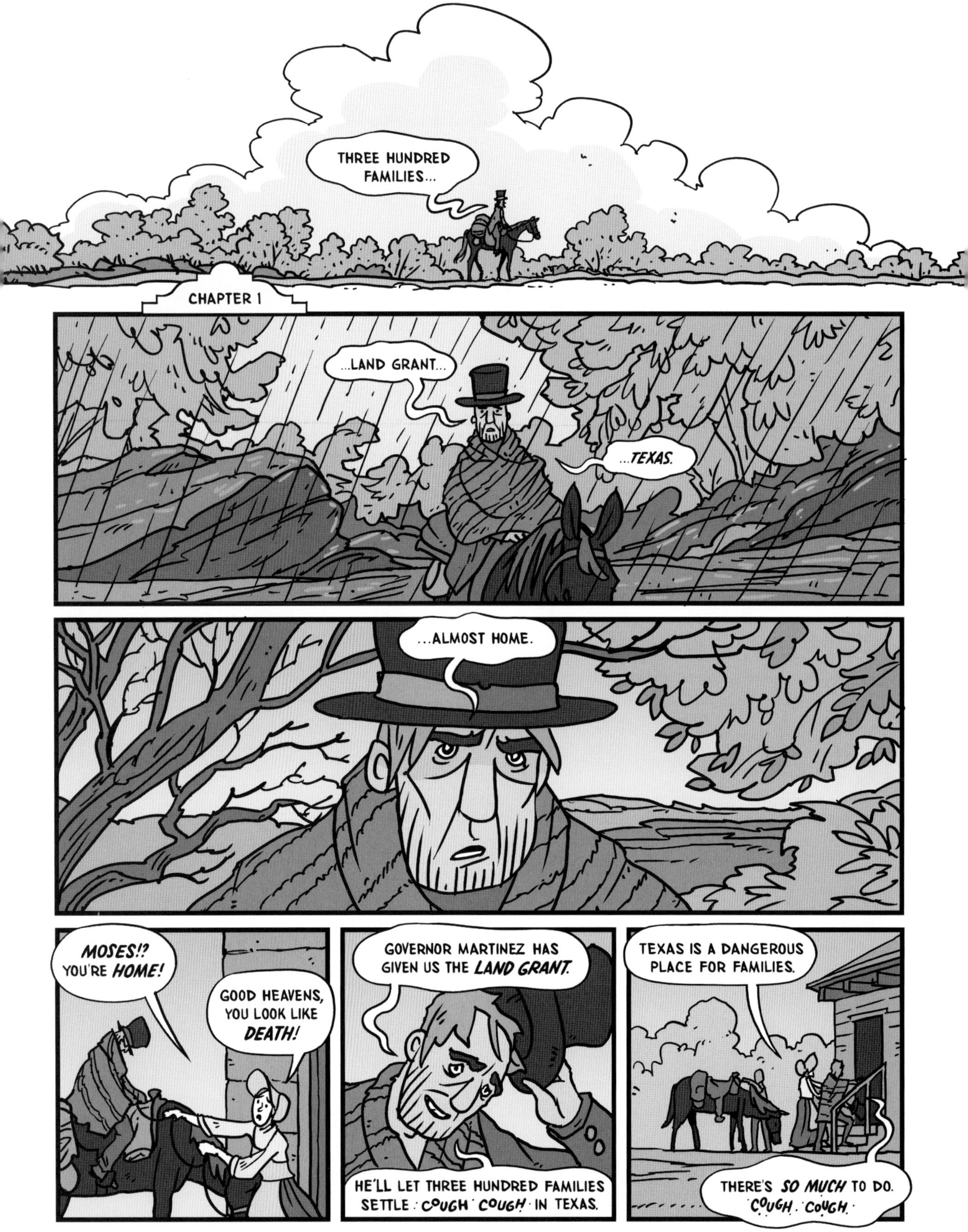
THREE HUNDRED FAMILIES...
CHAPTER 1
...LAND GRANT...
...TEXAS.
...ALMOST HOME.
MOSES!? YOU'RE HOME!
GOOD HEAVENS, YOU LOOK LIKE DEATH!
GOVERNOR MARTINEZ HAS GIVEN US THE LAND GRANT.
HE'LL LET THREE HUNDRED FAMILIES SETTLE COUGH COUGH IN TEXAS.
TEXAS IS A DANGEROUS PLACE FOR FAMILIES.
THERE'S SO MUCH TO DO. COUGH. COUGH.

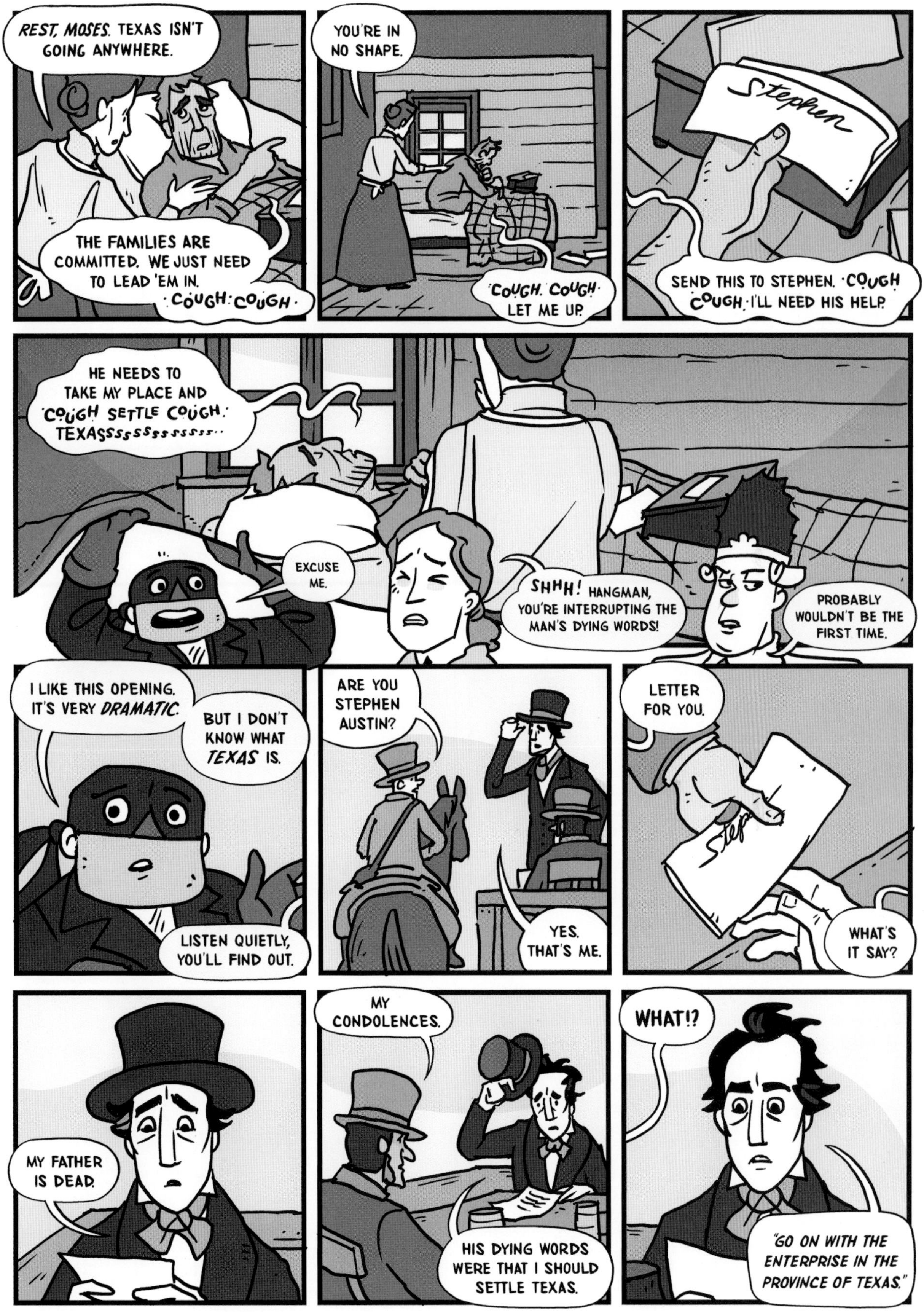
REST, MOSES. TEXAS ISN'T GOING ANYWHERE.
THE FAMILIES ARE COMMITTED. WE JUST NEED TO LEAD 'EM IN.
COUGH COUGH
YOU'RE IN NO SHAPE.
COUGH. COUGH LET ME UP.
Stephen
SEND THIS TO STEPHEN. COUGH COUGH. I'LL NEED HIS HELP.
HE NEEDS TO TAKE MY PLACE AND COUGH SETTLE COUGH. TEXASSSSSSSSSSSSS...
EXCUSE ME.
SHHH! HANGMAN, YOU'RE INTERRUPTING THE MAN'S DYING WORDS!
PROBABLY WOULDN'T BE THE FIRST TIME.
I LIKE THIS OPENING. IT'S VERY DRAMATIC.
BUT I DON'T KNOW WHAT TEXAS IS.
LISTEN QUIETLY, YOU'LL FIND OUT.
ARE YOU STEPHEN AUSTIN?
YES. THAT'S ME.
LETTER FOR YOU.
WHAT'S IT SAY?
MY FATHER IS DEAD.
MY CONDOLENCES.
HIS DYING WORDS WERE THAT I SHOULD SETTLE TEXAS.
WHAT!?
"GO ON WITH THE ENTERPRISE IN THE PROVINCE OF TEXAS."

MEXICAN TERRITORY IS DANGEROUS!

MY FATHER GOT PERMISSION FROM THE MEXICAN GOVERNMENT.

SPAIN OWNS MEXICO. DID HE GET PERMISSION FROM THE SPANISH CROWN?

I DON'T REALLY KNOW.

WHERE ARE YOU GOING?

I'M GONNA GO SETTLE TEXAS.

I STILL DON'T HAVE ANY IDEA WHAT'S GOING ON!

WHO IS THAT GUY?

WHAT IS TEXAS!?

WHY AREN'T YOU EXPLAINING THINGS BETTER?!

WE HAVEN'T INTRODUCED OURSELVES, OR SET UP THE THEME OF THE BOOK OR ANYTHING!

THIS ISN'T HOW WE START THESE BOOKS!

I'M S'POSED TO SAY, "WE HANG SPIES!"

YOUR S'POSED TO SAY, "I'M THE PATRIOT SPY NATHAN HALE AND MY LAST WORDS SENT ME INTO A GIANT MAGICAL HISTORY BOOK!"

AND HE'S S'POSED TO SAY, "HARRUMPH! HARRUMPH! MAGICAL HISTORY BOOKS ARE NONSENSE!"

I'VE NEVER SAID "HARRUMPH."

BUT MAGICAL HISTORY BOOKS ARE NONSENSE.

OH YEAH? THEN WHAT'S THAT!?

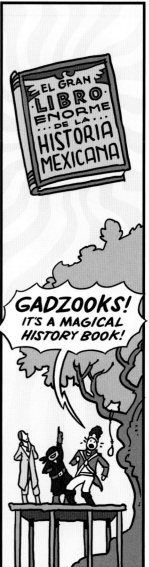

EL GRAN LIBRO ENORME DE LA HISTORIA MEXICANA

GADZOOKS! IT'S A MAGICAL HISTORY BOOK!

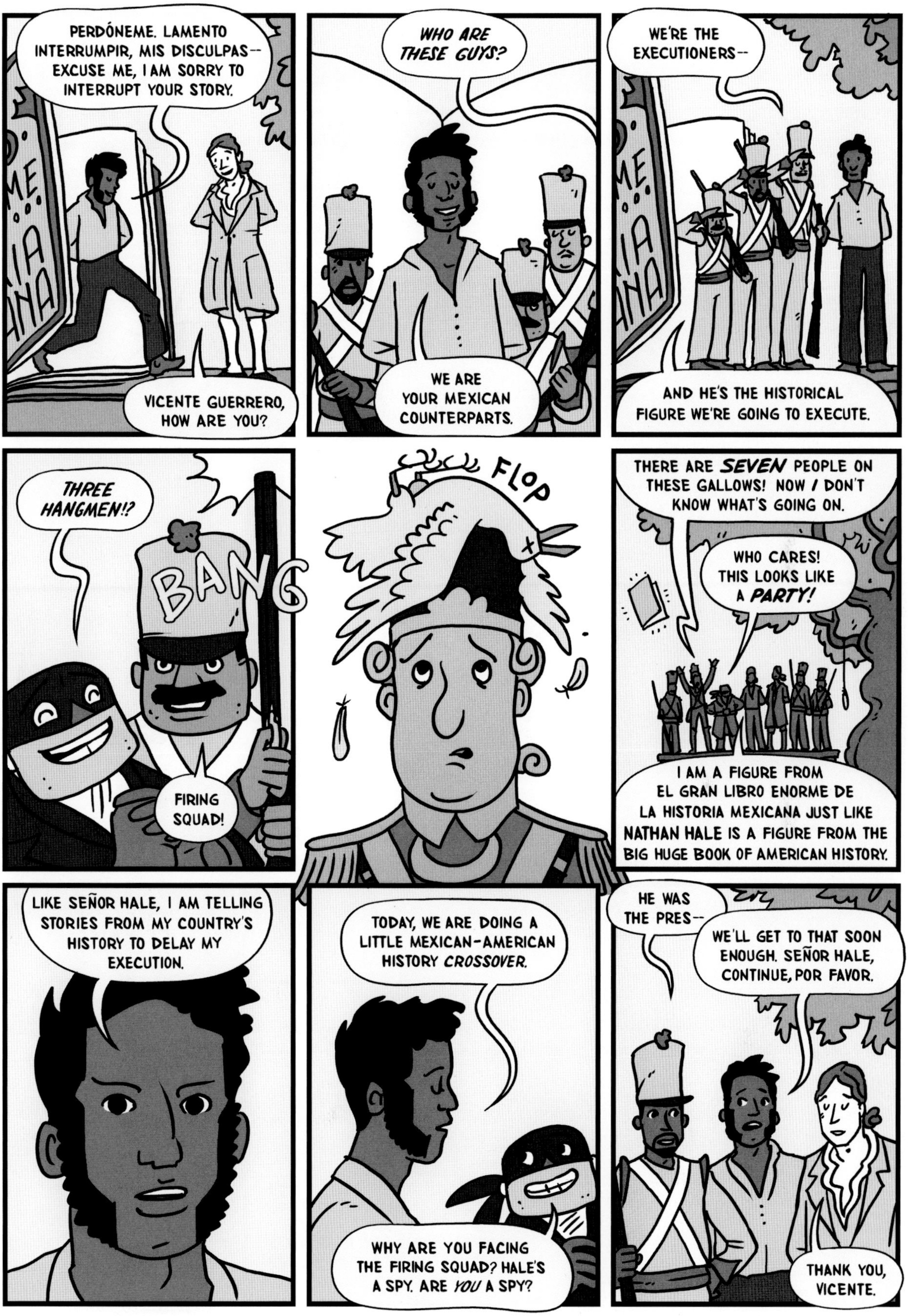
PERDÓNEME. LAMENTO INTERRUMPIR, MIS DISCULPAS-- EXCUSE ME, I AM SORRY TO INTERRUPT YOUR STORY.
VICENTE GUERRERO, HOW ARE YOU?
WHO ARE THESE GUYS?
WE ARE YOUR MEXICAN COUNTERPARTS.
WE'RE THE EXECUTIONERS--
AND HE'S THE HISTORICAL FIGURE WE'RE GOING TO EXECUTE.
THREE HANGMEN!?
BANG
FIRING SQUAD!
FLOP
THERE ARE SEVEN PEOPLE ON THESE GALLOWS! NOW I DON'T KNOW WHAT'S GOING ON.
WHO CARES! THIS LOOKS LIKE A PARTY!
I AM A FIGURE FROM EL GRAN LIBRO ENORME DE LA HISTORIA MEXICANA JUST LIKE NATHAN HALE IS A FIGURE FROM THE BIG HUGE BOOK OF AMERICAN HISTORY.
LIKE SEÑOR HALE, I AM TELLING STORIES FROM MY COUNTRY'S HISTORY TO DELAY MY EXECUTION.
TODAY, WE ARE DOING A LITTLE MEXICAN-AMERICAN HISTORY CROSSOVER.
WHY ARE YOU FACING THE FIRING SQUAD? HALE'S A SPY. ARE YOU A SPY?
HE WAS THE PRES--
WE'LL GET TO THAT SOON ENOUGH. SEÑOR HALE, CONTINUE, POR FAVOR.
THANK YOU, VICENTE.

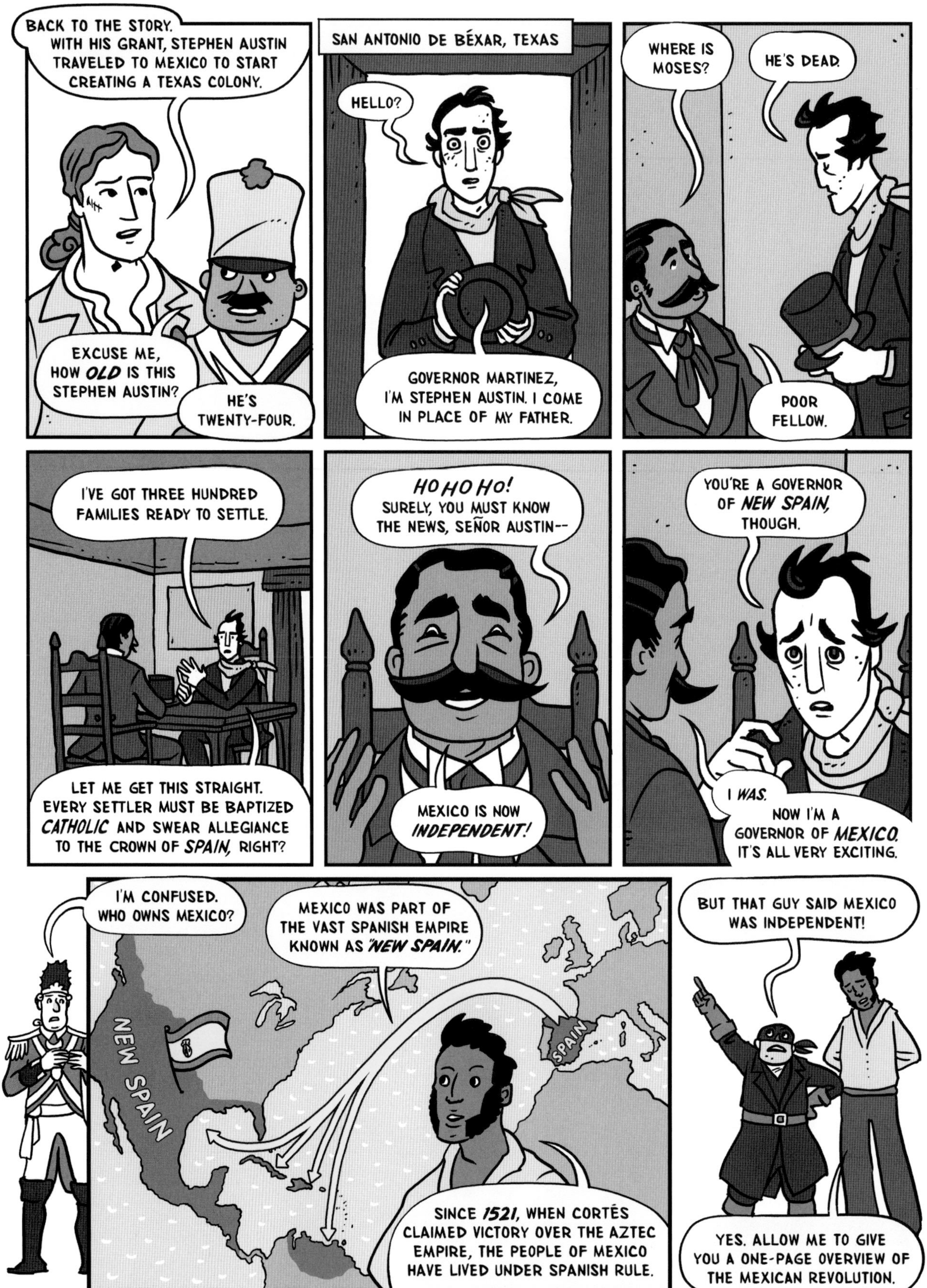
BACK TO THE STORY. WITH HIS GRANT, STEPHEN AUSTIN TRAVELED TO MEXICO TO START CREATING A TEXAS COLONY.
EXCUSE ME, HOW *OLD* IS THIS STEPHEN AUSTIN?
HE'S TWENTY-FOUR.
SAN ANTONIO DE BÉXAR, TEXAS
HELLO?
GOVERNOR MARTINEZ, I'M STEPHEN AUSTIN. I COME IN PLACE OF MY FATHER.
WHERE IS MOSES?
HE'S DEAD.
POOR FELLOW.
I'VE GOT THREE HUNDRED FAMILIES READY TO SETTLE.
LET ME GET THIS STRAIGHT. EVERY SETTLER MUST BE BAPTIZED *CATHOLIC* AND SWEAR ALLEGIANCE TO THE CROWN OF *SPAIN*, RIGHT?
HO HO HO! SURELY, YOU MUST KNOW THE NEWS, SEÑOR AUSTIN--
MEXICO IS NOW *INDEPENDENT!*
YOU'RE A GOVERNOR OF *NEW SPAIN*, THOUGH.
I *WAS*. NOW I'M A GOVERNOR OF *MEXICO*. IT'S ALL VERY EXCITING.
I'M CONFUSED. WHO OWNS MEXICO?
MEXICO WAS PART OF THE VAST SPANISH EMPIRE KNOWN AS *"NEW SPAIN."*
NEW SPAIN
SPAIN
SINCE *1521*, WHEN CORTÉS CLAIMED VICTORY OVER THE AZTEC EMPIRE, THE PEOPLE OF MEXICO HAVE LIVED UNDER SPANISH RULE.
BUT THAT GUY SAID MEXICO WAS INDEPENDENT!
YES. ALLOW ME TO GIVE YOU A ONE-PAGE OVERVIEW OF THE MEXICAN REVOLUTION.

IN *1810*, A CATHOLIC PRIEST NAMED MIGUEL HIDALGO BEGAN TO LEAD THE POOR FARMERS OF MEXICO AGAINST THEIR SPANISH RULERS.

HE WAS CAPTURED, KILLED, AND BEHEADED.

BUT THE SEEDS OF REVOLUTION WERE PLANTED. THE PEOPLE OF MEXICO ROSE UP.

AT FIRST, WE WERE JUST SMALL GUERRILLA GROUPS. BUT WE GREW.

AND GREW.

ON SEPTEMBER 27, *1821*, AFTER A DECADE OF FIGHTING,

AN ARMY OF REBELS AND FORMER ROYALISTS MARCHED INTO MEXICO CITY.

THE NEXT DAY, MEXICO WAS INDEPENDENT.

WE CALLED OURSELVES THE *EJERCITO DE LAS TRES GARANTIAS*

--THE ARMY OF THE THREE GUARANTEES.

I WAS ONE OF THOSE GENERALS.

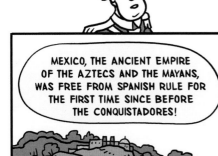

WHAT WERE THE THREE GUARANTEES?

INDEPENDENCE!

UNITY!

THE ROMAN CATHOLIC RELIGION!

WOW!

MEXICO, THE ANCIENT EMPIRE OF THE AZTECS AND THE MAYANS, WAS FREE FROM SPANISH RULE FOR THE FIRST TIME SINCE BEFORE THE CONQUISTADORES!

IT WAS INTO THIS NEWLY LIBERATED, WAR-TORN COUNTRY THAT YOUNG STEPHEN AUSTIN ARRIVED, WITH HIS FATHER'S GRANT.

HELLO?

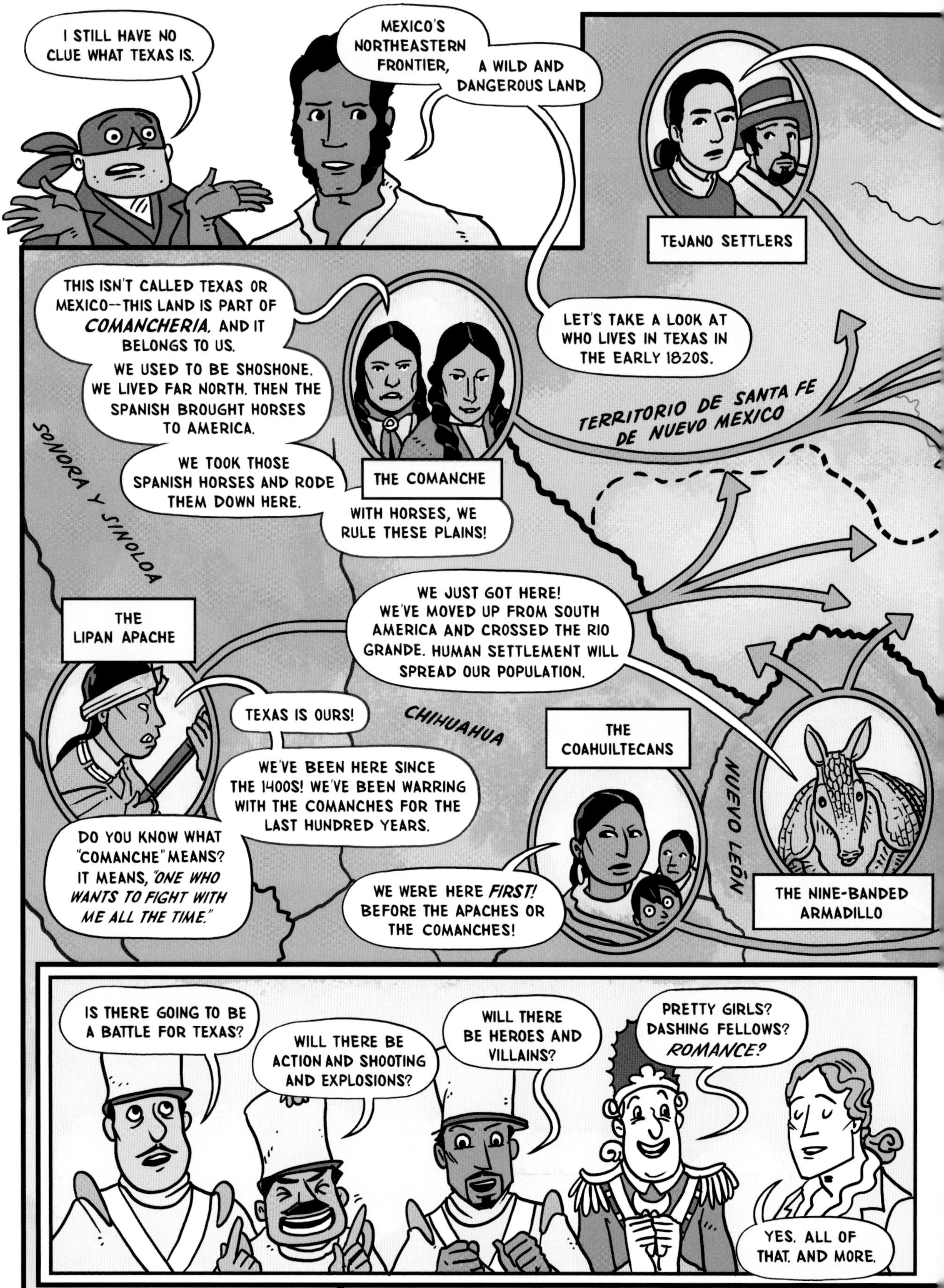
I STILL HAVE NO CLUE WHAT TEXAS IS.
MEXICO'S NORTHEASTERN FRONTIER,
A WILD AND DANGEROUS LAND.
TEJANO SETTLERS
LET'S TAKE A LOOK AT WHO LIVES IN TEXAS IN THE EARLY 1820S.
THIS ISN'T CALLED TEXAS OR MEXICO--THIS LAND IS PART OF *COMANCHERIA*, AND IT BELONGS TO US.
WE USED TO BE SHOSHONE. WE LIVED FAR NORTH. THEN THE SPANISH BROUGHT HORSES TO AMERICA.
WE TOOK THOSE SPANISH HORSES AND RODE THEM DOWN HERE.
WITH HORSES, WE RULE THESE PLAINS!
THE COMANCHE
TERRITORIO DE SANTA FE DE NUEVO MEXICO
SONORA Y SINOLOA
CHIHUAHUA
NUEVO LEÓN
THE LIPAN APACHE
TEXAS IS OURS!
WE'VE BEEN HERE SINCE THE 1400S! WE'VE BEEN WARRING WITH THE COMANCHES FOR THE LAST HUNDRED YEARS.
DO YOU KNOW WHAT "COMANCHE" MEANS? IT MEANS, *"ONE WHO WANTS TO FIGHT WITH ME ALL THE TIME."*
WE JUST GOT HERE! WE'VE MOVED UP FROM SOUTH AMERICA AND CROSSED THE RIO GRANDE. HUMAN SETTLEMENT WILL SPREAD OUR POPULATION.
THE NINE-BANDED ARMADILLO
THE COAHUILTECANS
WE WERE HERE *FIRST!* BEFORE THE APACHES OR THE COMANCHES!
IS THERE GOING TO BE A BATTLE FOR TEXAS?
WILL THERE BE ACTION AND SHOOTING AND EXPLOSIONS?
WILL THERE BE HEROES AND VILLAINS?
PRETTY GIRLS? DASHING FELLOWS? *ROMANCE?*
YES. ALL OF THAT. AND MORE.

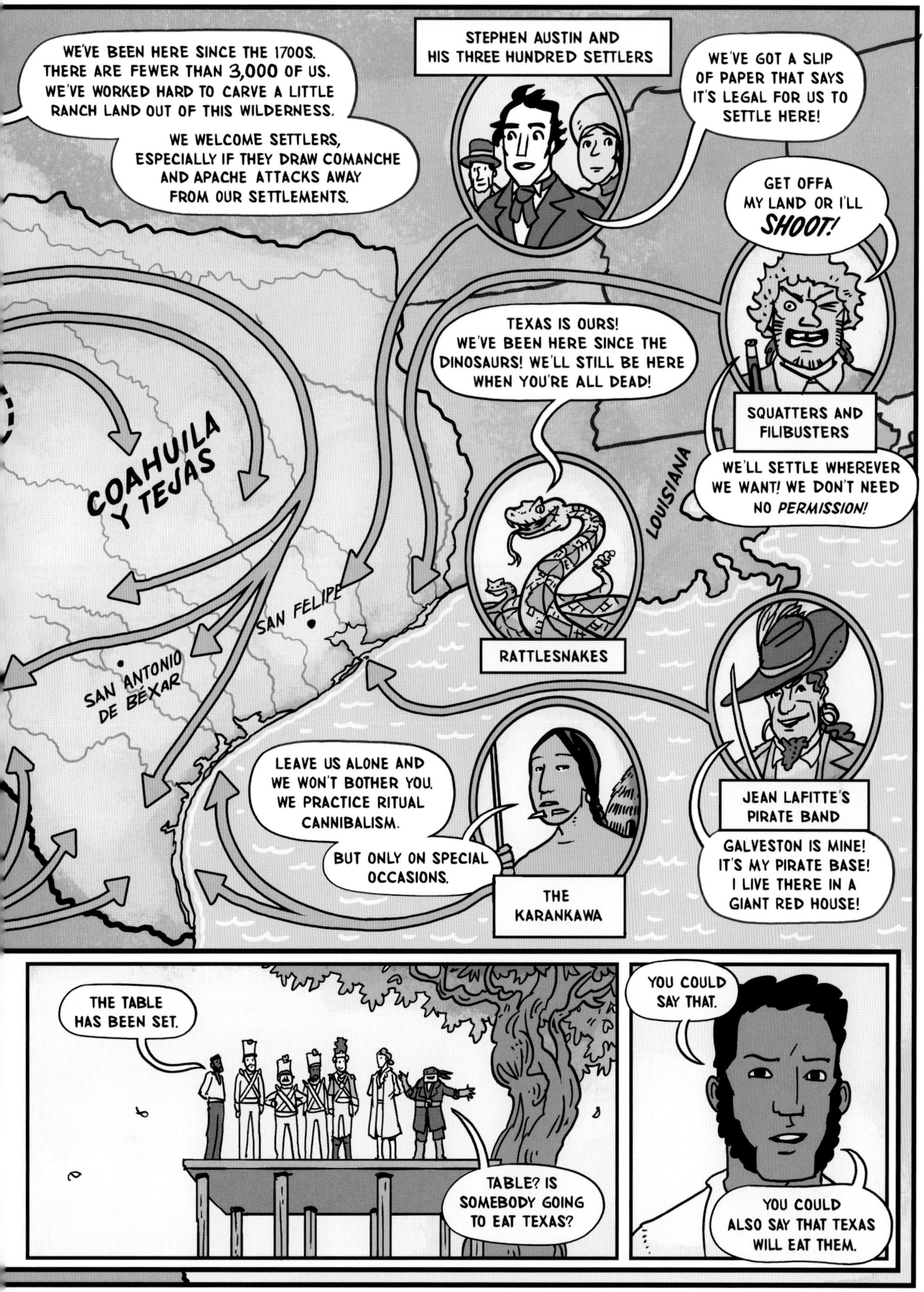
WE'VE BEEN HERE SINCE THE 1700S. THERE ARE FEWER THAN 3,000 OF US. WE'VE WORKED HARD TO CARVE A LITTLE RANCH LAND OUT OF THIS WILDERNESS.
WE WELCOME SETTLERS, ESPECIALLY IF THEY DRAW COMANCHE AND APACHE ATTACKS AWAY FROM OUR SETTLEMENTS.
STEPHEN AUSTIN AND HIS THREE HUNDRED SETTLERS
WE'VE GOT A SLIP OF PAPER THAT SAYS IT'S LEGAL FOR US TO SETTLE HERE!
GET OFFA MY LAND OR I'LL SHOOT!
SQUATTERS AND FILIBUSTERS
WE'LL SETTLE WHEREVER WE WANT! WE DON'T NEED NO PERMISSION!
TEXAS IS OURS! WE'VE BEEN HERE SINCE THE DINOSAURS! WE'LL STILL BE HERE WHEN YOU'RE ALL DEAD!
RATTLESNAKES
COAHUILA Y TEJAS
LOUISIANA
SAN FELIPE
SAN ANTONIO DE BÉXAR
JEAN LAFITTE'S PIRATE BAND
GALVESTON IS MINE! IT'S MY PIRATE BASE! I LIVE THERE IN A GIANT RED HOUSE!
LEAVE US ALONE AND WE WON'T BOTHER YOU. WE PRACTICE RITUAL CANNIBALISM.
BUT ONLY ON SPECIAL OCCASIONS.
THE KARANKAWA
THE TABLE HAS BEEN SET.
TABLE? IS SOMEBODY GOING TO EAT TEXAS?
YOU COULD SAY THAT.
YOU COULD ALSO SAY THAT TEXAS WILL EAT THEM.

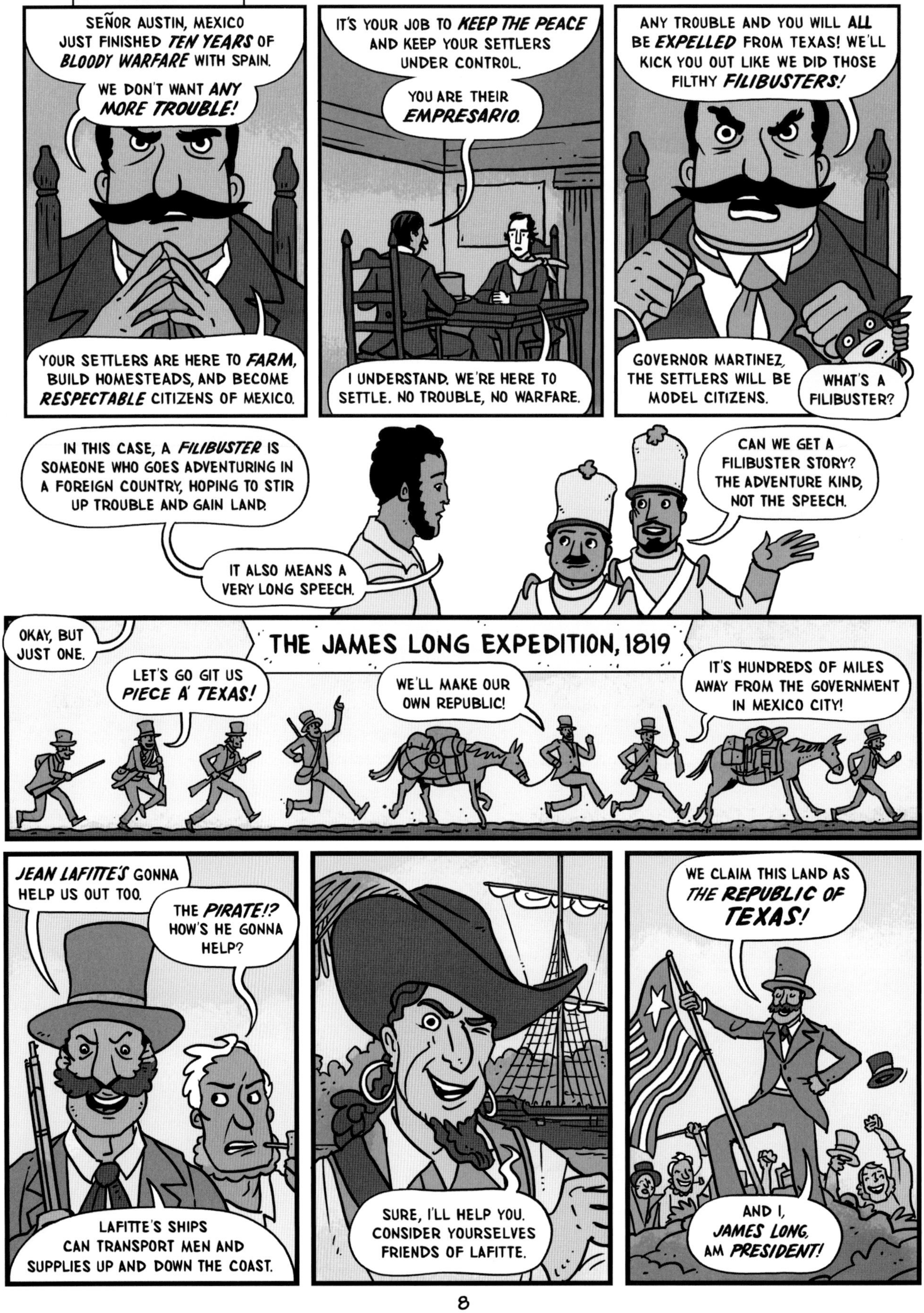
SEÑOR AUSTIN, MEXICO JUST FINISHED TEN YEARS OF BLOODY WARFARE WITH SPAIN.
WE DON'T WANT ANY MORE TROUBLE!
YOUR SETTLERS ARE HERE TO FARM, BUILD HOMESTEADS, AND BECOME RESPECTABLE CITIZENS OF MEXICO.
IT'S YOUR JOB TO KEEP THE PEACE AND KEEP YOUR SETTLERS UNDER CONTROL.
YOU ARE THEIR EMPRESARIO.
I UNDERSTAND. WE'RE HERE TO SETTLE. NO TROUBLE, NO WARFARE.
ANY TROUBLE AND YOU WILL ALL BE EXPELLED FROM TEXAS! WE'LL KICK YOU OUT LIKE WE DID THOSE FILTHY FILIBUSTERS!
GOVERNOR MARTINEZ, THE SETTLERS WILL BE MODEL CITIZENS.
WHAT'S A FILIBUSTER?
IN THIS CASE, A FILIBUSTER IS SOMEONE WHO GOES ADVENTURING IN A FOREIGN COUNTRY, HOPING TO STIR UP TROUBLE AND GAIN LAND.
IT ALSO MEANS A VERY LONG SPEECH.
CAN WE GET A FILIBUSTER STORY? THE ADVENTURE KIND, NOT THE SPEECH.
OKAY, BUT JUST ONE.
THE JAMES LONG EXPEDITION, 1819
LET'S GO GIT US PIECE A' TEXAS!
WE'LL MAKE OUR OWN REPUBLIC!
IT'S HUNDREDS OF MILES AWAY FROM THE GOVERNMENT IN MEXICO CITY!
JEAN LAFITTE'S GONNA HELP US OUT TOO.
THE PIRATE!? HOW'S HE GONNA HELP?
LAFITTE'S SHIPS CAN TRANSPORT MEN AND SUPPLIES UP AND DOWN THE COAST.
SURE, I'LL HELP YOU. CONSIDER YOURSELVES FRIENDS OF LAFITTE.
WE CLAIM THIS LAND AS THE REPUBLIC OF TEXAS!
AND I, JAMES LONG, AM PRESIDENT!

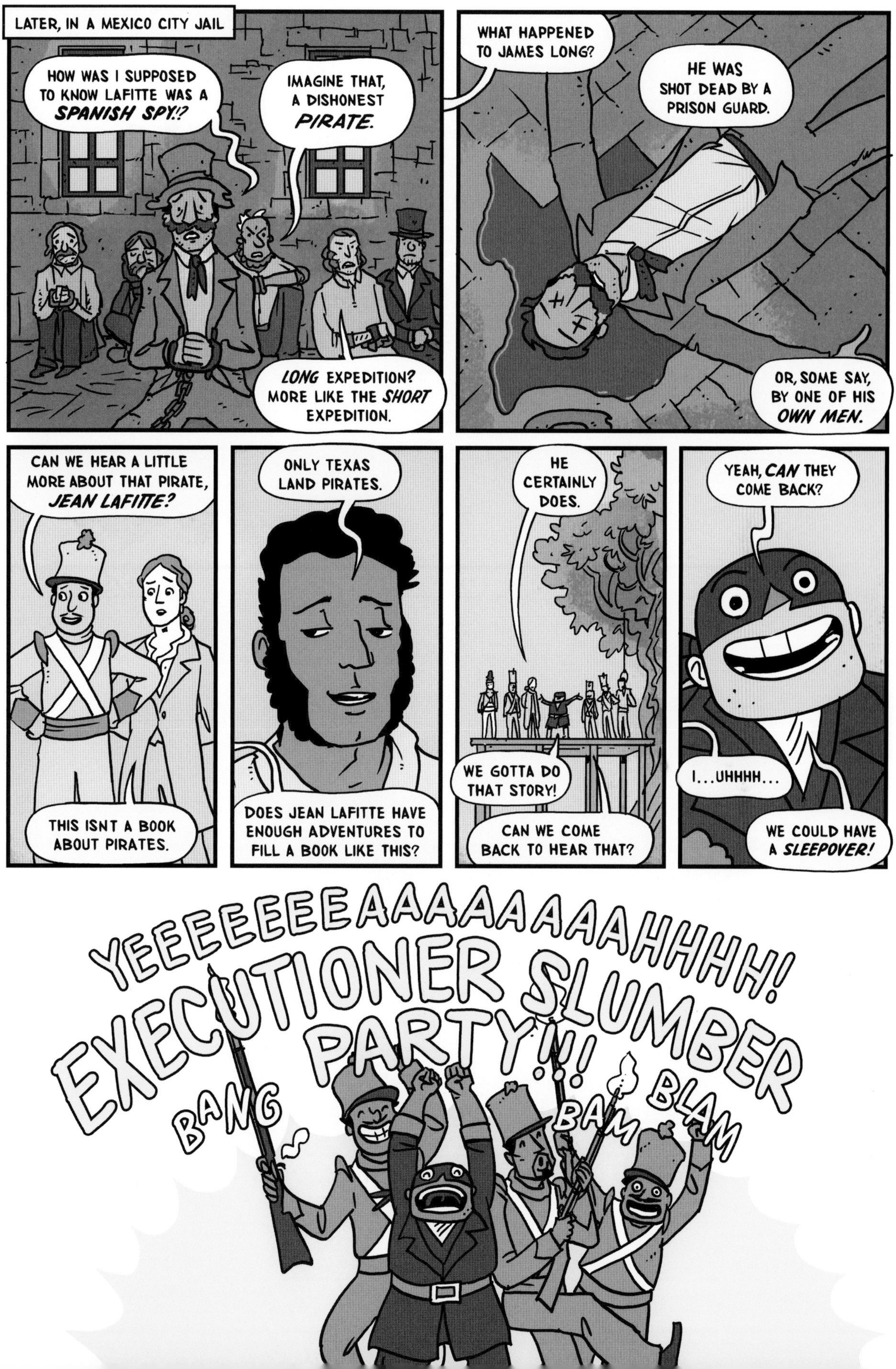
LATER, IN A MEXICO CITY JAIL
HOW WAS I SUPPOSED TO KNOW LAFITTE WAS A SPANISH SPY!?
IMAGINE THAT, A DISHONEST PIRATE.
LONG EXPEDITION? MORE LIKE THE SHORT EXPEDITION.
WHAT HAPPENED TO JAMES LONG?
HE WAS SHOT DEAD BY A PRISON GUARD.
OR, SOME SAY, BY ONE OF HIS OWN MEN.
CAN WE HEAR A LITTLE MORE ABOUT THAT PIRATE, JEAN LAFITTE?
THIS ISNT A BOOK ABOUT PIRATES.
ONLY TEXAS LAND PIRATES.
DOES JEAN LAFITTE HAVE ENOUGH ADVENTURES TO FILL A BOOK LIKE THIS?
HE CERTAINLY DOES.
WE GOTTA DO THAT STORY!
CAN WE COME BACK TO HEAR THAT?
YEAH, CAN THEY COME BACK?
I...UHHHH...
WE COULD HAVE A SLEEPOVER!
YEEEEEEEEAAAAAAAAAAHHHHH!
EXECUTIONER SLUMBER PARTY!!!
BANG
BAM
BLAM

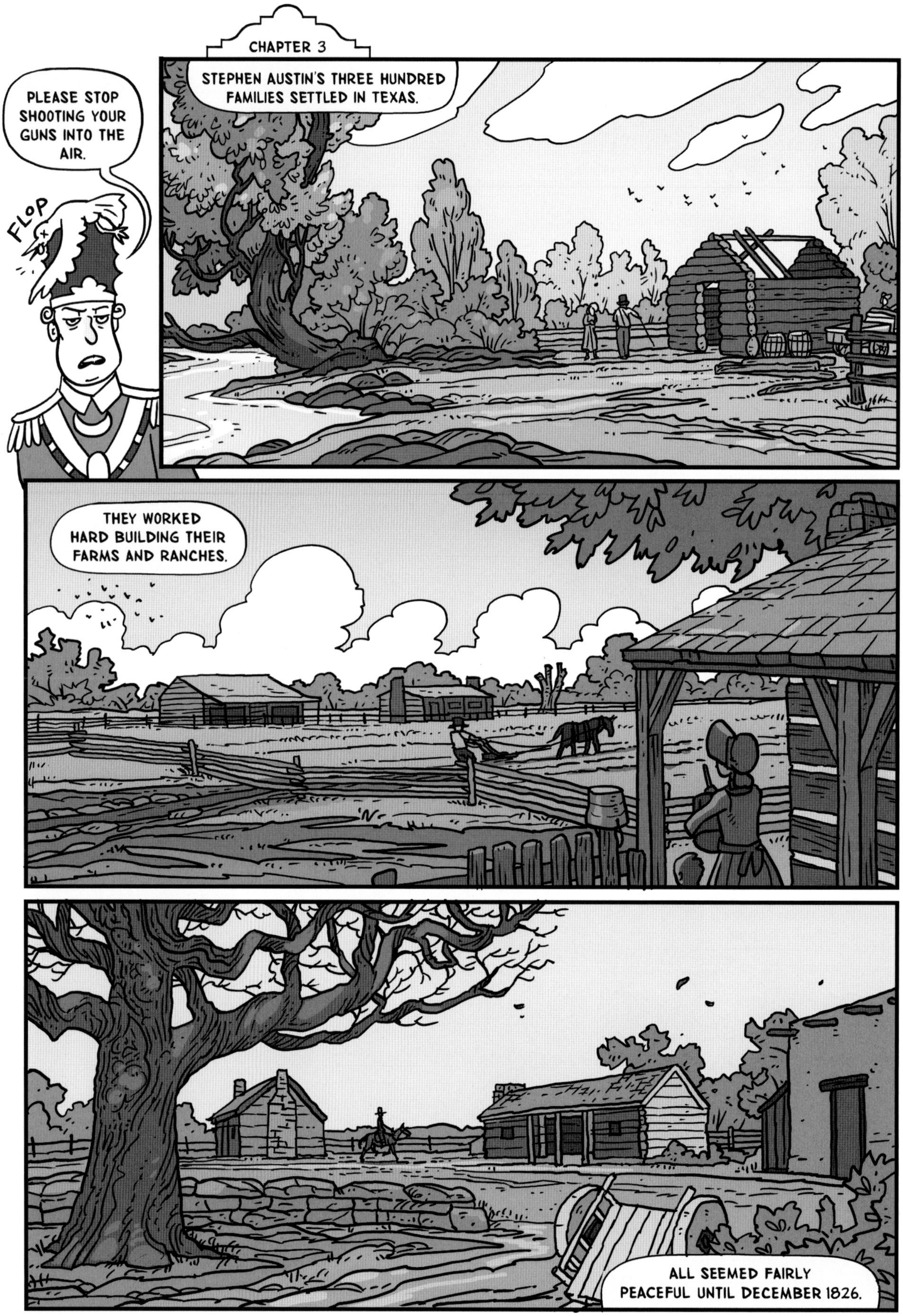
CHAPTER 3
PLEASE STOP SHOOTING YOUR GUNS INTO THE AIR.
FLOP
STEPHEN AUSTIN'S THREE HUNDRED FAMILIES SETTLED IN TEXAS.
THEY WORKED HARD BUILDING THEIR FARMS AND RANCHES.
ALL SEEMED FAIRLY PEACEFUL UNTIL DECEMBER 1826.

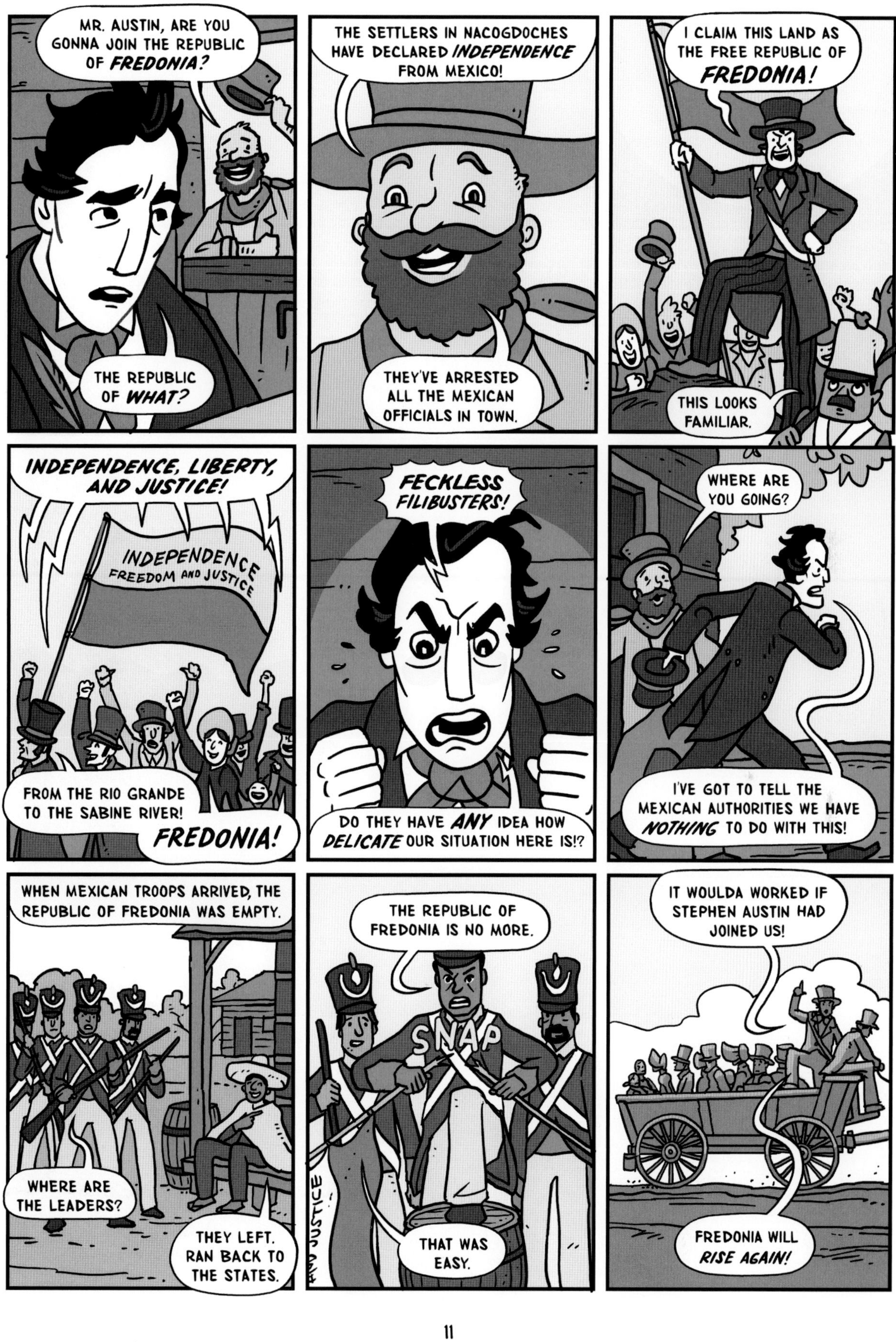
MR. AUSTIN, ARE YOU GONNA JOIN THE REPUBLIC OF FREDONIA?
THE REPUBLIC OF WHAT?
THE SETTLERS IN NACOGDOCHES HAVE DECLARED INDEPENDENCE FROM MEXICO!
THEY'VE ARRESTED ALL THE MEXICAN OFFICIALS IN TOWN.
I CLAIM THIS LAND AS THE FREE REPUBLIC OF FREDONIA!
THIS LOOKS FAMILIAR.
INDEPENDENCE, LIBERTY, AND JUSTICE!
INDEPENDENCE FREEDOM AND JUSTICE
FROM THE RIO GRANDE TO THE SABINE RIVER!
FREDONIA!
FECKLESS FILIBUSTERS!
DO THEY HAVE ANY IDEA HOW DELICATE OUR SITUATION HERE IS!?
WHERE ARE YOU GOING?
I'VE GOT TO TELL THE MEXICAN AUTHORITIES WE HAVE NOTHING TO DO WITH THIS!
WHEN MEXICAN TROOPS ARRIVED, THE REPUBLIC OF FREDONIA WAS EMPTY.
WHERE ARE THE LEADERS?
THEY LEFT. RAN BACK TO THE STATES.
THE REPUBLIC OF FREDONIA IS NO MORE.
SNAP
AND JUSTICE
THAT WAS EASY.
IT WOULDA WORKED IF STEPHEN AUSTIN HAD JOINED US!
FREDONIA WILL RISE AGAIN!

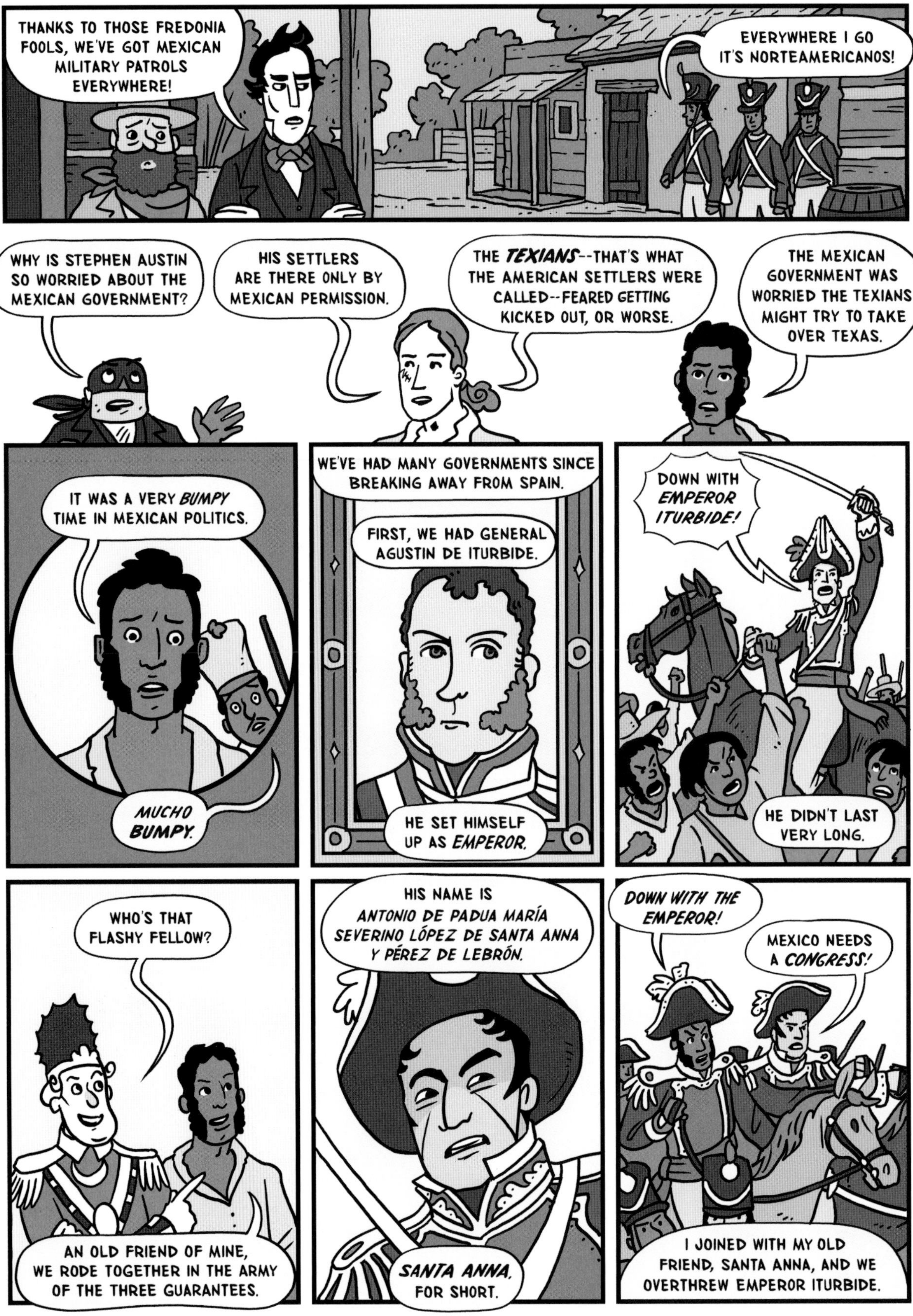
THANKS TO THOSE FREDONIA FOOLS, WE'VE GOT MEXICAN MILITARY PATROLS EVERYWHERE!
EVERYWHERE I GO IT'S NORTEAMERICANOS!
WHY IS STEPHEN AUSTIN SO WORRIED ABOUT THE MEXICAN GOVERNMENT?
HIS SETTLERS ARE THERE ONLY BY MEXICAN PERMISSION.
THE TEXIANS--THAT'S WHAT THE AMERICAN SETTLERS WERE CALLED--FEARED GETTING KICKED OUT, OR WORSE.
THE MEXICAN GOVERNMENT WAS WORRIED THE TEXIANS MIGHT TRY TO TAKE OVER TEXAS.
IT WAS A VERY BUMPY TIME IN MEXICAN POLITICS.
MUCHO BUMPY.
WE'VE HAD MANY GOVERNMENTS SINCE BREAKING AWAY FROM SPAIN.
FIRST, WE HAD GENERAL AGUSTIN DE ITURBIDE.
HE SET HIMSELF UP AS EMPEROR.
DOWN WITH EMPEROR ITURBIDE!
HE DIDN'T LAST VERY LONG.
WHO'S THAT FLASHY FELLOW?
AN OLD FRIEND OF MINE, WE RODE TOGETHER IN THE ARMY OF THE THREE GUARANTEES.
HIS NAME IS ANTONIO DE PADUA MARÍA SEVERINO LÓPEZ DE SANTA ANNA Y PÉREZ DE LEBRÓN.
SANTA ANNA, FOR SHORT.
DOWN WITH THE EMPEROR!
MEXICO NEEDS A CONGRESS!
I JOINED WITH MY OLD FRIEND, SANTA ANNA, AND WE OVERTHREW EMPEROR ITURBIDE.

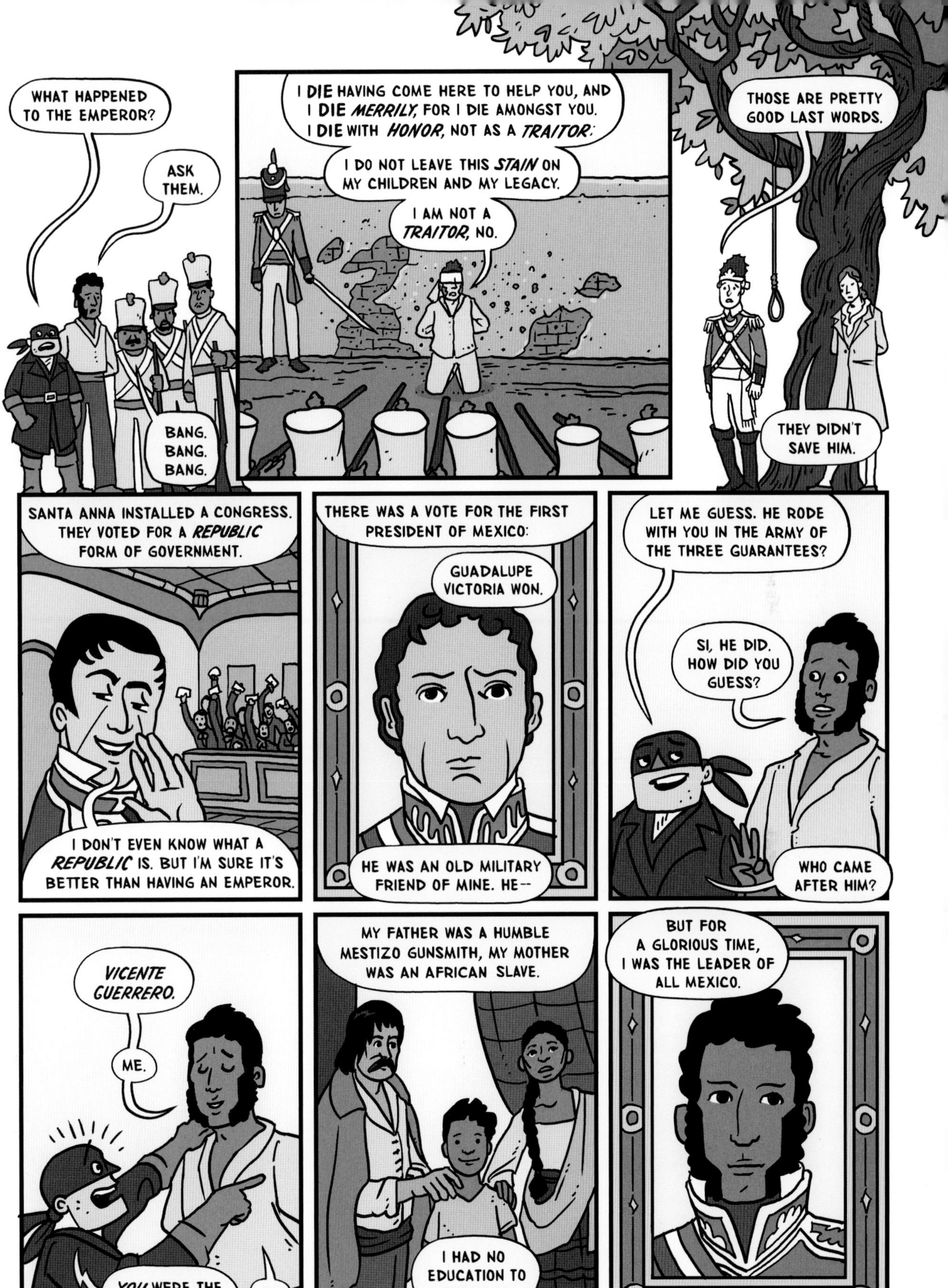

WHAT HAPPENED TO THE EMPEROR?
ASK THEM.
BANG. BANG. BANG.
I DIE HAVING COME HERE TO HELP YOU, AND I DIE MERRILY, FOR I DIE AMONGST YOU. I DIE WITH HONOR, NOT AS A TRAITOR.
I DO NOT LEAVE THIS STAIN ON MY CHILDREN AND MY LEGACY.
I AM NOT A TRAITOR, NO.
THOSE ARE PRETTY GOOD LAST WORDS.
THEY DIDN'T SAVE HIM.
SANTA ANNA INSTALLED A CONGRESS. THEY VOTED FOR A REPUBLIC FORM OF GOVERNMENT.
I DON'T EVEN KNOW WHAT A REPUBLIC IS. BUT I'M SURE IT'S BETTER THAN HAVING AN EMPEROR.
THERE WAS A VOTE FOR THE FIRST PRESIDENT OF MEXICO:
GUADALUPE VICTORIA WON.
HE WAS AN OLD MILITARY FRIEND OF MINE. HE--
LET ME GUESS. HE RODE WITH YOU IN THE ARMY OF THE THREE GUARANTEES?
SI, HE DID. HOW DID YOU GUESS?
WHO CAME AFTER HIM?
VICENTE GUERRERO.
ME.
YOU WERE THE PRESIDENT!?
SI.
MY FATHER WAS A HUMBLE MESTIZO GUNSMITH, MY MOTHER WAS AN AFRICAN SLAVE.
I HAD NO EDUCATION TO SPEAK OF.
BUT FOR A GLORIOUS TIME, I WAS THE LEADER OF ALL MEXICO.

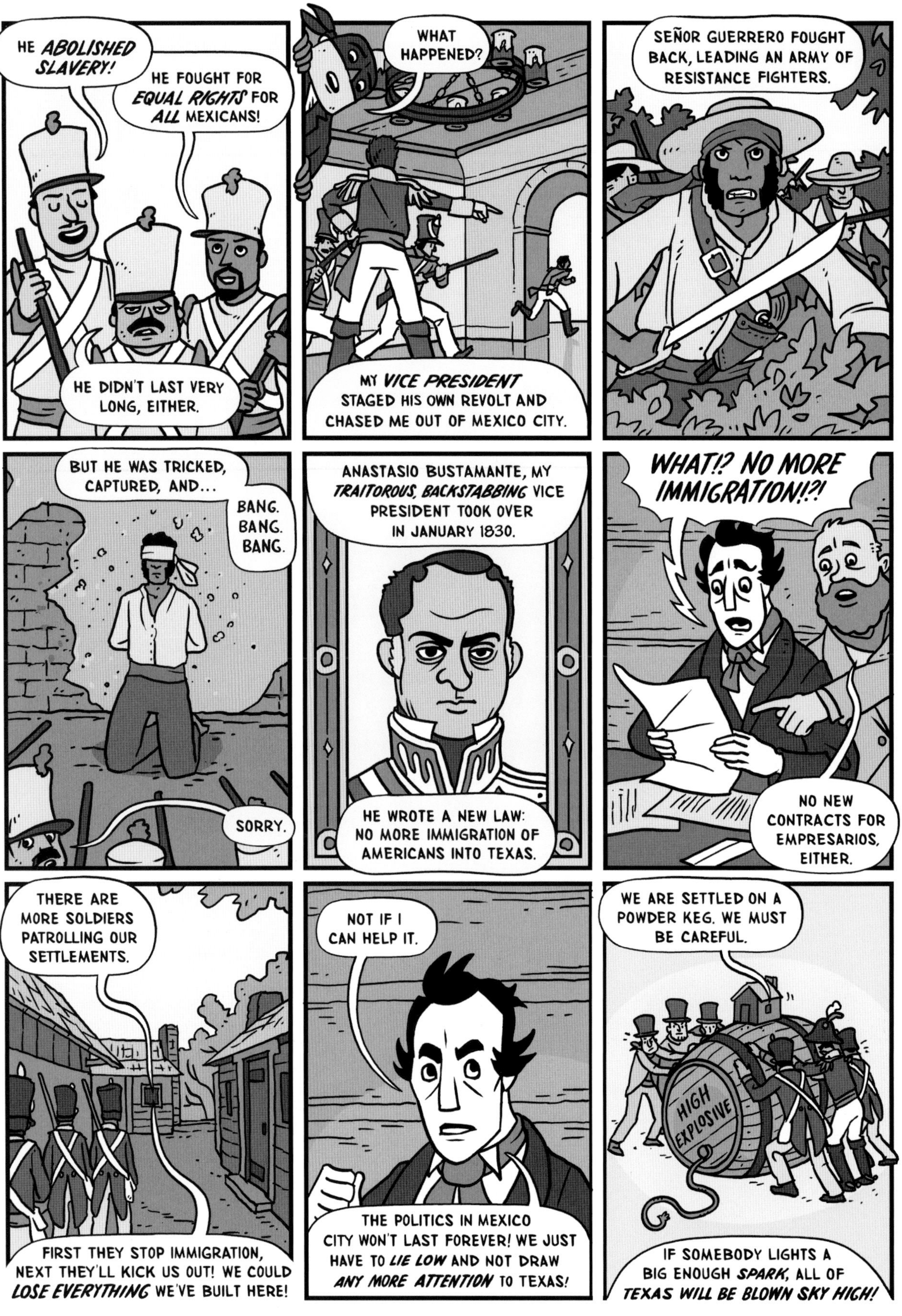
HE ABOLISHED SLAVERY!
HE FOUGHT FOR EQUAL RIGHTS FOR ALL MEXICANS!
HE DIDN'T LAST VERY LONG, EITHER.
WHAT HAPPENED?
MY VICE PRESIDENT STAGED HIS OWN REVOLT AND CHASED ME OUT OF MEXICO CITY.
SEÑOR GUERRERO FOUGHT BACK, LEADING AN ARMY OF RESISTANCE FIGHTERS.
BUT HE WAS TRICKED, CAPTURED, AND...
BANG. BANG. BANG.
SORRY.
ANASTASIO BUSTAMANTE, MY TRAITOROUS, BACKSTABBING VICE PRESIDENT TOOK OVER IN JANUARY 1830.
HE WROTE A NEW LAW: NO MORE IMMIGRATION OF AMERICANS INTO TEXAS.
WHAT!? NO MORE IMMIGRATION!?!
NO NEW CONTRACTS FOR EMPRESARIOS, EITHER.
THERE ARE MORE SOLDIERS PATROLLING OUR SETTLEMENTS.
FIRST THEY STOP IMMIGRATION, NEXT THEY'LL KICK US OUT! WE COULD LOSE EVERYTHING WE'VE BUILT HERE!
NOT IF I CAN HELP IT.
THE POLITICS IN MEXICO CITY WON'T LAST FOREVER! WE JUST HAVE TO LIE LOW AND NOT DRAW ANY MORE ATTENTION TO TEXAS!
WE ARE SETTLED ON A POWDER KEG. WE MUST BE CAREFUL.
HIGH EXPLOSIVE
IF SOMEBODY LIGHTS A BIG ENOUGH SPARK, ALL OF TEXAS WILL BE BLOWN SKY HIGH!

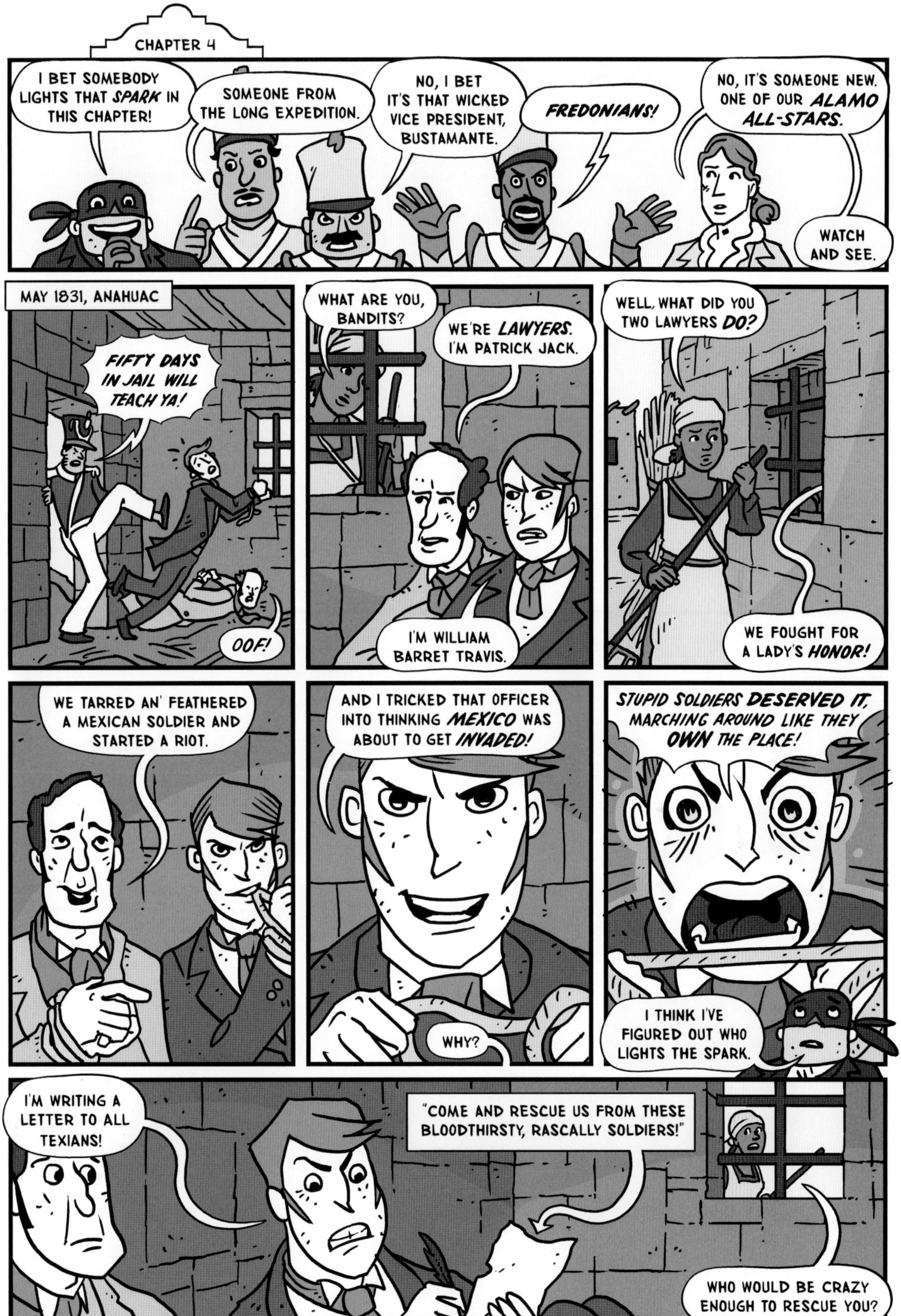
CHAPTER 4
I BET SOMEBODY LIGHTS THAT SPARK IN THIS CHAPTER!
SOMEONE FROM THE LONG EXPEDITION.
NO, I BET IT'S THAT WICKED VICE PRESIDENT, BUSTAMANTE.
FREDONIANS!
NO, IT'S SOMEONE NEW. ONE OF OUR ALAMO ALL-STARS.
WATCH AND SEE.
MAY 1831, ANAHUAC
FIFTY DAYS IN JAIL WILL TEACH YA!
OOF!
WHAT ARE YOU, BANDITS?
WE'RE LAWYERS. I'M PATRICK JACK.
I'M WILLIAM BARRET TRAVIS.
WELL, WHAT DID YOU TWO LAWYERS DO?
WE FOUGHT FOR A LADY'S HONOR!
WE TARRED AN' FEATHERED A MEXICAN SOLDIER AND STARTED A RIOT.
AND I TRICKED THAT OFFICER INTO THINKING MEXICO WAS ABOUT TO GET INVADED!
WHY?
STUPID SOLDIERS DESERVED IT, MARCHING AROUND LIKE THEY OWN THE PLACE!
I THINK I'VE FIGURED OUT WHO LIGHTS THE SPARK.
I'M WRITING A LETTER TO ALL TEXIANS!
"COME AND RESCUE US FROM THESE BLOODTHIRSTY, RASCALLY SOLDIERS!"
WHO WOULD BE CRAZY ENOUGH TO RESCUE YOU?

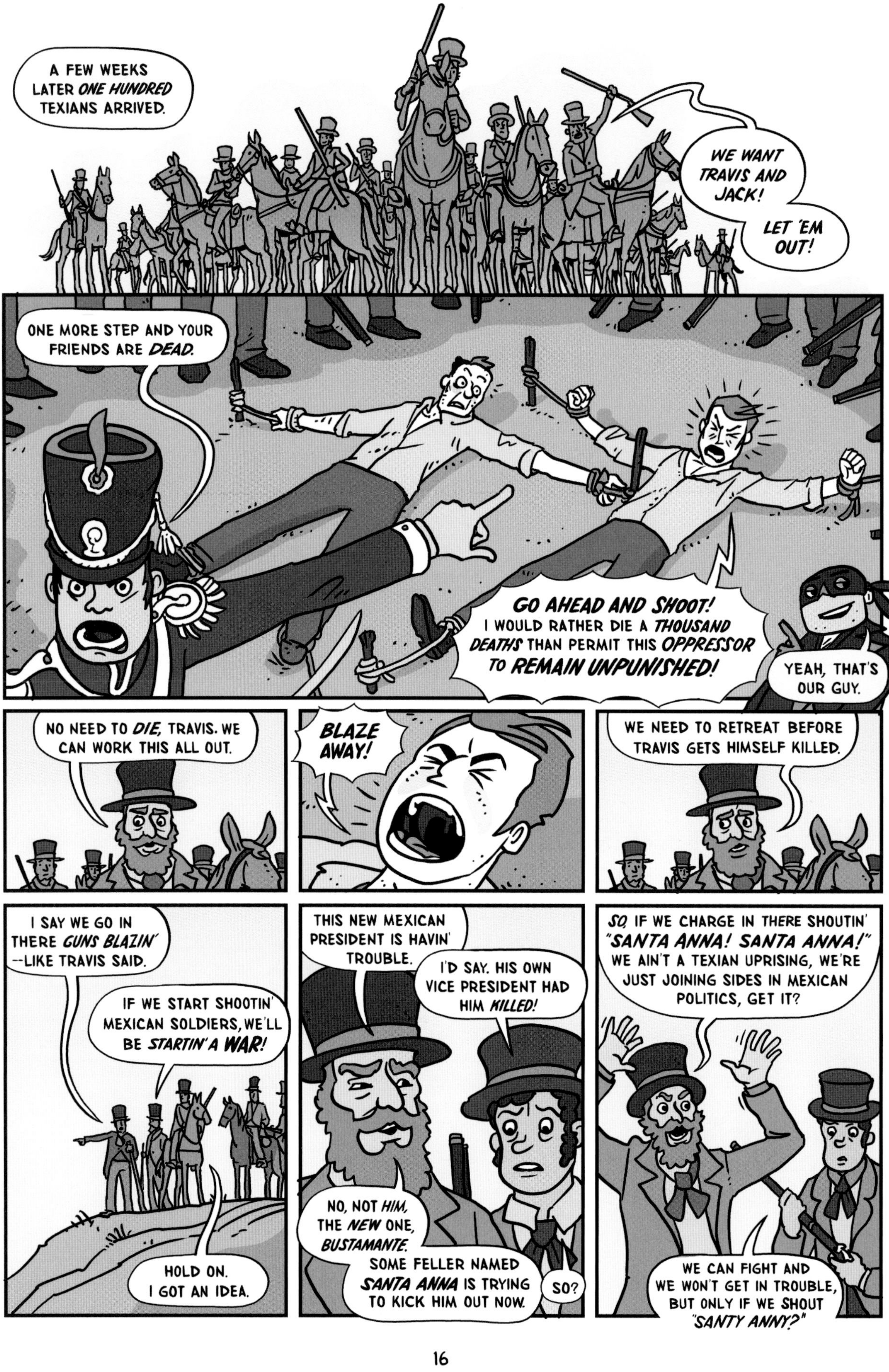
A FEW WEEKS LATER ONE HUNDRED TEXIANS ARRIVED.
WE WANT TRAVIS AND JACK!
LET 'EM OUT!
ONE MORE STEP AND YOUR FRIENDS ARE DEAD.
GO AHEAD AND SHOOT! I WOULD RATHER DIE A THOUSAND DEATHS THAN PERMIT THIS OPPRESSOR TO REMAIN UNPUNISHED!
YEAH, THAT'S OUR GUY.
NO NEED TO DIE, TRAVIS. WE CAN WORK THIS ALL OUT.
BLAZE AWAY!
WE NEED TO RETREAT BEFORE TRAVIS GETS HIMSELF KILLED.
I SAY WE GO IN THERE GUNS BLAZIN' --LIKE TRAVIS SAID.
IF WE START SHOOTIN' MEXICAN SOLDIERS, WE'LL BE STARTIN' A WAR!
HOLD ON. I GOT AN IDEA.
THIS NEW MEXICAN PRESIDENT IS HAVIN' TROUBLE.
I'D SAY. HIS OWN VICE PRESIDENT HAD HIM KILLED!
NO, NOT HIM, THE NEW ONE, BUSTAMANTE.
SOME FELLER NAMED SANTA ANNA IS TRYING TO KICK HIM OUT NOW.
SO?
SO, IF WE CHARGE IN THERE SHOUTIN' "SANTA ANNA! SANTA ANNA!" WE AIN'T A TEXIAN UPRISING, WE'RE JUST JOINING SIDES IN MEXICAN POLITICS, GET IT?
WE CAN FIGHT AND WE WON'T GET IN TROUBLE, BUT ONLY IF WE SHOUT "SANTY ANNY?"

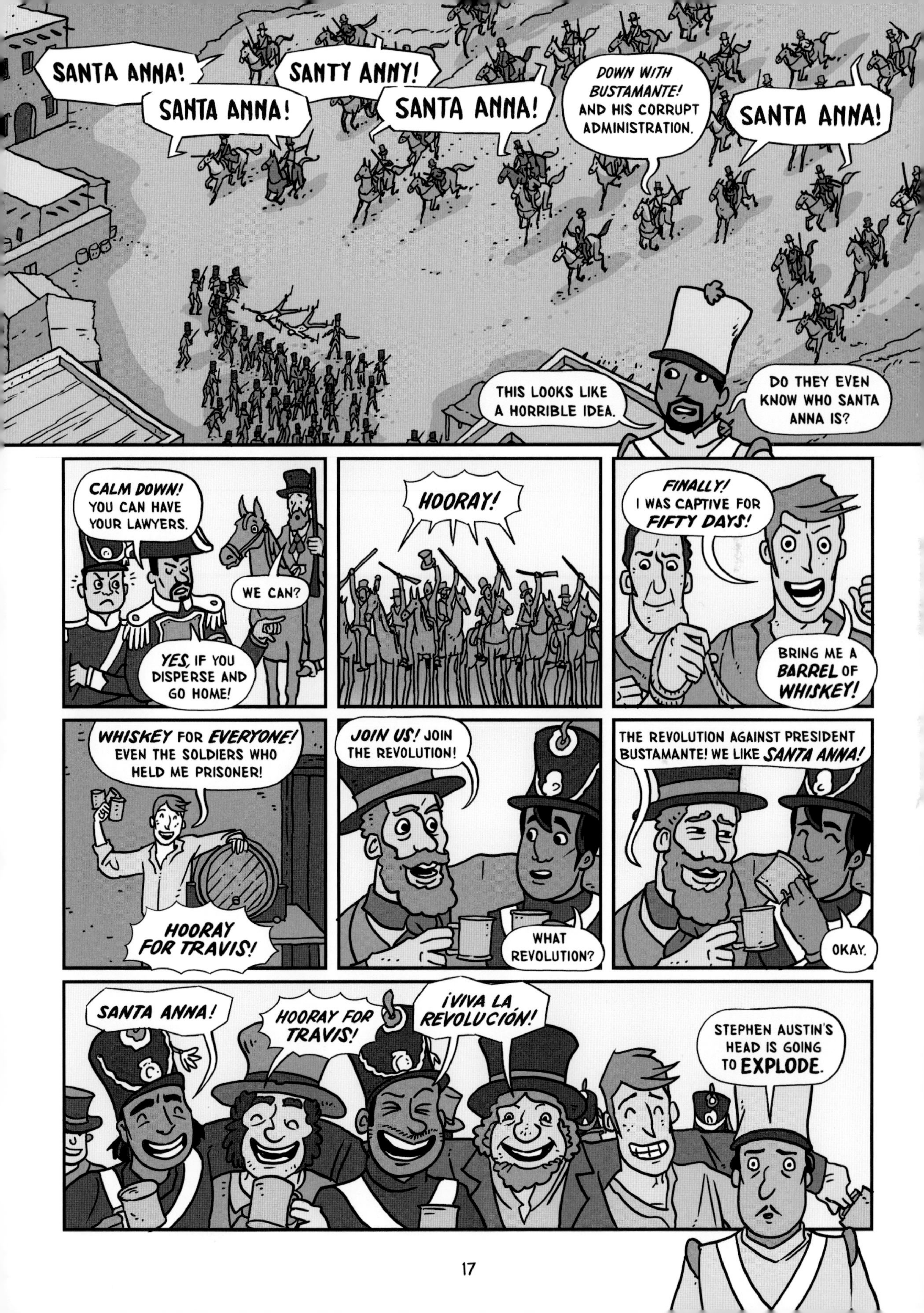
SANTA ANNA!
SANTY ANNY!
SANTA ANNA!
SANTA ANNA!
DOWN WITH BUSTAMANTE! AND HIS CORRUPT ADMINISTRATION.
SANTA ANNA!
THIS LOOKS LIKE A HORRIBLE IDEA.
DO THEY EVEN KNOW WHO SANTA ANNA IS?
CALM DOWN! YOU CAN HAVE YOUR LAWYERS.
WE CAN?
YES, IF YOU DISPERSE AND GO HOME!
HOORAY!
FINALLY! I WAS CAPTIVE FOR FIFTY DAYS!
BRING ME A BARREL OF WHISKEY!
WHISKEY FOR EVERYONE! EVEN THE SOLDIERS WHO HELD ME PRISONER!
HOORAY FOR TRAVIS!
JOIN US! JOIN THE REVOLUTION!
WHAT REVOLUTION?
THE REVOLUTION AGAINST PRESIDENT BUSTAMANTE! WE LIKE SANTA ANNA!
OKAY.
SANTA ANNA!
HOORAY FOR TRAVIS!
¡VIVA LA REVOLUCIÓN!
STEPHEN AUSTIN'S HEAD IS GOING TO EXPLODE.

CHAPTER 5

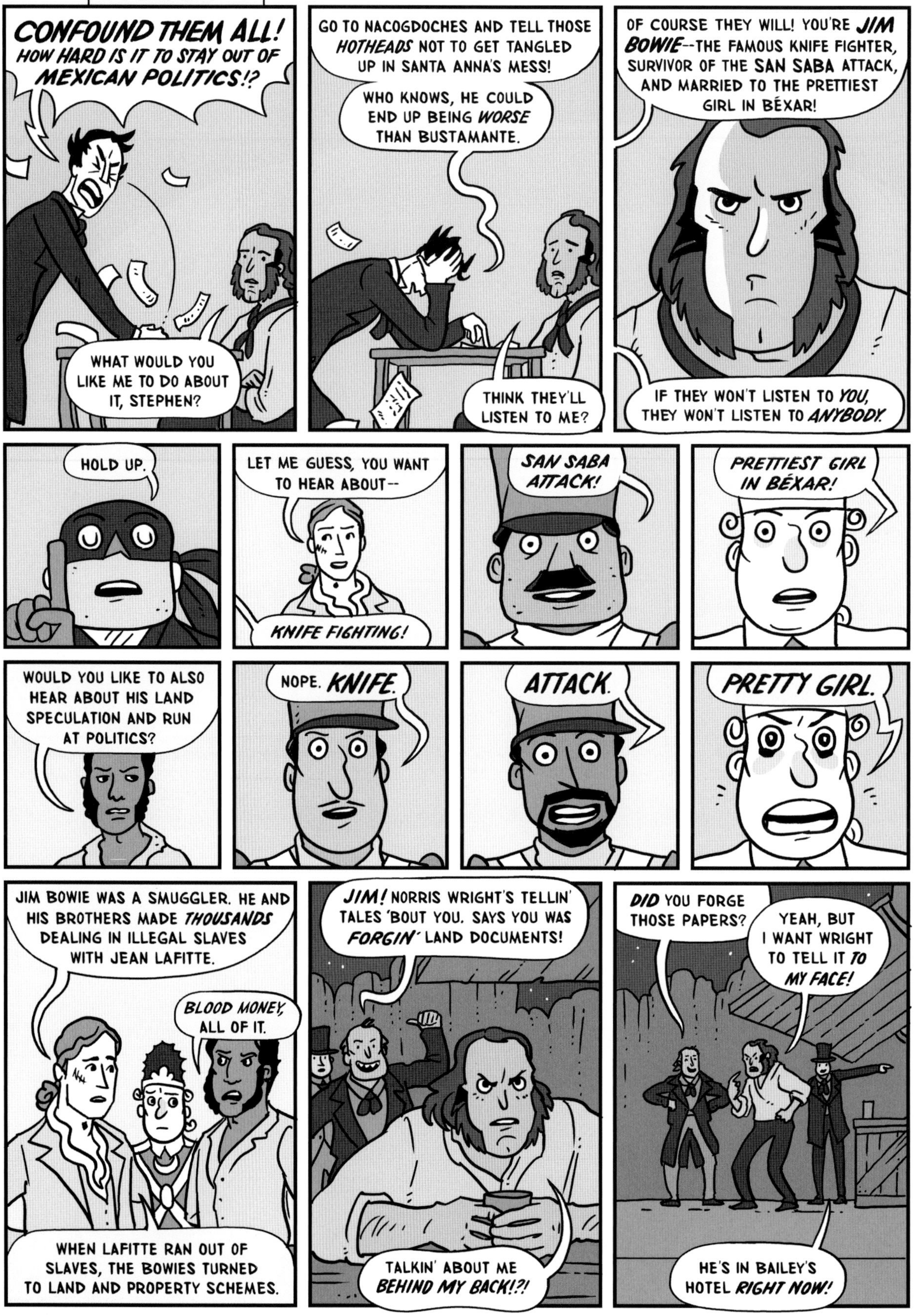

CONFOUND THEM ALL! HOW HARD IS IT TO STAY OUT OF MEXICAN POLITICS!?
WHAT WOULD YOU LIKE ME TO DO ABOUT IT, STEPHEN?
GO TO NACOGDOCHES AND TELL THOSE HOTHEADS NOT TO GET TANGLED UP IN SANTA ANNA'S MESS!
WHO KNOWS, HE COULD END UP BEING WORSE THAN BUSTAMANTE.
THINK THEY'LL LISTEN TO ME?
OF COURSE THEY WILL! YOU'RE JIM BOWIE--THE FAMOUS KNIFE FIGHTER, SURVIVOR OF THE SAN SABA ATTACK, AND MARRIED TO THE PRETTIEST GIRL IN BÉXAR!
IF THEY WON'T LISTEN TO YOU, THEY WON'T LISTEN TO ANYBODY.
HOLD UP.
LET ME GUESS, YOU WANT TO HEAR ABOUT--
KNIFE FIGHTING!
SAN SABA ATTACK!
PRETTIEST GIRL IN BÉXAR!
WOULD YOU LIKE TO ALSO HEAR ABOUT HIS LAND SPECULATION AND RUN AT POLITICS?
NOPE. KNIFE.
ATTACK.
PRETTY GIRL.
JIM BOWIE WAS A SMUGGLER. HE AND HIS BROTHERS MADE THOUSANDS DEALING IN ILLEGAL SLAVES WITH JEAN LAFITTE.
BLOOD MONEY, ALL OF IT.
WHEN LAFITTE RAN OUT OF SLAVES, THE BOWIES TURNED TO LAND AND PROPERTY SCHEMES.
JIM! NORRIS WRIGHT'S TELLIN' TALES 'BOUT YOU. SAYS YOU WAS FORGIN' LAND DOCUMENTS!
TALKIN' ABOUT ME BEHIND MY BACK!?!
DID YOU FORGE THOSE PAPERS?
YEAH, BUT I WANT WRIGHT TO TELL IT TO MY FACE!
HE'S IN BAILEY'S HOTEL RIGHT NOW!

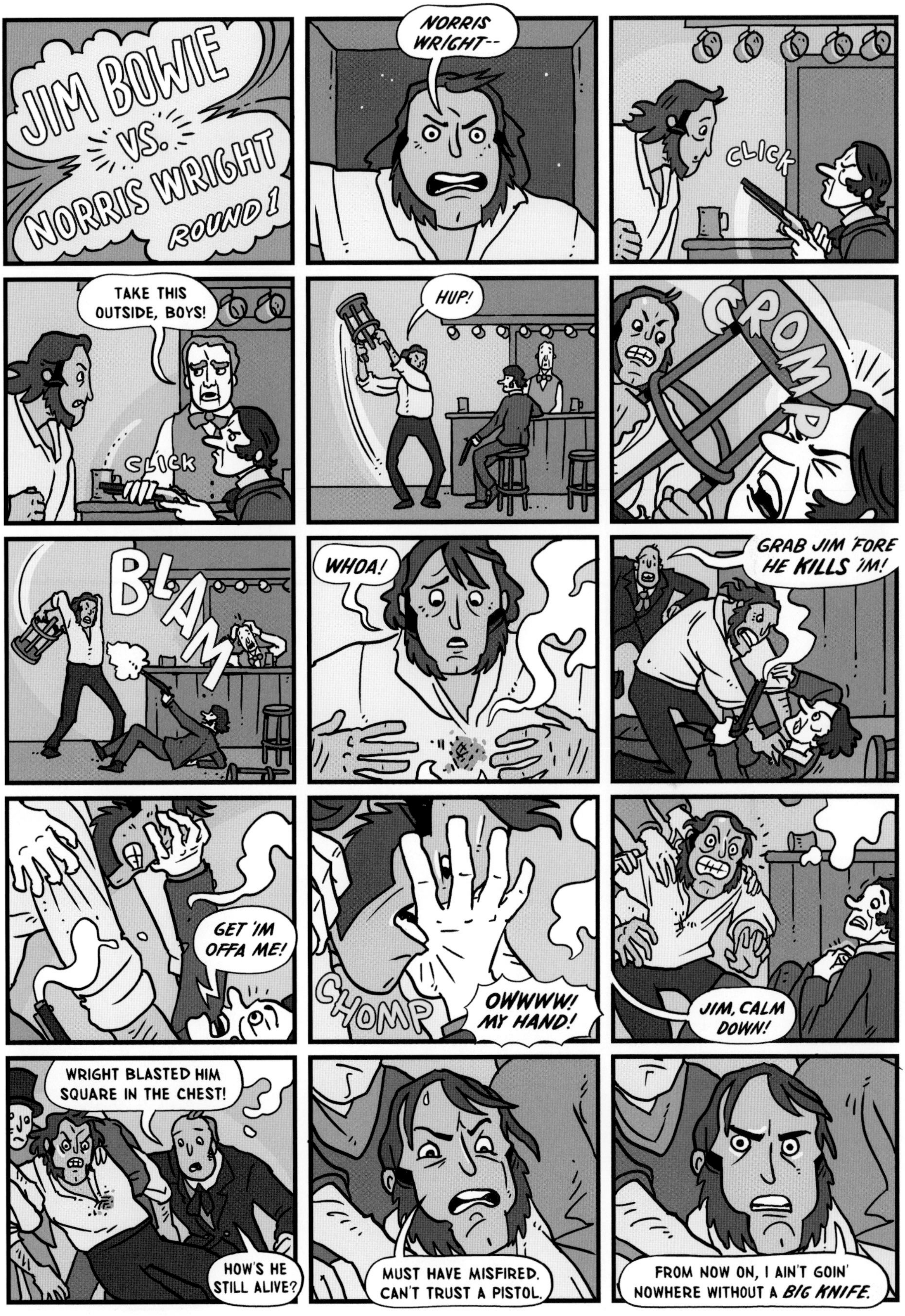
JIM BOWIE VS. NORRIS WRIGHT ROUND 1
NORRIS WRIGHT--
CLICK
TAKE THIS OUTSIDE, BOYS!
CLICK
HUP!
CROMP
BLAM
WHOA!
GRAB JIM 'FORE HE KILLS 'IM!
GET 'IM OFFA ME!
CHOMP
OWWWW! MY HAND!
JIM, CALM DOWN!
WRIGHT BLASTED HIM SQUARE IN THE CHEST!
HOW'S HE STILL ALIVE?
MUST HAVE MISFIRED. CAN'T TRUST A PISTOL.
FROM NOW ON, I AIN'T GOIN' NOWHERE WITHOUT A BIG KNIFE.

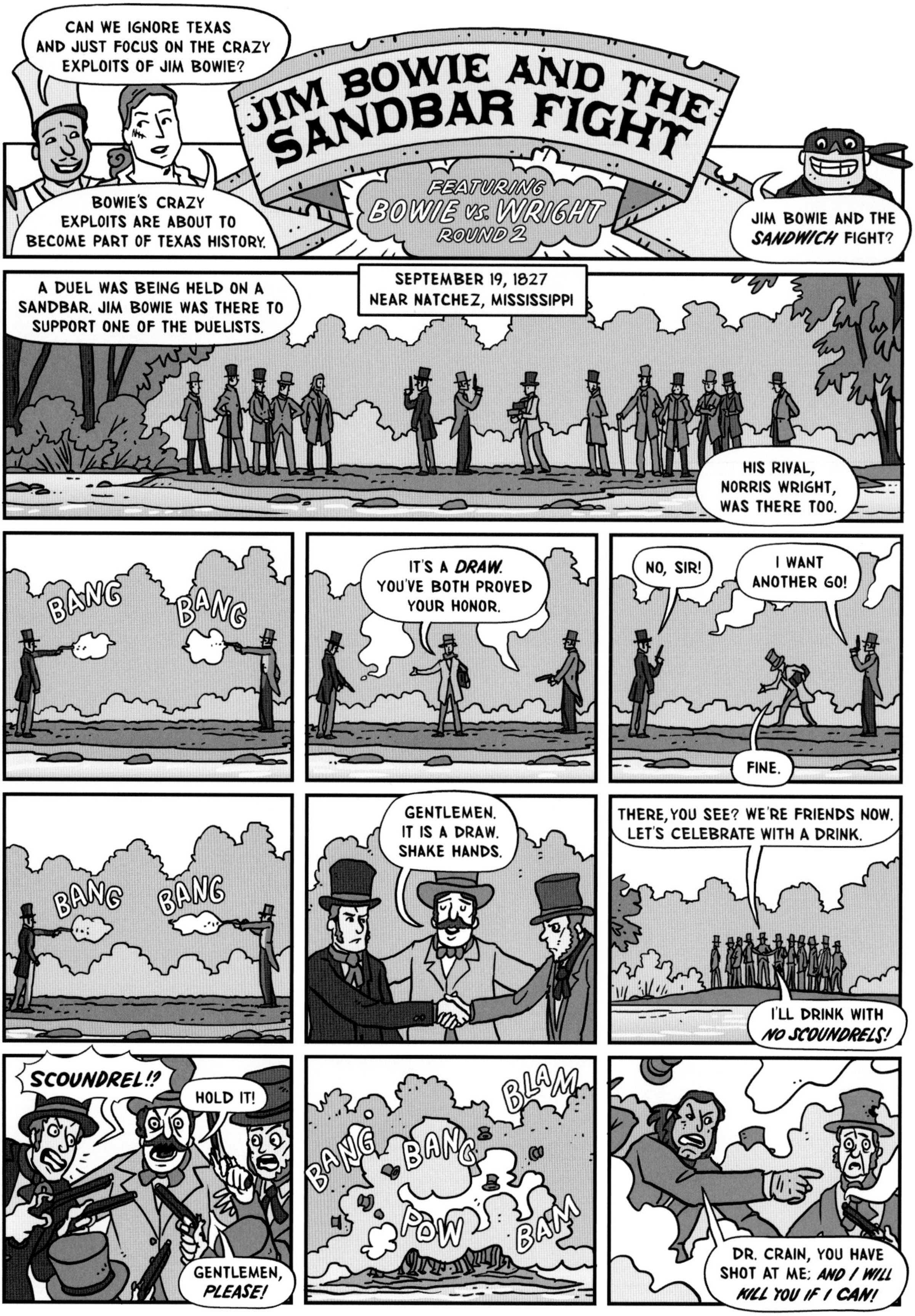
CAN WE IGNORE TEXAS AND JUST FOCUS ON THE CRAZY EXPLOITS OF JIM BOWIE?
JIM BOWIE AND THE SANDBAR FIGHT
FEATURING BOWIE VS. WRIGHT ROUND 2
BOWIE'S CRAZY EXPLOITS ARE ABOUT TO BECOME PART OF TEXAS HISTORY.
JIM BOWIE AND THE SANDWICH FIGHT?
A DUEL WAS BEING HELD ON A SANDBAR. JIM BOWIE WAS THERE TO SUPPORT ONE OF THE DUELISTS.
SEPTEMBER 19, 1827 NEAR NATCHEZ, MISSISSIPPI
HIS RIVAL, NORRIS WRIGHT, WAS THERE TOO.
BANG
BANG
IT'S A DRAW. YOU'VE BOTH PROVED YOUR HONOR.
NO, SIR!
I WANT ANOTHER GO!
FINE.
BANG
BANG
GENTLEMEN. IT IS A DRAW. SHAKE HANDS.
THERE, YOU SEE? WE'RE FRIENDS NOW. LET'S CELEBRATE WITH A DRINK.
I'LL DRINK WITH NO SCOUNDRELS!
SCOUNDREL!?
HOLD IT!
GENTLEMEN, PLEASE!
BLAM
BANG
BANG
POW
BAM
DR. CRAIN, YOU HAVE SHOT AT ME; AND I WILL KILL YOU IF I CAN!

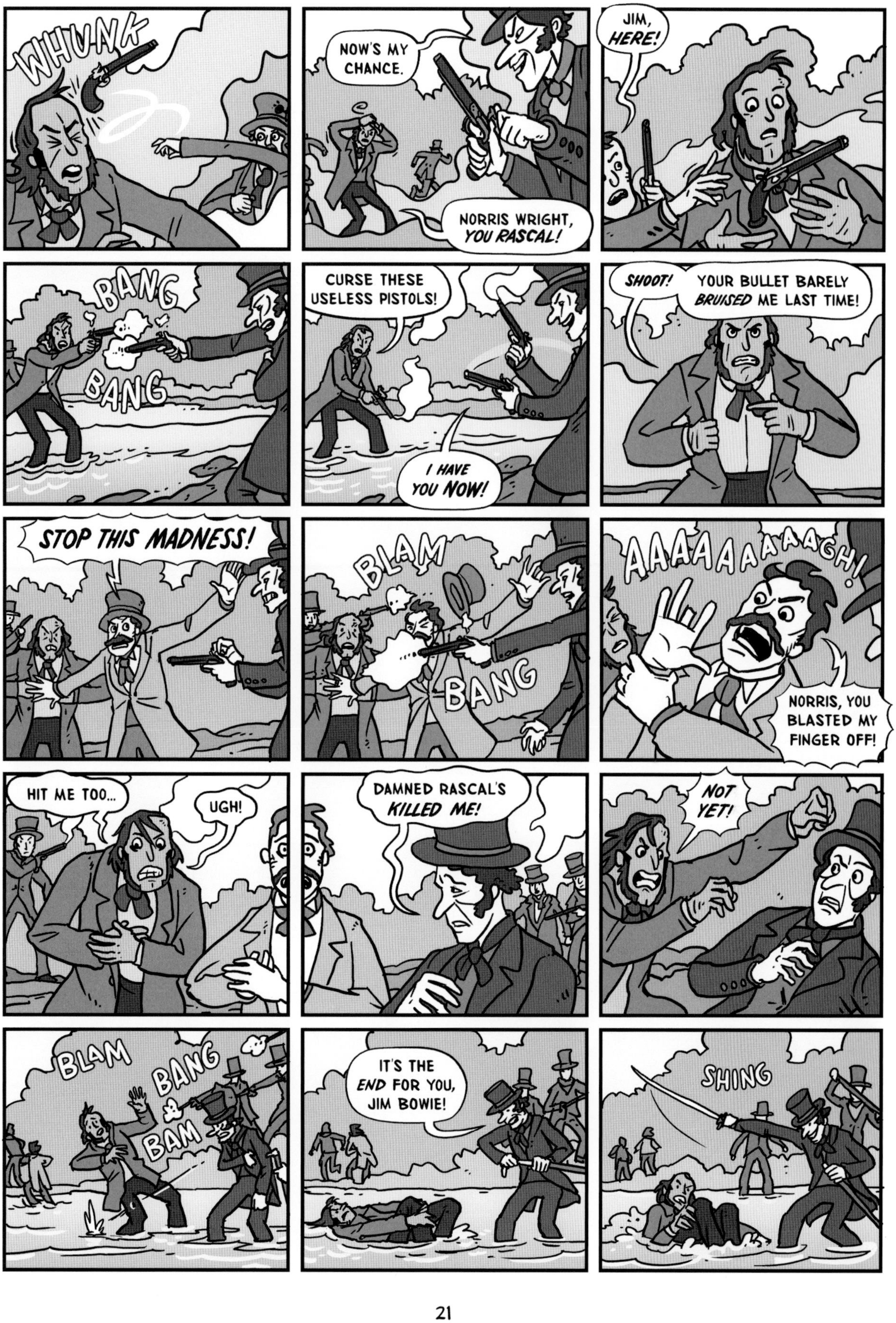
WHUNK
NOW'S MY CHANCE.
NORRIS WRIGHT, YOU RASCAL!
JIM, HERE!
BANG
BANG
CURSE THESE USELESS PISTOLS!
I HAVE YOU NOW!
SHOOT!
YOUR BULLET BARELY BRUISED ME LAST TIME!
STOP THIS MADNESS!
BLAM
BANG
AAAAAAAAAAGH!
NORRIS, YOU BLASTED MY FINGER OFF!
HIT ME TOO...
UGH!
DAMNED RASCAL'S KILLED ME!
NOT YET!
BLAM
BANG
BAM
IT'S THE END FOR YOU, JIM BOWIE!
SHING

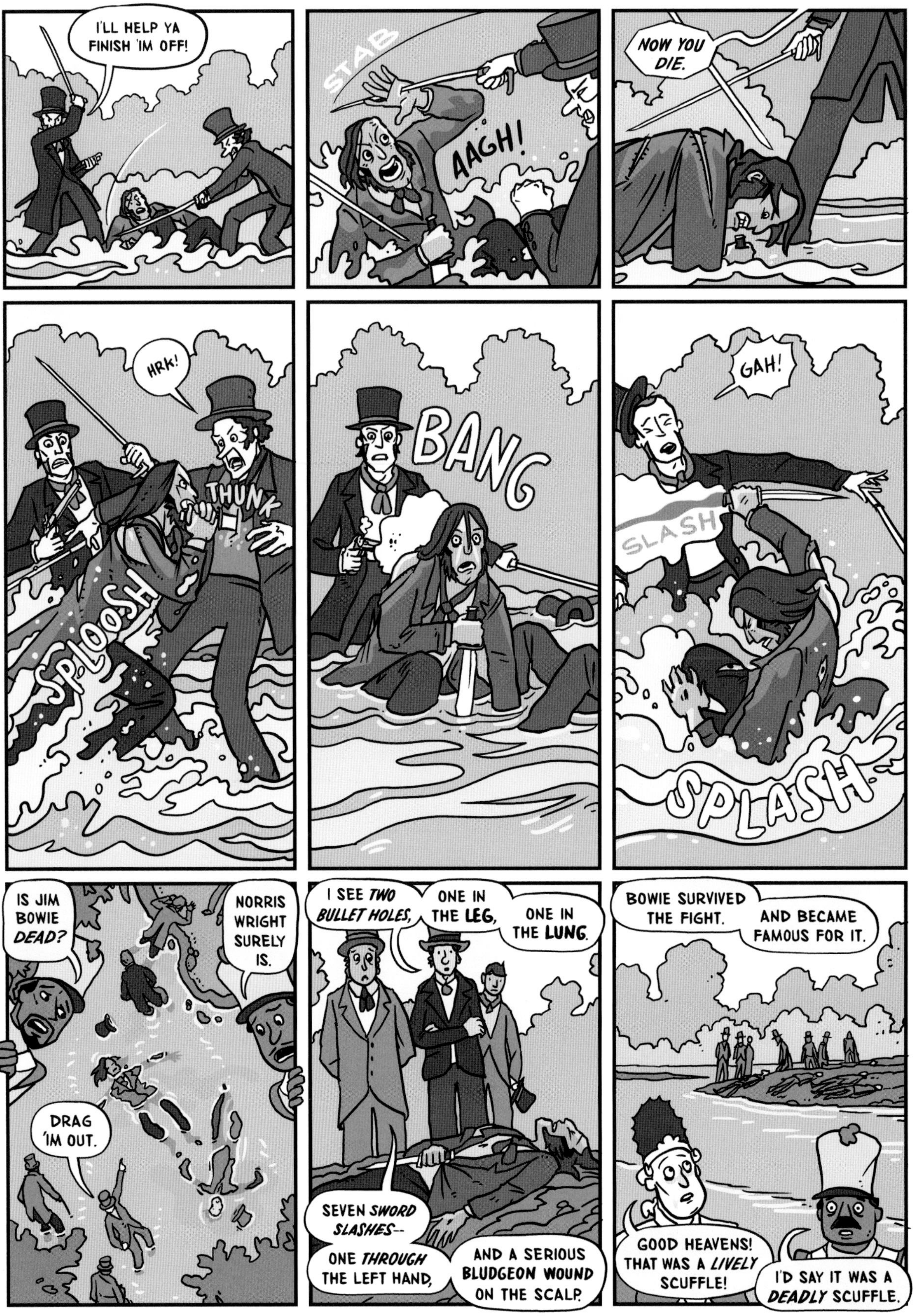

I'LL HELP YA FINISH 'IM OFF!
STAB
AAGH!
NOW YOU DIE.
HRK!
THUNK
SPLOOSH
BANG
GAH!
SLASH
SPLASH
IS JIM BOWIE DEAD?
NORRIS WRIGHT SURELY IS.
DRAG 'IM OUT.
I SEE TWO BULLET HOLES,
ONE IN THE LEG,
ONE IN THE LUNG.
SEVEN SWORD SLASHES--
ONE THROUGH THE LEFT HAND,
AND A SERIOUS BLUDGEON WOUND ON THE SCALP.
BOWIE SURVIVED THE FIGHT.
AND BECAME FAMOUS FOR IT.
GOOD HEAVENS! THAT WAS A LIVELY SCUFFLE!
I'D SAY IT WAS A DEADLY SCUFFLE.

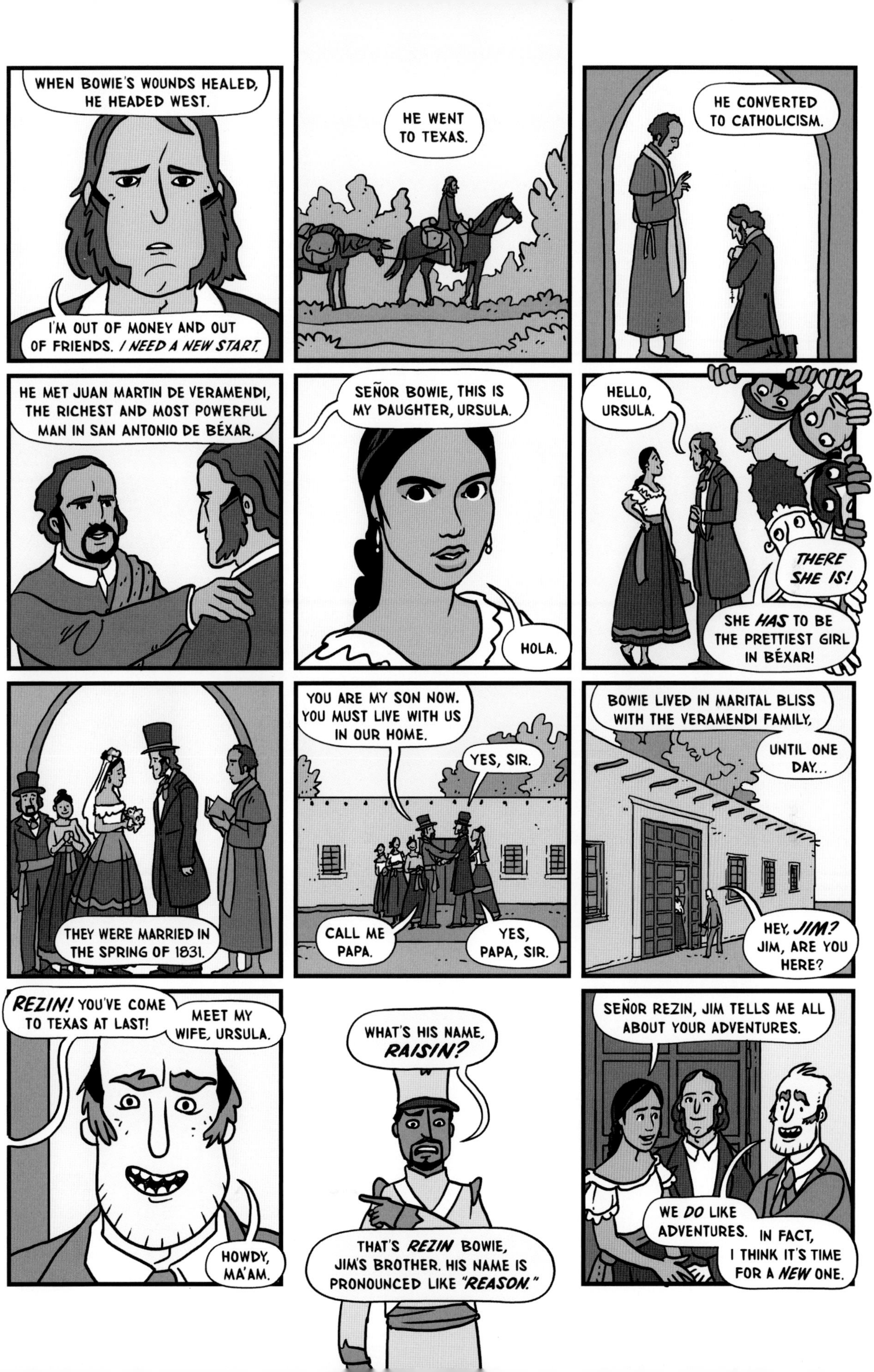
WHEN BOWIE'S WOUNDS HEALED, HE HEADED WEST.
I'M OUT OF MONEY AND OUT OF FRIENDS. I NEED A NEW START.
HE WENT TO TEXAS.
HE CONVERTED TO CATHOLICISM.
HE MET JUAN MARTIN DE VERAMENDI, THE RICHEST AND MOST POWERFUL MAN IN SAN ANTONIO DE BÉXAR.
SEÑOR BOWIE, THIS IS MY DAUGHTER, URSULA.
HOLA.
HELLO, URSULA.
THERE SHE IS!
SHE HAS TO BE THE PRETTIEST GIRL IN BÉXAR!
THEY WERE MARRIED IN THE SPRING OF 1831.
YOU ARE MY SON NOW. YOU MUST LIVE WITH US IN OUR HOME.
YES, SIR.
CALL ME PAPA.
YES, PAPA, SIR.
BOWIE LIVED IN MARITAL BLISS WITH THE VERAMENDI FAMILY,
UNTIL ONE DAY...
HEY, JIM? JIM, ARE YOU HERE?
REZIN! YOU'VE COME TO TEXAS AT LAST!
MEET MY WIFE, URSULA.
HOWDY, MA'AM.
WHAT'S HIS NAME, RAISIN?
THAT'S REZIN BOWIE, JIM'S BROTHER. HIS NAME IS PRONOUNCED LIKE "REASON."
SEÑOR REZIN, JIM TELLS ME ALL ABOUT YOUR ADVENTURES.
WE DO LIKE ADVENTURES.
IN FACT, I THINK IT'S TIME FOR A NEW ONE.

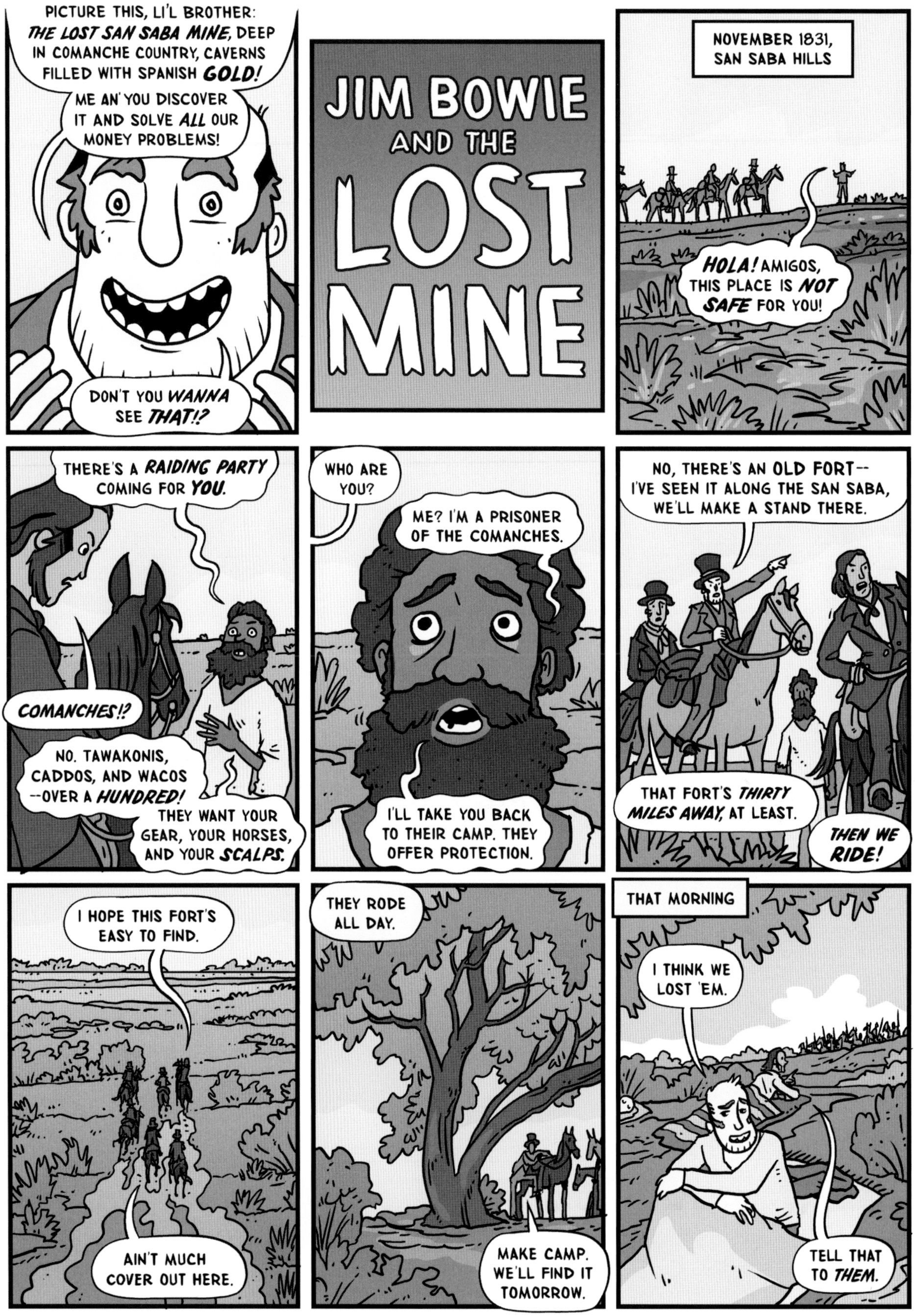
PICTURE THIS, LI'L BROTHER: THE LOST SAN SABA MINE, DEEP IN COMANCHE COUNTRY, CAVERNS FILLED WITH SPANISH GOLD!
ME AN' YOU DISCOVER IT AND SOLVE ALL OUR MONEY PROBLEMS!
DON'T YOU WANNA SEE THAT!?
JIM BOWIE AND THE LOST MINE
NOVEMBER 1831, SAN SABA HILLS
HOLA! AMIGOS, THIS PLACE IS NOT SAFE FOR YOU!
THERE'S A RAIDING PARTY COMING FOR YOU.
COMANCHES!?
NO. TAWAKONIS, CADDOS, AND WACOS --OVER A HUNDRED!
THEY WANT YOUR GEAR, YOUR HORSES, AND YOUR SCALPS.
WHO ARE YOU?
ME? I'M A PRISONER OF THE COMANCHES.
I'LL TAKE YOU BACK TO THEIR CAMP. THEY OFFER PROTECTION.
NO, THERE'S AN OLD FORT-- I'VE SEEN IT ALONG THE SAN SABA, WE'LL MAKE A STAND THERE.
THAT FORT'S THIRTY MILES AWAY, AT LEAST.
THEN WE RIDE!
I HOPE THIS FORT'S EASY TO FIND.
AIN'T MUCH COVER OUT HERE.
THEY RODE ALL DAY.
MAKE CAMP. WE'LL FIND IT TOMORROW.
THAT MORNING
I THINK WE LOST 'EM.
TELL THAT TO THEM.

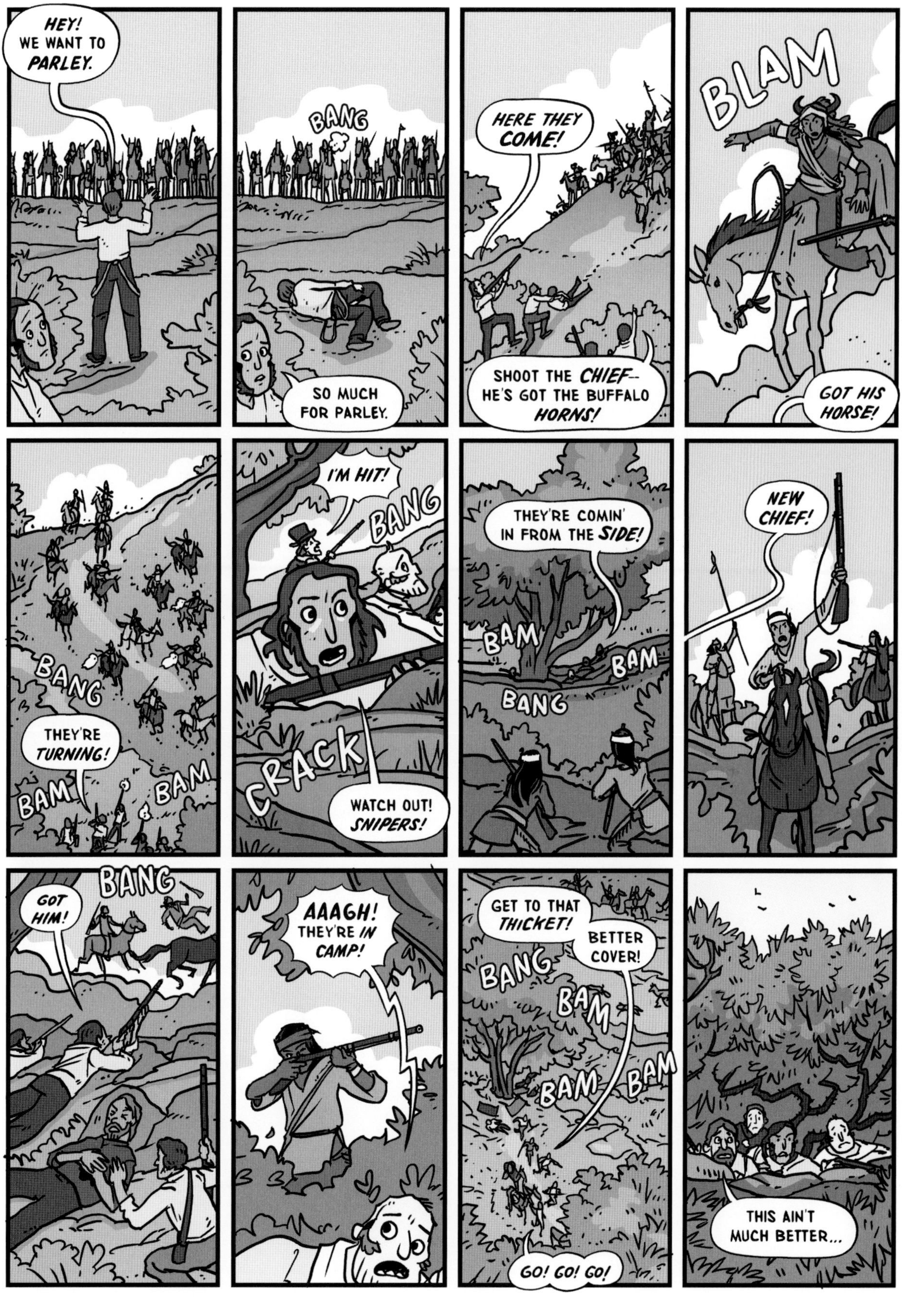
HEY! WE WANT TO PARLEY.
BANG
SO MUCH FOR PARLEY.
HERE THEY COME!
SHOOT THE CHIEF-- HE'S GOT THE BUFFALO HORNS!
BLAM
GOT HIS HORSE!
BANG
THEY'RE TURNING!
BAM
BAM
I'M HIT!
BANG
CRACK
WATCH OUT! SNIPERS!
THEY'RE COMIN' IN FROM THE SIDE!
BAM
BAM
BANG
NEW CHIEF!
BANG
GOT HIM!
AAAGH! THEY'RE IN CAMP!
GET TO THAT THICKET!
BETTER COVER!
BANG
BAM
BAM
BAM
GO! GO! GO!
THIS AIN'T MUCH BETTER...

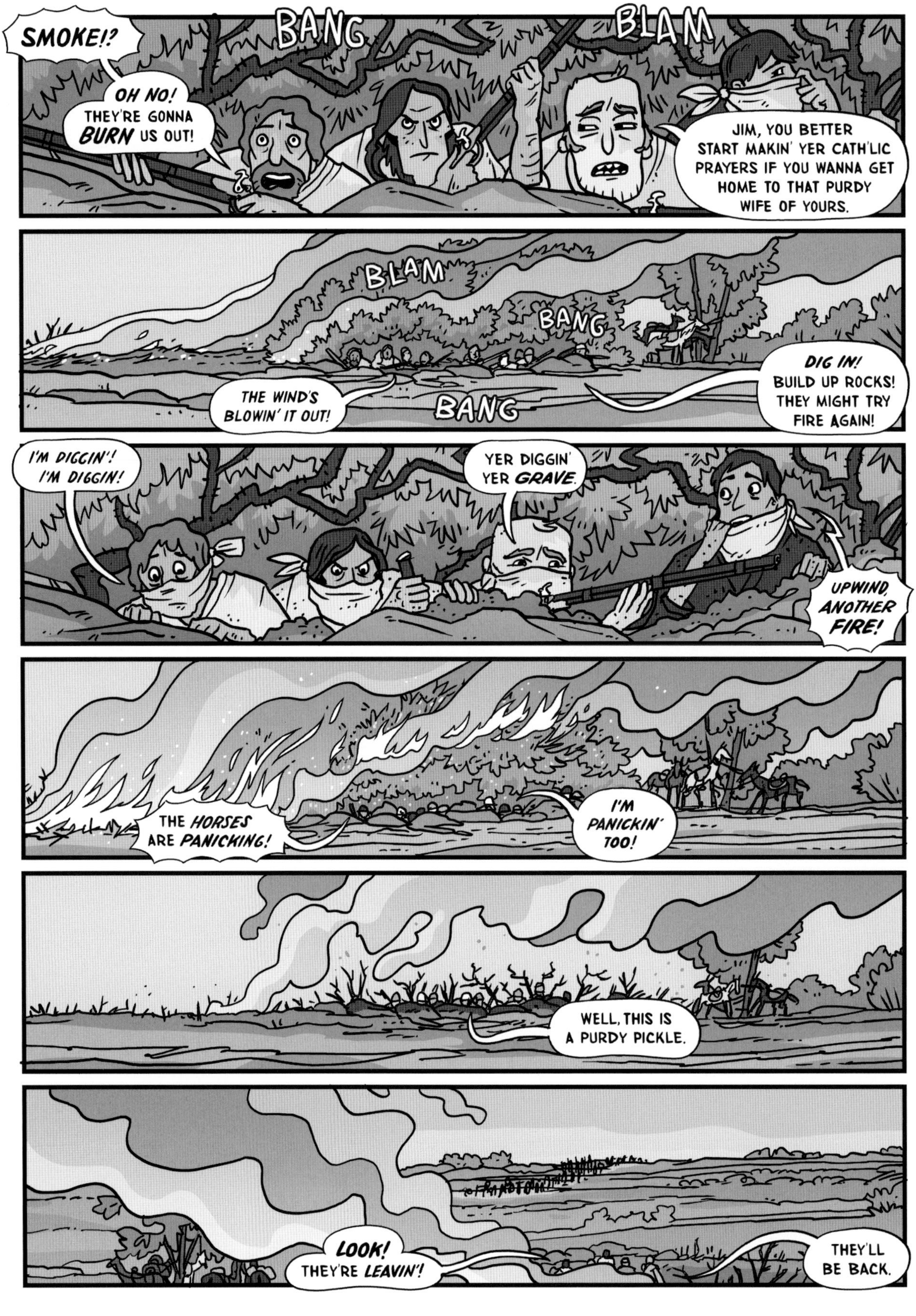

BANG
BLAM
SMOKE!?
OH NO! THEY'RE GONNA BURN US OUT!
JIM, YOU BETTER START MAKIN' YER CATH'LIC PRAYERS IF YOU WANNA GET HOME TO THAT PURDY WIFE OF YOURS.
BLAM
BANG
THE WIND'S BLOWIN' IT OUT!
BANG
DIG IN! BUILD UP ROCKS! THEY MIGHT TRY FIRE AGAIN!
I'M DIGGIN'! I'M DIGGIN!
YER DIGGIN' YER GRAVE.
UPWIND, ANOTHER FIRE!
THE HORSES ARE PANICKING!
I'M PANICKIN' TOO!
WELL, THIS IS A PURDY PICKLE.
LOOK! THEY'RE LEAVIN'!
THEY'LL BE BACK.

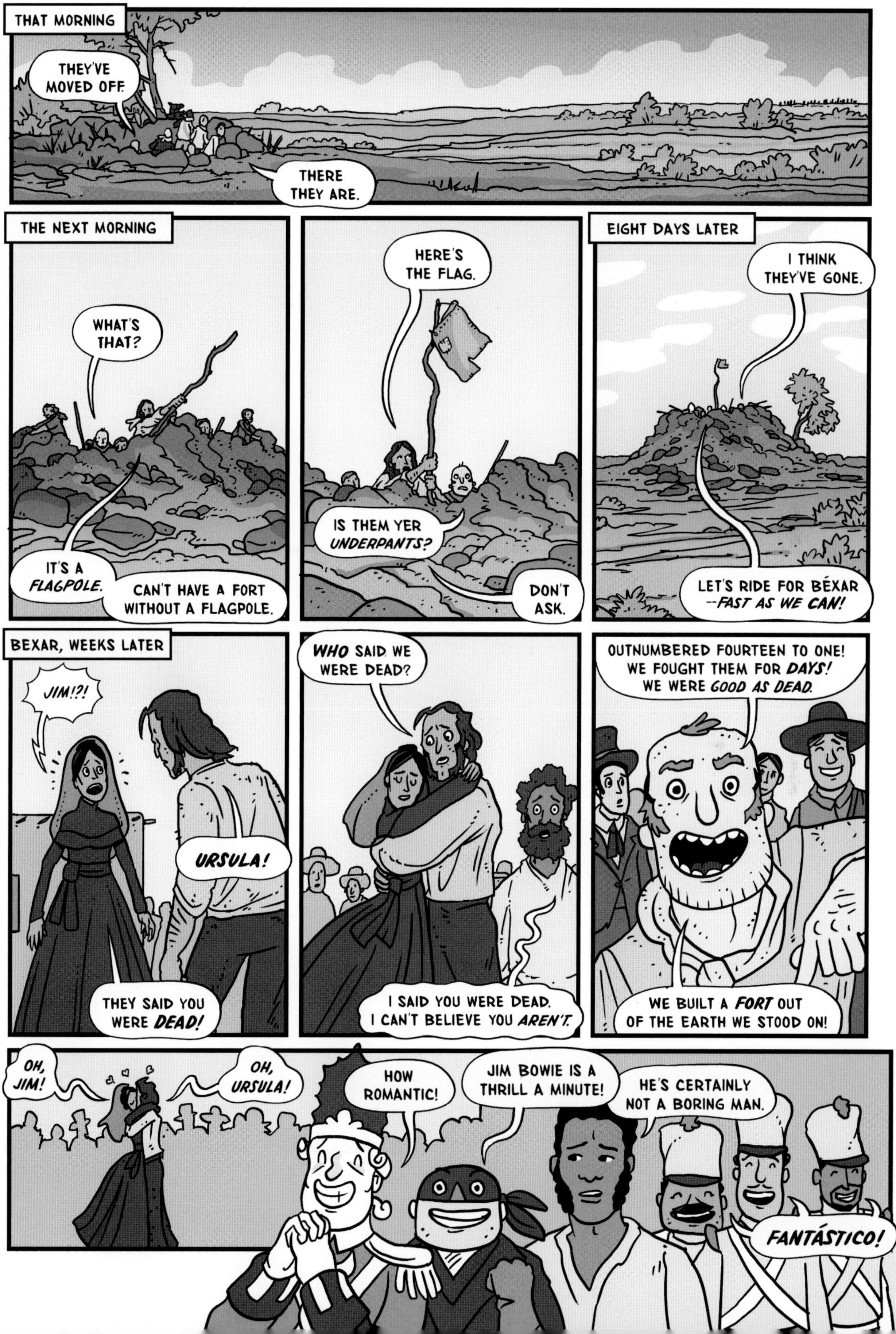
THAT MORNING
THEY'VE MOVED OFF.
THERE THEY ARE.
THE NEXT MORNING
WHAT'S THAT?
IT'S A FLAGPOLE.
CAN'T HAVE A FORT WITHOUT A FLAGPOLE.
HERE'S THE FLAG.
IS THEM YER UNDERPANTS?
DON'T ASK.
EIGHT DAYS LATER
I THINK THEY'VE GONE.
LET'S RIDE FOR BÉXAR --FAST AS WE CAN!
BEXAR, WEEKS LATER
JIM!?!
URSULA!
THEY SAID YOU WERE DEAD!
WHO SAID WE WERE DEAD?
I SAID YOU WERE DEAD. I CAN'T BELIEVE YOU AREN'T.
OUTNUMBERED FOURTEEN TO ONE! WE FOUGHT THEM FOR DAYS! WE WERE GOOD AS DEAD.
WE BUILT A FORT OUT OF THE EARTH WE STOOD ON!
OH, JIM!
OH, URSULA!
HOW ROMANTIC!
JIM BOWIE IS A THRILL A MINUTE!
HE'S CERTAINLY NOT A BORING MAN.
FANTÁSTICO!

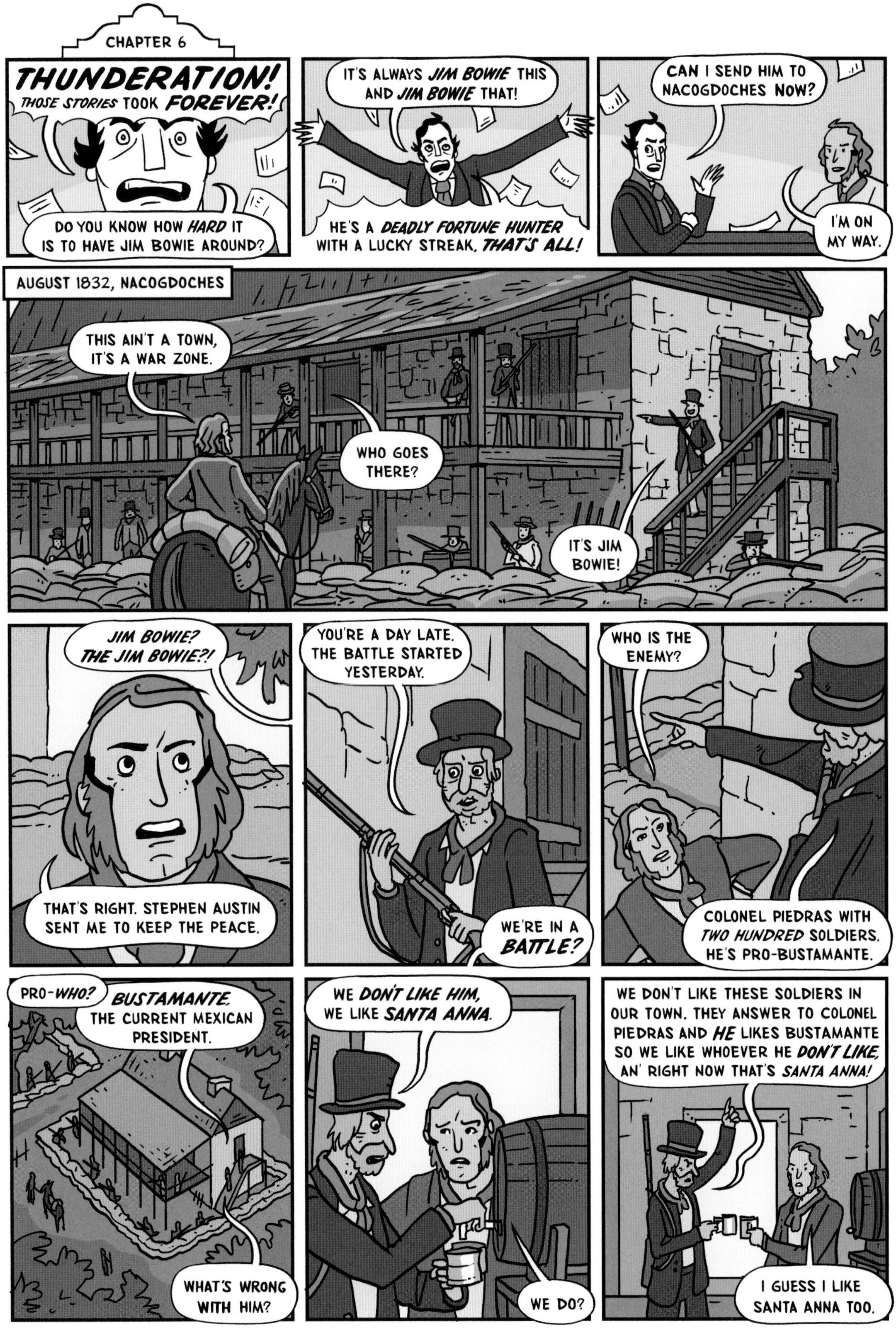
CHAPTER 6
THUNDERATION! THOSE STORIES TOOK FOREVER!
DO YOU KNOW HOW HARD IT IS TO HAVE JIM BOWIE AROUND?
IT'S ALWAYS JIM BOWIE THIS AND JIM BOWIE THAT!
HE'S A DEADLY FORTUNE HUNTER WITH A LUCKY STREAK, THAT'S ALL!
CAN I SEND HIM TO NACOGDOCHES NOW?
I'M ON MY WAY.
AUGUST 1832, NACOGDOCHES
THIS AIN'T A TOWN, IT'S A WAR ZONE.
WHO GOES THERE?
IT'S JIM BOWIE!
JIM BOWIE? THE JIM BOWIE?!
THAT'S RIGHT. STEPHEN AUSTIN SENT ME TO KEEP THE PEACE.
YOU'RE A DAY LATE. THE BATTLE STARTED YESTERDAY.
WE'RE IN A BATTLE?
WHO IS THE ENEMY?
COLONEL PIEDRAS WITH TWO HUNDRED SOLDIERS. HE'S PRO-BUSTAMANTE.
PRO-WHO?
BUSTAMANTE, THE CURRENT MEXICAN PRESIDENT.
WHAT'S WRONG WITH HIM?
WE DON'T LIKE HIM, WE LIKE SANTA ANNA.
WE DO?
WE DON'T LIKE THESE SOLDIERS IN OUR TOWN. THEY ANSWER TO COLONEL PIEDRAS AND HE LIKES BUSTAMANTE SO WE LIKE WHOEVER HE DON'T LIKE, AN' RIGHT NOW THAT'S SANTA ANNA!
I GUESS I LIKE SANTA ANNA TOO.

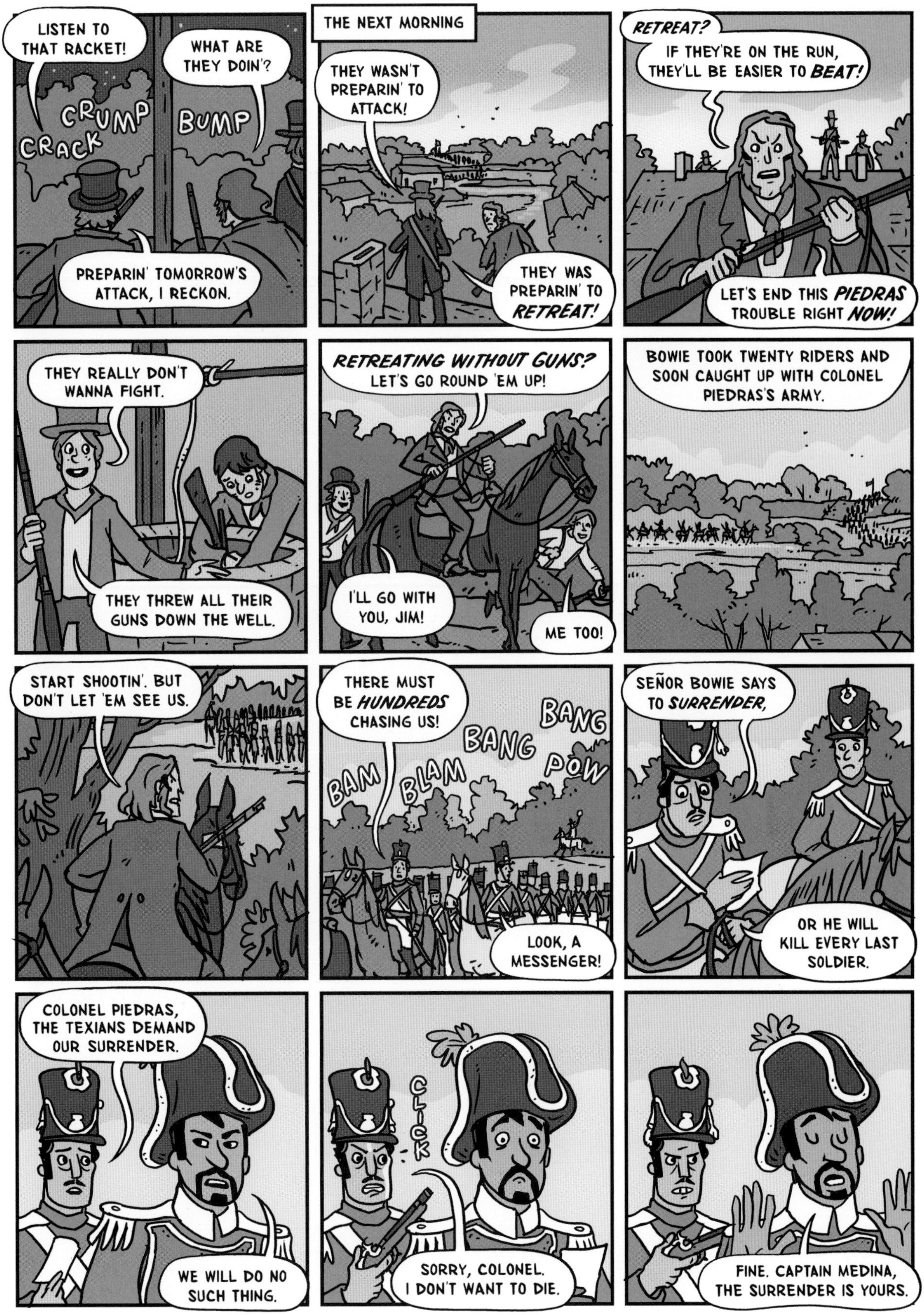
LISTEN TO THAT RACKET!
CRUMP
CRACK
WHAT ARE THEY DOIN'?
BUMP
PREPARIN' TOMORROW'S ATTACK, I RECKON.
THE NEXT MORNING
THEY WASN'T PREPARIN' TO ATTACK!
THEY WAS PREPARIN' TO RETREAT!
RETREAT?
IF THEY'RE ON THE RUN, THEY'LL BE EASIER TO BEAT!
LET'S END THIS PIEDRAS TROUBLE RIGHT NOW!
THEY REALLY DON'T WANNA FIGHT.
THEY THREW ALL THEIR GUNS DOWN THE WELL.
RETREATING WITHOUT GUNS? LET'S GO ROUND 'EM UP!
I'LL GO WITH YOU, JIM!
ME TOO!
BOWIE TOOK TWENTY RIDERS AND SOON CAUGHT UP WITH COLONEL PIEDRAS'S ARMY.
START SHOOTIN'. BUT DON'T LET 'EM SEE US.
THERE MUST BE HUNDREDS CHASING US!
BAM
BLAM
BANG
BANG
POW
LOOK, A MESSENGER!
SEÑOR BOWIE SAYS TO SURRENDER,
OR HE WILL KILL EVERY LAST SOLDIER.
COLONEL PIEDRAS, THE TEXIANS DEMAND OUR SURRENDER.
WE WILL DO NO SUCH THING.
CLICK
SORRY, COLONEL. I DON'T WANT TO DIE.
FINE. CAPTAIN MEDINA, THE SURRENDER IS YOURS.

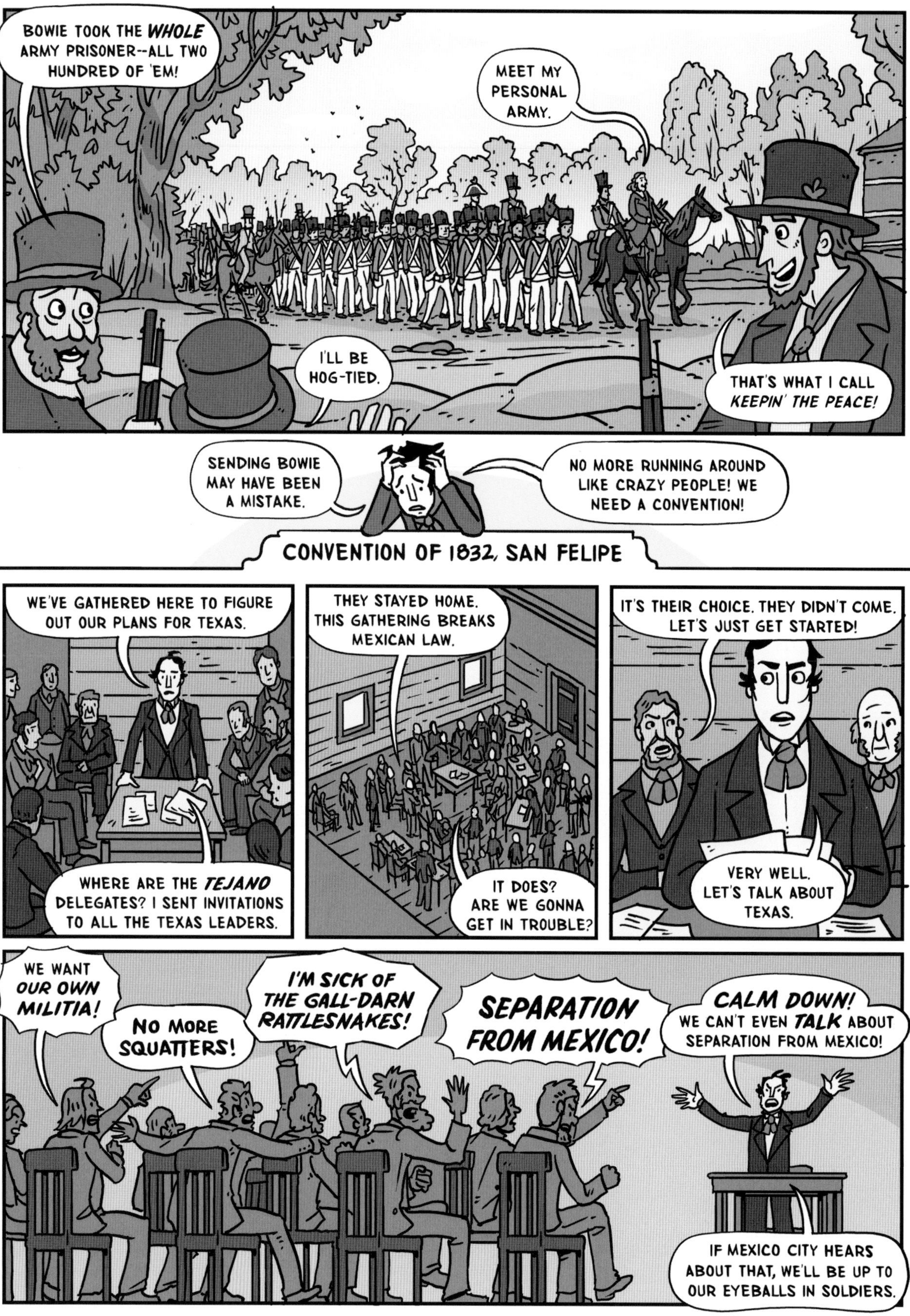
BOWIE TOOK THE *WHOLE* ARMY PRISONER--ALL TWO HUNDRED OF 'EM!
MEET MY PERSONAL ARMY.
I'LL BE HOG-TIED.
THAT'S WHAT I CALL *KEEPIN' THE PEACE!*
SENDING BOWIE MAY HAVE BEEN A MISTAKE.
NO MORE RUNNING AROUND LIKE CRAZY PEOPLE! WE NEED A CONVENTION!
CONVENTION OF 1832, SAN FELIPE
WE'VE GATHERED HERE TO FIGURE OUT OUR PLANS FOR TEXAS.
WHERE ARE THE *TEJANO* DELEGATES? I SENT INVITATIONS TO ALL THE TEXAS LEADERS.
THEY STAYED HOME. THIS GATHERING BREAKS MEXICAN LAW.
IT DOES? ARE WE GONNA GET IN TROUBLE?
IT'S THEIR CHOICE. THEY DIDN'T COME. LET'S JUST GET STARTED!
VERY WELL. LET'S TALK ABOUT TEXAS.
WE WANT *OUR OWN MILITIA!*
NO MORE SQUATTERS!
I'M SICK OF THE GALL-DARN RATTLESNAKES!
SEPARATION FROM MEXICO!
CALM DOWN! WE CAN'T EVEN *TALK* ABOUT SEPARATION FROM MEXICO!
IF MEXICO CITY HEARS ABOUT THAT, WE'LL BE UP TO OUR EYEBALLS IN SOLDIERS.

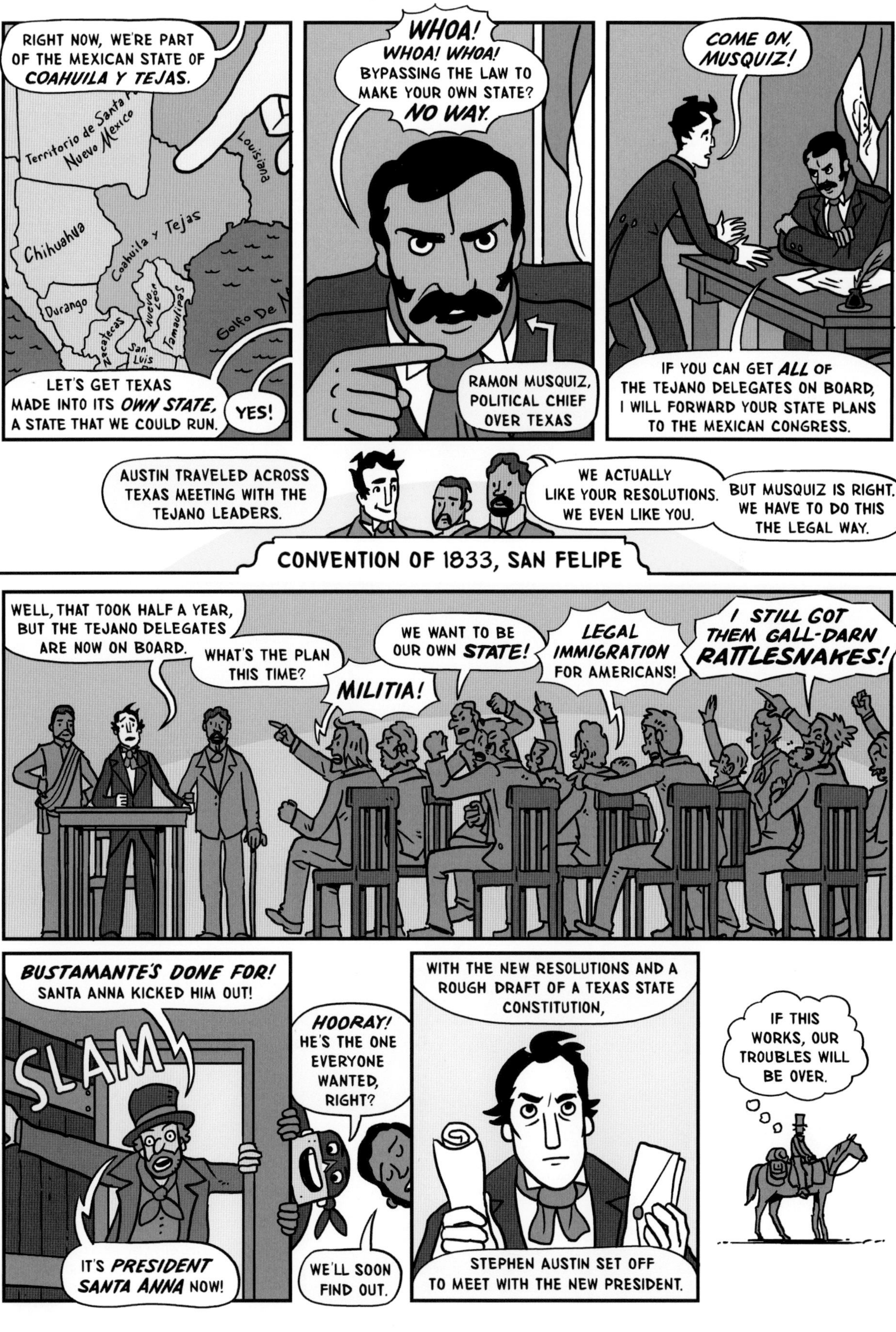
RIGHT NOW, WE'RE PART OF THE MEXICAN STATE OF *COAHUILA Y TEJAS.*
Territorio de Santa Fe Nuevo Mexico
Louisiana
Chihuahua
Coahuila y Tejas
Durango
Nuevo Leon
Tamaulipas
Zacatecas
LET'S GET TEXAS MADE INTO ITS *OWN STATE,* A STATE THAT WE COULD RUN.
YES!
WHOA! WHOA! WHOA! BYPASSING THE LAW TO MAKE YOUR OWN STATE? *NO WAY.*
RAMON MUSQUIZ, POLITICAL CHIEF OVER TEXAS
COME ON, MUSQUIZ!
IF YOU CAN GET *ALL* OF THE TEJANO DELEGATES ON BOARD, I WILL FORWARD YOUR STATE PLANS TO THE MEXICAN CONGRESS.
AUSTIN TRAVELED ACROSS TEXAS MEETING WITH THE TEJANO LEADERS.
WE ACTUALLY LIKE YOUR RESOLUTIONS. WE EVEN LIKE YOU.
BUT MUSQUIZ IS RIGHT. WE HAVE TO DO THIS THE LEGAL WAY.
CONVENTION OF 1833, SAN FELIPE
WELL, THAT TOOK HALF A YEAR, BUT THE TEJANO DELEGATES ARE NOW ON BOARD.
WHAT'S THE PLAN THIS TIME?
MILITIA!
WE WANT TO BE OUR OWN *STATE!*
LEGAL IMMIGRATION FOR AMERICANS!
I STILL GOT THEM GALL-DARN RATTLESNAKES!
BUSTAMANTE'S DONE FOR! SANTA ANNA KICKED HIM OUT!
SLAM
IT'S *PRESIDENT SANTA ANNA* NOW!
HOORAY! HE'S THE ONE EVERYONE WANTED, RIGHT?
WE'LL SOON FIND OUT.
WITH THE NEW RESOLUTIONS AND A ROUGH DRAFT OF A TEXAS STATE CONSTITUTION,
STEPHEN AUSTIN SET OFF TO MEET WITH THE NEW PRESIDENT.
IF THIS WORKS, OUR TROUBLES WILL BE OVER.

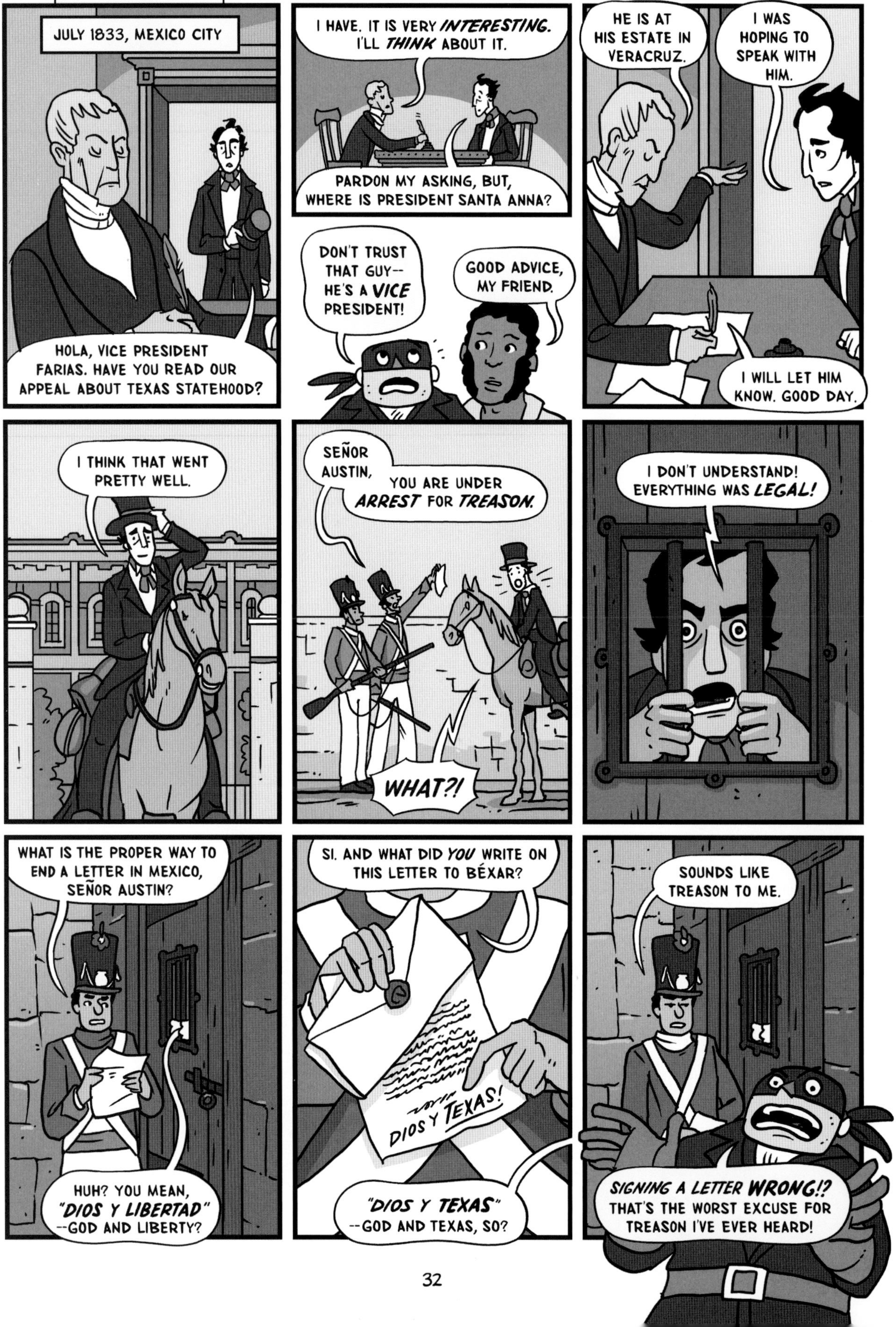
JULY 1833, MEXICO CITY
HOLA, VICE PRESIDENT FARIAS. HAVE YOU READ OUR APPEAL ABOUT TEXAS STATEHOOD?
I HAVE. IT IS VERY *INTERESTING*. I'LL *THINK* ABOUT IT.
PARDON MY ASKING, BUT, WHERE IS PRESIDENT SANTA ANNA?
DON'T TRUST THAT GUY-- HE'S A *VICE* PRESIDENT!
GOOD ADVICE, MY FRIEND.
HE IS AT HIS ESTATE IN VERACRUZ.
I WAS HOPING TO SPEAK WITH HIM.
I WILL LET HIM KNOW. GOOD DAY.
I THINK THAT WENT PRETTY WELL.
SEÑOR AUSTIN,
YOU ARE UNDER *ARREST* FOR *TREASON*.
WHAT?!
I DON'T UNDERSTAND! EVERYTHING WAS *LEGAL!*
WHAT IS THE PROPER WAY TO END A LETTER IN MEXICO, SEÑOR AUSTIN?
HUH? YOU MEAN, *"DIOS Y LIBERTAD"* --GOD AND LIBERTY?
SI. AND WHAT DID *YOU* WRITE ON THIS LETTER TO BÉXAR?
DIOS Y TEXAS!
"DIOS Y TEXAS" --GOD AND TEXAS, SO?
SOUNDS LIKE TREASON TO ME.
SIGNING A LETTER WRONG!? THAT'S THE WORST EXCUSE FOR TREASON I'VE EVER HEARD!

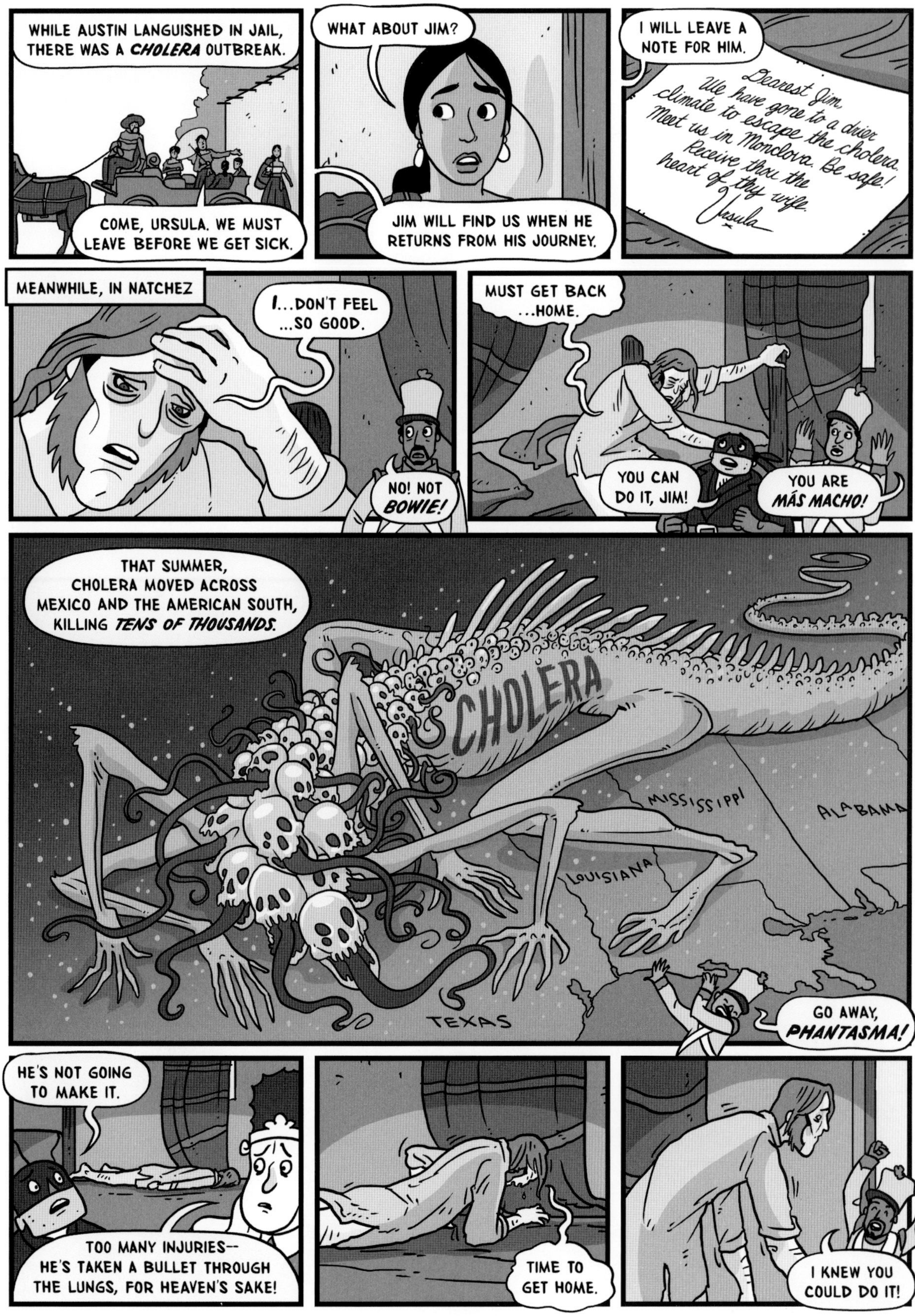

WHILE AUSTIN LANGUISHED IN JAIL, THERE WAS A CHOLERA OUTBREAK.
COME, URSULA. WE MUST LEAVE BEFORE WE GET SICK.
WHAT ABOUT JIM?
JIM WILL FIND US WHEN HE RETURNS FROM HIS JOURNEY.
I WILL LEAVE A NOTE FOR HIM.
Dearest Jim, We have gone to a drier climate to escape the cholera. Meet us in Monclova. Be safe! Receive thou the heart of thy wife. Ursula
MEANWHILE, IN NATCHEZ
I...DON'T FEEL ...SO GOOD.
NO! NOT BOWIE!
MUST GET BACK ...HOME.
YOU CAN DO IT, JIM!
YOU ARE MÁS MACHO!
THAT SUMMER, CHOLERA MOVED ACROSS MEXICO AND THE AMERICAN SOUTH, KILLING TENS OF THOUSANDS.
CHOLERA
MISSISSIPPI
ALABAMA
LOUISIANA
TEXAS
GO AWAY, PHANTASMA!
HE'S NOT GOING TO MAKE IT.
TOO MANY INJURIES-- HE'S TAKEN A BULLET THROUGH THE LUNGS, FOR HEAVEN'S SAKE!
TIME TO GET HOME.
I KNEW YOU COULD DO IT!

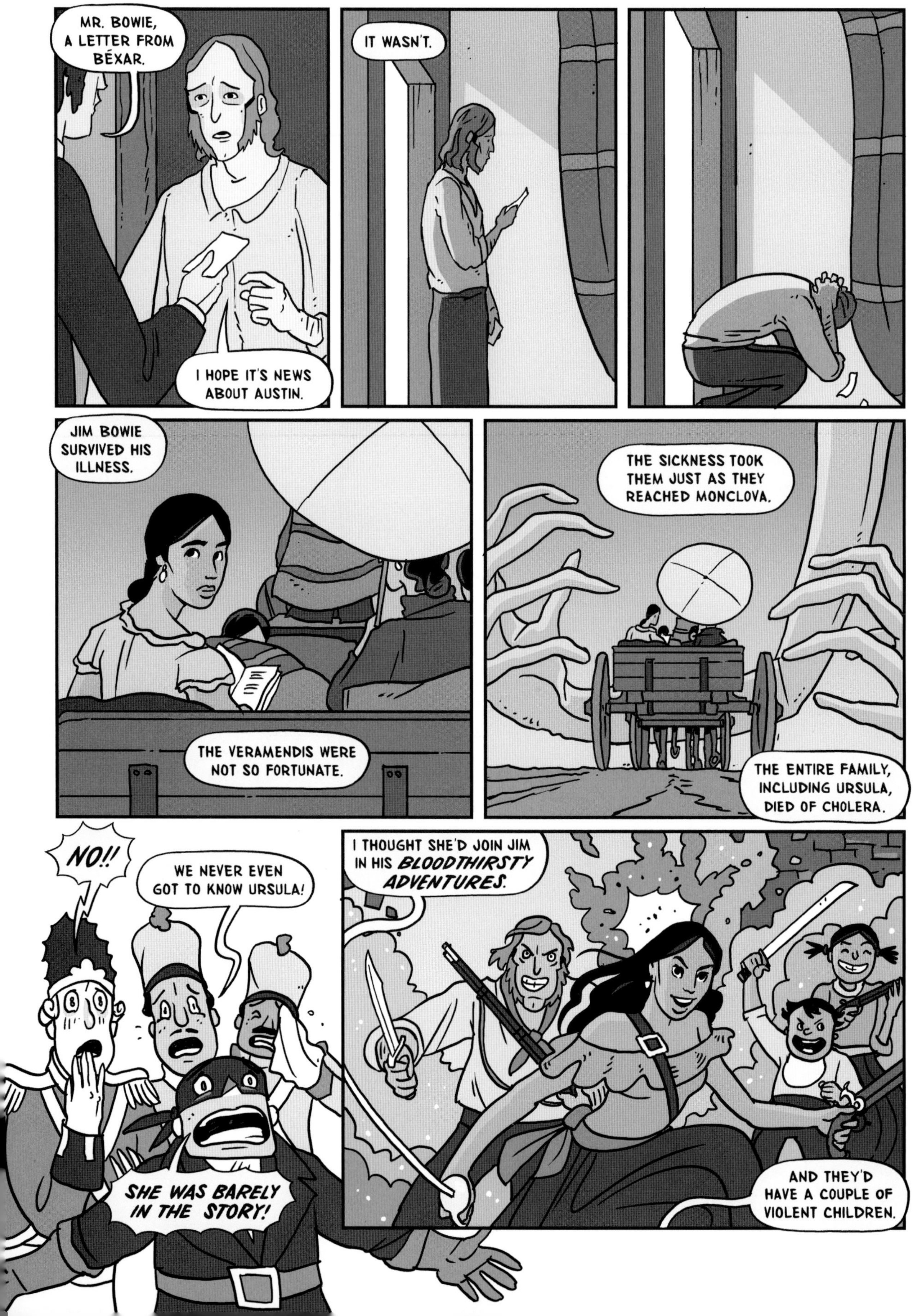
MR. BOWIE, A LETTER FROM BÉXAR.
I HOPE IT'S NEWS ABOUT AUSTIN.
IT WASN'T.
JIM BOWIE SURVIVED HIS ILLNESS.
THE VERAMENDIS WERE NOT SO FORTUNATE.
THE SICKNESS TOOK THEM JUST AS THEY REACHED MONCLOVA.
THE ENTIRE FAMILY, INCLUDING URSULA, DIED OF CHOLERA.
NO!!
WE NEVER EVEN GOT TO KNOW URSULA!
SHE WAS BARELY IN THE STORY!
I THOUGHT SHE'D JOIN JIM IN HIS BLOODTHIRSTY ADVENTURES.
AND THEY'D HAVE A COUPLE OF VIOLENT CHILDREN.

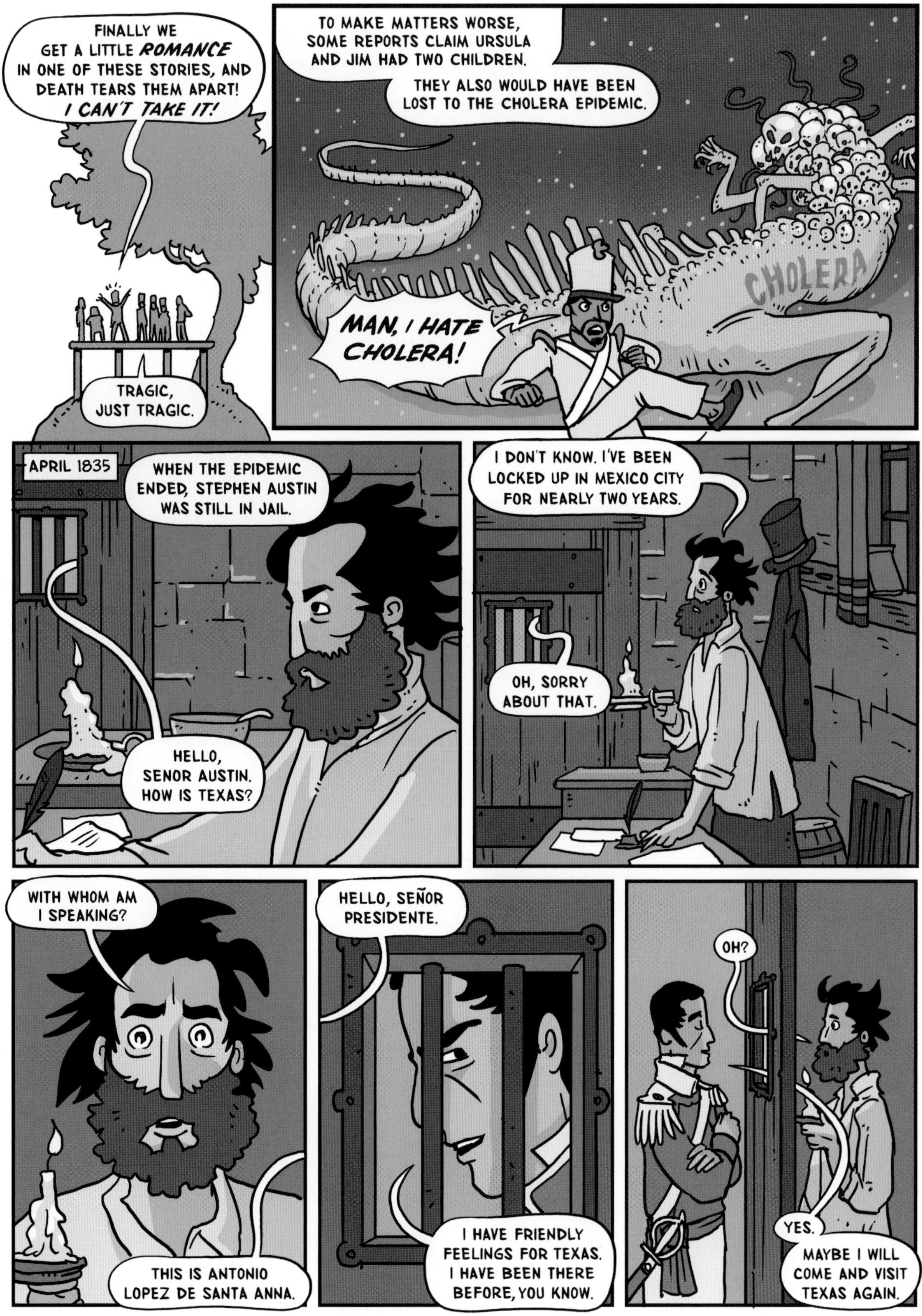
FINALLY WE GET A LITTLE ROMANCE IN ONE OF THESE STORIES, AND DEATH TEARS THEM APART! I CAN'T TAKE IT!
TRAGIC, JUST TRAGIC.
TO MAKE MATTERS WORSE, SOME REPORTS CLAIM URSULA AND JIM HAD TWO CHILDREN.
THEY ALSO WOULD HAVE BEEN LOST TO THE CHOLERA EPIDEMIC.
CHOLERA
MAN, I HATE CHOLERA!
APRIL 1835
WHEN THE EPIDEMIC ENDED, STEPHEN AUSTIN WAS STILL IN JAIL.
HELLO, SENOR AUSTIN. HOW IS TEXAS?
I DON'T KNOW. I'VE BEEN LOCKED UP IN MEXICO CITY FOR NEARLY TWO YEARS.
OH, SORRY ABOUT THAT.
WITH WHOM AM I SPEAKING?
THIS IS ANTONIO LOPEZ DE SANTA ANNA.
HELLO, SEÑOR PRESIDENTE.
I HAVE FRIENDLY FEELINGS FOR TEXAS. I HAVE BEEN THERE BEFORE, YOU KNOW.
OH?
YES.
MAYBE I WILL COME AND VISIT TEXAS AGAIN.

CHAPTER 8

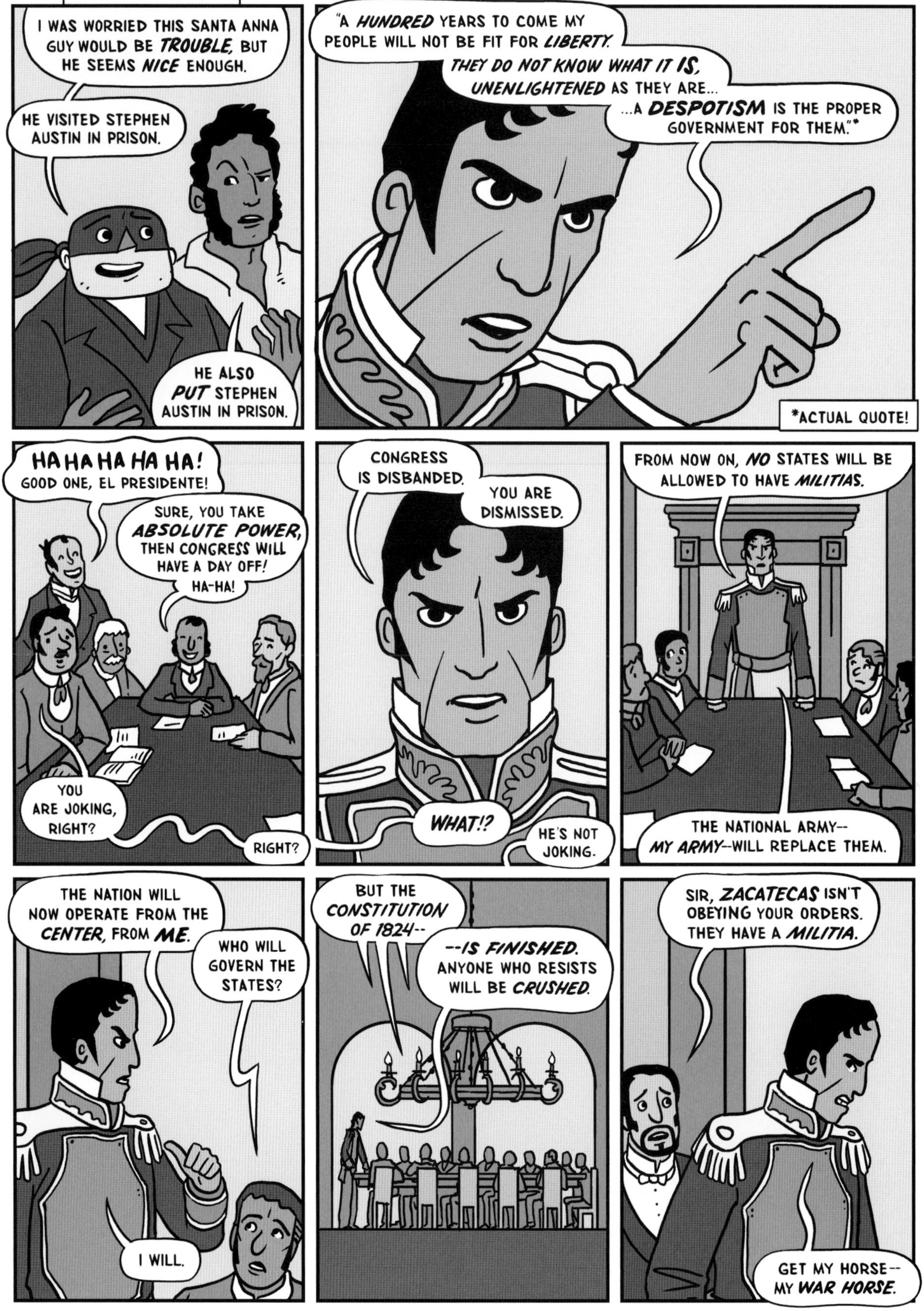

I WAS WORRIED THIS SANTA ANNA GUY WOULD BE TROUBLE, BUT HE SEEMS NICE ENOUGH.
HE VISITED STEPHEN AUSTIN IN PRISON.
HE ALSO PUT STEPHEN AUSTIN IN PRISON.
"A HUNDRED YEARS TO COME MY PEOPLE WILL NOT BE FIT FOR LIBERTY.
THEY DO NOT KNOW WHAT IT IS, UNENLIGHTENED AS THEY ARE...
...A DESPOTISM IS THE PROPER GOVERNMENT FOR THEM."*
*ACTUAL QUOTE!
HA HA HA HA HA HA! GOOD ONE, EL PRESIDENTE!
SURE, YOU TAKE ABSOLUTE POWER, THEN CONGRESS WILL HAVE A DAY OFF! HA-HA!
YOU ARE JOKING, RIGHT?
RIGHT?
CONGRESS IS DISBANDED.
YOU ARE DISMISSED.
WHAT!?
HE'S NOT JOKING.
FROM NOW ON, NO STATES WILL BE ALLOWED TO HAVE MILITIAS.
THE NATIONAL ARMY-- MY ARMY--WILL REPLACE THEM.
THE NATION WILL NOW OPERATE FROM THE CENTER, FROM ME.
WHO WILL GOVERN THE STATES?
I WILL.
BUT THE CONSTITUTION OF 1824--
--IS FINISHED. ANYONE WHO RESISTS WILL BE CRUSHED.
SIR, ZACATECAS ISN'T OBEYING YOUR ORDERS. THEY HAVE A MILITIA.
GET MY HORSE-- MY WAR HORSE.

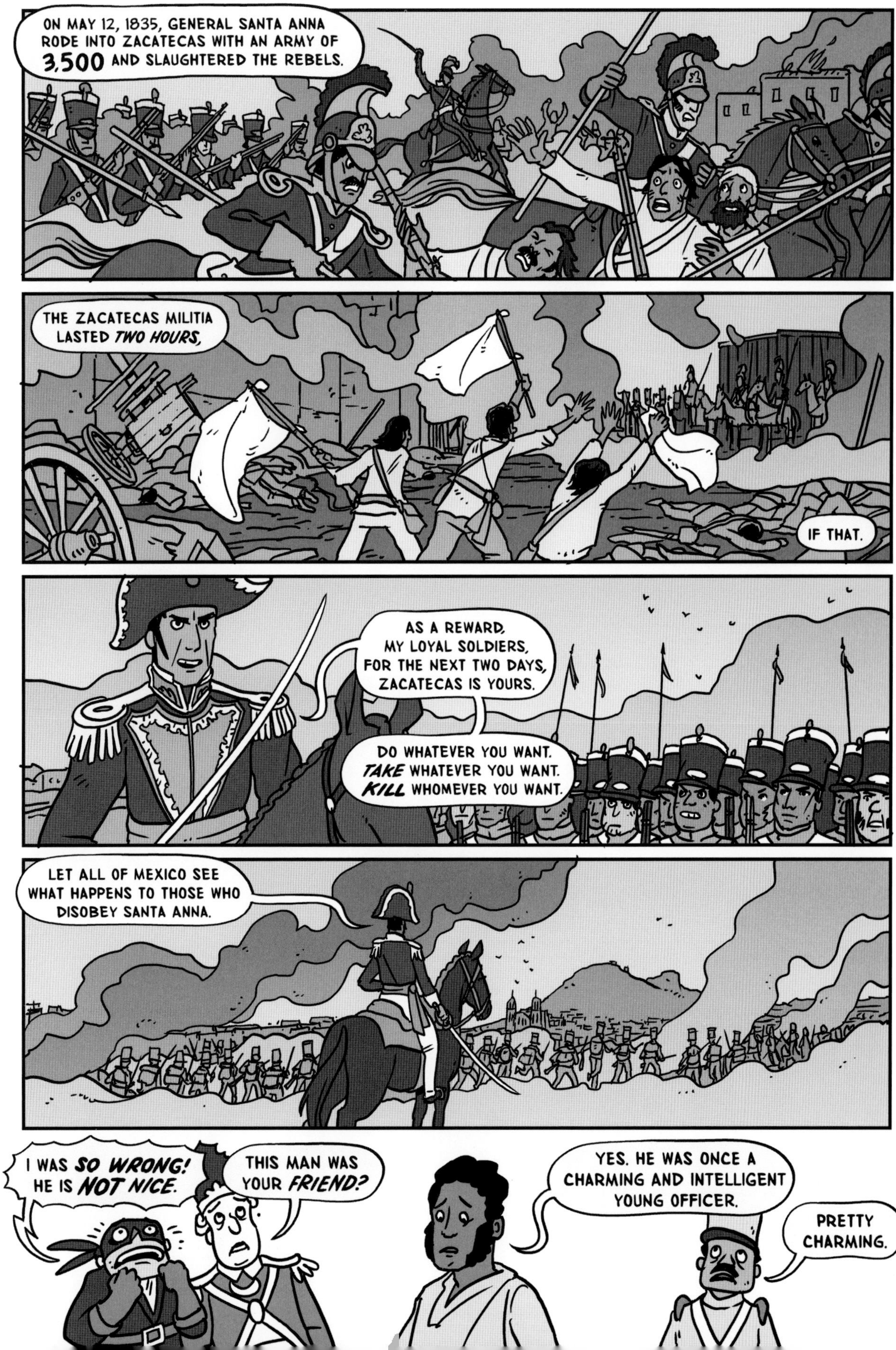
ON MAY 12, 1835, GENERAL SANTA ANNA RODE INTO ZACATECAS WITH AN ARMY OF 3,500 AND SLAUGHTERED THE REBELS.
THE ZACATECAS MILITIA LASTED *TWO HOURS*,
IF THAT.
AS A REWARD, MY LOYAL SOLDIERS, FOR THE NEXT TWO DAYS, ZACATECAS IS YOURS.
DO WHATEVER YOU WANT. ***TAKE*** WHATEVER YOU WANT. ***KILL*** WHOMEVER YOU WANT.
LET ALL OF MEXICO SEE WHAT HAPPENS TO THOSE WHO DISOBEY SANTA ANNA.
I WAS ***SO WRONG!*** HE IS ***NOT NICE***.
THIS MAN WAS YOUR *FRIEND?*
YES. HE WAS ONCE A CHARMING AND INTELLIGENT YOUNG OFFICER.
PRETTY CHARMING.

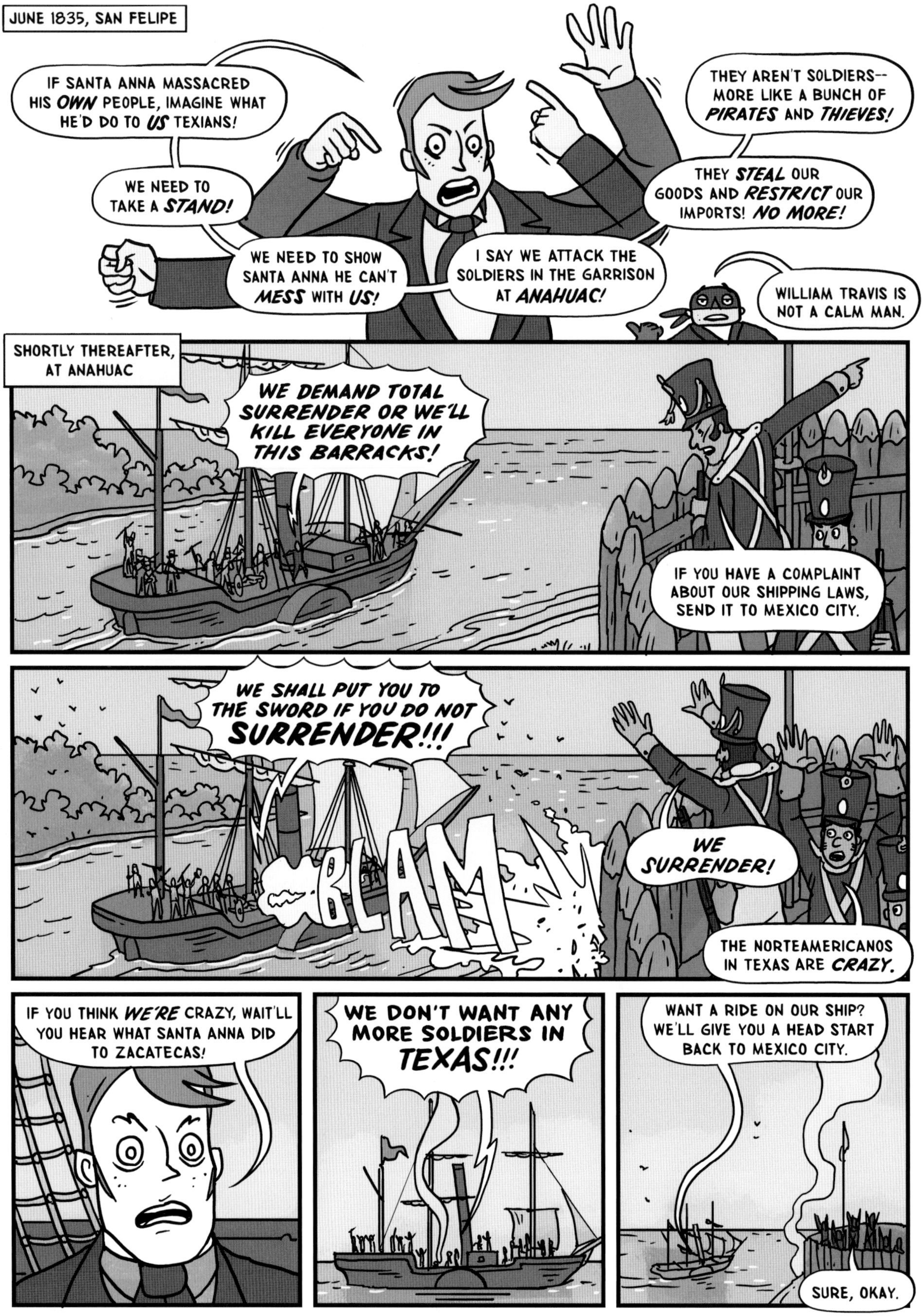
JUNE 1835, SAN FELIPE
IF SANTA ANNA MASSACRED HIS OWN PEOPLE, IMAGINE WHAT HE'D DO TO US TEXIANS!
WE NEED TO TAKE A STAND!
WE NEED TO SHOW SANTA ANNA HE CAN'T MESS WITH US!
I SAY WE ATTACK THE SOLDIERS IN THE GARRISON AT ANAHUAC!
THEY AREN'T SOLDIERS-- MORE LIKE A BUNCH OF PIRATES AND THIEVES!
THEY STEAL OUR GOODS AND RESTRICT OUR IMPORTS! NO MORE!
WILLIAM TRAVIS IS NOT A CALM MAN.
SHORTLY THEREAFTER, AT ANAHUAC
WE DEMAND TOTAL SURRENDER OR WE'LL KILL EVERYONE IN THIS BARRACKS!
IF YOU HAVE A COMPLAINT ABOUT OUR SHIPPING LAWS, SEND IT TO MEXICO CITY.
WE SHALL PUT YOU TO THE SWORD IF YOU DO NOT SURRENDER!!!
BLAM
WE SURRENDER!
THE NORTEAMERICANOS IN TEXAS ARE CRAZY.
IF YOU THINK WE'RE CRAZY, WAIT'LL YOU HEAR WHAT SANTA ANNA DID TO ZACATECAS!
WE DON'T WANT ANY MORE SOLDIERS IN TEXAS!!!
WANT A RIDE ON OUR SHIP? WE'LL GIVE YOU A HEAD START BACK TO MEXICO CITY.
SURE, OKAY.

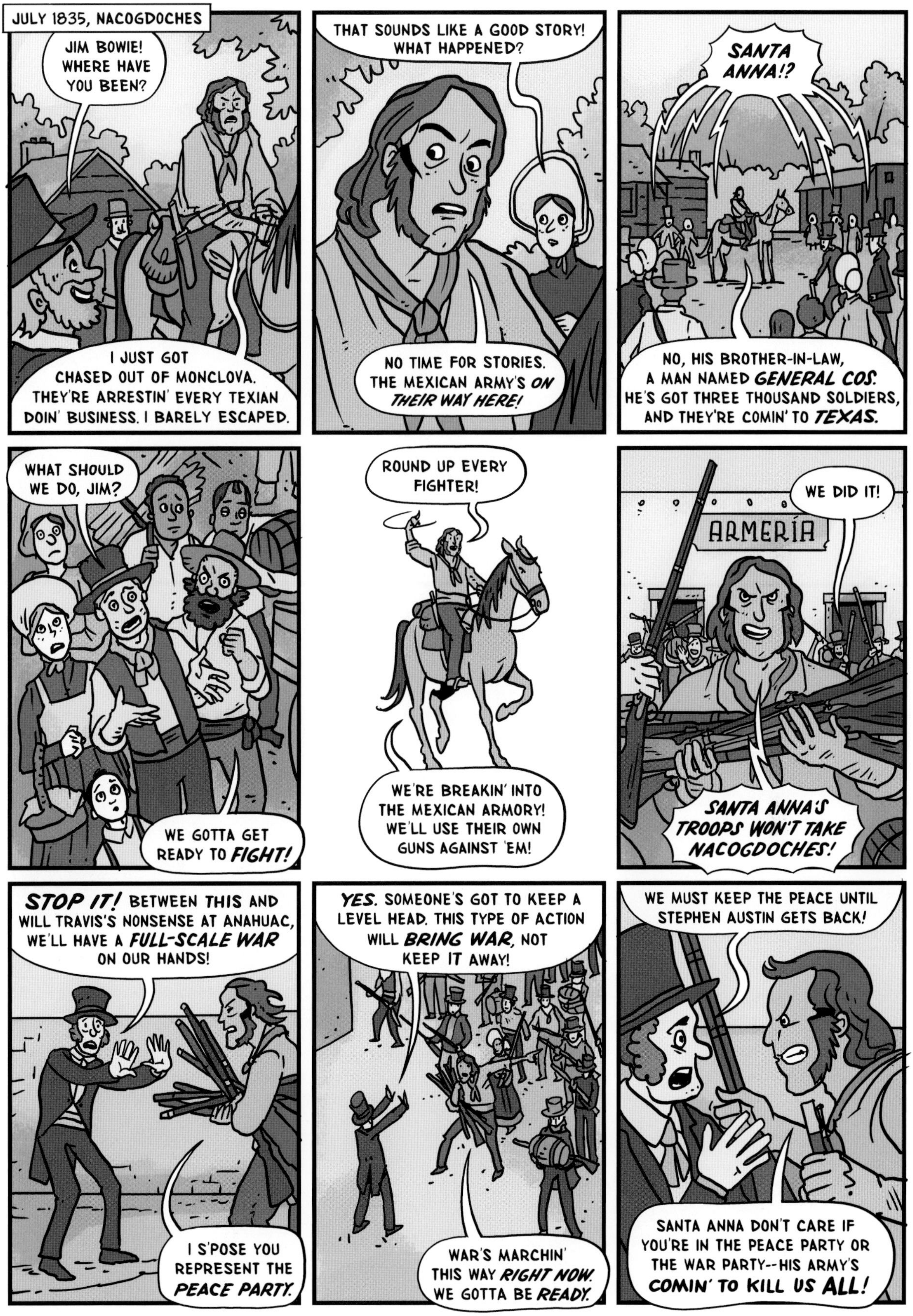
JULY 1835, NACOGDOCHES
JIM BOWIE! WHERE HAVE YOU BEEN?
I JUST GOT CHASED OUT OF MONCLOVA. THEY'RE ARRESTIN' EVERY TEXIAN DOIN' BUSINESS. I BARELY ESCAPED.
THAT SOUNDS LIKE A GOOD STORY! WHAT HAPPENED?
NO TIME FOR STORIES. THE MEXICAN ARMY'S *ON THEIR WAY HERE!*
SANTA ANNA!?
NO, HIS BROTHER-IN-LAW, A MAN NAMED ***GENERAL COS.*** HE'S GOT THREE THOUSAND SOLDIERS, AND THEY'RE COMIN' TO ***TEXAS.***
WHAT SHOULD WE DO, JIM?
WE GOTTA GET READY TO ***FIGHT!***
ROUND UP EVERY FIGHTER!
WE'RE BREAKIN' INTO THE MEXICAN ARMORY! WE'LL USE THEIR OWN GUNS AGAINST 'EM!
ARMERÍA
WE DID IT!
SANTA ANNA'S TROOPS WON'T TAKE NACOGDOCHES!
STOP IT! BETWEEN THIS AND WILL TRAVIS'S NONSENSE AT ANAHUAC, WE'LL HAVE A ***FULL-SCALE WAR*** ON OUR HANDS!
I S'POSE YOU REPRESENT THE ***PEACE PARTY.***
YES. SOMEONE'S GOT TO KEEP A LEVEL HEAD. THIS TYPE OF ACTION WILL ***BRING WAR,*** NOT KEEP IT AWAY!
WAR'S MARCHIN' THIS WAY ***RIGHT NOW.*** WE GOTTA BE ***READY.***
WE MUST KEEP THE PEACE UNTIL STEPHEN AUSTIN GETS BACK!
SANTA ANNA DON'T CARE IF YOU'RE IN THE PEACE PARTY OR THE WAR PARTY--HIS ARMY'S **COMIN' TO KILL US ALL!**

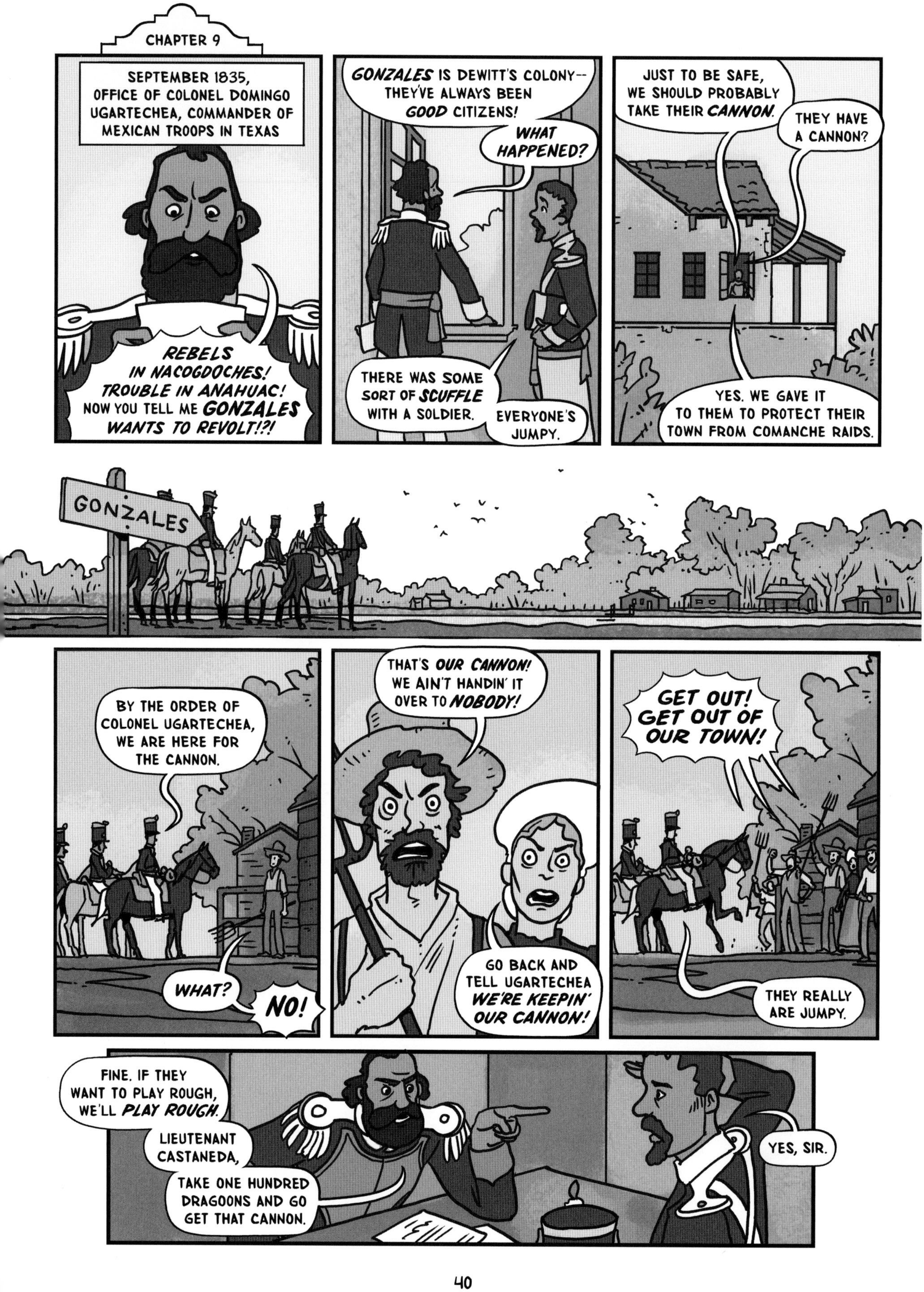
CHAPTER 9
SEPTEMBER 1835, OFFICE OF COLONEL DOMINGO UGARTECHEA, COMMANDER OF MEXICAN TROOPS IN TEXAS
REBELS IN NACOGDOCHES! TROUBLE IN ANAHUAC! NOW YOU TELL ME GONZALES WANTS TO REVOLT!?!
GONZALES IS DEWITT'S COLONY-- THEY'VE ALWAYS BEEN GOOD CITIZENS!
WHAT HAPPENED?
THERE WAS SOME SORT OF SCUFFLE WITH A SOLDIER.
EVERYONE'S JUMPY.
JUST TO BE SAFE, WE SHOULD PROBABLY TAKE THEIR CANNON.
THEY HAVE A CANNON?
YES. WE GAVE IT TO THEM TO PROTECT THEIR TOWN FROM COMANCHE RAIDS.
GONZALES
BY THE ORDER OF COLONEL UGARTECHEA, WE ARE HERE FOR THE CANNON.
WHAT?
NO!
THAT'S OUR CANNON! WE AIN'T HANDIN' IT OVER TO NOBODY!
GO BACK AND TELL UGARTECHEA WE'RE KEEPIN' OUR CANNON!
GET OUT! GET OUT OF OUR TOWN!
THEY REALLY ARE JUMPY.
FINE. IF THEY WANT TO PLAY ROUGH, WE'LL PLAY ROUGH.
LIEUTENANT CASTANEDA,
TAKE ONE HUNDRED DRAGOONS AND GO GET THAT CANNON.
YES, SIR.

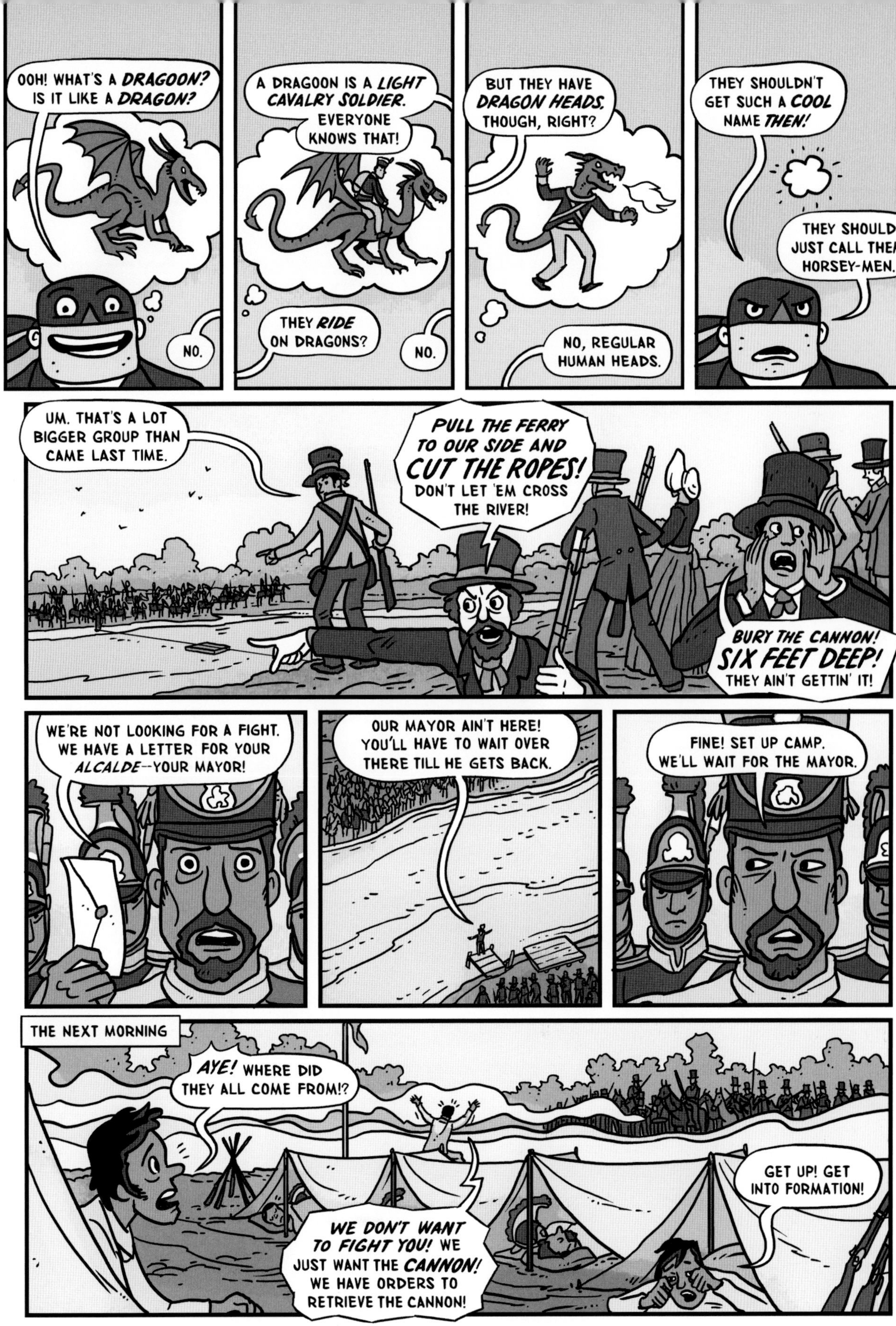
OOH! WHAT'S A DRAGOON? IS IT LIKE A DRAGON?
NO.
A DRAGOON IS A LIGHT CAVALRY SOLDIER.
EVERYONE KNOWS THAT!
THEY RIDE ON DRAGONS?
NO.
BUT THEY HAVE DRAGON HEADS, THOUGH, RIGHT?
NO, REGULAR HUMAN HEADS.
THEY SHOULDN'T GET SUCH A COOL NAME THEN!
THEY SHOULD JUST CALL THEM HORSEY-MEN.
UM. THAT'S A LOT BIGGER GROUP THAN CAME LAST TIME.
PULL THE FERRY TO OUR SIDE AND CUT THE ROPES! DON'T LET 'EM CROSS THE RIVER!
BURY THE CANNON! SIX FEET DEEP! THEY AIN'T GETTIN' IT!
WE'RE NOT LOOKING FOR A FIGHT. WE HAVE A LETTER FOR YOUR ALCALDE--YOUR MAYOR!
OUR MAYOR AIN'T HERE! YOU'LL HAVE TO WAIT OVER THERE TILL HE GETS BACK.
FINE! SET UP CAMP. WE'LL WAIT FOR THE MAYOR.
THE NEXT MORNING
AYE! WHERE DID THEY ALL COME FROM!?
WE DON'T WANT TO FIGHT YOU! WE JUST WANT THE CANNON! WE HAVE ORDERS TO RETRIEVE THE CANNON!
GET UP! GET INTO FORMATION!

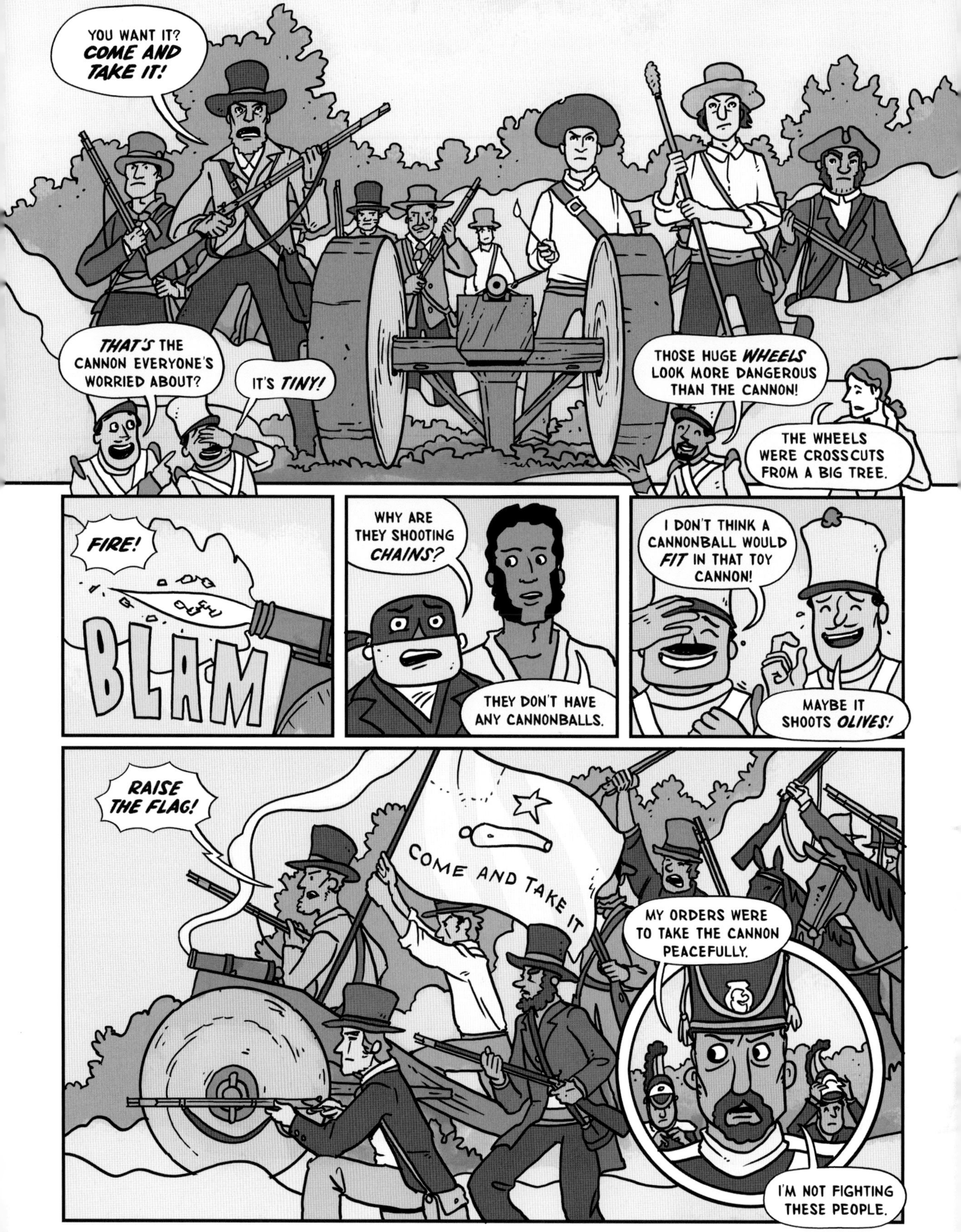
YOU WANT IT? COME AND TAKE IT!
THAT'S THE CANNON EVERYONE'S WORRIED ABOUT?
IT'S TINY!
THOSE HUGE WHEELS LOOK MORE DANGEROUS THAN THE CANNON!
THE WHEELS WERE CROSSCUTS FROM A BIG TREE.
FIRE!
BLAM
WHY ARE THEY SHOOTING CHAINS?
THEY DON'T HAVE ANY CANNONBALLS.
I DON'T THINK A CANNONBALL WOULD FIT IN THAT TOY CANNON!
MAYBE IT SHOOTS OLIVES!
RAISE THE FLAG!
COME AND TAKE IT
MY ORDERS WERE TO TAKE THE CANNON PEACEFULLY.
I'M NOT FIGHTING THESE PEOPLE.

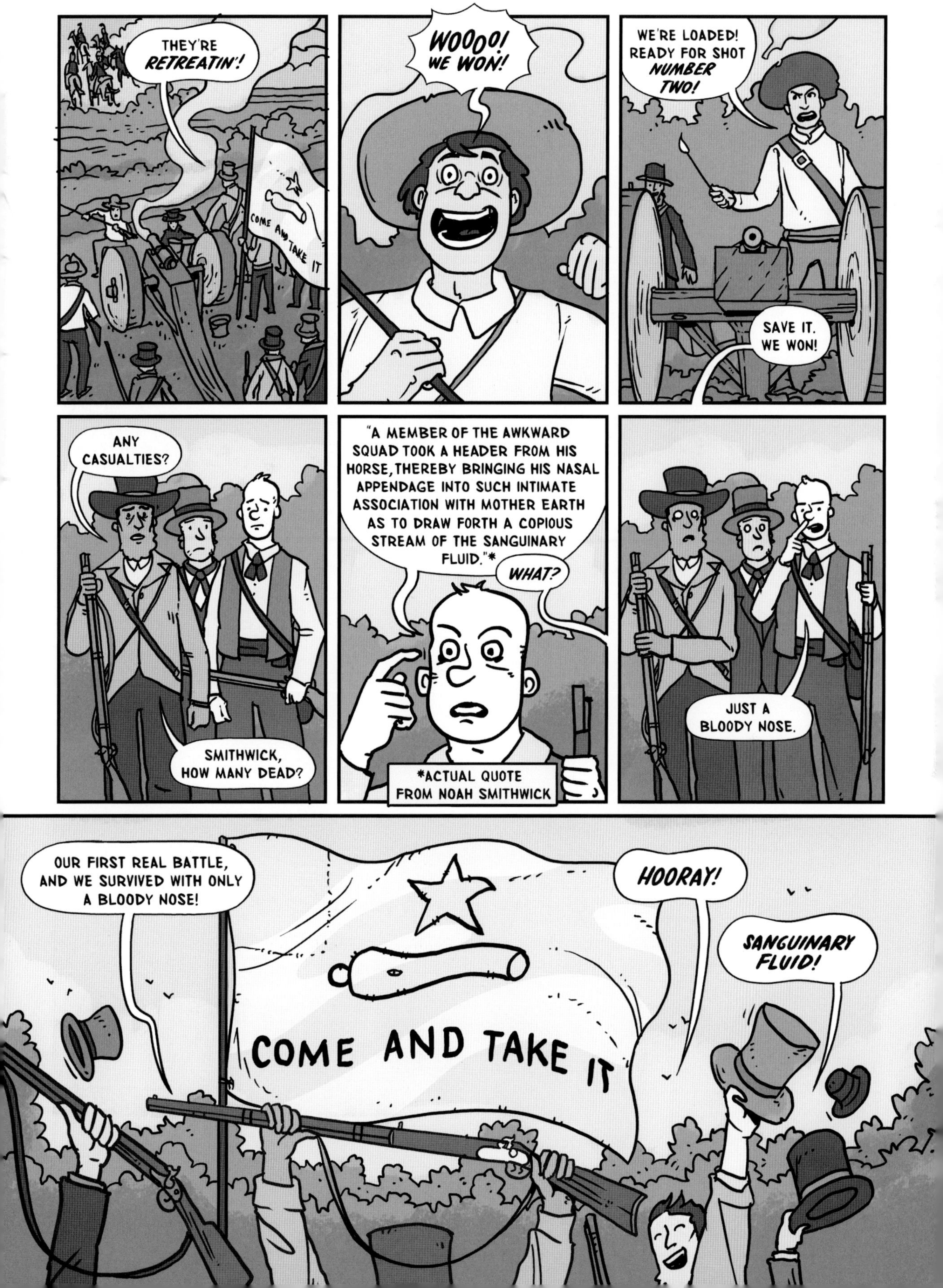

THEY'RE *RETREATIN'*!
COME AND TAKE IT
WOOOO! WE WON!
WE'RE LOADED! READY FOR SHOT *NUMBER TWO!*
SAVE IT. WE WON!
ANY CASUALTIES?
SMITHWICK, HOW MANY DEAD?
"A MEMBER OF THE AWKWARD SQUAD TOOK A HEADER FROM HIS HORSE, THEREBY BRINGING HIS NASAL APPENDAGE INTO SUCH INTIMATE ASSOCIATION WITH MOTHER EARTH AS TO DRAW FORTH A COPIOUS STREAM OF THE SANGUINARY FLUID."*
WHAT?
*ACTUAL QUOTE FROM NOAH SMITHWICK
JUST A BLOODY NOSE.
OUR FIRST REAL BATTLE, AND WE SURVIVED WITH ONLY A BLOODY NOSE!
COME AND TAKE IT
HOORAY!
SANGUINARY FLUID!

CHAPTER 10

SEPTEMBER 1835, SAN FELIPE

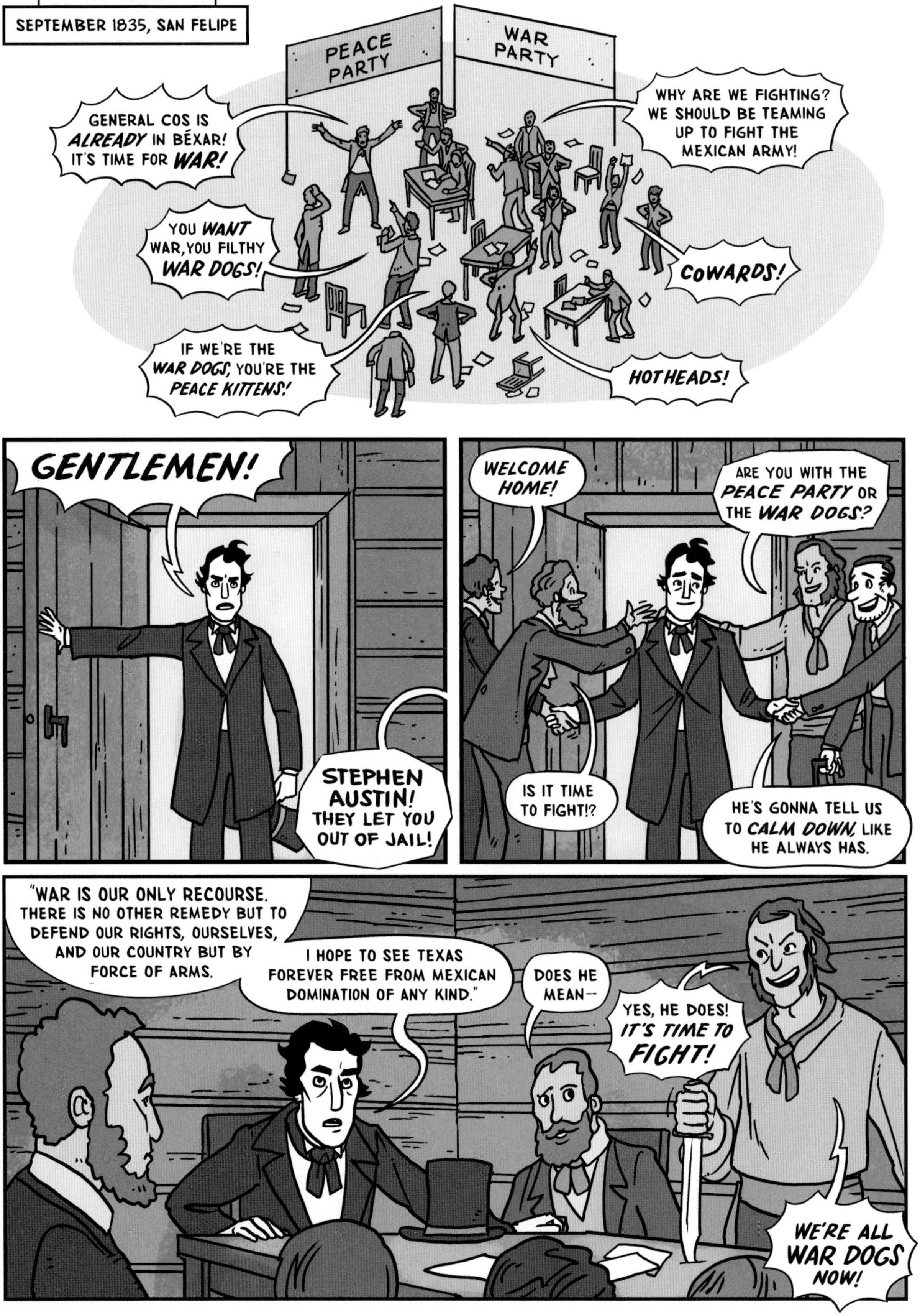

PEACE PARTY
WAR PARTY
GENERAL COS IS ALREADY IN BÉXAR! IT'S TIME FOR WAR!
WHY ARE WE FIGHTING? WE SHOULD BE TEAMING UP TO FIGHT THE MEXICAN ARMY!
YOU WANT WAR, YOU FILTHY WAR DOGS!
COWARDS!
IF WE'RE THE WAR DOGS, YOU'RE THE PEACE KITTENS!
HOTHEADS!
GENTLEMEN!
STEPHEN AUSTIN! THEY LET YOU OUT OF JAIL!
WELCOME HOME!
ARE YOU WITH THE PEACE PARTY OR THE WAR DOGS?
IS IT TIME TO FIGHT!?
HE'S GONNA TELL US TO CALM DOWN, LIKE HE ALWAYS HAS.
"WAR IS OUR ONLY RECOURSE. THERE IS NO OTHER REMEDY BUT TO DEFEND OUR RIGHTS, OURSELVES, AND OUR COUNTRY BUT BY FORCE OF ARMS.
I HOPE TO SEE TEXAS FOREVER FREE FROM MEXICAN DOMINATION OF ANY KIND."
DOES HE MEAN--
YES, HE DOES! IT'S TIME TO FIGHT!
WE'RE ALL WAR DOGS NOW!

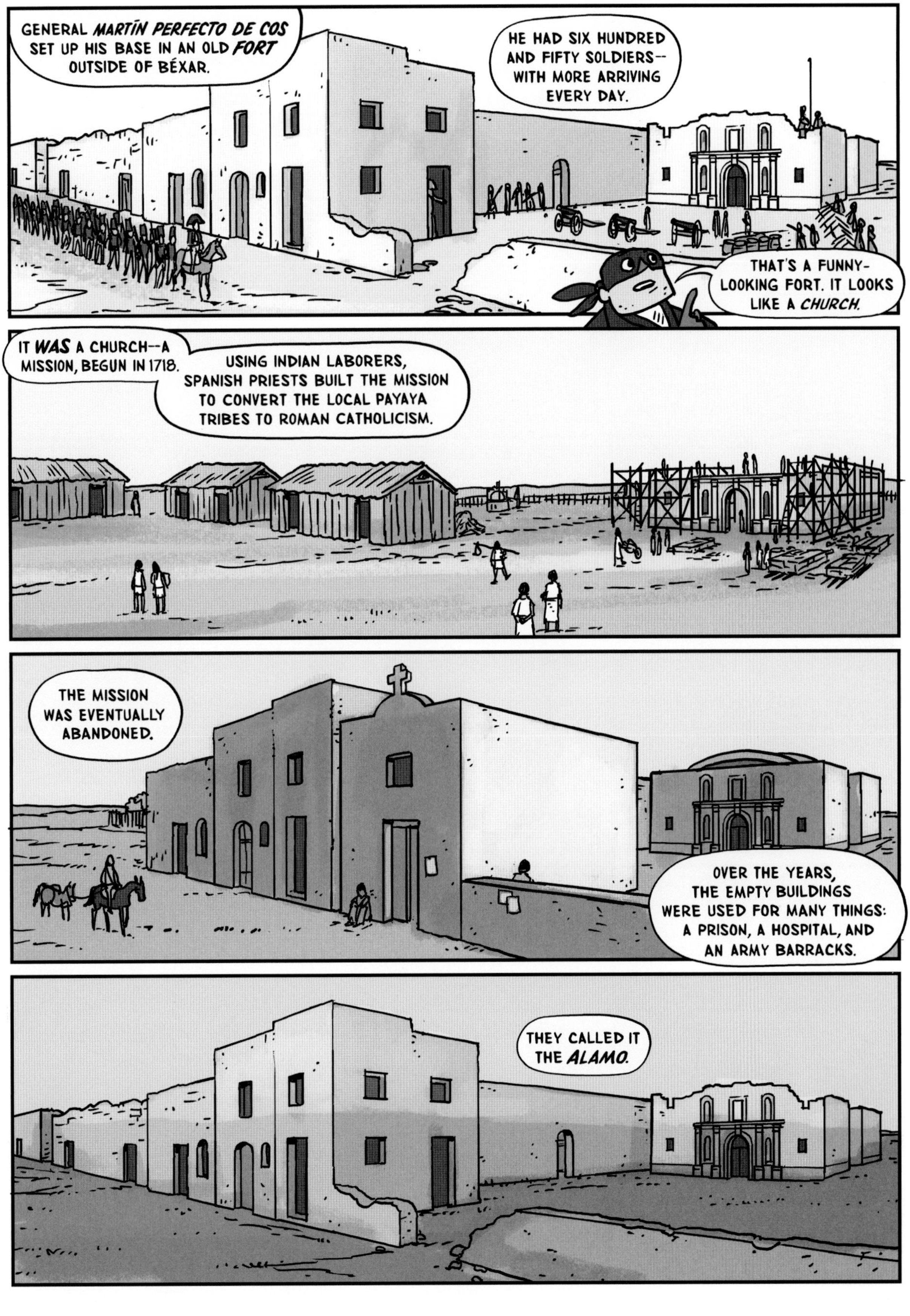
GENERAL *MARTÍN PERFECTO DE COS* SET UP HIS BASE IN AN OLD *FORT* OUTSIDE OF BÉXAR.
HE HAD SIX HUNDRED AND FIFTY SOLDIERS-- WITH MORE ARRIVING EVERY DAY.
THAT'S A FUNNY-LOOKING FORT. IT LOOKS LIKE A *CHURCH.*
IT ***WAS*** A CHURCH--A MISSION, BEGUN IN 1718.
USING INDIAN LABORERS, SPANISH PRIESTS BUILT THE MISSION TO CONVERT THE LOCAL PAYAYA TRIBES TO ROMAN CATHOLICISM.
THE MISSION WAS EVENTUALLY ABANDONED.
OVER THE YEARS, THE EMPTY BUILDINGS WERE USED FOR MANY THINGS: A PRISON, A HOSPITAL, AND AN ARMY BARRACKS.
THEY CALLED IT THE *ALAMO.*

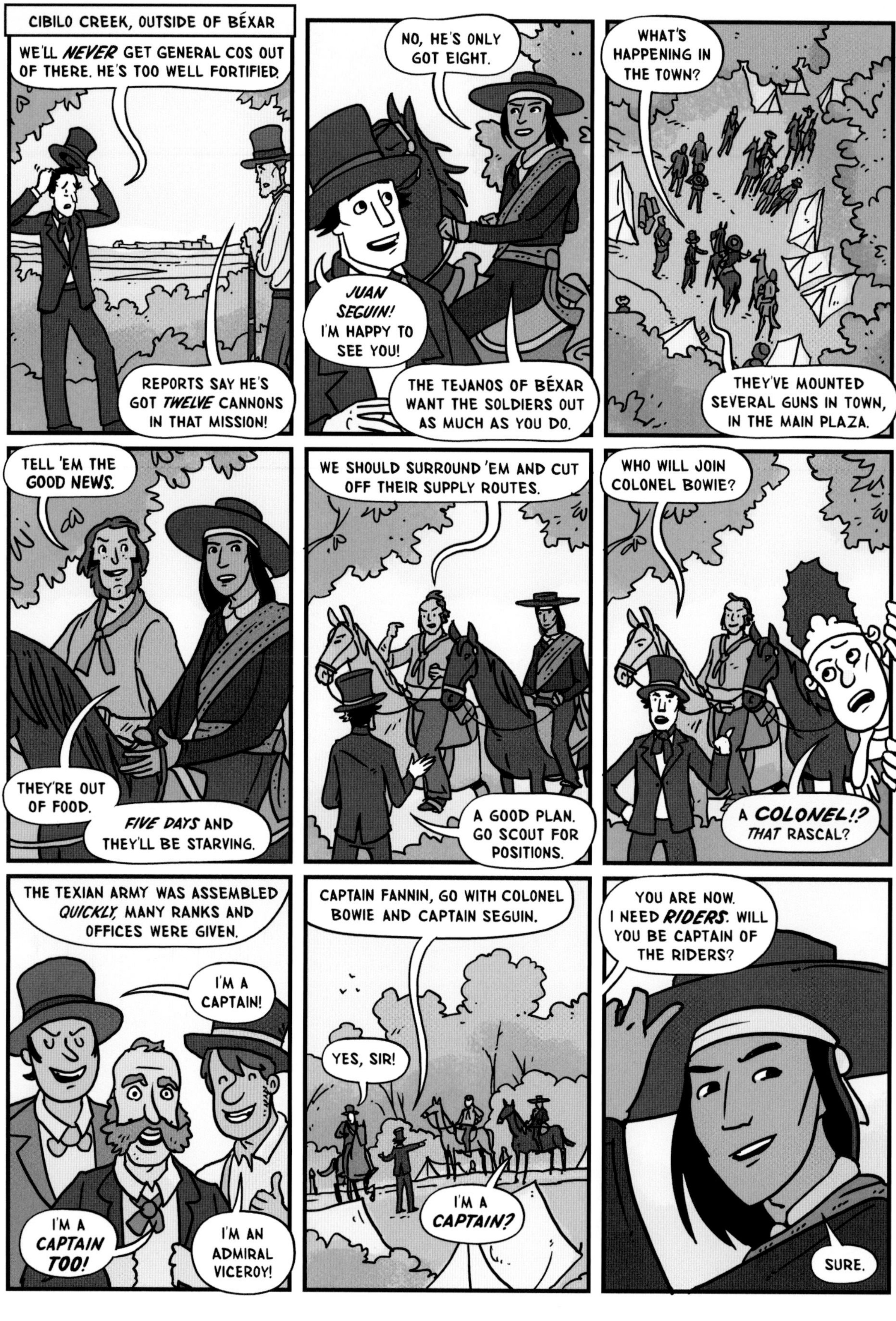
CIBILO CREEK, OUTSIDE OF BÉXAR
WE'LL *NEVER* GET GENERAL COS OUT OF THERE. HE'S TOO WELL FORTIFIED.
REPORTS SAY HE'S GOT *TWELVE* CANNONS IN THAT MISSION!
NO, HE'S ONLY GOT EIGHT.
JUAN SEGUIN! I'M HAPPY TO SEE YOU!
THE TEJANOS OF BÉXAR WANT THE SOLDIERS OUT AS MUCH AS YOU DO.
WHAT'S HAPPENING IN THE TOWN?
THEY'VE MOUNTED SEVERAL GUNS IN TOWN, IN THE MAIN PLAZA.
TELL 'EM THE GOOD NEWS.
THEY'RE OUT OF FOOD.
FIVE DAYS AND THEY'LL BE STARVING.
WE SHOULD SURROUND 'EM AND CUT OFF THEIR SUPPLY ROUTES.
A GOOD PLAN. GO SCOUT FOR POSITIONS.
WHO WILL JOIN COLONEL BOWIE?
A *COLONEL!?* *THAT* RASCAL?
THE TEXIAN ARMY WAS ASSEMBLED *QUICKLY*, MANY RANKS AND OFFICES WERE GIVEN.
I'M A CAPTAIN!
I'M A *CAPTAIN TOO!*
I'M AN ADMIRAL VICEROY!
CAPTAIN FANNIN, GO WITH COLONEL BOWIE AND CAPTAIN SEGUIN.
YES, SIR!
I'M A *CAPTAIN?*
YOU ARE NOW. I NEED *RIDERS*. WILL YOU BE CAPTAIN OF THE RIDERS?
SURE.

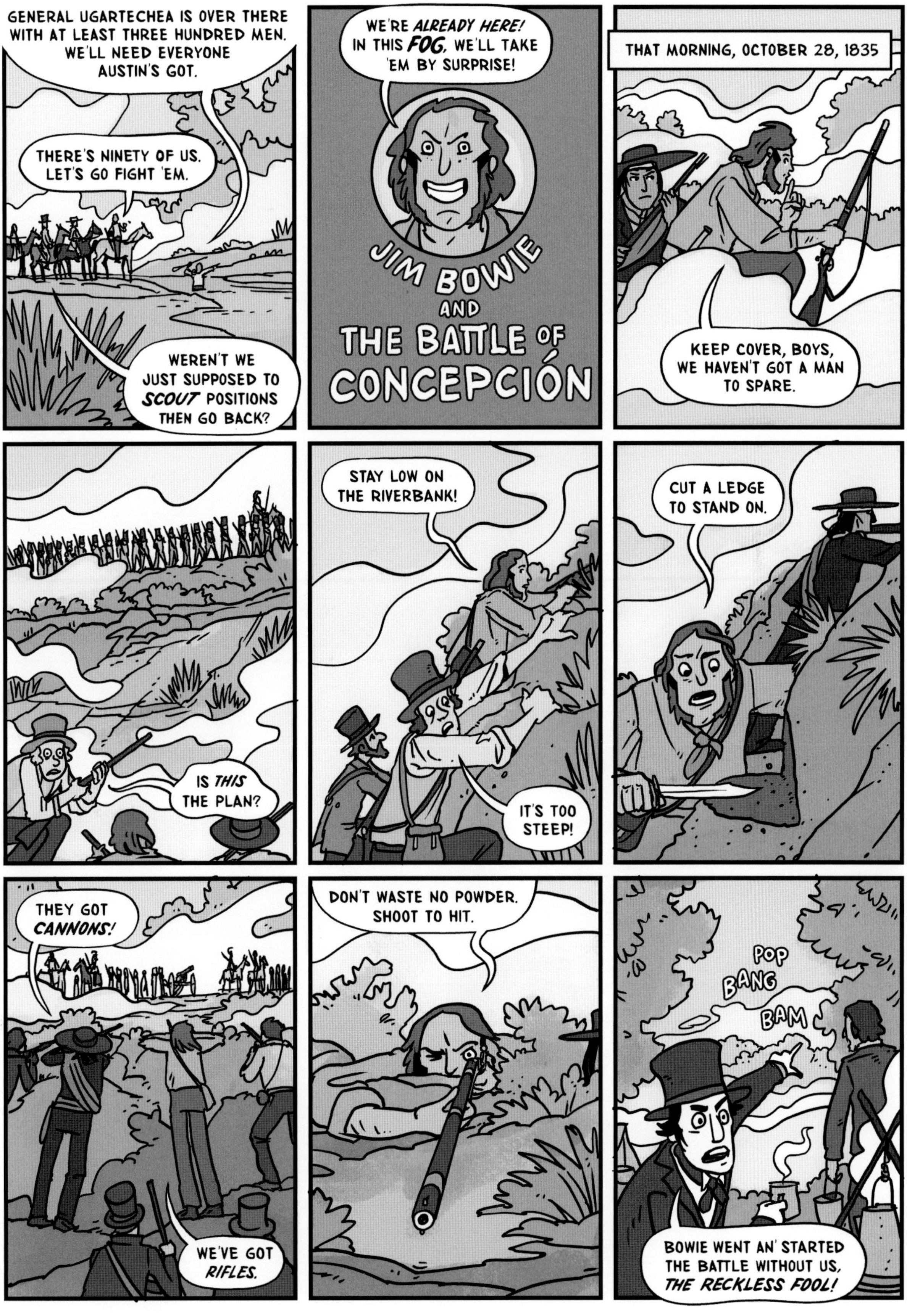
GENERAL UGARTECHEA IS OVER THERE WITH AT LEAST THREE HUNDRED MEN. WE'LL NEED EVERYONE AUSTIN'S GOT.
THERE'S NINETY OF US. LET'S GO FIGHT 'EM.
WEREN'T WE JUST SUPPOSED TO SCOUT POSITIONS THEN GO BACK?
WE'RE ALREADY HERE! IN THIS FOG, WE'LL TAKE 'EM BY SURPRISE!
JIM BOWIE AND THE BATTLE OF CONCEPCIÓN
THAT MORNING, OCTOBER 28, 1835
KEEP COVER, BOYS, WE HAVEN'T GOT A MAN TO SPARE.
IS THIS THE PLAN?
STAY LOW ON THE RIVERBANK!
IT'S TOO STEEP!
CUT A LEDGE TO STAND ON.
THEY GOT CANNONS!
WE'VE GOT RIFLES.
DON'T WASTE NO POWDER. SHOOT TO HIT.
POP
BANG
BAM
BOWIE WENT AN' STARTED THE BATTLE WITHOUT US, THE RECKLESS FOOL!

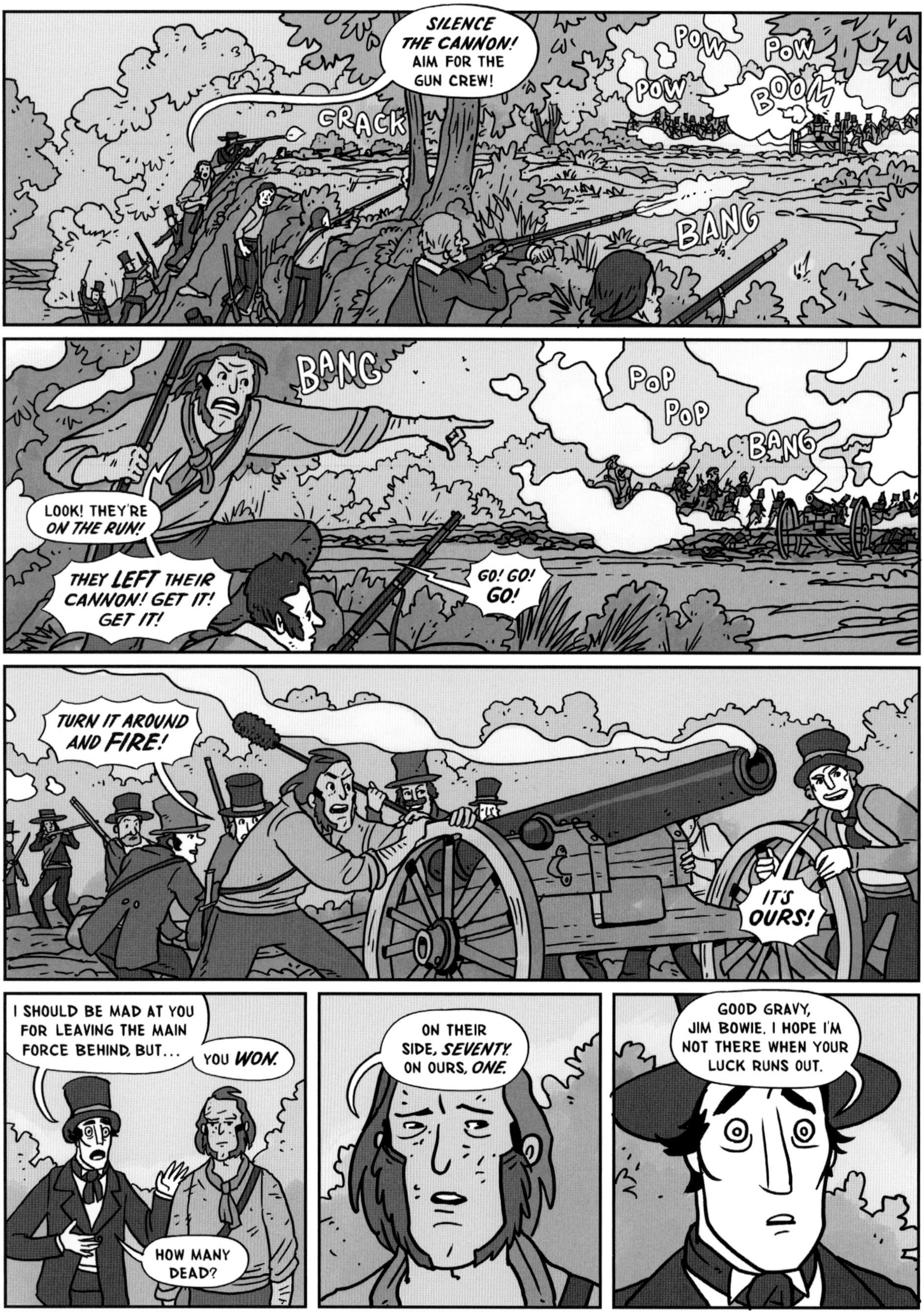

SILENCE THE CANNON! AIM FOR THE GUN CREW!
POW
POW
POW
BOOM
CRACK
BANG
BANG
POP
POP
BANG
LOOK! THEY'RE ON THE RUN!
THEY LEFT THEIR CANNON! GET IT! GET IT!
GO! GO! GO!
TURN IT AROUND AND FIRE!
IT'S OURS!
I SHOULD BE MAD AT YOU FOR LEAVING THE MAIN FORCE BEHIND, BUT...
YOU WON.
HOW MANY DEAD?
ON THEIR SIDE, SEVENTY. ON OURS, ONE.
GOOD GRAVY, JIM BOWIE. I HOPE I'M NOT THERE WHEN YOUR LUCK RUNS OUT.

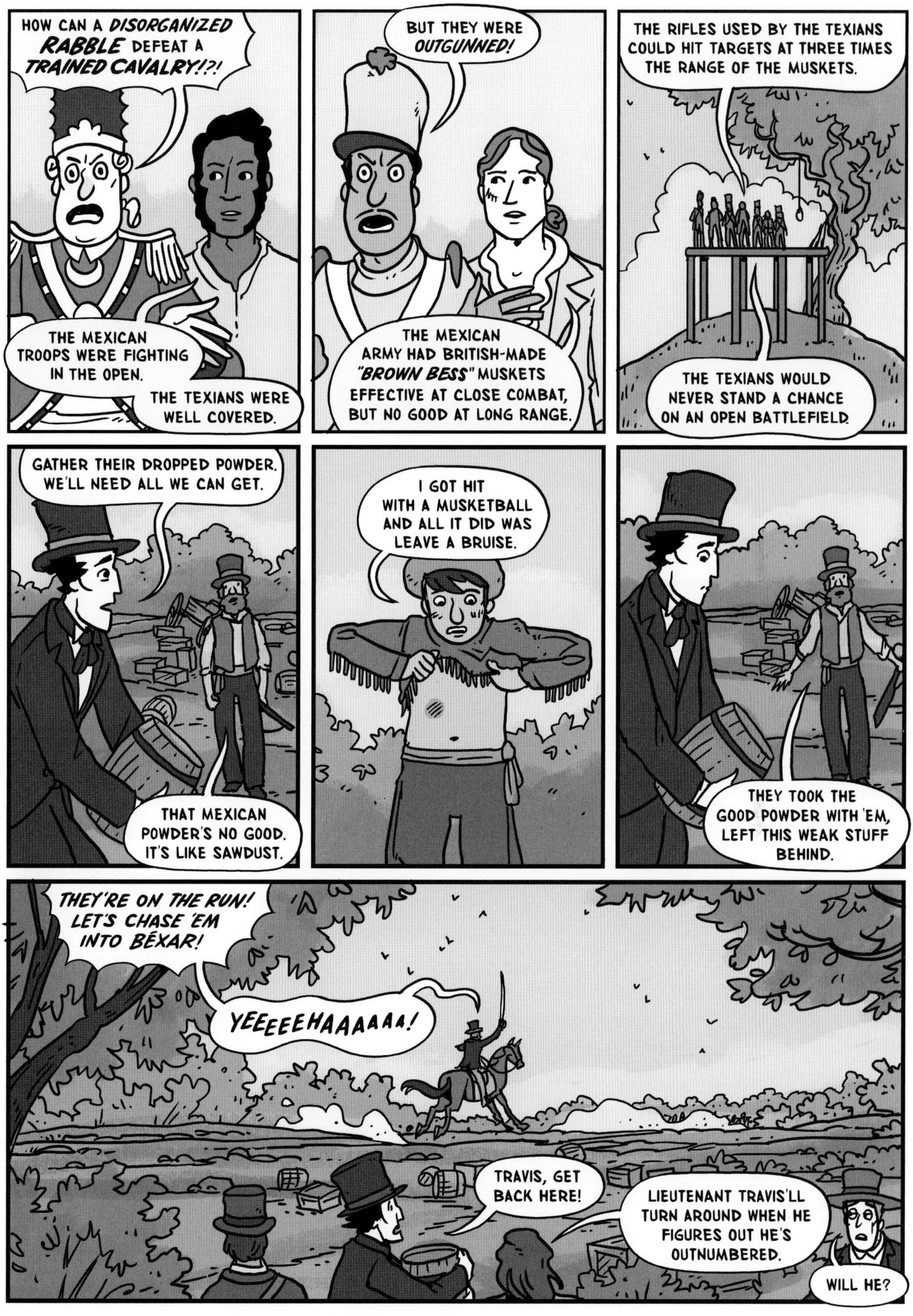
HOW CAN A *DISORGANIZED* *RABBLE* DEFEAT A *TRAINED CAVALRY!?!*
THE MEXICAN TROOPS WERE FIGHTING IN THE OPEN.
THE TEXIANS WERE WELL COVERED.
BUT THEY WERE *OUTGUNNED!*
THE MEXICAN ARMY HAD BRITISH-MADE *"BROWN BESS"* MUSKETS EFFECTIVE AT CLOSE COMBAT, BUT NO GOOD AT LONG RANGE.
THE RIFLES USED BY THE TEXIANS COULD HIT TARGETS AT THREE TIMES THE RANGE OF THE MUSKETS.
THE TEXIANS WOULD NEVER STAND A CHANCE ON AN OPEN BATTLEFIELD.
GATHER THEIR DROPPED POWDER. WE'LL NEED ALL WE CAN GET.
THAT MEXICAN POWDER'S NO GOOD. IT'S LIKE SAWDUST.
I GOT HIT WITH A MUSKETBALL AND ALL IT DID WAS LEAVE A BRUISE.
THEY TOOK THE GOOD POWDER WITH 'EM, LEFT THIS WEAK STUFF BEHIND.
THEY'RE ON THE RUN! LET'S CHASE 'EM INTO BÉXAR!
YEEEEEHAAAAAA!
TRAVIS, GET BACK HERE!
LIEUTENANT TRAVIS'LL TURN AROUND WHEN HE FIGURES OUT HE'S OUTNUMBERED.
WILL HE?

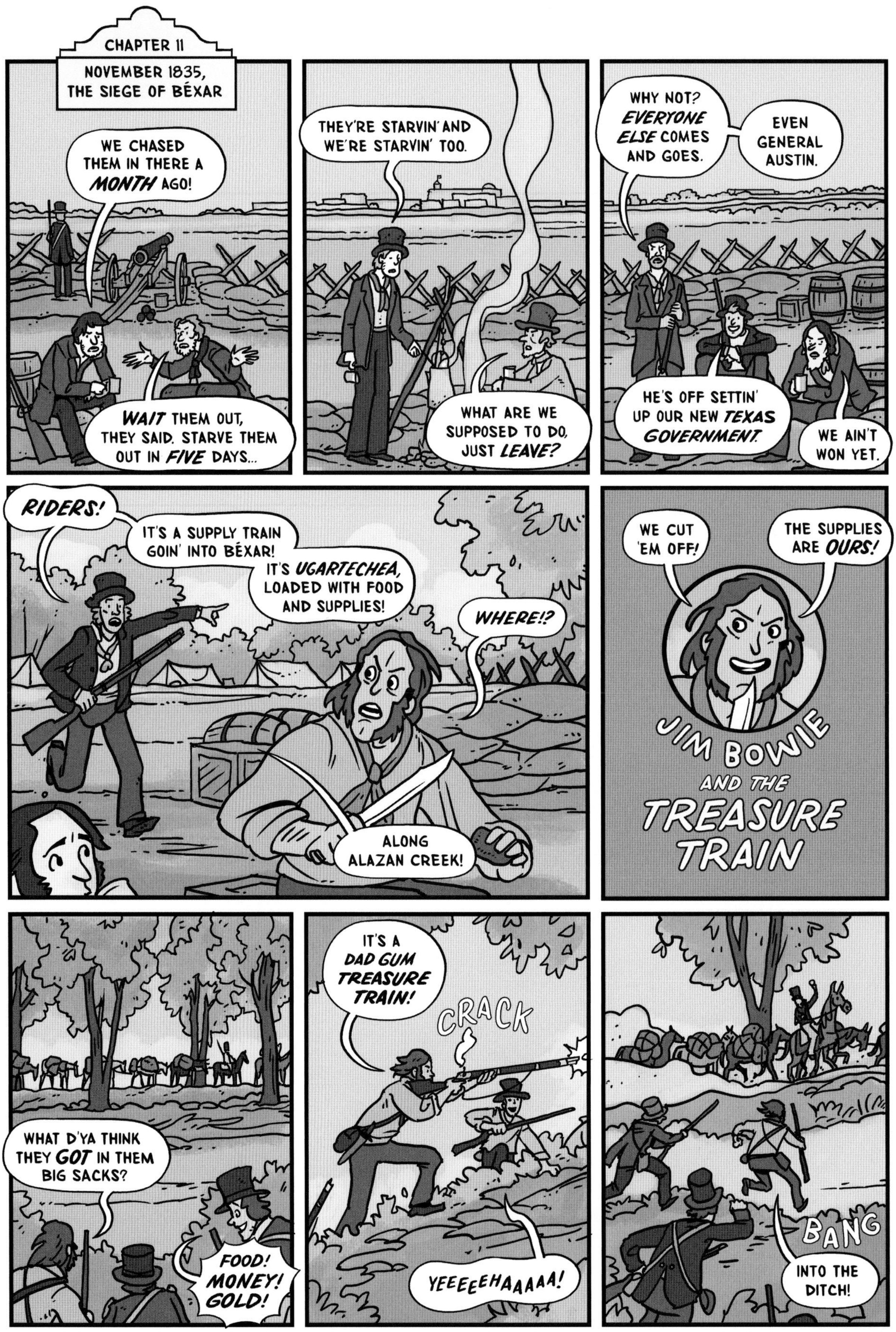

CHAPTER 11
NOVEMBER 1835, THE SIEGE OF BÉXAR
WE CHASED THEM IN THERE A MONTH AGO!
WAIT THEM OUT, THEY SAID. STARVE THEM OUT IN FIVE DAYS...
THEY'RE STARVIN' AND WE'RE STARVIN' TOO.
WHAT ARE WE SUPPOSED TO DO, JUST LEAVE?
WHY NOT? EVERYONE ELSE COMES AND GOES.
EVEN GENERAL AUSTIN.
HE'S OFF SETTIN' UP OUR NEW TEXAS GOVERNMENT.
WE AIN'T WON YET.
RIDERS!
IT'S A SUPPLY TRAIN GOIN' INTO BÉXAR!
IT'S UGARTECHEA, LOADED WITH FOOD AND SUPPLIES!
WHERE!?
ALONG ALAZAN CREEK!
WE CUT 'EM OFF!
THE SUPPLIES ARE OURS!
JIM BOWIE AND THE TREASURE TRAIN
WHAT D'YA THINK THEY GOT IN THEM BIG SACKS?
FOOD! MONEY! GOLD!
IT'S A DAD GUM TREASURE TRAIN!
CRACK
YEEEEEHAAAAA!
BANG
INTO THE DITCH!

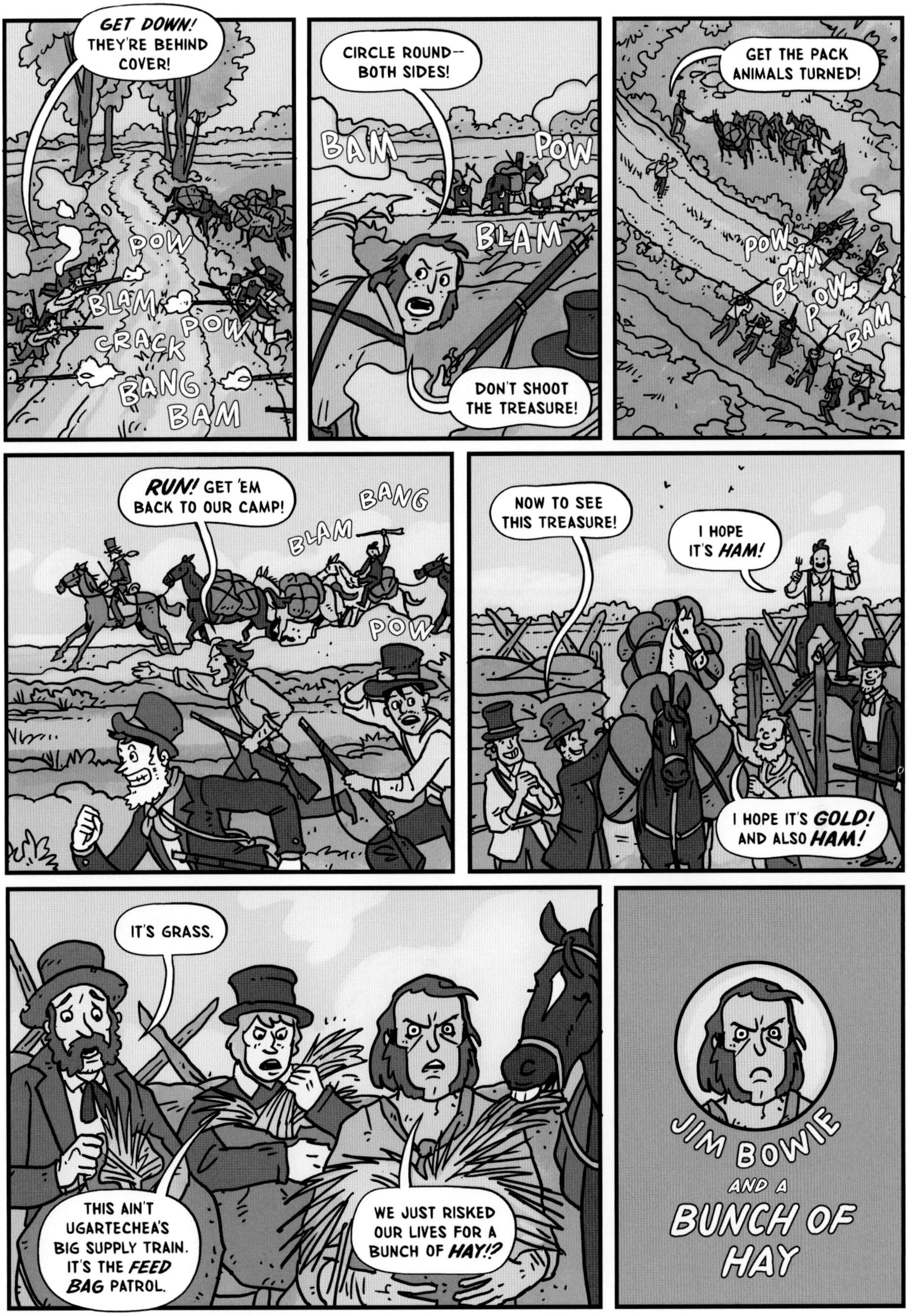
GET DOWN! THEY'RE BEHIND COVER!
POW
BLAM
CRACK
POW
BANG
BAM
CIRCLE ROUND-- BOTH SIDES!
BAM
POW
BLAM
DON'T SHOOT THE TREASURE!
GET THE PACK ANIMALS TURNED!
POW
BLAM
POW
BAM
RUN! GET 'EM BACK TO OUR CAMP!
BANG
BLAM
POW
NOW TO SEE THIS TREASURE!
I HOPE IT'S HAM!
I HOPE IT'S GOLD! AND ALSO HAM!
IT'S GRASS.
THIS AIN'T UGARTECHEA'S BIG SUPPLY TRAIN. IT'S THE FEED BAG PATROL.
WE JUST RISKED OUR LIVES FOR A BUNCH OF HAY!?
JIM BOWIE AND A BUNCH OF HAY

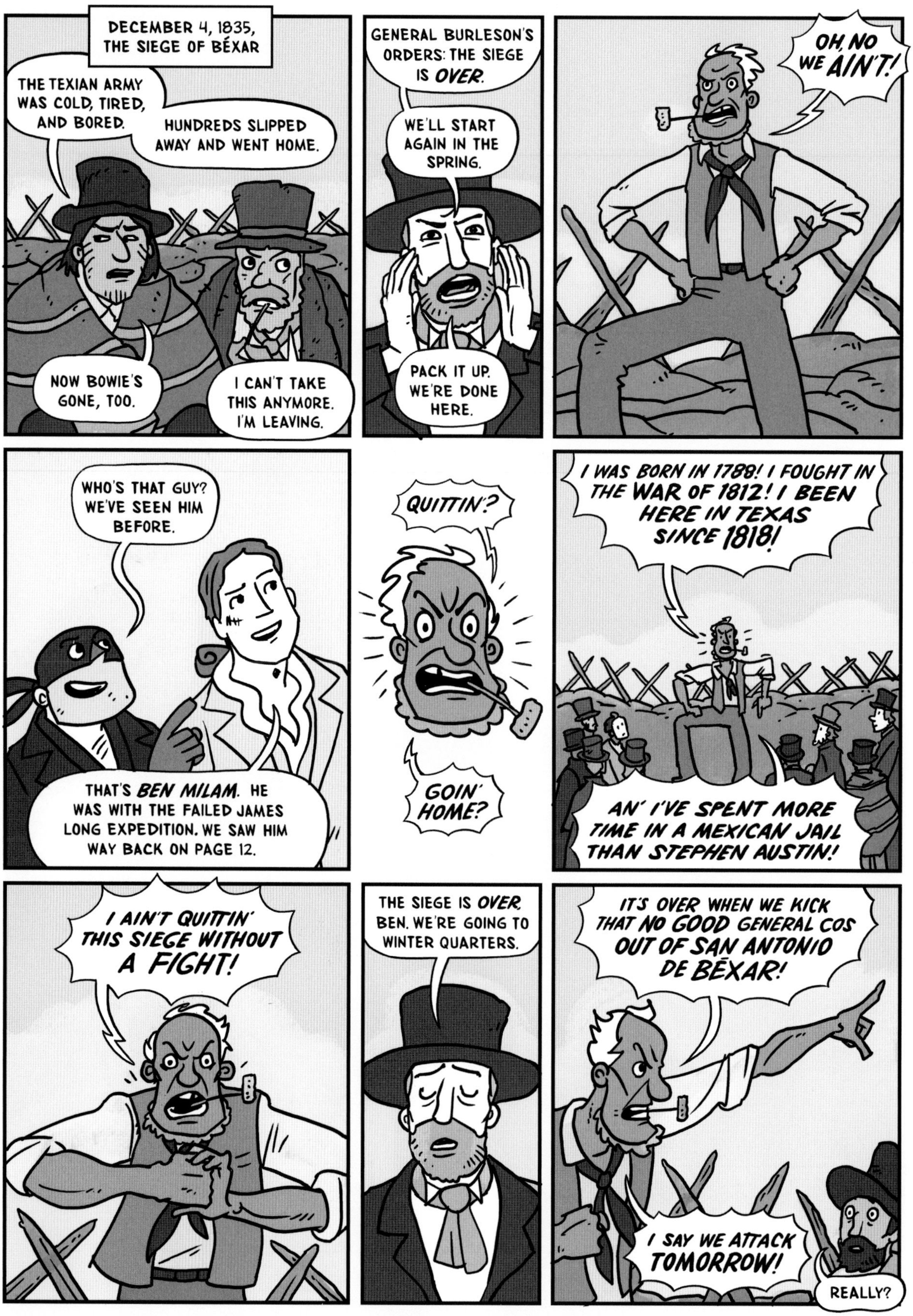
DECEMBER 4, 1835, THE SIEGE OF BÉXAR
THE TEXIAN ARMY WAS COLD, TIRED, AND BORED.
HUNDREDS SLIPPED AWAY AND WENT HOME.
NOW BOWIE'S GONE, TOO.
I CAN'T TAKE THIS ANYMORE. I'M LEAVING.
GENERAL BURLESON'S ORDERS: THE SIEGE IS *OVER*.
WE'LL START AGAIN IN THE SPRING.
PACK IT UP. WE'RE DONE HERE.
OH, NO WE AIN'T!
WHO'S THAT GUY? WE'VE SEEN HIM BEFORE.
THAT'S *BEN MILAM*. HE WAS WITH THE FAILED JAMES LONG EXPEDITION. WE SAW HIM WAY BACK ON PAGE 12.
QUITTIN'?
GOIN' HOME?
I WAS BORN IN 1788! I FOUGHT IN THE WAR OF 1812! I BEEN HERE IN TEXAS SINCE 1818!
AN' I'VE SPENT MORE TIME IN A MEXICAN JAIL THAN STEPHEN AUSTIN!
I AIN'T QUITTIN' THIS SIEGE WITHOUT A FIGHT!
THE SIEGE IS *OVER*, BEN. WE'RE GOING TO WINTER QUARTERS.
IT'S OVER WHEN WE KICK THAT NO GOOD GENERAL COS OUT OF SAN ANTONIO DE BĒXAR!
I SAY WE ATTACK TOMORROW!
REALLY?

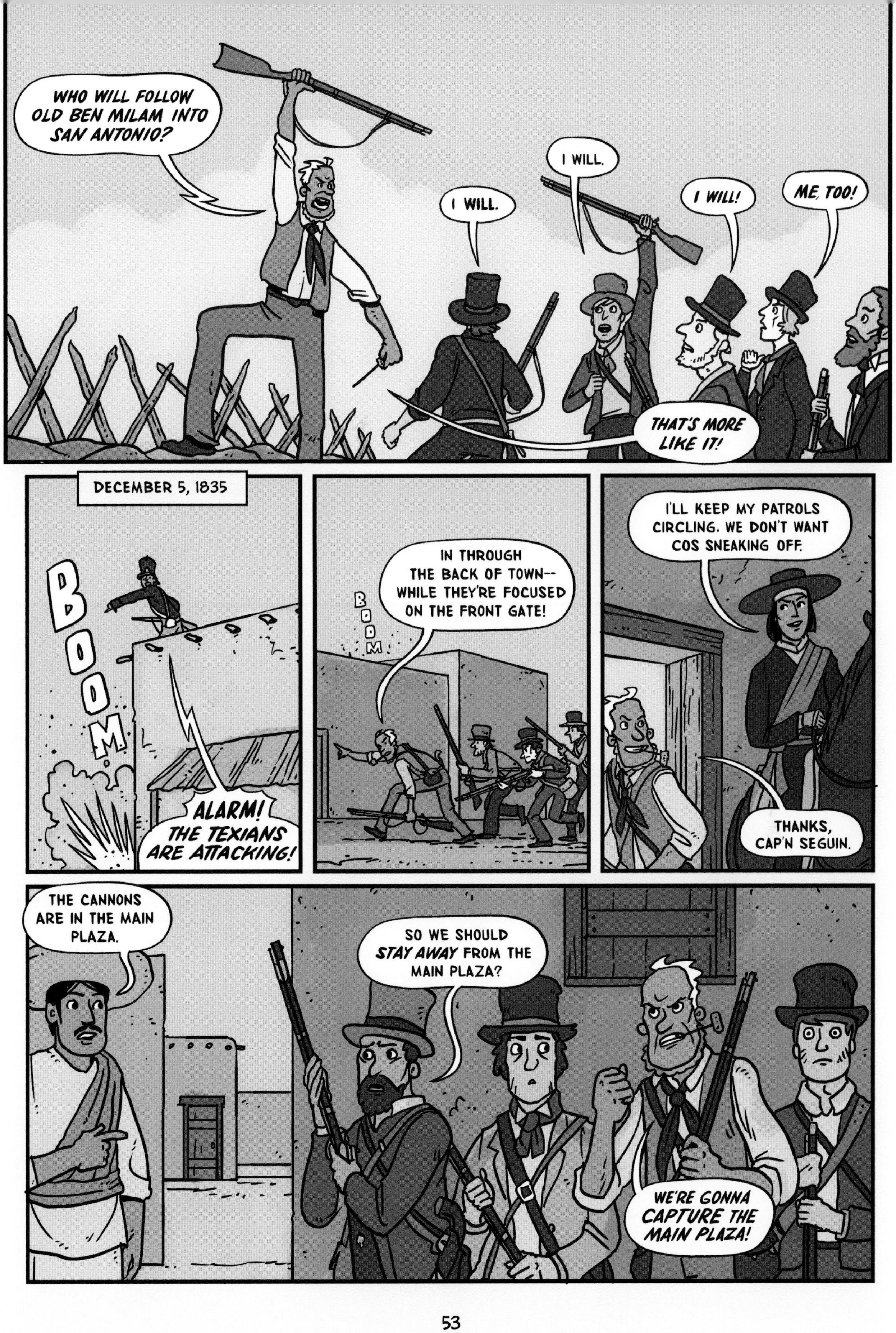
WHO WILL FOLLOW OLD BEN MILAM INTO SAN ANTONIO?
I WILL.
I WILL.
I WILL!
ME, TOO!
THAT'S MORE LIKE IT!
DECEMBER 5, 1835
BOOM
ALARM! THE TEXIANS ARE ATTACKING!
BOOM
IN THROUGH THE BACK OF TOWN-- WHILE THEY'RE FOCUSED ON THE FRONT GATE!
I'LL KEEP MY PATROLS CIRCLING. WE DON'T WANT COS SNEAKING OFF.
THANKS, CAP'N SEGUIN.
THE CANNONS ARE IN THE MAIN PLAZA.
SO WE SHOULD STAY AWAY FROM THE MAIN PLAZA?
WE'RE GONNA CAPTURE THE MAIN PLAZA!

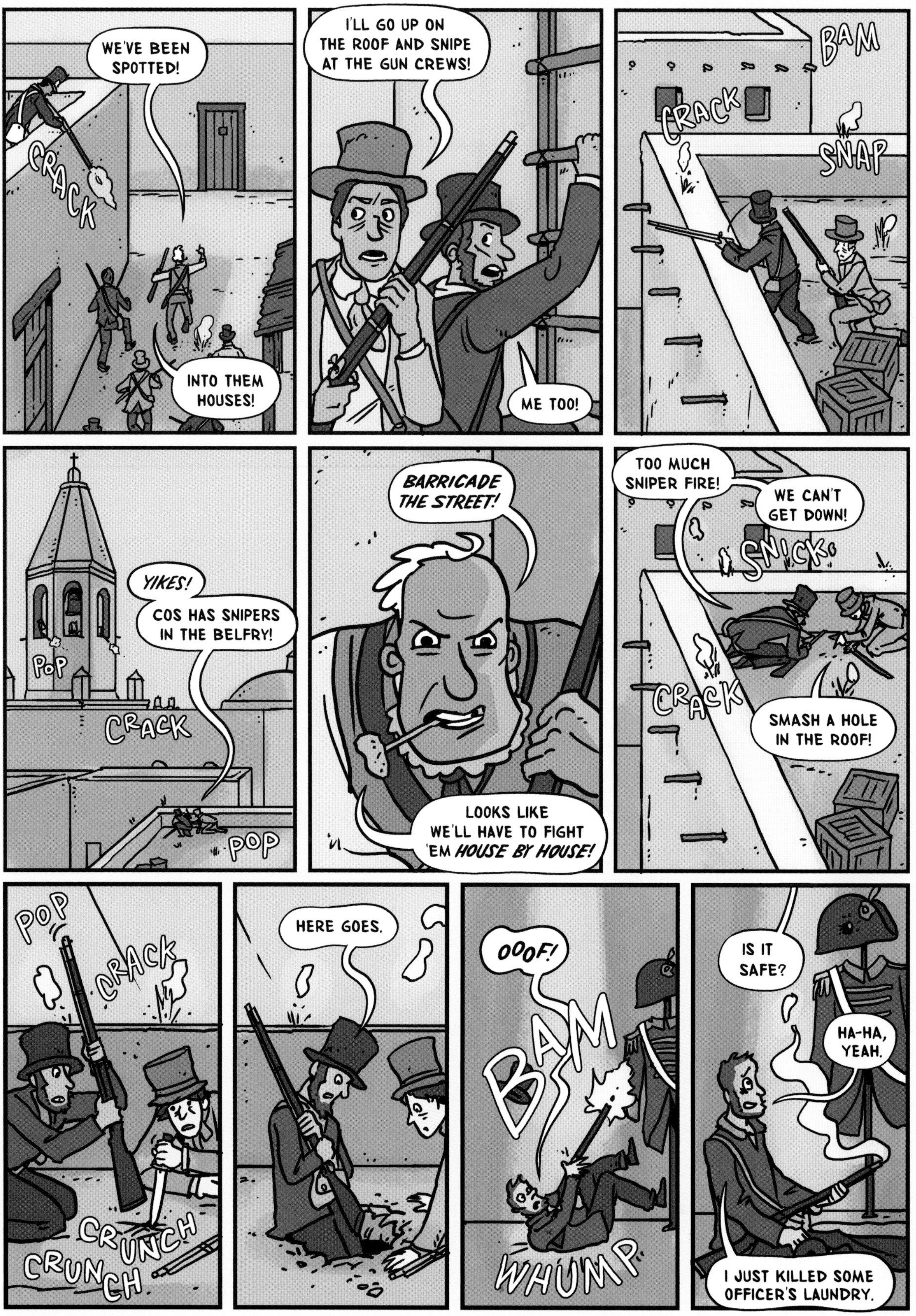
WE'VE BEEN SPOTTED!
CRACK
INTO THEM HOUSES!
I'LL GO UP ON THE ROOF AND SNIPE AT THE GUN CREWS!
ME TOO!
BAM
CRACK
SNAP
YIKES!
COS HAS SNIPERS IN THE BELFRY!
POP
CRACK
POP
BARRICADE THE STREET!
LOOKS LIKE WE'LL HAVE TO FIGHT 'EM HOUSE BY HOUSE!
TOO MUCH SNIPER FIRE!
WE CAN'T GET DOWN!
SNICK
CRACK
SMASH A HOLE IN THE ROOF!
POP
CRACK
CRUNCH
CRUNCH
HERE GOES.
OOOF!
BAM
WHUMP
IS IT SAFE?
HA-HA, YEAH.
I JUST KILLED SOME OFFICER'S LAUNDRY.

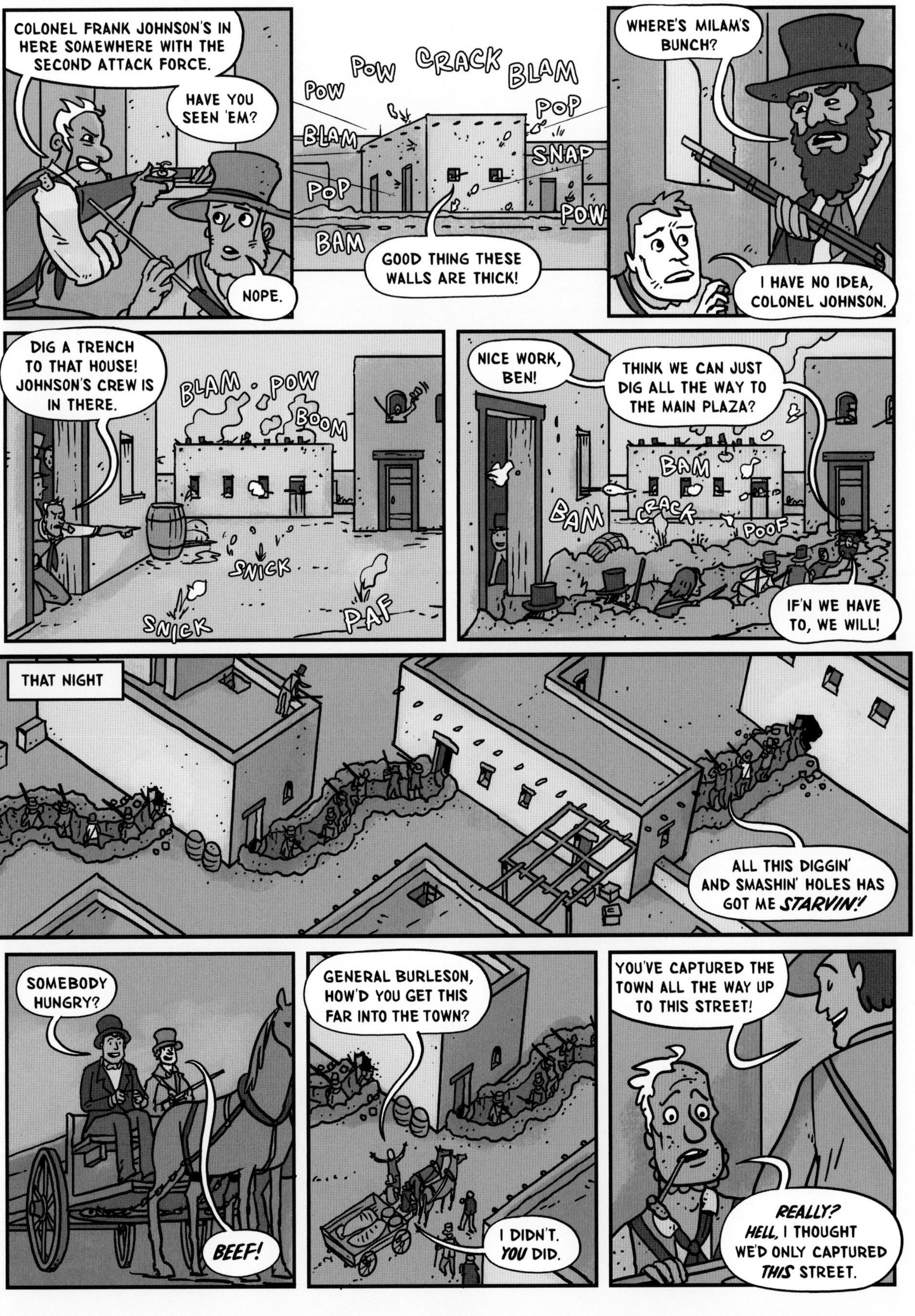
COLONEL FRANK JOHNSON'S IN HERE SOMEWHERE WITH THE SECOND ATTACK FORCE.
HAVE YOU SEEN 'EM?
NOPE.
POW POW CRACK BLAM
BLAM POP
POP SNAP
BAM POW
GOOD THING THESE WALLS ARE THICK!
WHERE'S MILAM'S BUNCH?
I HAVE NO IDEA, COLONEL JOHNSON.
DIG A TRENCH TO THAT HOUSE! JOHNSON'S CREW IS IN THERE.
BLAM POW
BOOM
SNICK
SNICK
PAF
NICE WORK, BEN!
THINK WE CAN JUST DIG ALL THE WAY TO THE MAIN PLAZA?
BAM
BAM
CRACK
POOF
IF'N WE HAVE TO, WE WILL!
THAT NIGHT
ALL THIS DIGGIN' AND SMASHIN' HOLES HAS GOT ME STARVIN'!
SOMEBODY HUNGRY?
BEEF!
GENERAL BURLESON, HOW'D YOU GET THIS FAR INTO THE TOWN?
I DIDN'T. YOU DID.
YOU'VE CAPTURED THE TOWN ALL THE WAY UP TO THIS STREET!
REALLY? HELL, I THOUGHT WE'D ONLY CAPTURED THIS STREET.

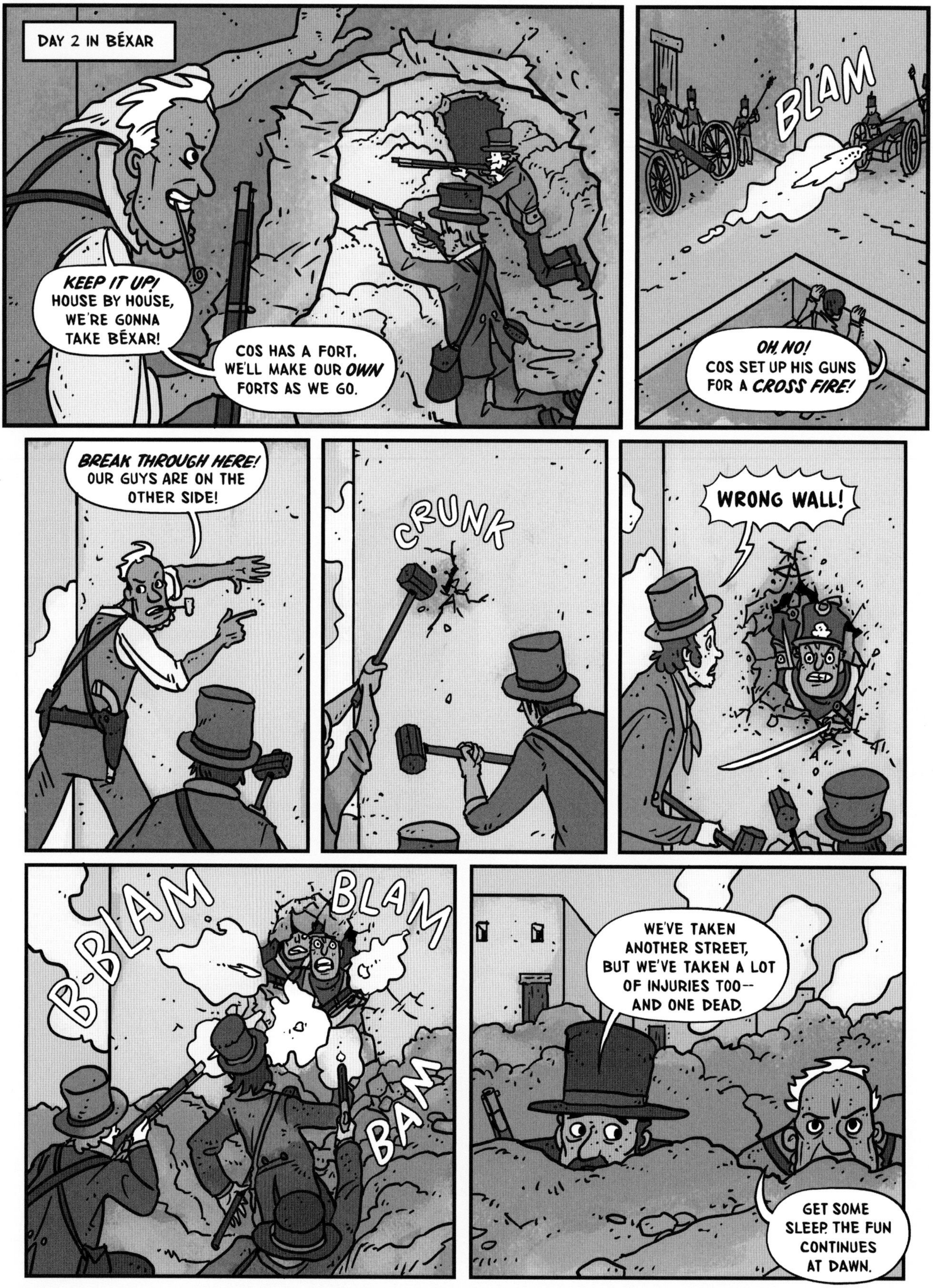
DAY 2 IN BÉXAR
KEEP IT UP! HOUSE BY HOUSE, WE'RE GONNA TAKE BÉXAR!
COS HAS A FORT. WE'LL MAKE OUR OWN FORTS AS WE GO.
BLAM
OH, NO! COS SET UP HIS GUNS FOR A CROSS FIRE!
BREAK THROUGH HERE! OUR GUYS ARE ON THE OTHER SIDE!
CRUNK
WRONG WALL!
B-BLAM
BLAM
BAM
WE'VE TAKEN ANOTHER STREET, BUT WE'VE TAKEN A LOT OF INJURIES TOO-- AND ONE DEAD.
GET SOME SLEEP. THE FUN CONTINUES AT DAWN.

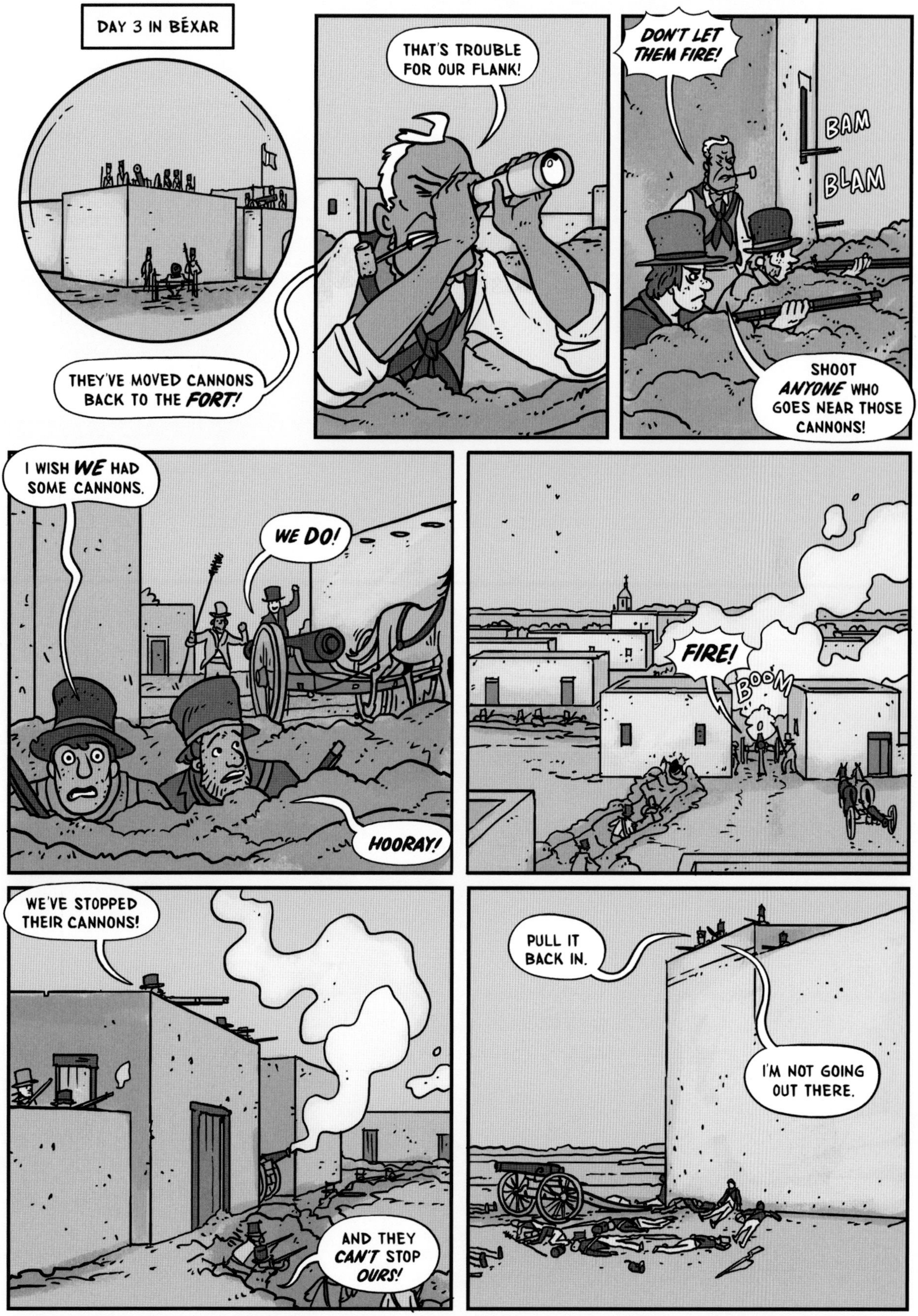
DAY 3 IN BÉXAR
THEY'VE MOVED CANNONS BACK TO THE FORT!
THAT'S TROUBLE FOR OUR FLANK!
DON'T LET THEM FIRE!
BAM
BLAM
SHOOT ANYONE WHO GOES NEAR THOSE CANNONS!
I WISH WE HAD SOME CANNONS.
WE DO!
HOORAY!
FIRE!
BOOM
WE'VE STOPPED THEIR CANNONS!
AND THEY CAN'T STOP OURS!
PULL IT BACK IN.
I'M NOT GOING OUT THERE.

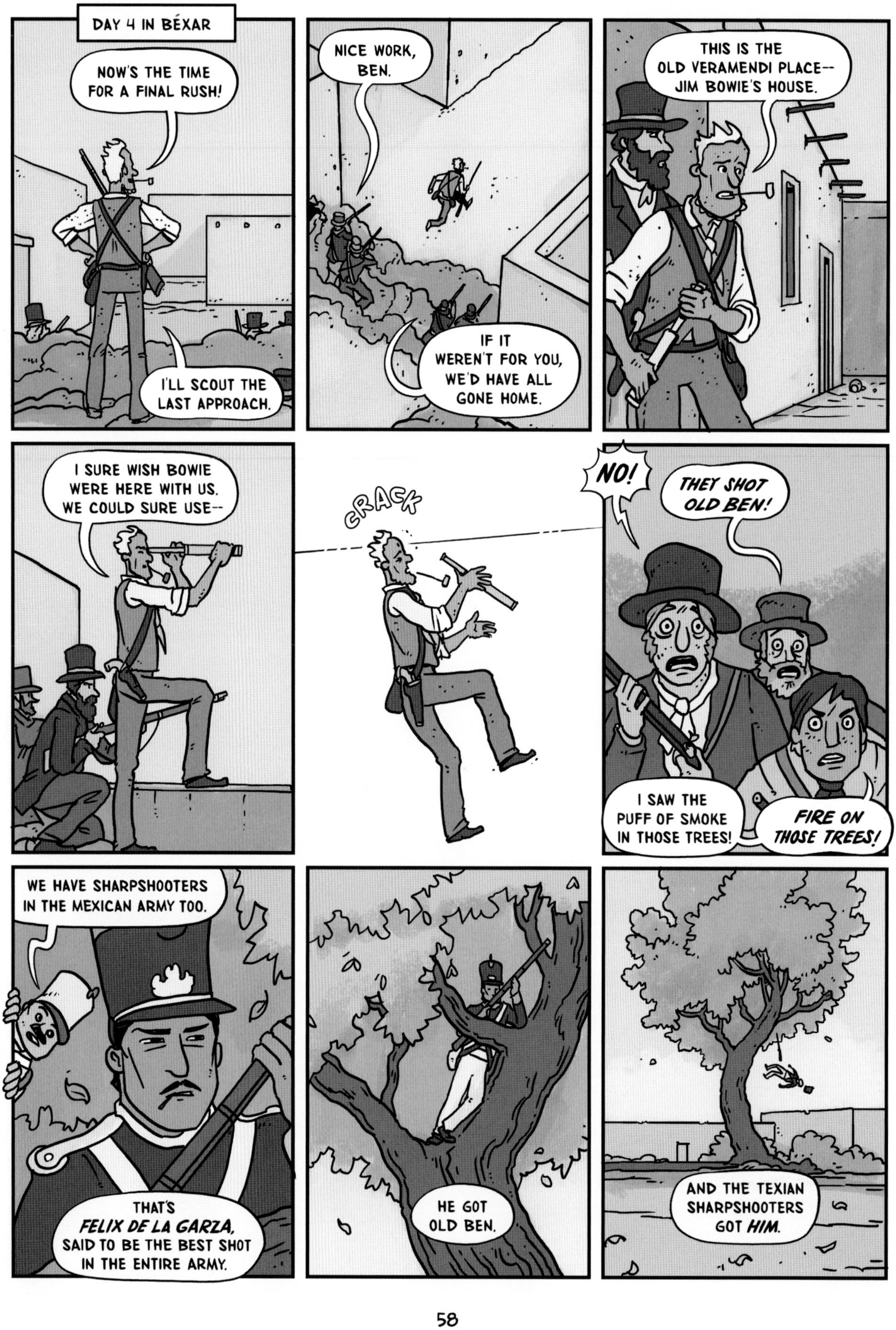
DAY 4 IN BÉXAR
NOW'S THE TIME FOR A FINAL RUSH!
I'LL SCOUT THE LAST APPROACH.
NICE WORK, BEN.
IF IT WEREN'T FOR YOU, WE'D HAVE ALL GONE HOME.
THIS IS THE OLD VERAMENDI PLACE-- JIM BOWIE'S HOUSE.
I SURE WISH BOWIE WERE HERE WITH US. WE COULD SURE USE--
CRACK
NO!
THEY SHOT OLD BEN!
I SAW THE PUFF OF SMOKE IN THOSE TREES!
FIRE ON THOSE TREES!
WE HAVE SHARPSHOOTERS IN THE MEXICAN ARMY TOO.
THAT'S *FELIX DE LA GARZA,* SAID TO BE THE BEST SHOT IN THE ENTIRE ARMY.
HE GOT OLD BEN.
AND THE TEXIAN SHARPSHOOTERS GOT *HIM.*

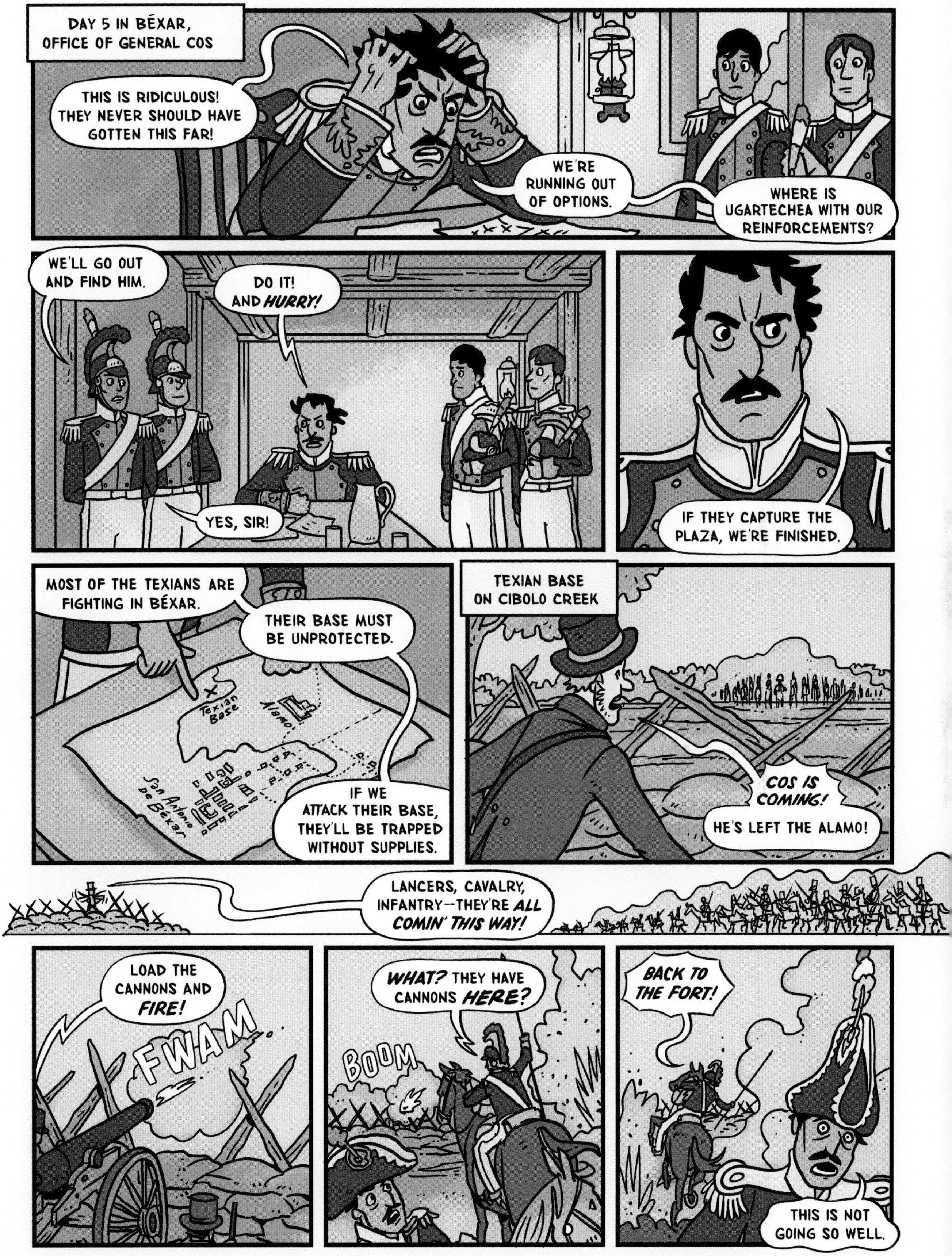
DAY 5 IN BÉXAR, OFFICE OF GENERAL COS
THIS IS RIDICULOUS! THEY NEVER SHOULD HAVE GOTTEN THIS FAR!
WE'RE RUNNING OUT OF OPTIONS.
WHERE IS UGARTECHEA WITH OUR REINFORCEMENTS?
WE'LL GO OUT AND FIND HIM.
DO IT! AND HURRY!
YES, SIR!
IF THEY CAPTURE THE PLAZA, WE'RE FINISHED.
MOST OF THE TEXIANS ARE FIGHTING IN BÉXAR.
THEIR BASE MUST BE UNPROTECTED.
Texian Base
Alamo
San Antonio de Béxar
IF WE ATTACK THEIR BASE, THEY'LL BE TRAPPED WITHOUT SUPPLIES.
TEXIAN BASE ON CIBOLO CREEK
COS IS COMING!
HE'S LEFT THE ALAMO!
LANCERS, CAVALRY, INFANTRY--THEY'RE ALL COMIN' THIS WAY!
LOAD THE CANNONS AND FIRE!
FWAM
WHAT? THEY HAVE CANNONS HERE?
BOOM
BACK TO THE FORT!
THIS IS NOT GOING SO WELL.

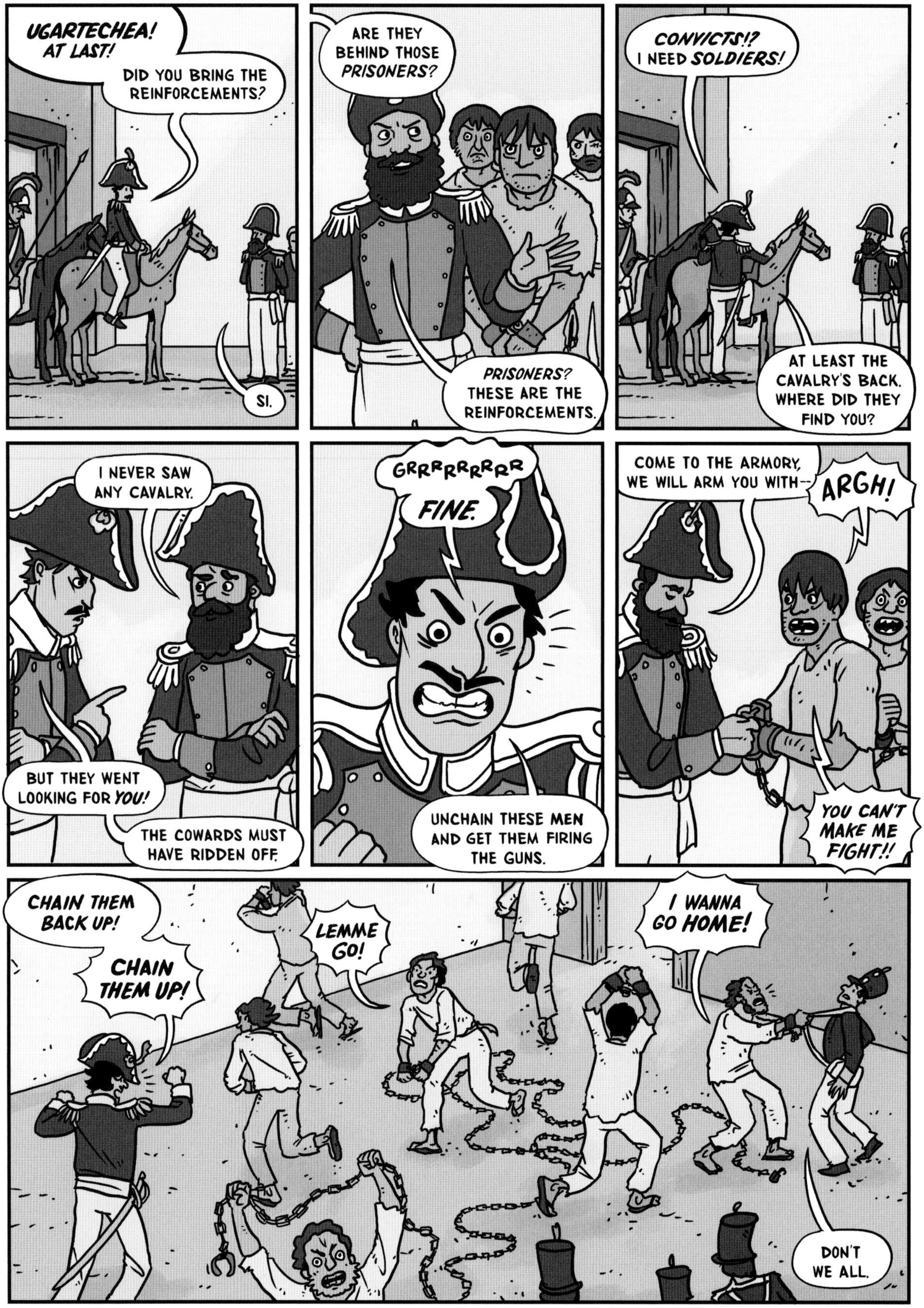
UGARTECHEA! AT LAST!
DID YOU BRING THE REINFORCEMENTS?
SI.
ARE THEY BEHIND THOSE PRISONERS?
PRISONERS? THESE ARE THE REINFORCEMENTS.
CONVICTS!? I NEED SOLDIERS!
AT LEAST THE CAVALRY'S BACK. WHERE DID THEY FIND YOU?
I NEVER SAW ANY CAVALRY.
BUT THEY WENT LOOKING FOR YOU!
THE COWARDS MUST HAVE RIDDEN OFF.
GRRRRRRRRR
FINE.
UNCHAIN THESE MEN AND GET THEM FIRING THE GUNS.
COME TO THE ARMORY, WE WILL ARM YOU WITH--
ARGH!
YOU CAN'T MAKE ME FIGHT!!
CHAIN THEM BACK UP!
CHAIN THEM UP!
LEMME GO!
I WANNA GO HOME!
DON'T WE ALL.

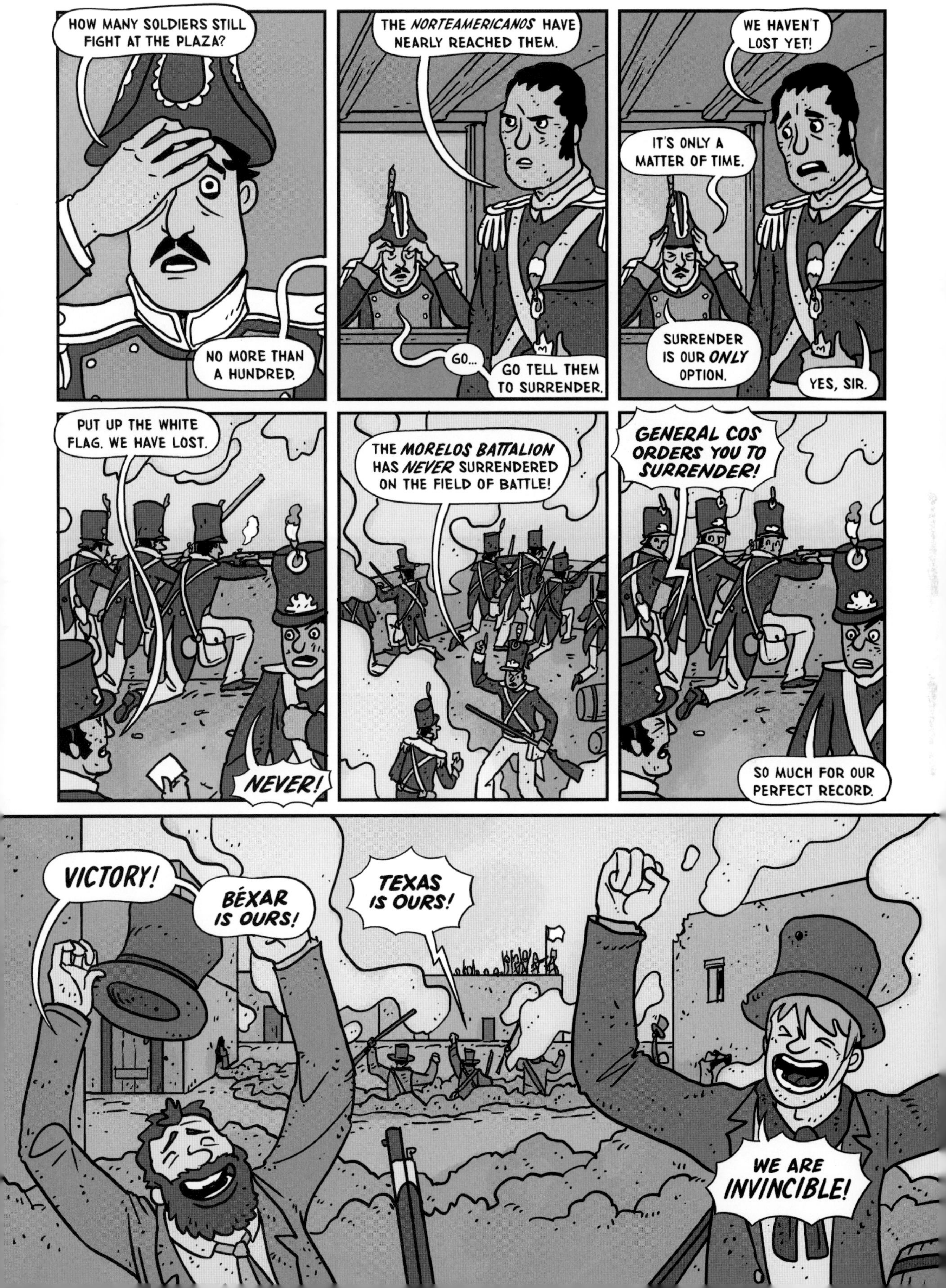

HOW MANY SOLDIERS STILL FIGHT AT THE PLAZA?
NO MORE THAN A HUNDRED.
THE *NORTEAMERICANOS* HAVE NEARLY REACHED THEM.
GO...
GO TELL THEM TO SURRENDER.
WE HAVEN'T LOST YET!
IT'S ONLY A MATTER OF TIME.
SURRENDER IS OUR *ONLY* OPTION.
YES, SIR.
PUT UP THE WHITE FLAG. WE HAVE LOST.
NEVER!
THE *MORELOS BATTALION* HAS *NEVER* SURRENDERED ON THE FIELD OF BATTLE!
GENERAL COS ORDERS YOU TO SURRENDER!
SO MUCH FOR OUR PERFECT RECORD.
VICTORY!
BÉXAR IS OURS!
TEXAS IS OURS!
WE ARE INVINCIBLE!

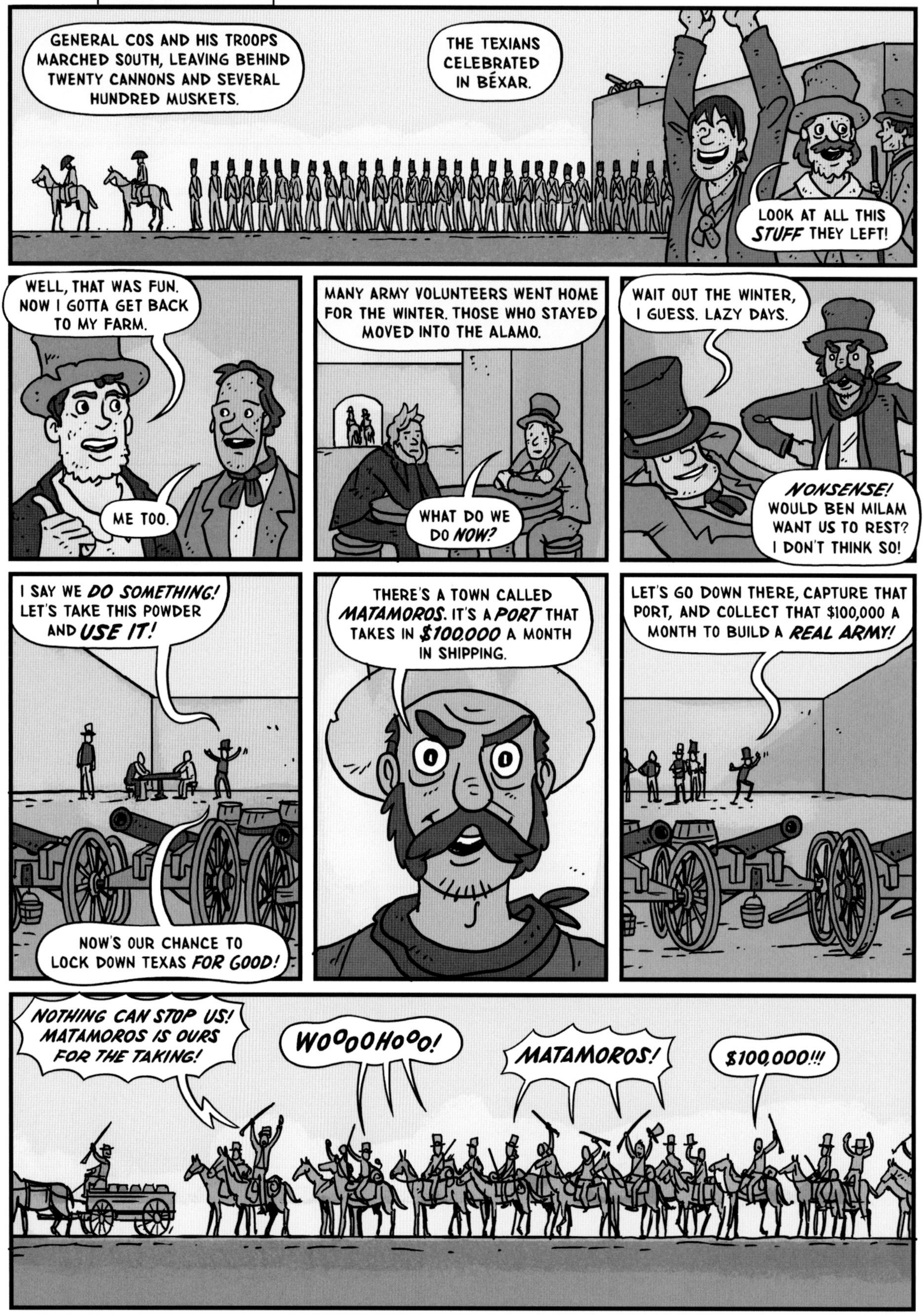
GENERAL COS AND HIS TROOPS MARCHED SOUTH, LEAVING BEHIND TWENTY CANNONS AND SEVERAL HUNDRED MUSKETS.
THE TEXIANS CELEBRATED IN BÉXAR.
LOOK AT ALL THIS *STUFF* THEY LEFT!
WELL, THAT WAS FUN. NOW I GOTTA GET BACK TO MY FARM.
ME TOO.
MANY ARMY VOLUNTEERS WENT HOME FOR THE WINTER. THOSE WHO STAYED MOVED INTO THE ALAMO.
WHAT DO WE DO *NOW?*
WAIT OUT THE WINTER, I GUESS. LAZY DAYS.
NONSENSE! WOULD BEN MILAM WANT US TO REST? I DON'T THINK SO!
I SAY WE *DO SOMETHING!* LET'S TAKE THIS POWDER AND *USE IT!*
NOW'S OUR CHANCE TO LOCK DOWN TEXAS *FOR GOOD!*
THERE'S A TOWN CALLED *MATAMOROS.* IT'S A *PORT* THAT TAKES IN *$100,000* A MONTH IN SHIPPING.
LET'S GO DOWN THERE, CAPTURE THAT PORT, AND COLLECT THAT $100,000 A MONTH TO BUILD A *REAL ARMY!*
NOTHING CAN STOP US! MATAMOROS IS OURS FOR THE TAKING!
WOoOOHOoO!
MATAMOROS!
$100,000!!!

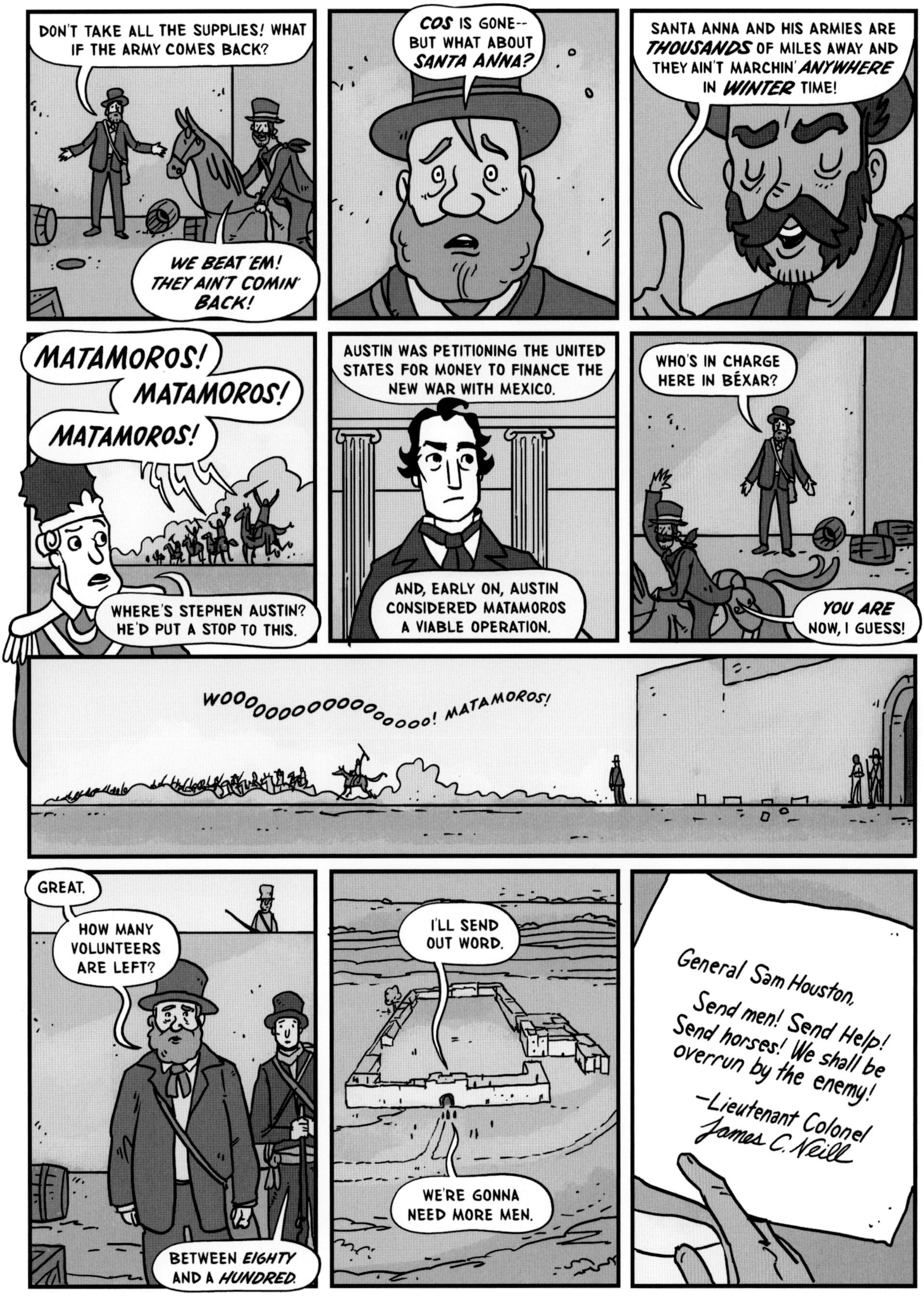
DON'T TAKE ALL THE SUPPLIES! WHAT IF THE ARMY COMES BACK?
WE BEAT 'EM! THEY AIN'T COMIN' BACK!
COS IS GONE-- BUT WHAT ABOUT SANTA ANNA?
SANTA ANNA AND HIS ARMIES ARE THOUSANDS OF MILES AWAY AND THEY AIN'T MARCHIN' ANYWHERE IN WINTER TIME!
MATAMOROS!
MATAMOROS!
MATAMOROS!
WHERE'S STEPHEN AUSTIN? HE'D PUT A STOP TO THIS.
AUSTIN WAS PETITIONING THE UNITED STATES FOR MONEY TO FINANCE THE NEW WAR WITH MEXICO.
AND, EARLY ON, AUSTIN CONSIDERED MATAMOROS A VIABLE OPERATION.
WHO'S IN CHARGE HERE IN BÉXAR?
YOU ARE NOW, I GUESS!
WOOOOOOOOOOOOOOOOO! MATAMOROS!
GREAT.
HOW MANY VOLUNTEERS ARE LEFT?
BETWEEN EIGHTY AND A HUNDRED.
I'LL SEND OUT WORD.
WE'RE GONNA NEED MORE MEN.
General Sam Houston,
Send men! Send Help! Send horses! We shall be overrun by the enemy!
—Lieutenant Colonel James C. Neill

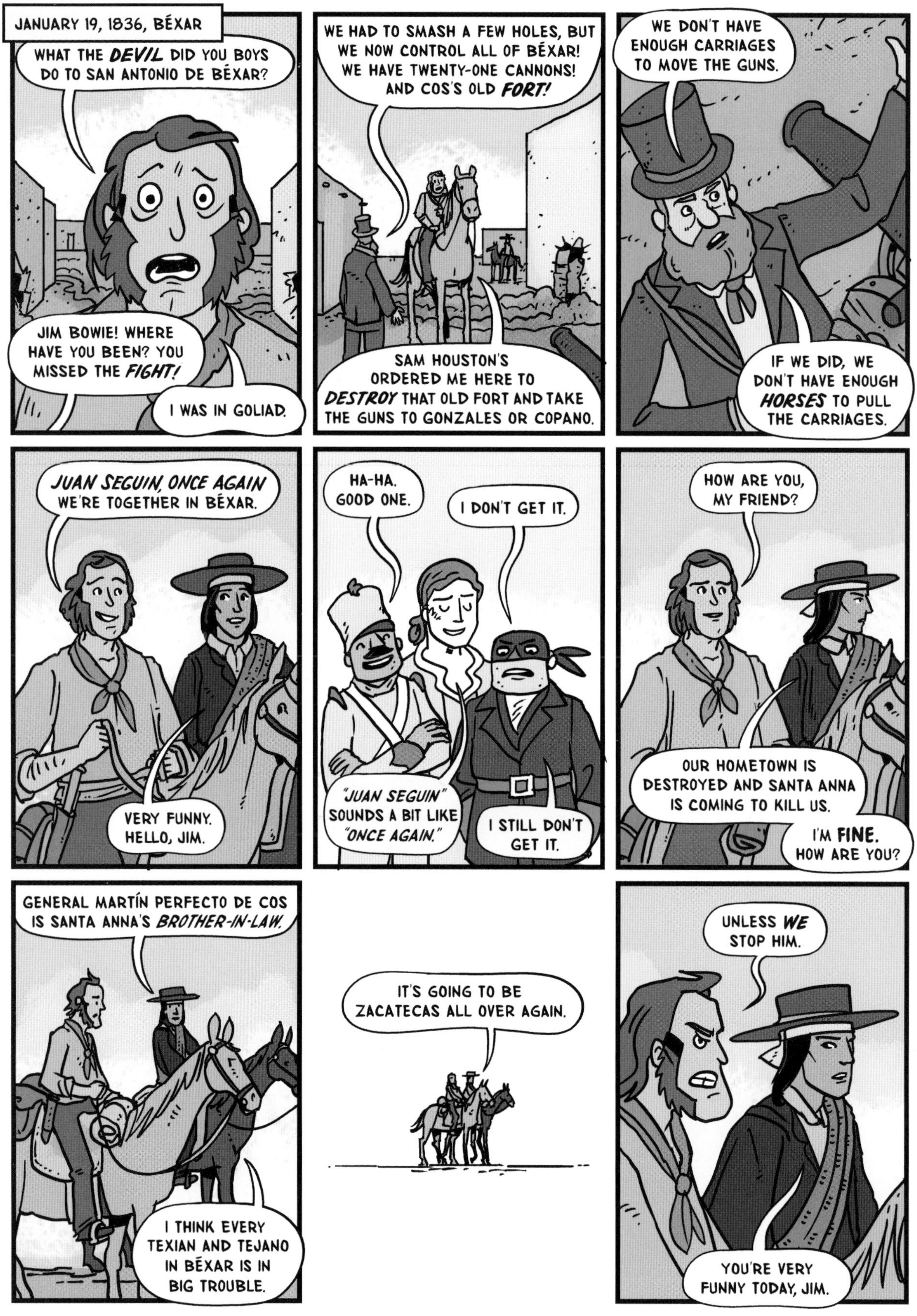

JANUARY 19, 1836, BÉXAR
WHAT THE DEVIL DID YOU BOYS DO TO SAN ANTONIO DE BÉXAR?
JIM BOWIE! WHERE HAVE YOU BEEN? YOU MISSED THE FIGHT!
I WAS IN GOLIAD.
WE HAD TO SMASH A FEW HOLES, BUT WE NOW CONTROL ALL OF BÉXAR! WE HAVE TWENTY-ONE CANNONS! AND COS'S OLD FORT!
SAM HOUSTON'S ORDERED ME HERE TO DESTROY THAT OLD FORT AND TAKE THE GUNS TO GONZALES OR COPANO.
WE DON'T HAVE ENOUGH CARRIAGES TO MOVE THE GUNS.
IF WE DID, WE DON'T HAVE ENOUGH HORSES TO PULL THE CARRIAGES.
JUAN SEGUIN, ONCE AGAIN WE'RE TOGETHER IN BÉXAR.
VERY FUNNY. HELLO, JIM.
HA-HA. GOOD ONE.
I DON'T GET IT.
"JUAN SEGUIN" SOUNDS A BIT LIKE "ONCE AGAIN."
I STILL DON'T GET IT.
HOW ARE YOU, MY FRIEND?
OUR HOMETOWN IS DESTROYED AND SANTA ANNA IS COMING TO KILL US.
I'M FINE. HOW ARE YOU?
GENERAL MARTÍN PERFECTO DE COS IS SANTA ANNA'S BROTHER-IN-LAW.
I THINK EVERY TEXIAN AND TEJANO IN BÉXAR IS IN BIG TROUBLE.
IT'S GOING TO BE ZACATECAS ALL OVER AGAIN.
UNLESS WE STOP HIM.
YOU'RE VERY FUNNY TODAY, JIM.

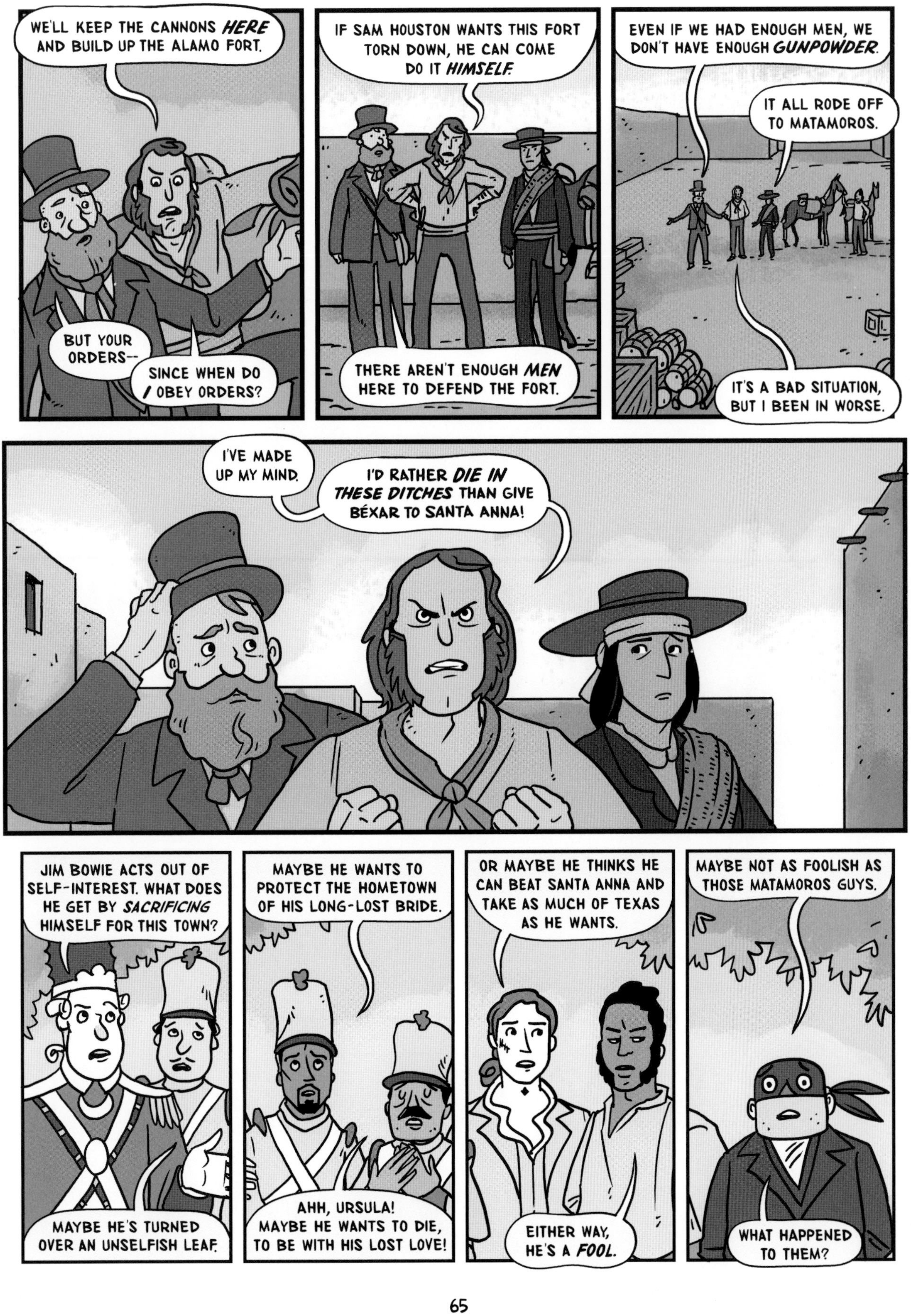
WE'LL KEEP THE CANNONS HERE AND BUILD UP THE ALAMO FORT.
BUT YOUR ORDERS--
SINCE WHEN DO I OBEY ORDERS?
IF SAM HOUSTON WANTS THIS FORT TORN DOWN, HE CAN COME DO IT HIMSELF.
THERE AREN'T ENOUGH MEN HERE TO DEFEND THE FORT.
EVEN IF WE HAD ENOUGH MEN, WE DON'T HAVE ENOUGH GUNPOWDER.
IT ALL RODE OFF TO MATAMOROS.
IT'S A BAD SITUATION, BUT I BEEN IN WORSE.
I'VE MADE UP MY MIND.
I'D RATHER DIE IN THESE DITCHES THAN GIVE BÉXAR TO SANTA ANNA!
JIM BOWIE ACTS OUT OF SELF-INTEREST. WHAT DOES HE GET BY SACRIFICING HIMSELF FOR THIS TOWN?
MAYBE HE'S TURNED OVER AN UNSELFISH LEAF.
MAYBE HE WANTS TO PROTECT THE HOMETOWN OF HIS LONG-LOST BRIDE.
AHH, URSULA! MAYBE HE WANTS TO DIE, TO BE WITH HIS LOST LOVE!
OR MAYBE HE THINKS HE CAN BEAT SANTA ANNA AND TAKE AS MUCH OF TEXAS AS HE WANTS.
EITHER WAY, HE'S A FOOL.
MAYBE NOT AS FOOLISH AS THOSE MATAMOROS GUYS.
WHAT HAPPENED TO THEM?

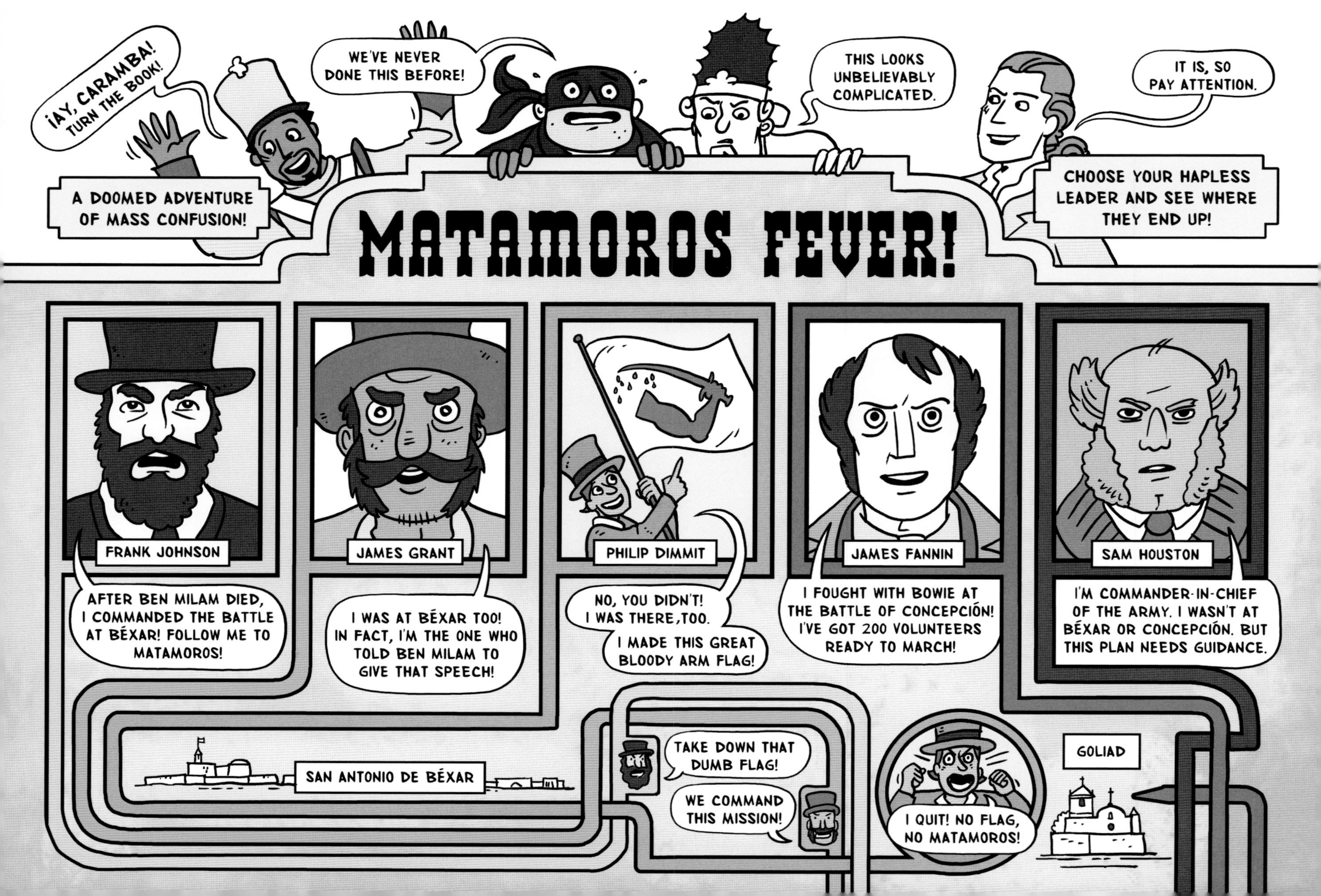

¡AY, CARAMBA! TURN THE BOOK!
WE'VE NEVER DONE THIS BEFORE!
THIS LOOKS UNBELIEVABLY COMPLICATED.
IT IS, SO PAY ATTENTION.
A DOOMED ADVENTURE OF MASS CONFUSION!
MATAMOROS FEVER!
CHOOSE YOUR HAPLESS LEADER AND SEE WHERE THEY END UP!
FRANK JOHNSON
AFTER BEN MILAM DIED, I COMMANDED THE BATTLE AT BÉXAR! FOLLOW ME TO MATAMOROS!
JAMES GRANT
I WAS AT BÉXAR TOO! IN FACT, I'M THE ONE WHO TOLD BEN MILAM TO GIVE THAT SPEECH!
PHILIP DIMMIT
NO, YOU DIDN'T! I WAS THERE, TOO.
I MADE THIS GREAT BLOODY ARM FLAG!
JAMES FANNIN
I FOUGHT WITH BOWIE AT THE BATTLE OF CONCEPCIÓN! I'VE GOT 200 VOLUNTEERS READY TO MARCH!
SAM HOUSTON
I'M COMMANDER-IN-CHIEF OF THE ARMY. I WASN'T AT BÉXAR OR CONCEPCIÓN. BUT THIS PLAN NEEDS GUIDANCE.
SAN ANTONIO DE BÉXAR
TAKE DOWN THAT DUMB FLAG!
WE COMMAND THIS MISSION!
I QUIT! NO FLAG, NO MATAMOROS!
GOLIAD

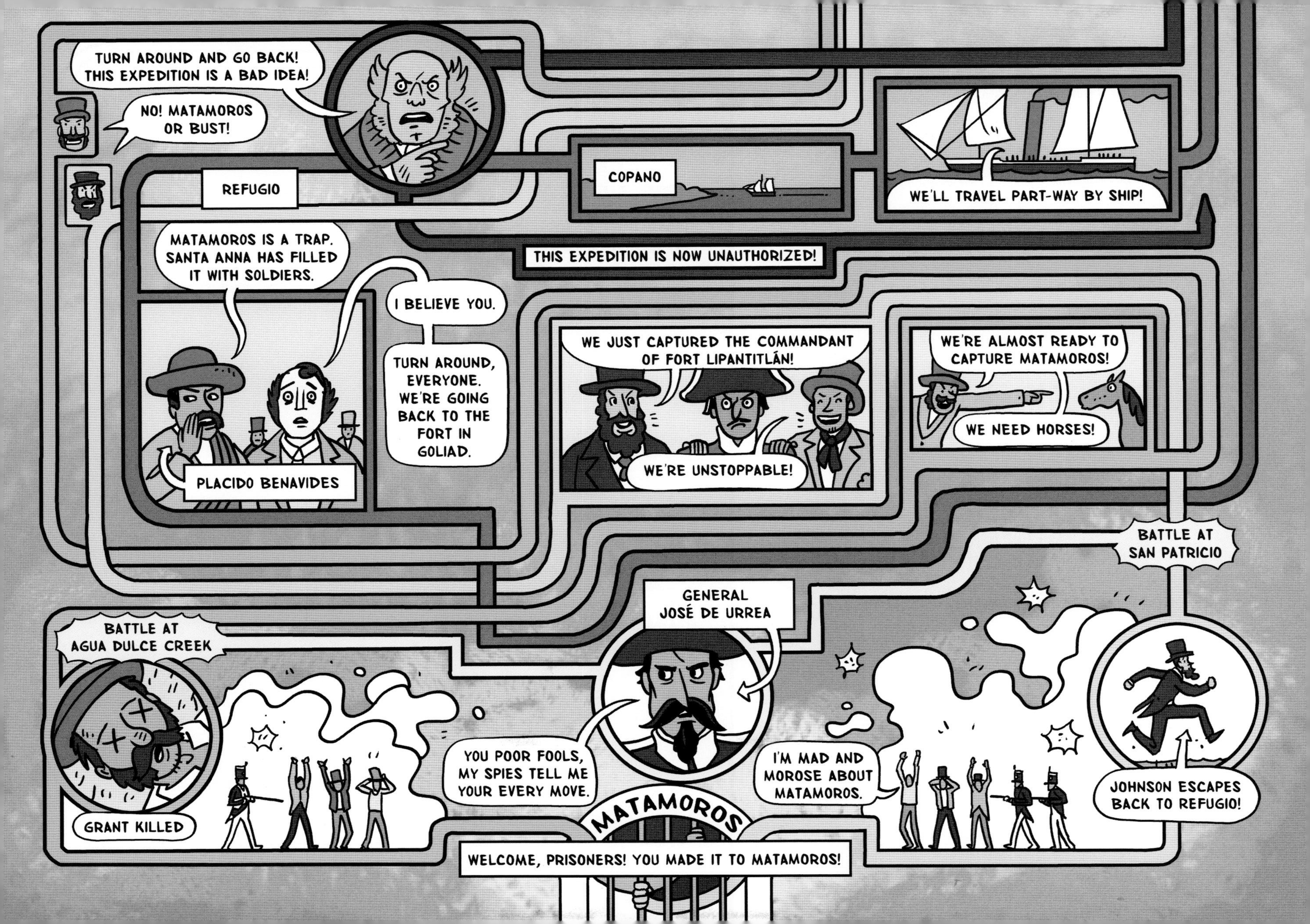
TURN AROUND AND GO BACK! THIS EXPEDITION IS A BAD IDEA!
NO! MATAMOROS OR BUST!
REFUGIO
COPANO
WE'LL TRAVEL PART-WAY BY SHIP!
THIS EXPEDITION IS NOW UNAUTHORIZED!
MATAMOROS IS A TRAP. SANTA ANNA HAS FILLED IT WITH SOLDIERS.
I BELIEVE YOU.
TURN AROUND, EVERYONE. WE'RE GOING BACK TO THE FORT IN GOLIAD.
PLACIDO BENAVIDES
WE JUST CAPTURED THE COMMANDANT OF FORT LIPANTITLÁN!
WE'RE UNSTOPPABLE!
WE'RE ALMOST READY TO CAPTURE MATAMOROS!
WE NEED HORSES!
BATTLE AT SAN PATRICIO
GENERAL JOSÉ DE URREA
BATTLE AT AGUA DULCE CREEK
GRANT KILLED
YOU POOR FOOLS, MY SPIES TELL ME YOUR EVERY MOVE.
I'M MAD AND MOROSE ABOUT MATAMOROS.
JOHNSON ESCAPES BACK TO REFUGIO!
MATAMOROS
WELCOME, PRISONERS! YOU MADE IT TO MATAMOROS!

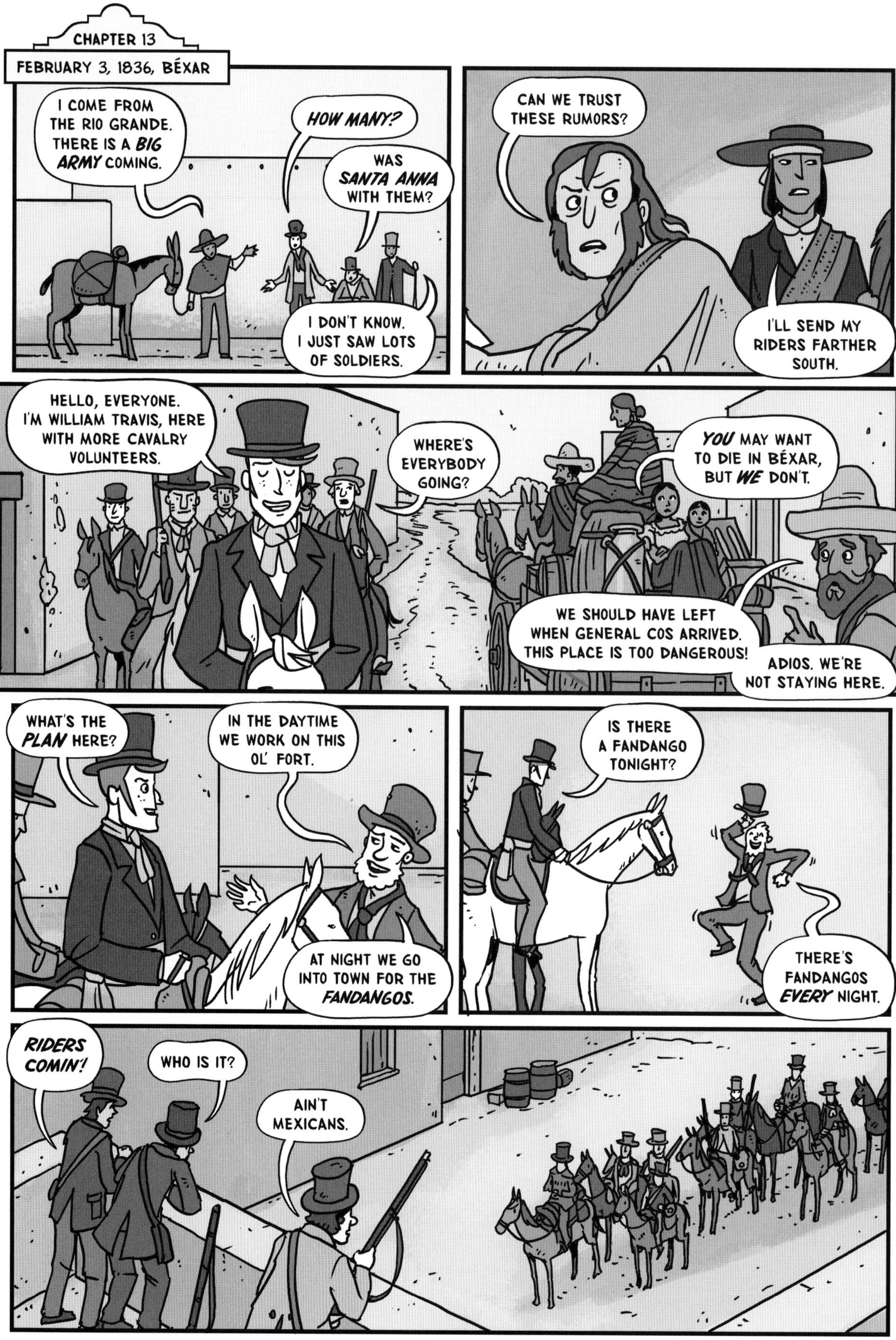
CHAPTER 13
FEBRUARY 3, 1836, BÉXAR
I COME FROM THE RIO GRANDE. THERE IS A *BIG ARMY* COMING.
HOW MANY?
WAS *SANTA ANNA* WITH THEM?
I DON'T KNOW. I JUST SAW LOTS OF SOLDIERS.
CAN WE TRUST THESE RUMORS?
I'LL SEND MY RIDERS FARTHER SOUTH.
HELLO, EVERYONE. I'M WILLIAM TRAVIS, HERE WITH MORE CAVALRY VOLUNTEERS.
WHERE'S EVERYBODY GOING?
YOU MAY WANT TO DIE IN BÉXAR, BUT *WE* DON'T.
WE SHOULD HAVE LEFT WHEN GENERAL COS ARRIVED. THIS PLACE IS TOO DANGEROUS!
ADIOS. WE'RE NOT STAYING HERE.
WHAT'S THE *PLAN* HERE?
IN THE DAYTIME WE WORK ON THIS OL' FORT.
AT NIGHT WE GO INTO TOWN FOR THE *FANDANGOS.*
IS THERE A FANDANGO TONIGHT?
THERE'S FANDANGOS *EVERY* NIGHT.
RIDERS COMIN'!
WHO IS IT?
AIN'T MEXICANS.

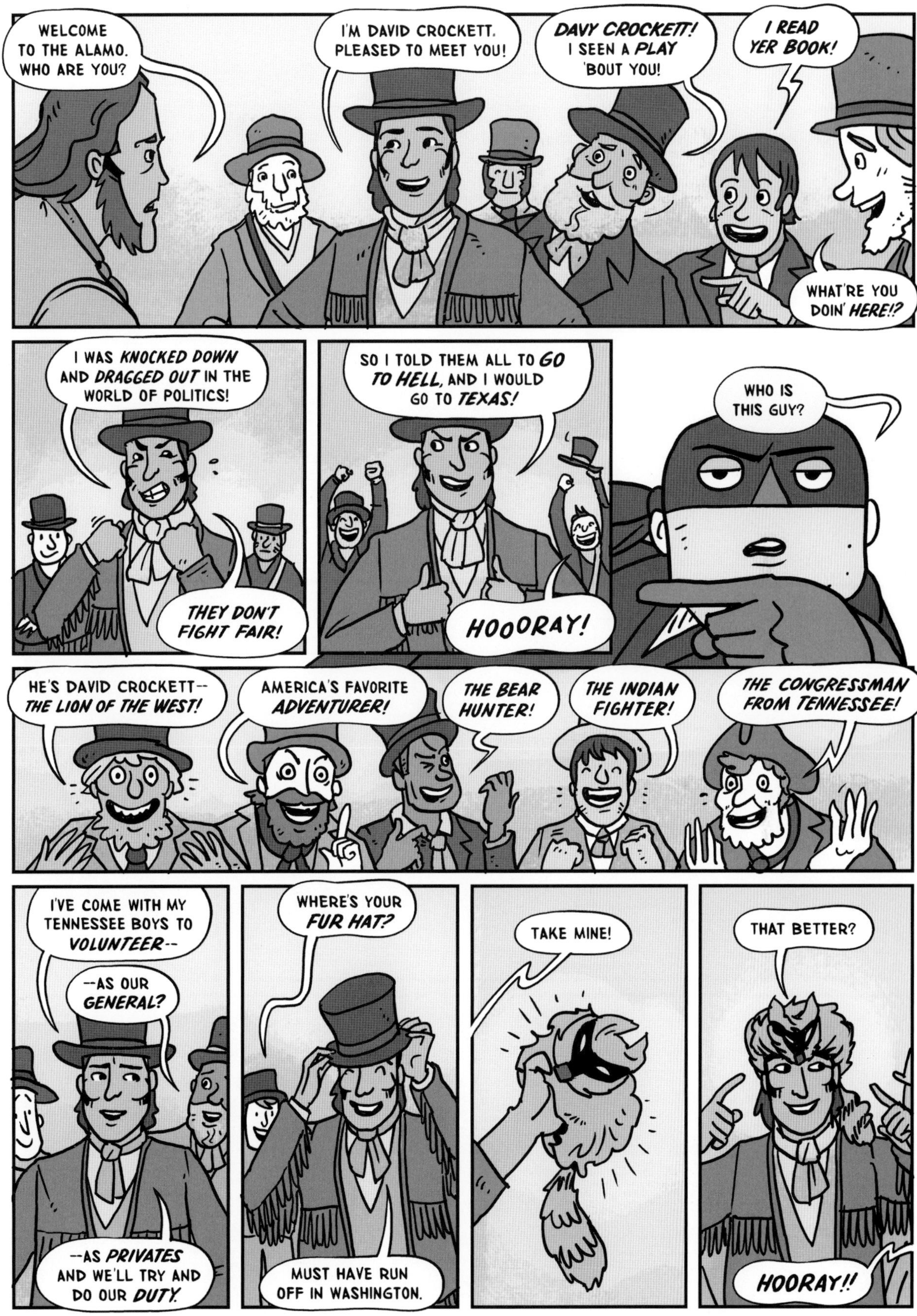
WELCOME TO THE ALAMO. WHO ARE YOU?
I'M DAVID CROCKETT. PLEASED TO MEET YOU!
DAVY CROCKETT! I SEEN A PLAY 'BOUT YOU!
I READ YER BOOK!
WHAT'RE YOU DOIN' HERE!?
I WAS KNOCKED DOWN AND DRAGGED OUT IN THE WORLD OF POLITICS!
THEY DON'T FIGHT FAIR!
SO I TOLD THEM ALL TO GO TO HELL, AND I WOULD GO TO TEXAS!
HOOORAY!
WHO IS THIS GUY?
HE'S DAVID CROCKETT-- THE LION OF THE WEST!
AMERICA'S FAVORITE ADVENTURER!
THE BEAR HUNTER!
THE INDIAN FIGHTER!
THE CONGRESSMAN FROM TENNESSEE!
I'VE COME WITH MY TENNESSEE BOYS TO VOLUNTEER--
--AS OUR GENERAL?
--AS PRIVATES AND WE'LL TRY AND DO OUR DUTY.
WHERE'S YOUR FUR HAT?
MUST HAVE RUN OFF IN WASHINGTON.
TAKE MINE!
THAT BETTER?
HOORAY!!

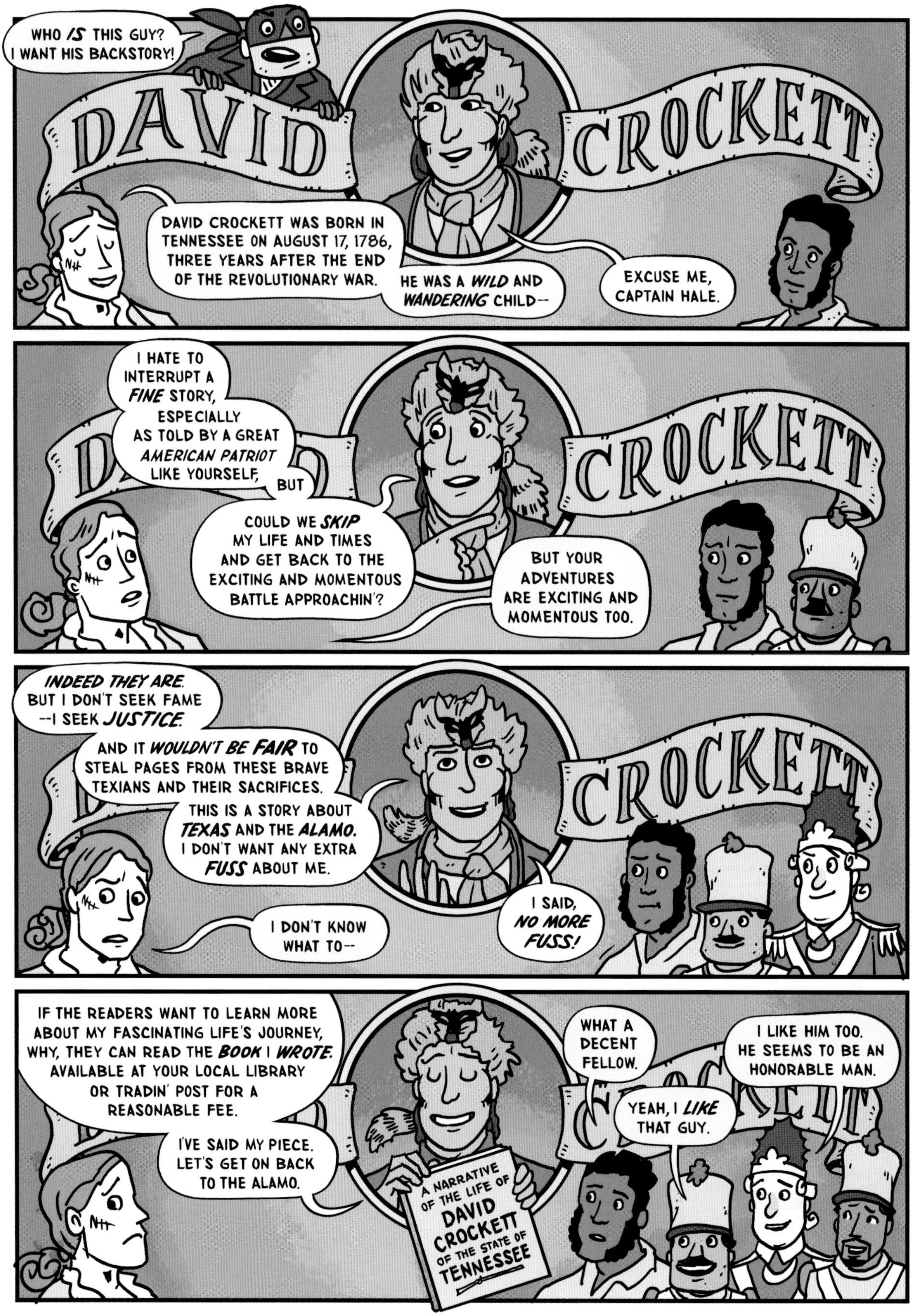
WHO IS THIS GUY? I WANT HIS BACKSTORY!
DAVID CROCKETT
DAVID CROCKETT WAS BORN IN TENNESSEE ON AUGUST 17, 1786, THREE YEARS AFTER THE END OF THE REVOLUTIONARY WAR.
HE WAS A WILD AND WANDERING CHILD--
EXCUSE ME, CAPTAIN HALE.
I HATE TO INTERRUPT A FINE STORY, ESPECIALLY AS TOLD BY A GREAT AMERICAN PATRIOT LIKE YOURSELF, BUT
COULD WE SKIP MY LIFE AND TIMES AND GET BACK TO THE EXCITING AND MOMENTOUS BATTLE APPROACHIN'?
BUT YOUR ADVENTURES ARE EXCITING AND MOMENTOUS TOO.
INDEED THEY ARE. BUT I DON'T SEEK FAME --I SEEK JUSTICE.
AND IT WOULDN'T BE FAIR TO STEAL PAGES FROM THESE BRAVE TEXIANS AND THEIR SACRIFICES.
THIS IS A STORY ABOUT TEXAS AND THE ALAMO. I DON'T WANT ANY EXTRA FUSS ABOUT ME.
I DON'T KNOW WHAT TO--
I SAID, NO MORE FUSS!
IF THE READERS WANT TO LEARN MORE ABOUT MY FASCINATING LIFE'S JOURNEY, WHY, THEY CAN READ THE BOOK I WROTE. AVAILABLE AT YOUR LOCAL LIBRARY OR TRADIN' POST FOR A REASONABLE FEE.
I'VE SAID MY PIECE. LET'S GET ON BACK TO THE ALAMO.
A NARRATIVE OF THE LIFE OF DAVID CROCKETT OF THE STATE OF TENNESSEE
WHAT A DECENT FELLOW.
YEAH, I LIKE THAT GUY.
I LIKE HIM TOO. HE SEEMS TO BE AN HONORABLE MAN.

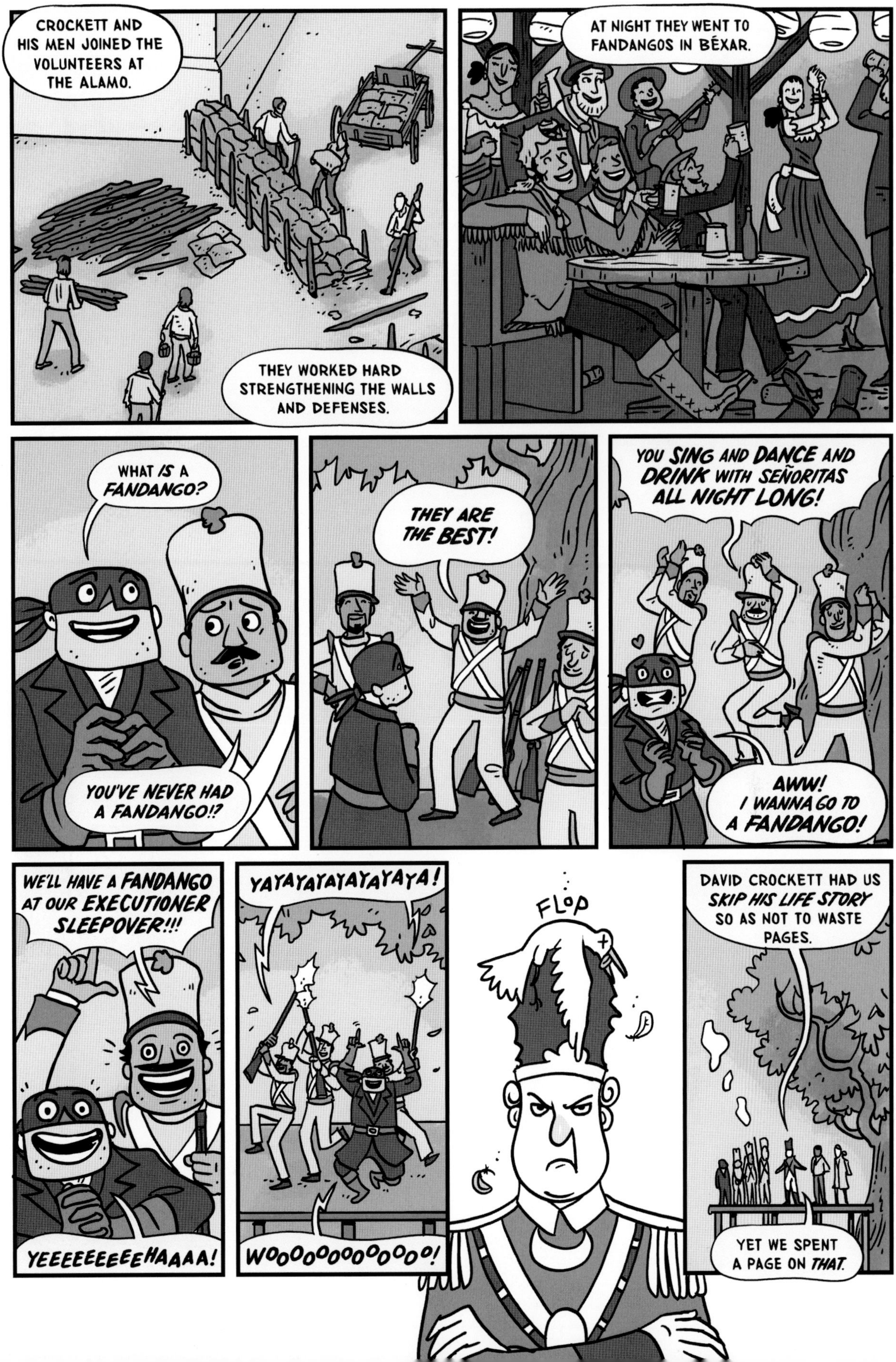
CROCKETT AND HIS MEN JOINED THE VOLUNTEERS AT THE ALAMO.
THEY WORKED HARD STRENGTHENING THE WALLS AND DEFENSES.
AT NIGHT THEY WENT TO FANDANGOS IN BÉXAR.
WHAT IS A FANDANGO?
YOU'VE NEVER HAD A FANDANGO!?
THEY ARE THE BEST!
YOU SING AND DANCE AND DRINK WITH SEÑORITAS ALL NIGHT LONG!
AWW! I WANNA GO TO A FANDANGO!
WE'LL HAVE A FANDANGO AT OUR EXECUTIONER SLEEPOVER!!!
YEEEEEEEEEHAAAA!
YAYAYAYAYAYAYAYA!
WOOOOOOOOOOOOO!
FLOP
DAVID CROCKETT HAD US SKIP HIS LIFE STORY SO AS NOT TO WASTE PAGES.
YET WE SPENT A PAGE ON THAT.

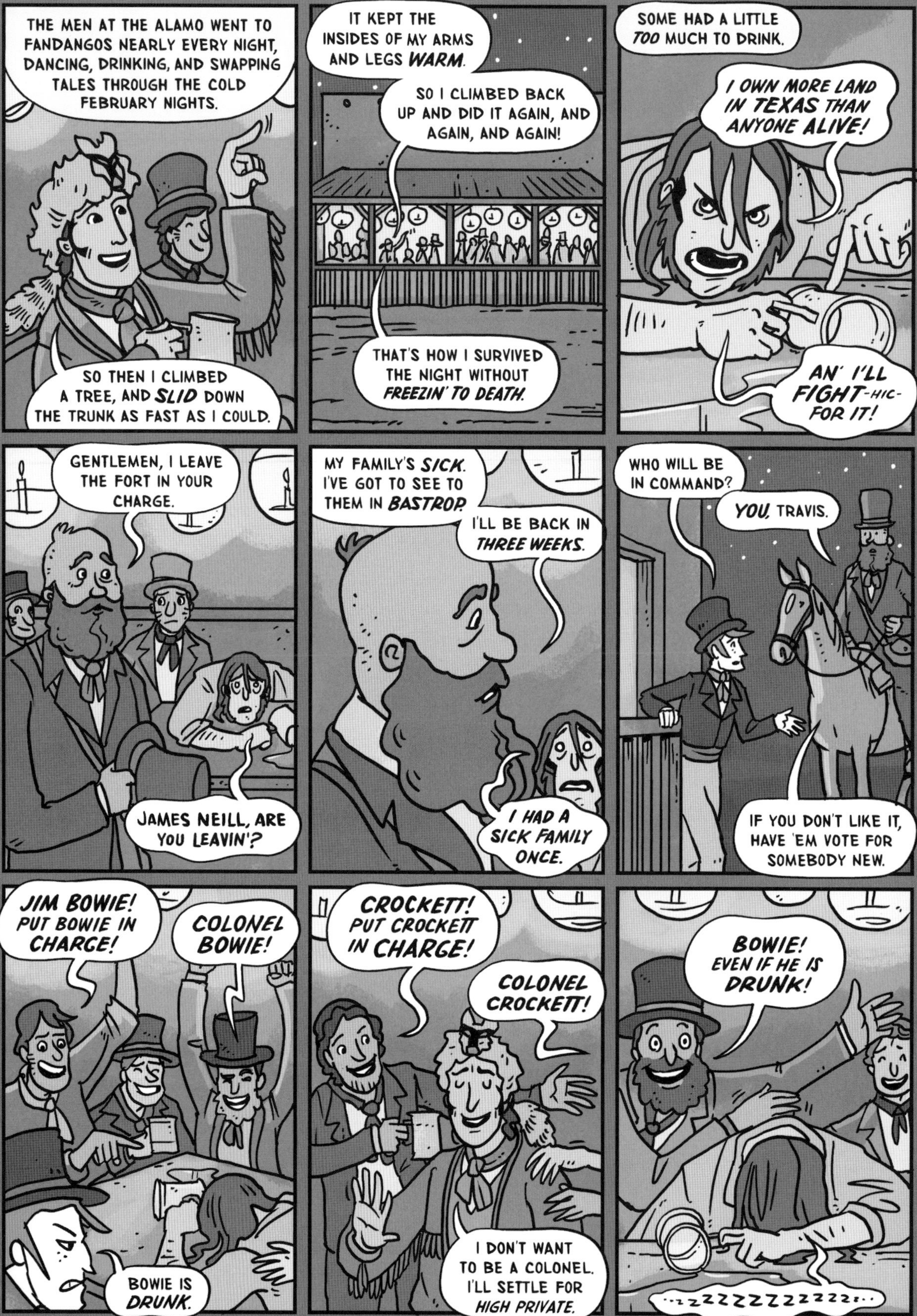
THE MEN AT THE ALAMO WENT TO FANDANGOS NEARLY EVERY NIGHT, DANCING, DRINKING, AND SWAPPING TALES THROUGH THE COLD FEBRUARY NIGHTS.
SO THEN I CLIMBED A TREE, AND SLID DOWN THE TRUNK AS FAST AS I COULD.
IT KEPT THE INSIDES OF MY ARMS AND LEGS WARM.
SO I CLIMBED BACK UP AND DID IT AGAIN, AND AGAIN, AND AGAIN!
THAT'S HOW I SURVIVED THE NIGHT WITHOUT FREEZIN' TO DEATH.
SOME HAD A LITTLE TOO MUCH TO DRINK.
I OWN MORE LAND IN TEXAS THAN ANYONE ALIVE!
AN' I'LL FIGHT-HIC-FOR IT!
GENTLEMEN, I LEAVE THE FORT IN YOUR CHARGE.
JAMES NEILL, ARE YOU LEAVIN'?
MY FAMILY'S SICK. I'VE GOT TO SEE TO THEM IN BASTROP.
I'LL BE BACK IN THREE WEEKS.
I HAD A SICK FAMILY ONCE.
WHO WILL BE IN COMMAND?
YOU, TRAVIS.
IF YOU DON'T LIKE IT, HAVE 'EM VOTE FOR SOMEBODY NEW.
JIM BOWIE! PUT BOWIE IN CHARGE!
COLONEL BOWIE!
BOWIE IS DRUNK.
CROCKETT! PUT CROCKETT IN CHARGE!
COLONEL CROCKETT!
I DON'T WANT TO BE A COLONEL. I'LL SETTLE FOR HIGH PRIVATE.
BOWIE! EVEN IF HE IS DRUNK!
..zzZZZZZZZzzzz...

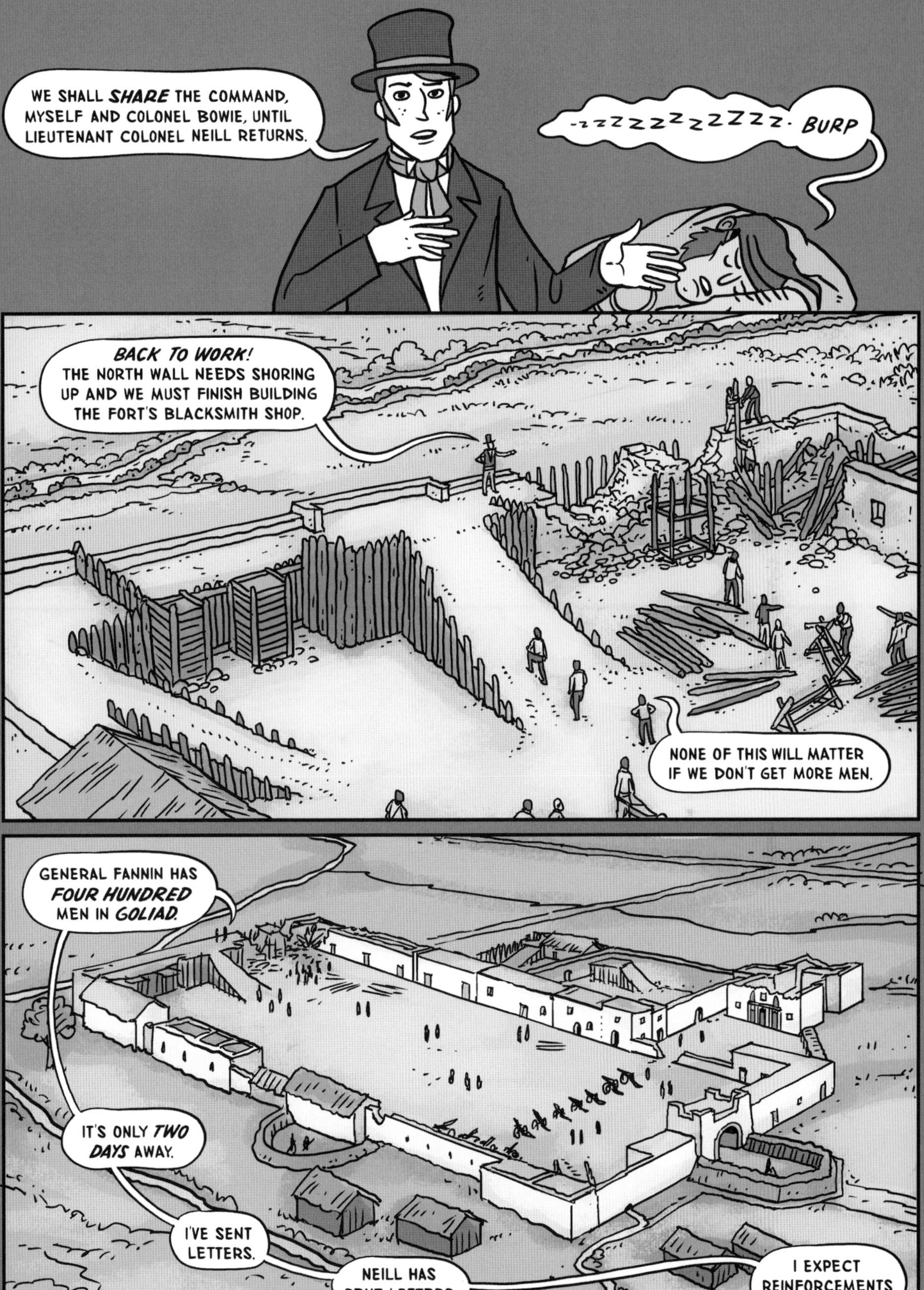
WE SHALL SHARE THE COMMAND, MYSELF AND COLONEL BOWIE, UNTIL LIEUTENANT COLONEL NEILL RETURNS.
-zzzzzzzzzzz- BURP
BACK TO WORK! THE NORTH WALL NEEDS SHORING UP AND WE MUST FINISH BUILDING THE FORT'S BLACKSMITH SHOP.
NONE OF THIS WILL MATTER IF WE DON'T GET MORE MEN.
GENERAL FANNIN HAS FOUR HUNDRED MEN IN GOLIAD.
IT'S ONLY TWO DAYS AWAY.
I'VE SENT LETTERS.
NEILL HAS SENT LETTERS.
I EXPECT REINFORCEMENTS ANY DAY.

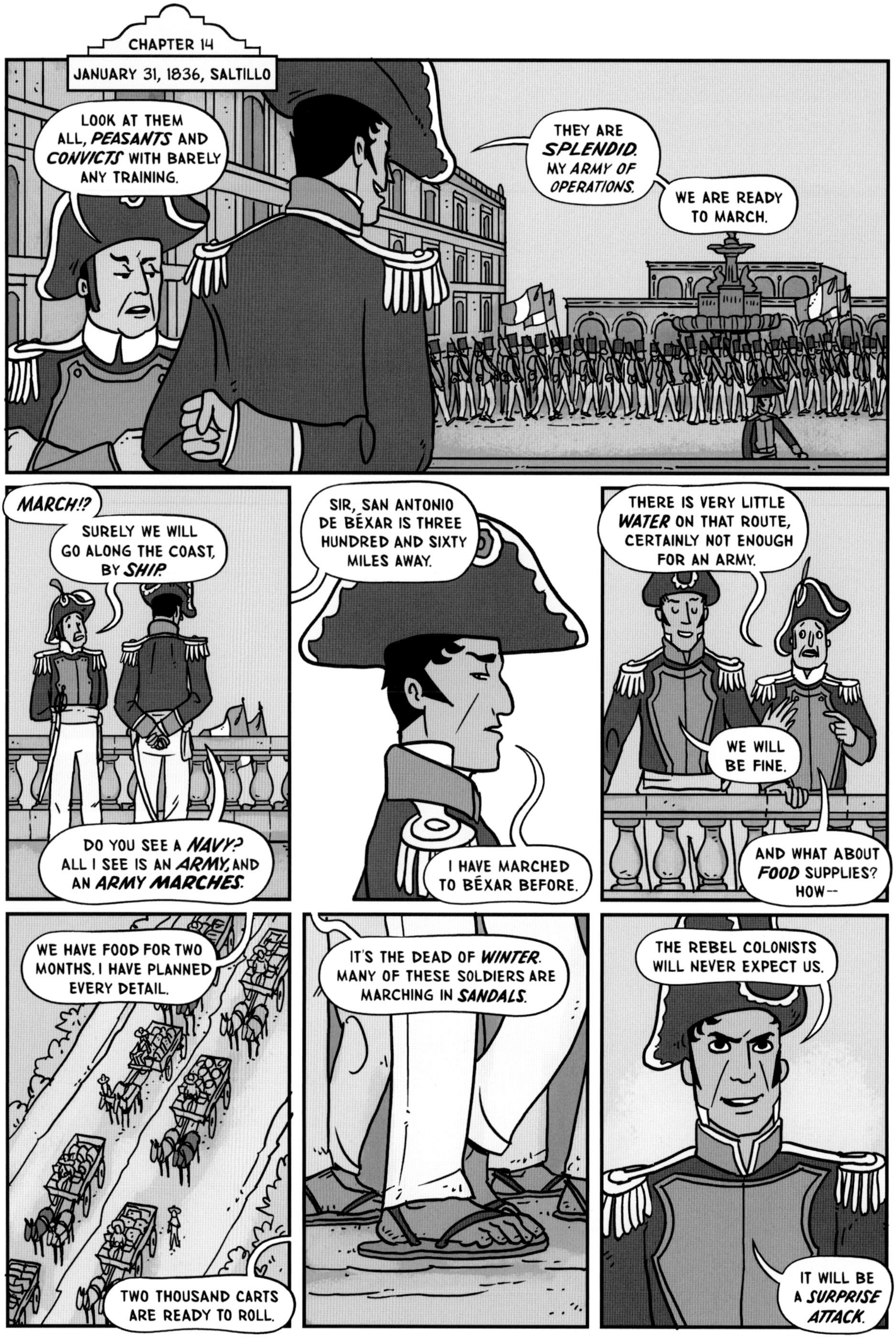
CHAPTER 14
JANUARY 31, 1836, SALTILLO
LOOK AT THEM ALL, PEASANTS AND CONVICTS WITH BARELY ANY TRAINING.
THEY ARE SPLENDID. MY ARMY OF OPERATIONS.
WE ARE READY TO MARCH.
MARCH!?
SURELY WE WILL GO ALONG THE COAST, BY SHIP.
DO YOU SEE A NAVY? ALL I SEE IS AN ARMY, AND AN ARMY MARCHES.
SIR, SAN ANTONIO DE BÉXAR IS THREE HUNDRED AND SIXTY MILES AWAY.
I HAVE MARCHED TO BÉXAR BEFORE.
THERE IS VERY LITTLE WATER ON THAT ROUTE, CERTAINLY NOT ENOUGH FOR AN ARMY.
WE WILL BE FINE.
AND WHAT ABOUT FOOD SUPPLIES? HOW--
WE HAVE FOOD FOR TWO MONTHS. I HAVE PLANNED EVERY DETAIL.
TWO THOUSAND CARTS ARE READY TO ROLL.
IT'S THE DEAD OF WINTER. MANY OF THESE SOLDIERS ARE MARCHING IN SANDALS.
THE REBEL COLONISTS WILL NEVER EXPECT US.
IT WILL BE A SURPRISE ATTACK.

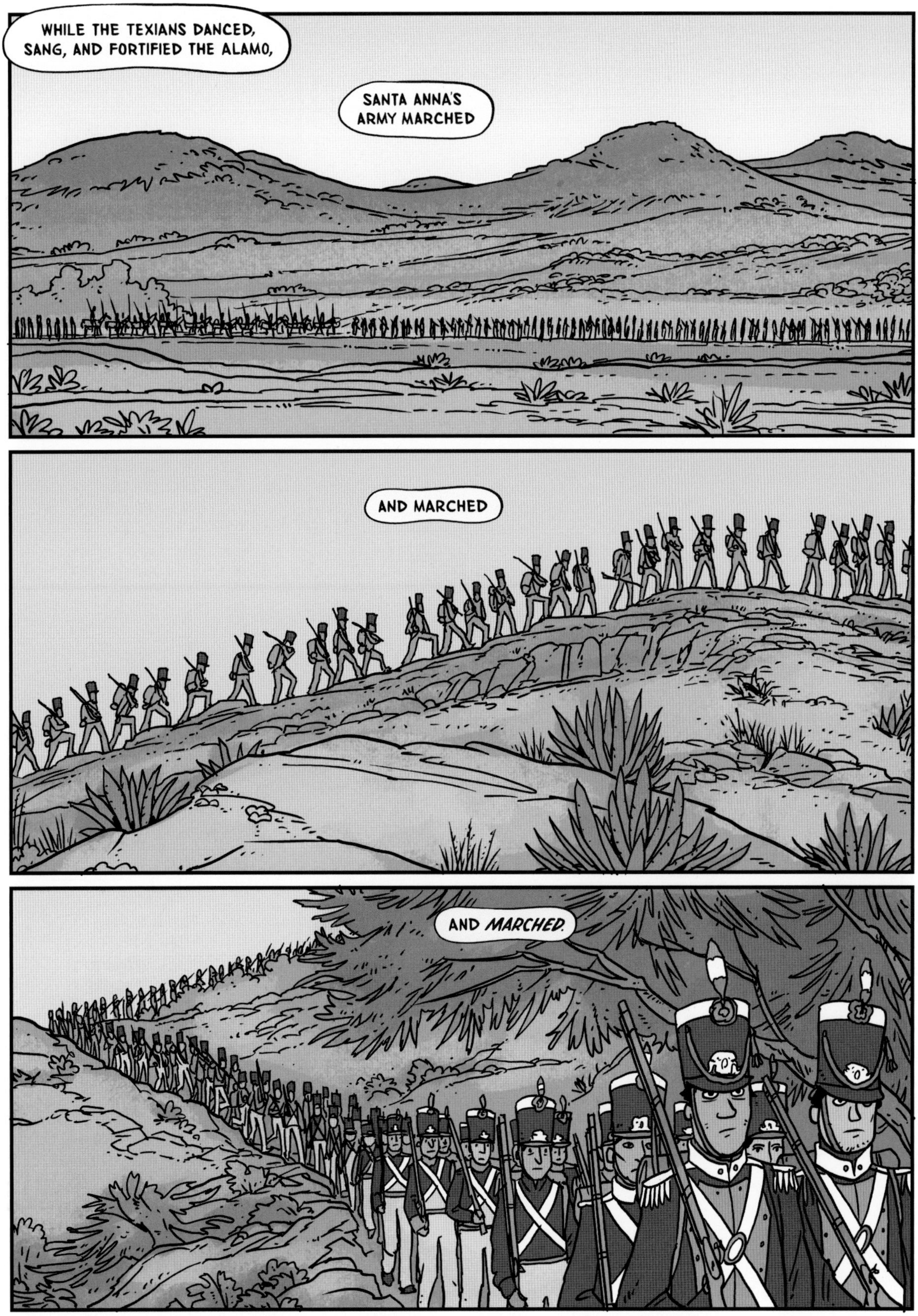
WHILE THE TEXIANS DANCED, SANG, AND FORTIFIED THE ALAMO,
SANTA ANNA'S ARMY MARCHED
AND MARCHED
AND *MARCHED.*

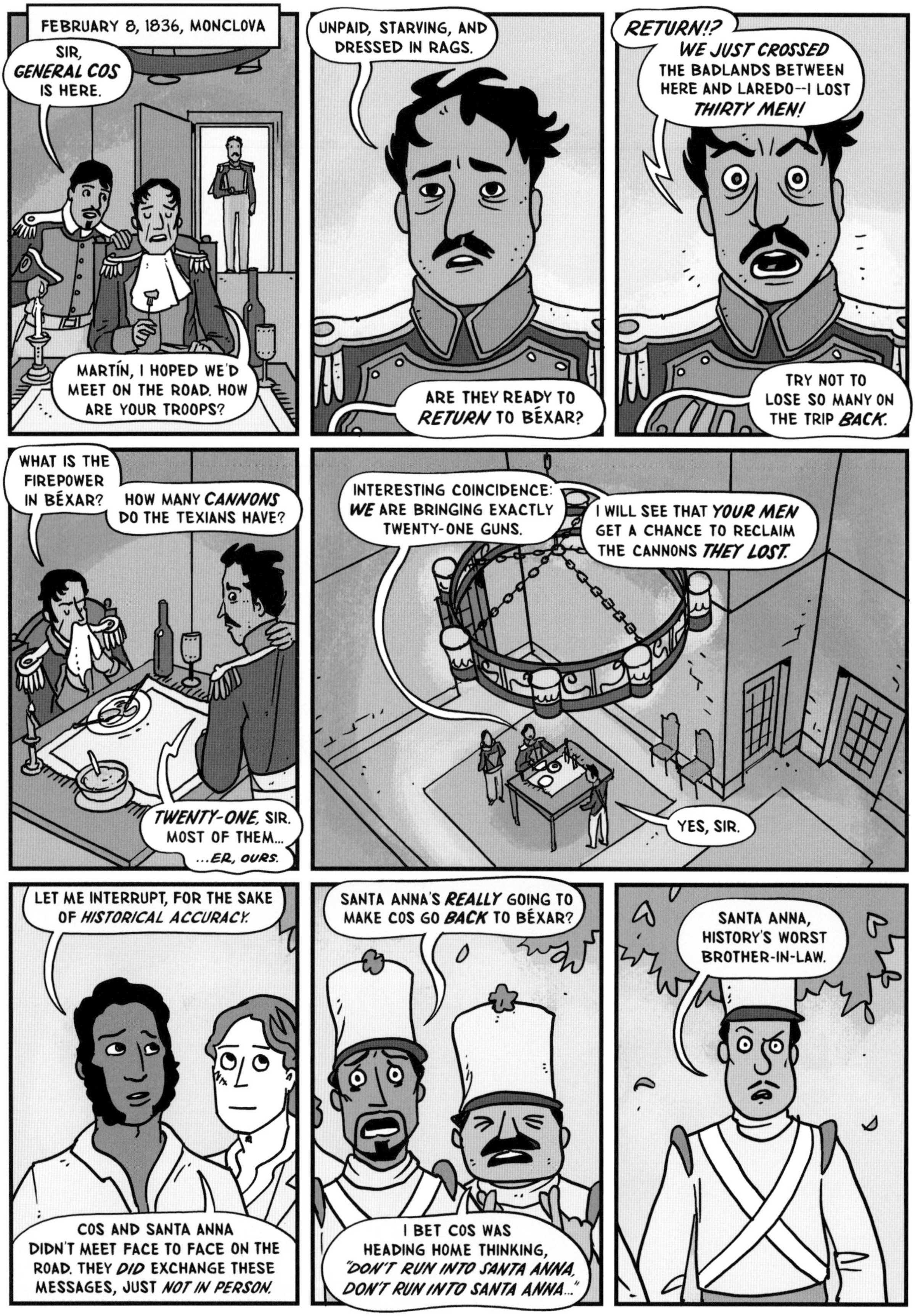
FEBRUARY 8, 1836, MONCLOVA
SIR, GENERAL COS IS HERE.
MARTÍN, I HOPED WE'D MEET ON THE ROAD. HOW ARE YOUR TROOPS?
UNPAID, STARVING, AND DRESSED IN RAGS.
ARE THEY READY TO RETURN TO BÉXAR?
RETURN!? WE JUST CROSSED THE BADLANDS BETWEEN HERE AND LAREDO--I LOST THIRTY MEN!
TRY NOT TO LOSE SO MANY ON THE TRIP BACK.
WHAT IS THE FIREPOWER IN BÉXAR?
HOW MANY CANNONS DO THE TEXIANS HAVE?
TWENTY-ONE, SIR. MOST OF THEM... ...ER, OURS.
INTERESTING COINCIDENCE: WE ARE BRINGING EXACTLY TWENTY-ONE GUNS.
I WILL SEE THAT YOUR MEN GET A CHANCE TO RECLAIM THE CANNONS THEY LOST.
YES, SIR.
LET ME INTERRUPT, FOR THE SAKE OF HISTORICAL ACCURACY.
COS AND SANTA ANNA DIDN'T MEET FACE TO FACE ON THE ROAD. THEY DID EXCHANGE THESE MESSAGES, JUST NOT IN PERSON.
SANTA ANNA'S REALLY GOING TO MAKE COS GO BACK TO BÉXAR?
I BET COS WAS HEADING HOME THINKING, "DON'T RUN INTO SANTA ANNA, DON'T RUN INTO SANTA ANNA..."
SANTA ANNA, HISTORY'S WORST BROTHER-IN-LAW.

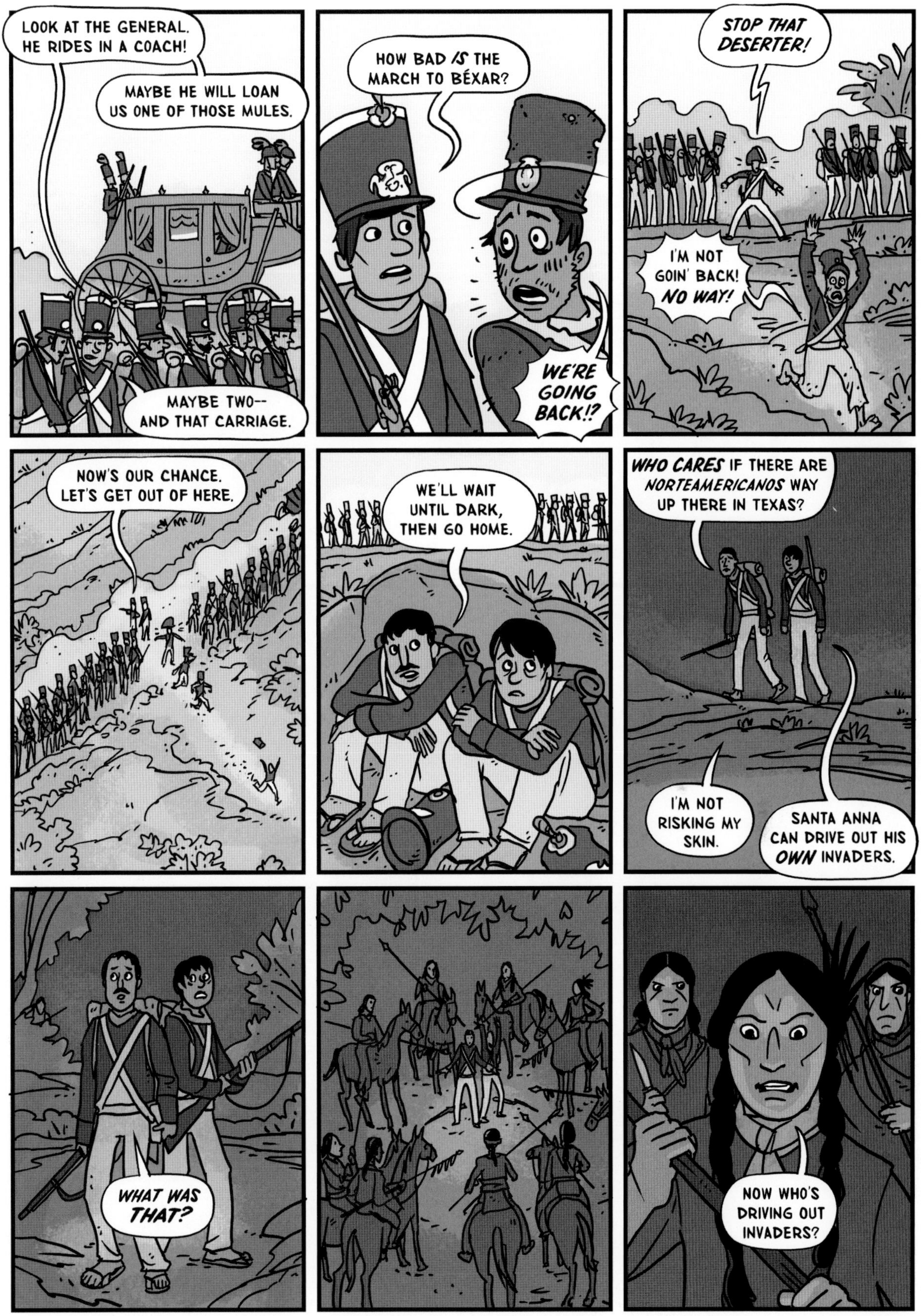
LOOK AT THE GENERAL. HE RIDES IN A COACH!
MAYBE HE WILL LOAN US ONE OF THOSE MULES.
MAYBE TWO-- AND THAT CARRIAGE.
HOW BAD *IS* THE MARCH TO BÉXAR?
WE'RE GOING BACK!?
STOP THAT DESERTER!
I'M NOT GOIN' BACK! *NO WAY!*
NOW'S OUR CHANCE. LET'S GET OUT OF HERE.
WE'LL WAIT UNTIL DARK, THEN GO HOME.
WHO CARES IF THERE ARE *NORTEAMERICANOS* WAY UP THERE IN TEXAS?
I'M NOT RISKING MY SKIN.
SANTA ANNA CAN DRIVE OUT HIS *OWN* INVADERS.
WHAT WAS THAT?
NOW WHO'S DRIVING OUT INVADERS?

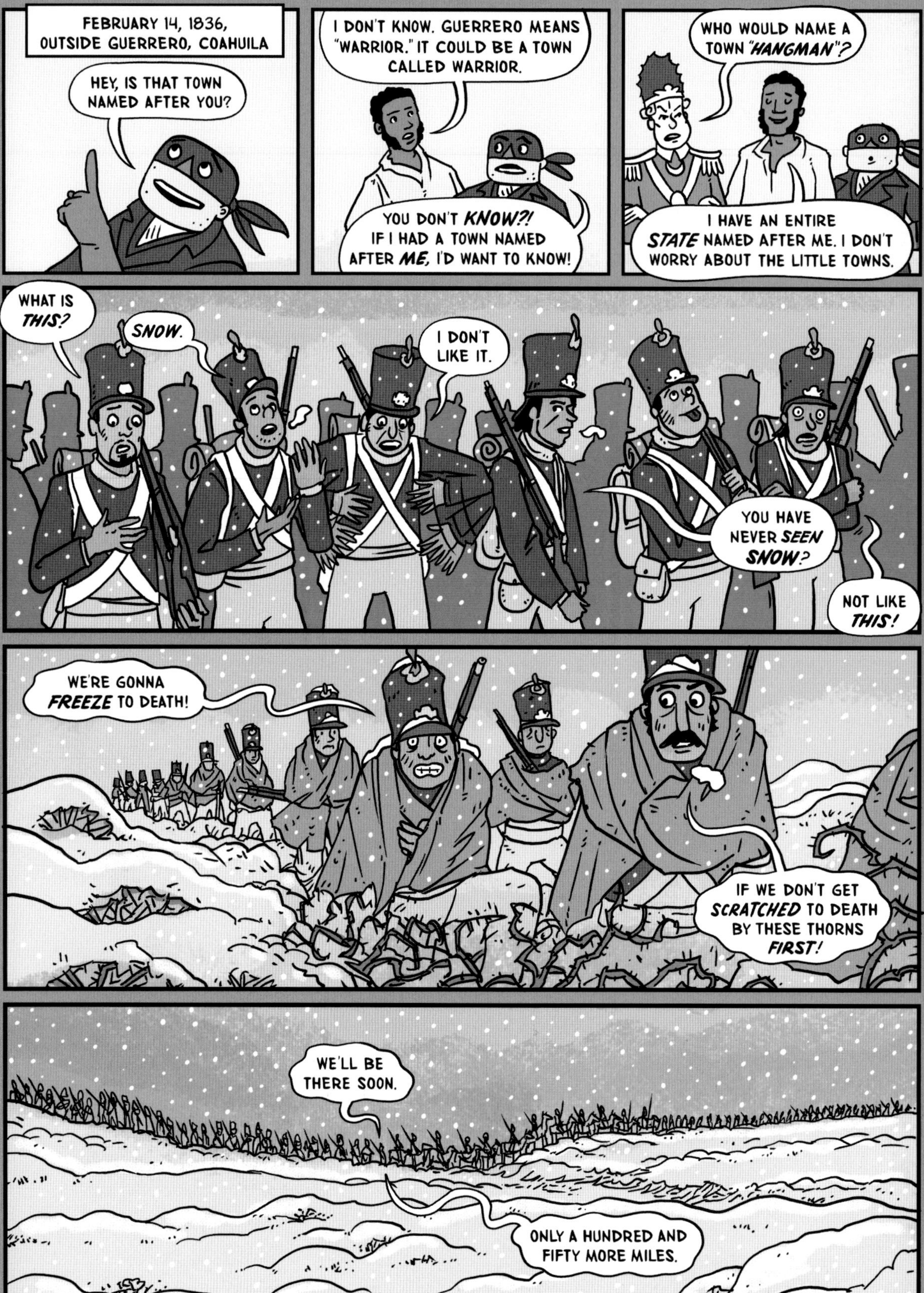
FEBRUARY 14, 1836, OUTSIDE GUERRERO, COAHUILA
HEY, IS THAT TOWN NAMED AFTER YOU?
I DON'T KNOW. GUERRERO MEANS "WARRIOR." IT COULD BE A TOWN CALLED WARRIOR.
YOU DON'T KNOW?! IF I HAD A TOWN NAMED AFTER ME, I'D WANT TO KNOW!
WHO WOULD NAME A TOWN "HANGMAN"?
I HAVE AN ENTIRE STATE NAMED AFTER ME. I DON'T WORRY ABOUT THE LITTLE TOWNS.
WHAT IS THIS?
SNOW.
I DON'T LIKE IT.
YOU HAVE NEVER SEEN SNOW?
NOT LIKE THIS!
WE'RE GONNA FREEZE TO DEATH!
IF WE DON'T GET SCRATCHED TO DEATH BY THESE THORNS FIRST!
WE'LL BE THERE SOON.
ONLY A HUNDRED AND FIFTY MORE MILES.

CHAPTER 15

FEBRUARY 22, 1836, BÉXAR

RAISE A GLASS, BOYS! TODAY'S THE BIRTHDAY OF GEORGE WASHINGTON!

GEORGE!

GEORGE!

JORGE!

HAPPY BIRTHDAY TO GEORGE WASHINGTON!

THERE HE WAS, THIS BIG OL' *RACCOON*, GRINNIN' DOWN AT ME FROM THE TOP OF A TREE.

SO I *GRINNED* RIGHT BACK.

DID YA SHOOT 'IM DOWN, DAVY?

NO, I TRIED TO *GRIN* HIM DOWN, LIKE THIS.

I *GRINNED* AT THAT 'COON FOR *FIVE* MINUTES!

WHAT DID THE 'COON *DO?*

IT JUST KEPT *GRINNIN' RIGHT BACK.*

I WAS SO MAD, I GOT MY *AX* AND *CUT THE WHOLE TREE DOWN!*

CHOP

DID YOU GIT 'IM THEN?

IT WASN'T A 'COON. IT WAS A *KNOT* THAT *LOOKED* LIKE A 'COON!

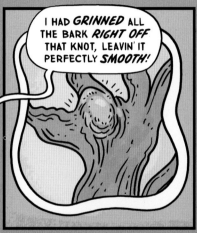

I HAD *GRINNED* ALL THE BARK *RIGHT OFF* THAT KNOT, LEAVIN' IT PERFECTLY *SMOOTH!*

IS THAT WHAT YOU'RE GONNA DO TO *SANTY ANNY?*

THAT'S RIGHT, I'LL *GRIN* HIM RIGHT OUTTA TEXAS!

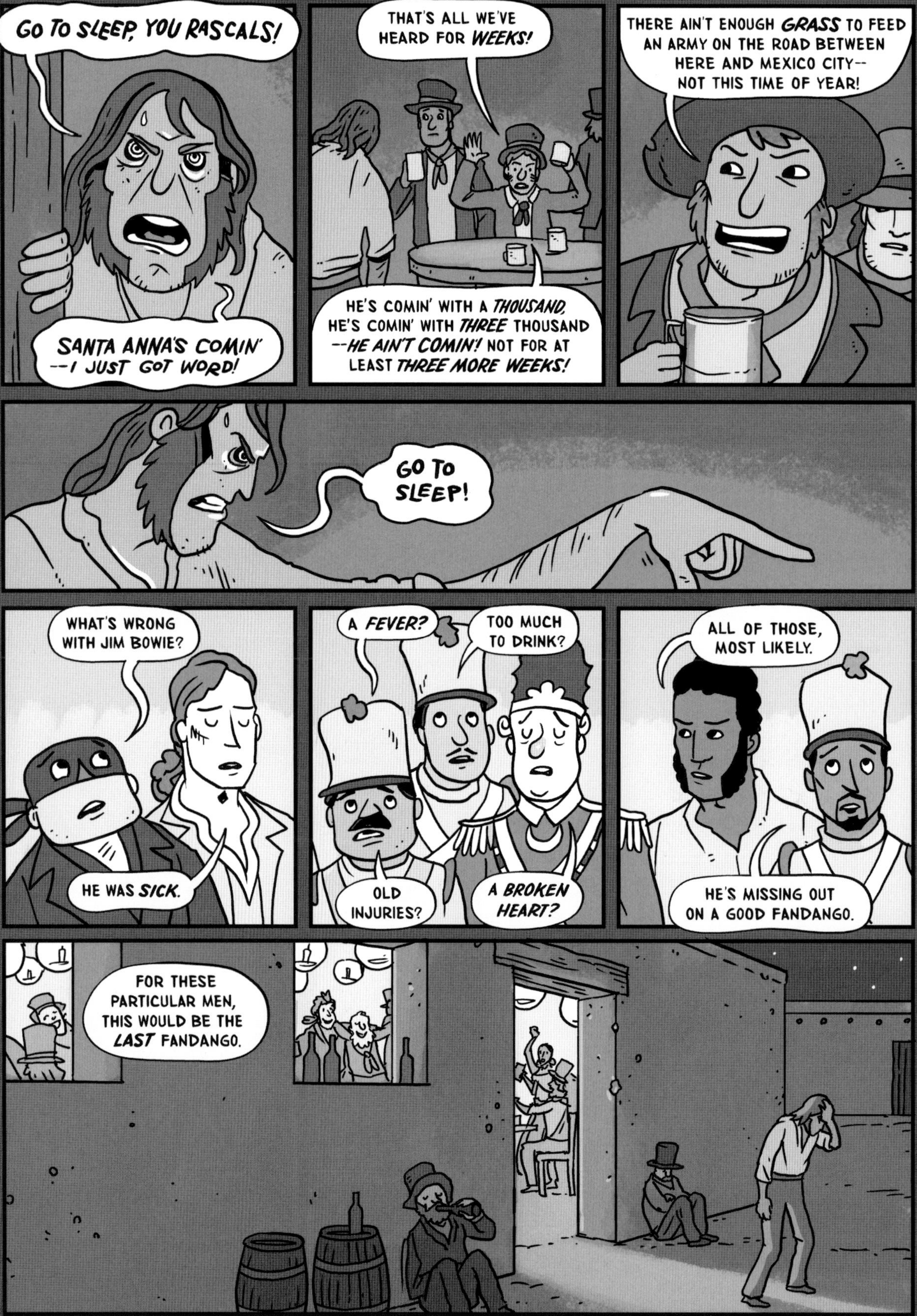
GO TO SLEEP, YOU RASCALS!
SANTA ANNA'S COMIN' --I JUST GOT WORD!
THAT'S ALL WE'VE HEARD FOR WEEKS!
HE'S COMIN' WITH A THOUSAND, HE'S COMIN' WITH THREE THOUSAND --HE AIN'T COMIN'! NOT FOR AT LEAST THREE MORE WEEKS!
THERE AIN'T ENOUGH GRASS TO FEED AN ARMY ON THE ROAD BETWEEN HERE AND MEXICO CITY-- NOT THIS TIME OF YEAR!
GO TO SLEEP!
WHAT'S WRONG WITH JIM BOWIE?
HE WAS SICK.
A FEVER?
TOO MUCH TO DRINK?
OLD INJURIES?
A BROKEN HEART?
ALL OF THOSE, MOST LIKELY.
HE'S MISSING OUT ON A GOOD FANDANGO.
FOR THESE PARTICULAR MEN, THIS WOULD BE THE LAST FANDANGO.

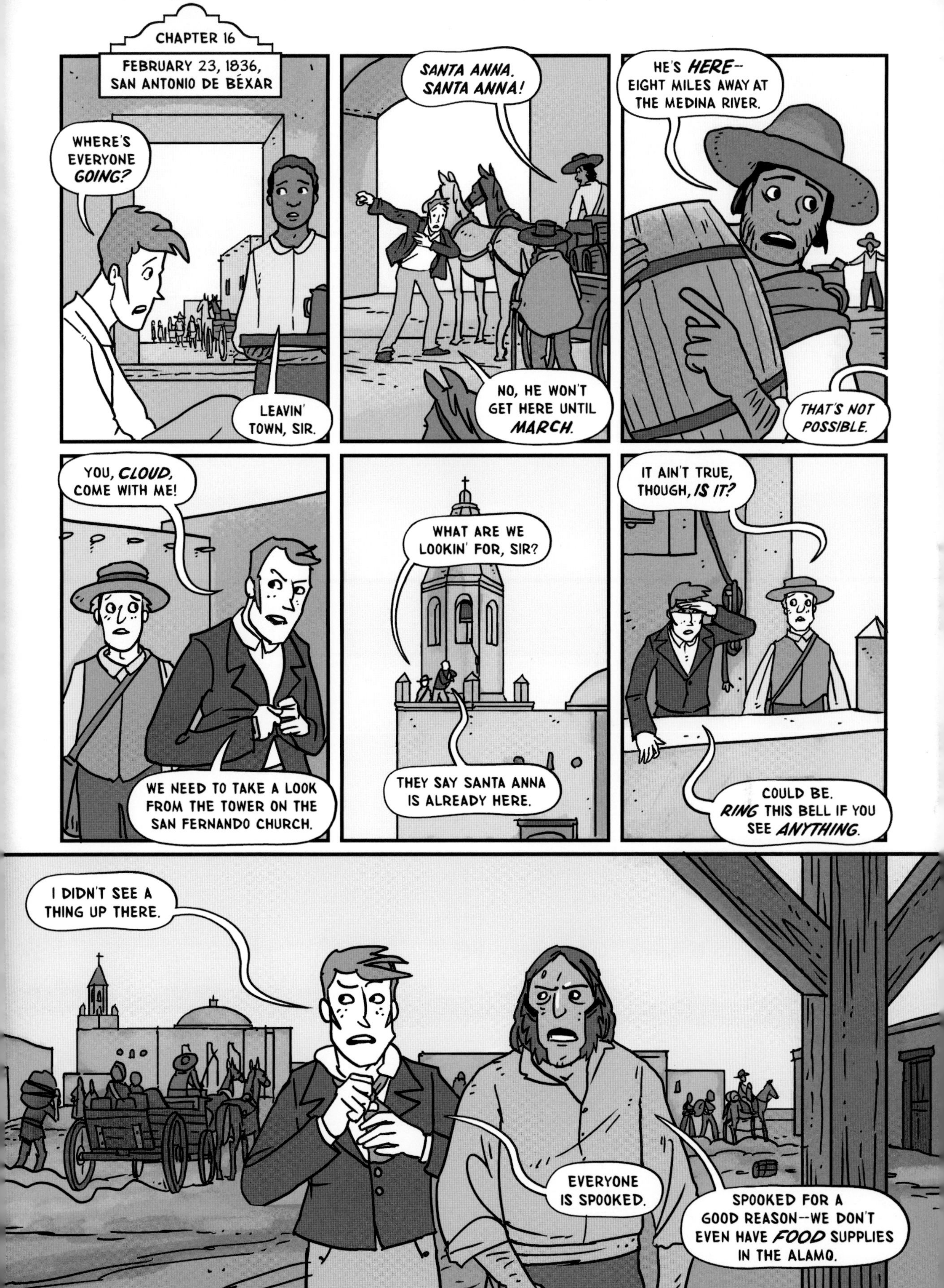

CHAPTER 16
FEBRUARY 23, 1836, SAN ANTONIO DE BÉXAR
WHERE'S EVERYONE *GOING?*
LEAVIN' TOWN, SIR.
SANTA ANNA. SANTA ANNA!
NO, HE WON'T GET HERE UNTIL ***MARCH.***
HE'S ***HERE***-- EIGHT MILES AWAY AT THE MEDINA RIVER.
THAT'S NOT POSSIBLE.
YOU, ***CLOUD,*** COME WITH ME!
WE NEED TO TAKE A LOOK FROM THE TOWER ON THE SAN FERNANDO CHURCH.
WHAT ARE WE LOOKIN' FOR, SIR?
THEY SAY SANTA ANNA IS ALREADY HERE.
IT AIN'T TRUE, THOUGH, ***IS IT?***
COULD BE. ***RING*** THIS BELL IF YOU SEE ***ANYTHING.***
I DIDN'T SEE A THING UP THERE.
EVERYONE IS SPOOKED.
SPOOKED FOR A GOOD REASON--WE DON'T EVEN HAVE ***FOOD*** SUPPLIES IN THE ALAMO.

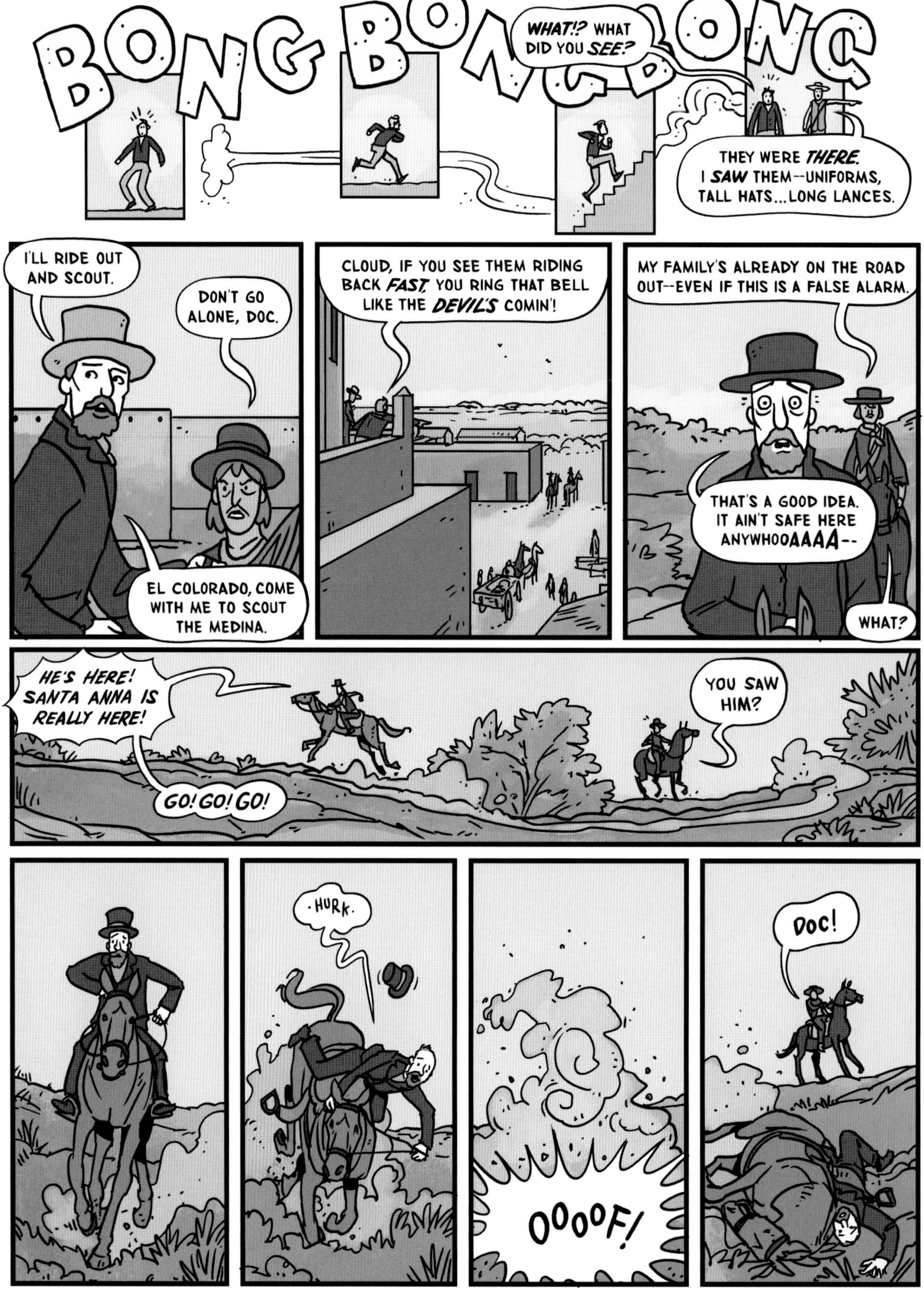
BONG BONG BONG
WHAT!? WHAT DID YOU SEE?
THEY WERE THERE. I SAW THEM--UNIFORMS, TALL HATS...LONG LANCES.
I'LL RIDE OUT AND SCOUT.
DON'T GO ALONE, DOC.
EL COLORADO, COME WITH ME TO SCOUT THE MEDINA.
CLOUD, IF YOU SEE THEM RIDING BACK FAST, YOU RING THAT BELL LIKE THE DEVIL'S COMIN'!
MY FAMILY'S ALREADY ON THE ROAD OUT--EVEN IF THIS IS A FALSE ALARM.
THAT'S A GOOD IDEA. IT AIN'T SAFE HERE ANYWHOOAAAA--
WHAT?
HE'S HERE! SANTA ANNA IS REALLY HERE!
GO! GO! GO!
YOU SAW HIM?
HURK.
OOOOF!
DOC!

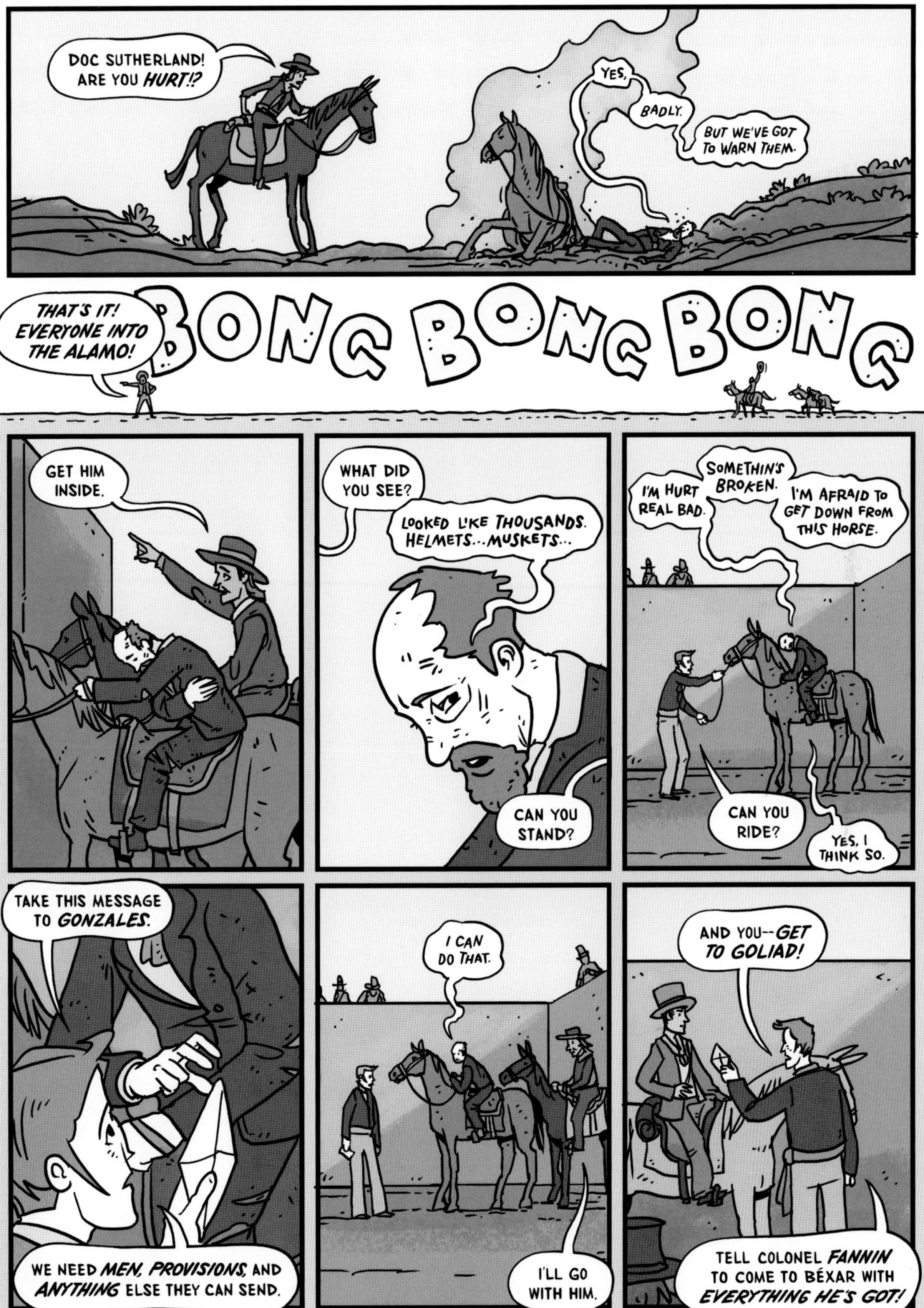
DOC SUTHERLAND! ARE YOU HURT!?
YES,
BADLY.
BUT WE'VE GOT TO WARN THEM.
THAT'S IT! EVERYONE INTO THE ALAMO!
BONG BONG BONG
GET HIM INSIDE.
WHAT DID YOU SEE?
LOOKED LIKE THOUSANDS. HELMETS...MUSKETS...
CAN YOU STAND?
I'M HURT REAL BAD.
SOMETHIN'S BROKEN.
I'M AFRAID TO GET DOWN FROM THIS HORSE.
CAN YOU RIDE?
YES, I THINK SO.
TAKE THIS MESSAGE TO GONZALES.
WE NEED MEN, PROVISIONS, AND ANYTHING ELSE THEY CAN SEND.
I CAN DO THAT.
I'LL GO WITH HIM.
AND YOU--GET TO GOLIAD!
TELL COLONEL FANNIN TO COME TO BÉXAR WITH EVERYTHING HE'S GOT!

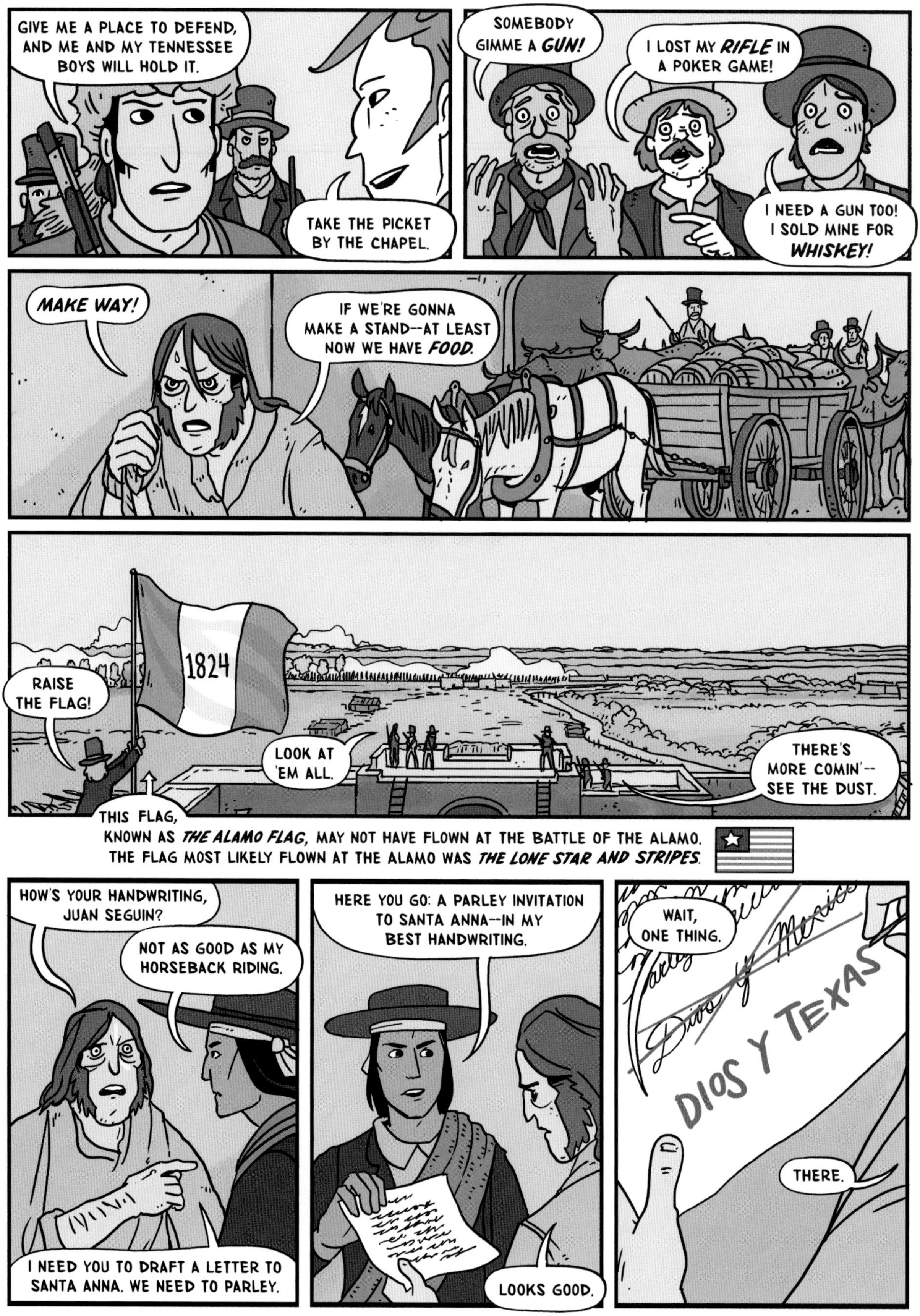
GIVE ME A PLACE TO DEFEND, AND ME AND MY TENNESSEE BOYS WILL HOLD IT.
TAKE THE PICKET BY THE CHAPEL.
SOMEBODY GIMME A GUN!
I LOST MY RIFLE IN A POKER GAME!
I NEED A GUN TOO! I SOLD MINE FOR WHISKEY!
MAKE WAY!
IF WE'RE GONNA MAKE A STAND--AT LEAST NOW WE HAVE FOOD.
1824
RAISE THE FLAG!
LOOK AT 'EM ALL.
THERE'S MORE COMIN'-- SEE THE DUST.
THIS FLAG, KNOWN AS THE ALAMO FLAG, MAY NOT HAVE FLOWN AT THE BATTLE OF THE ALAMO. THE FLAG MOST LIKELY FLOWN AT THE ALAMO WAS THE LONE STAR AND STRIPES.
HOW'S YOUR HANDWRITING, JUAN SEGUIN?
NOT AS GOOD AS MY HORSEBACK RIDING.
I NEED YOU TO DRAFT A LETTER TO SANTA ANNA. WE NEED TO PARLEY.
HERE YOU GO: A PARLEY INVITATION TO SANTA ANNA--IN MY BEST HANDWRITING.
LOOKS GOOD.
WAIT, ONE THING.
Dios y Mexico
DIOS Y TEXAS
THERE.

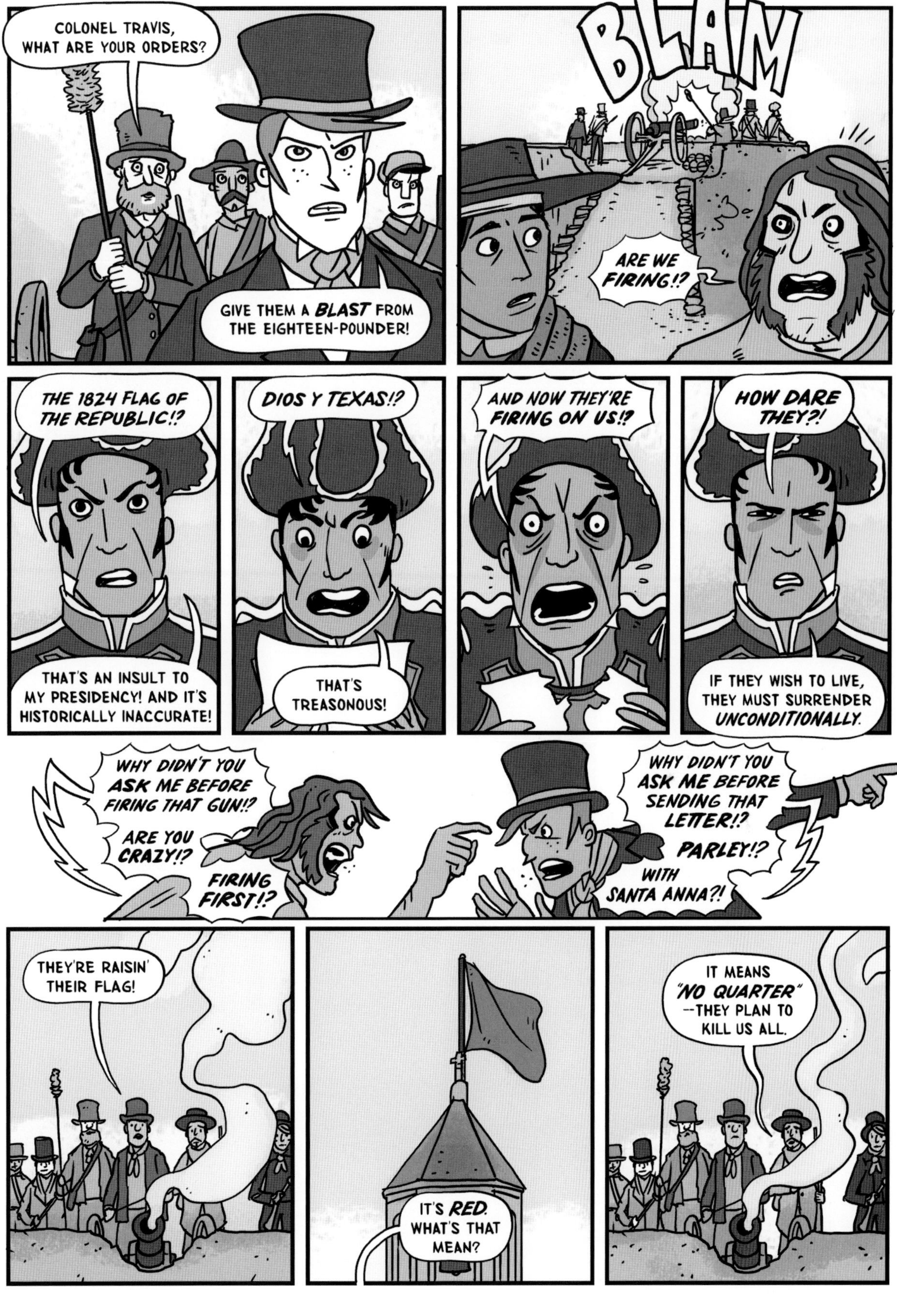

COLONEL TRAVIS, WHAT ARE YOUR ORDERS?
GIVE THEM A BLAST FROM THE EIGHTEEN-POUNDER!
BLAM
ARE WE FIRING!?
THE 1824 FLAG OF THE REPUBLIC!?
THAT'S AN INSULT TO MY PRESIDENCY! AND IT'S HISTORICALLY INACCURATE!
DIOS Y TEXAS!?
THAT'S TREASONOUS!
AND NOW THEY'RE FIRING ON US!?
HOW DARE THEY?!
IF THEY WISH TO LIVE, THEY MUST SURRENDER UNCONDITIONALLY.
WHY DIDN'T YOU ASK ME BEFORE FIRING THAT GUN!?
ARE YOU CRAZY!?
FIRING FIRST!?
WHY DIDN'T YOU ASK ME BEFORE SENDING THAT LETTER!?
PARLEY!?
WITH SANTA ANNA?!
THEY'RE RAISIN' THEIR FLAG!
IT'S RED. WHAT'S THAT MEAN?
IT MEANS "NO QUARTER" --THEY PLAN TO KILL US ALL.

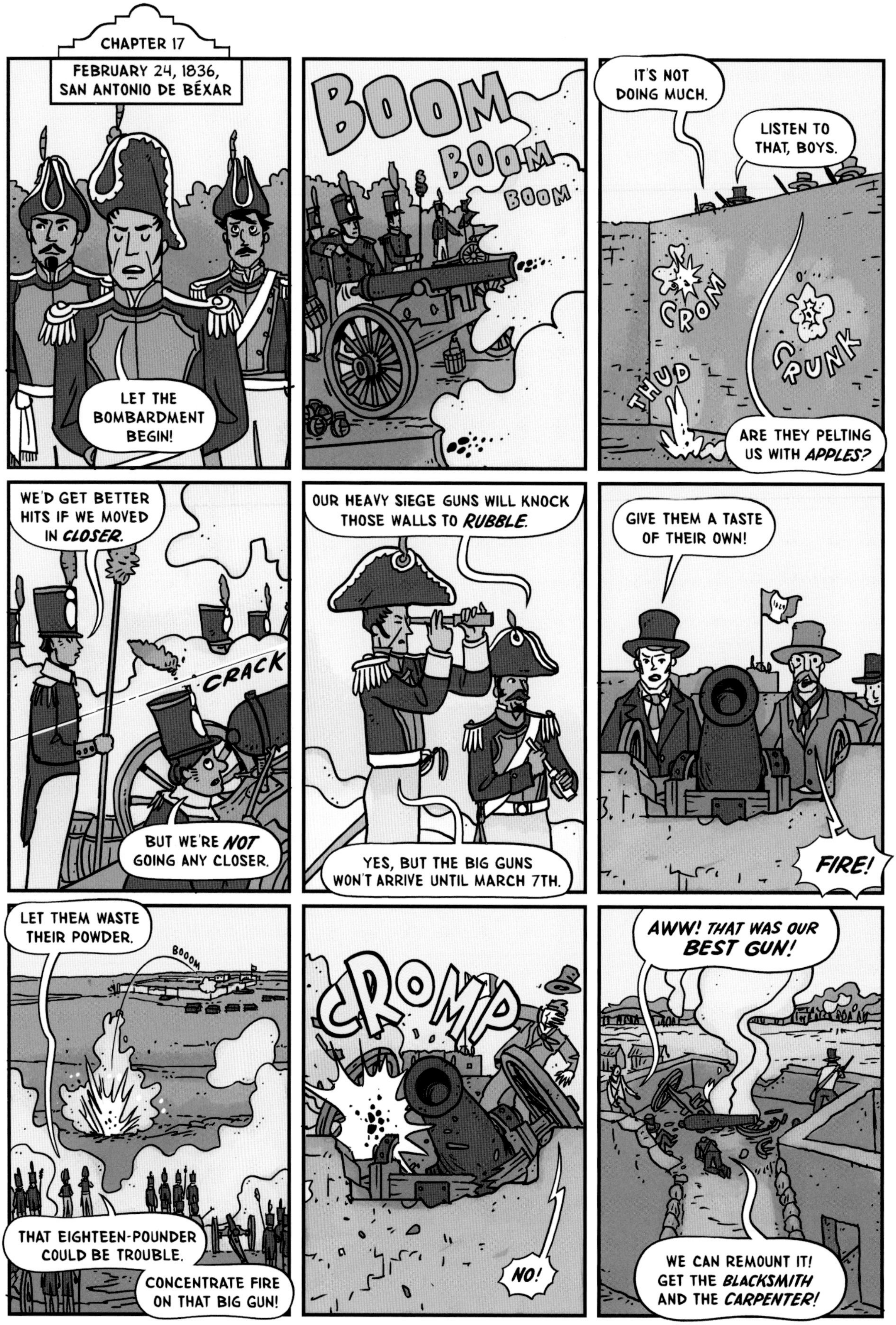
CHAPTER 17
FEBRUARY 24, 1836, SAN ANTONIO DE BÉXAR
LET THE BOMBARDMENT BEGIN!
BOOM
BOOM
BOOM
IT'S NOT DOING MUCH.
LISTEN TO THAT, BOYS.
CROM
CRUNK
THUD
ARE THEY PELTING US WITH APPLES?
WE'D GET BETTER HITS IF WE MOVED IN CLOSER.
CRACK
BUT WE'RE NOT GOING ANY CLOSER.
OUR HEAVY SIEGE GUNS WILL KNOCK THOSE WALLS TO RUBBLE.
YES, BUT THE BIG GUNS WON'T ARRIVE UNTIL MARCH 7TH.
GIVE THEM A TASTE OF THEIR OWN!
FIRE!
LET THEM WASTE THEIR POWDER.
BOOOM
THAT EIGHTEEN-POUNDER COULD BE TROUBLE.
CONCENTRATE FIRE ON THAT BIG GUN!
CROMP
NO!
AWW! THAT WAS OUR BEST GUN!
WE CAN REMOUNT IT! GET THE BLACKSMITH AND THE CARPENTER!

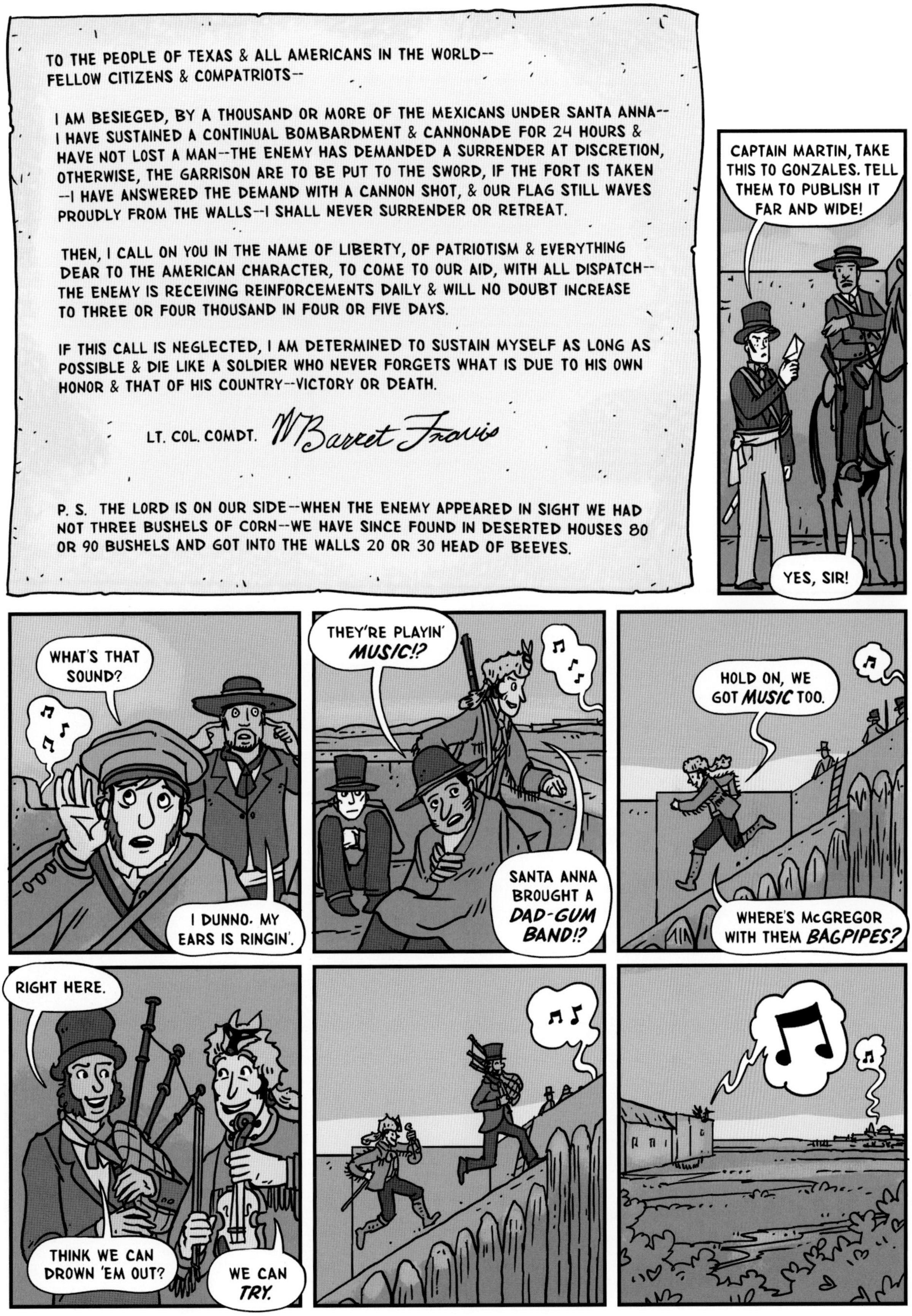
TO THE PEOPLE OF TEXAS & ALL AMERICANS IN THE WORLD--
FELLOW CITIZENS & COMPATRIOTS--
I AM BESIEGED, BY A THOUSAND OR MORE OF THE MEXICANS UNDER SANTA ANNA--I HAVE SUSTAINED A CONTINUAL BOMBARDMENT & CANNONADE FOR 24 HOURS & HAVE NOT LOST A MAN--THE ENEMY HAS DEMANDED A SURRENDER AT DISCRETION, OTHERWISE, THE GARRISON ARE TO BE PUT TO THE SWORD, IF THE FORT IS TAKEN --I HAVE ANSWERED THE DEMAND WITH A CANNON SHOT, & OUR FLAG STILL WAVES PROUDLY FROM THE WALLS--I SHALL NEVER SURRENDER OR RETREAT.
THEN, I CALL ON YOU IN THE NAME OF LIBERTY, OF PATRIOTISM & EVERYTHING DEAR TO THE AMERICAN CHARACTER, TO COME TO OUR AID, WITH ALL DISPATCH--THE ENEMY IS RECEIVING REINFORCEMENTS DAILY & WILL NO DOUBT INCREASE TO THREE OR FOUR THOUSAND IN FOUR OR FIVE DAYS.
IF THIS CALL IS NEGLECTED, I AM DETERMINED TO SUSTAIN MYSELF AS LONG AS POSSIBLE & DIE LIKE A SOLDIER WHO NEVER FORGETS WHAT IS DUE TO HIS OWN HONOR & THAT OF HIS COUNTRY--VICTORY OR DEATH.
LT. COL. COMDT. W Barret Travis
P. S. THE LORD IS ON OUR SIDE--WHEN THE ENEMY APPEARED IN SIGHT WE HAD NOT THREE BUSHELS OF CORN--WE HAVE SINCE FOUND IN DESERTED HOUSES 80 OR 90 BUSHELS AND GOT INTO THE WALLS 20 OR 30 HEAD OF BEEVES.
CAPTAIN MARTIN, TAKE THIS TO GONZALES. TELL THEM TO PUBLISH IT FAR AND WIDE!
YES, SIR!
WHAT'S THAT SOUND?
I DUNNO. MY EARS IS RINGIN'.
THEY'RE PLAYIN' *MUSIC!?*
SANTA ANNA BROUGHT A *DAD-GUM BAND!?*
HOLD ON, WE GOT *MUSIC* TOO.
WHERE'S McGREGOR WITH THEM *BAGPIPES?*
RIGHT HERE.
THINK WE CAN DROWN 'EM OUT?
WE CAN *TRY.*

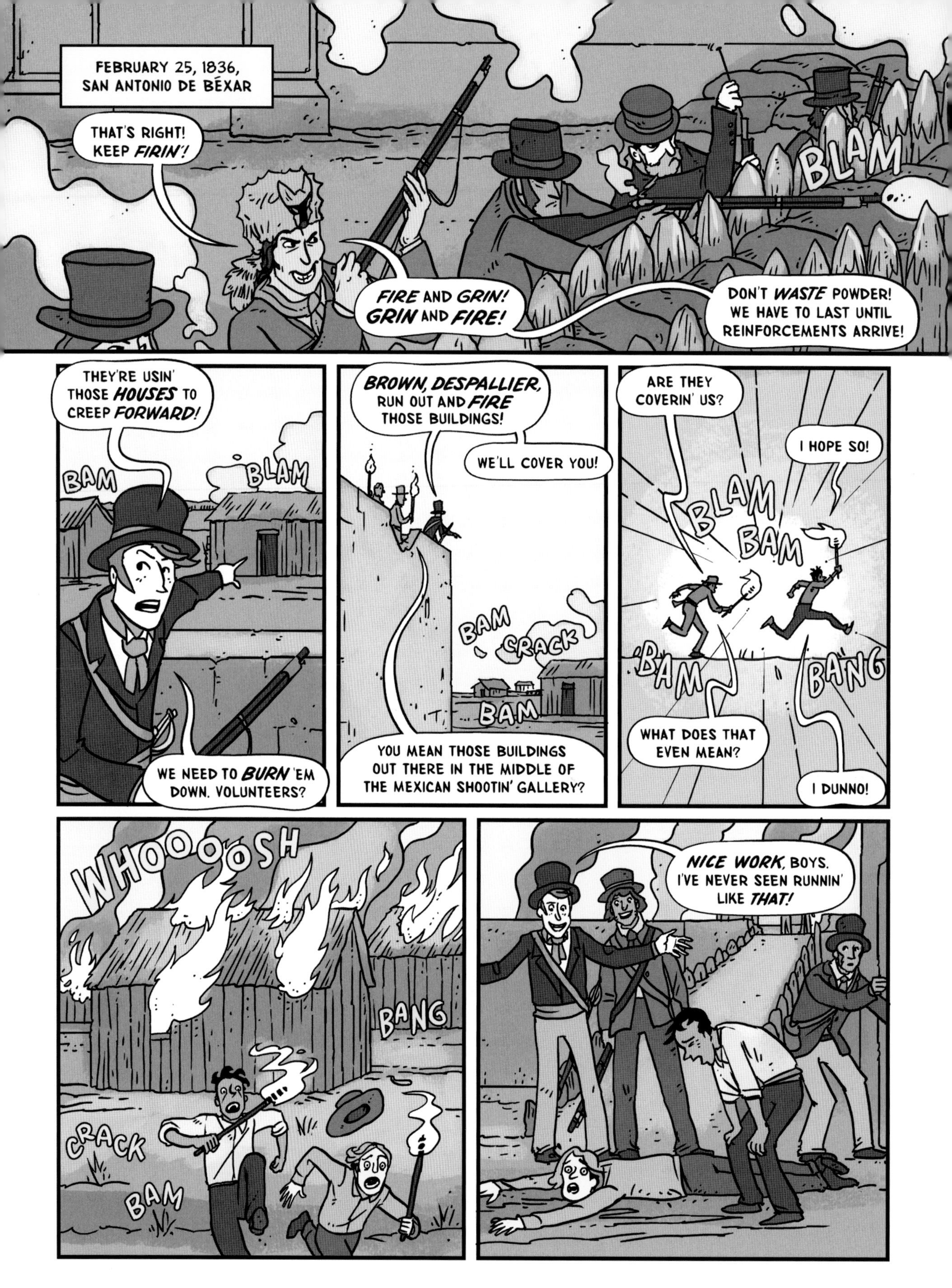

FEBRUARY 25, 1836, SAN ANTONIO DE BÉXAR
THAT'S RIGHT! KEEP *FIRIN'*!
BLAM
FIRE AND *GRIN*! *GRIN* AND *FIRE*!
DON'T *WASTE* POWDER! WE HAVE TO LAST UNTIL REINFORCEMENTS ARRIVE!
THEY'RE USIN' THOSE *HOUSES* TO CREEP *FORWARD*!
BAM
BLAM
WE NEED TO *BURN* 'EM DOWN. VOLUNTEERS?
BROWN, DESPALLIER, RUN OUT AND *FIRE* THOSE BUILDINGS!
WE'LL COVER YOU!
BAM
CRACK
BAM
YOU MEAN THOSE BUILDINGS OUT THERE IN THE MIDDLE OF THE MEXICAN SHOOTIN' GALLERY?
ARE THEY COVERIN' US?
I HOPE SO!
BLAM
BAM
BAM
BANG
WHAT DOES THAT EVEN MEAN?
I DUNNO!
WHOOOOOSH
BANG
CRACK
BAM
NICE WORK, BOYS. I'VE NEVER SEEN RUNNIN' LIKE *THAT*!

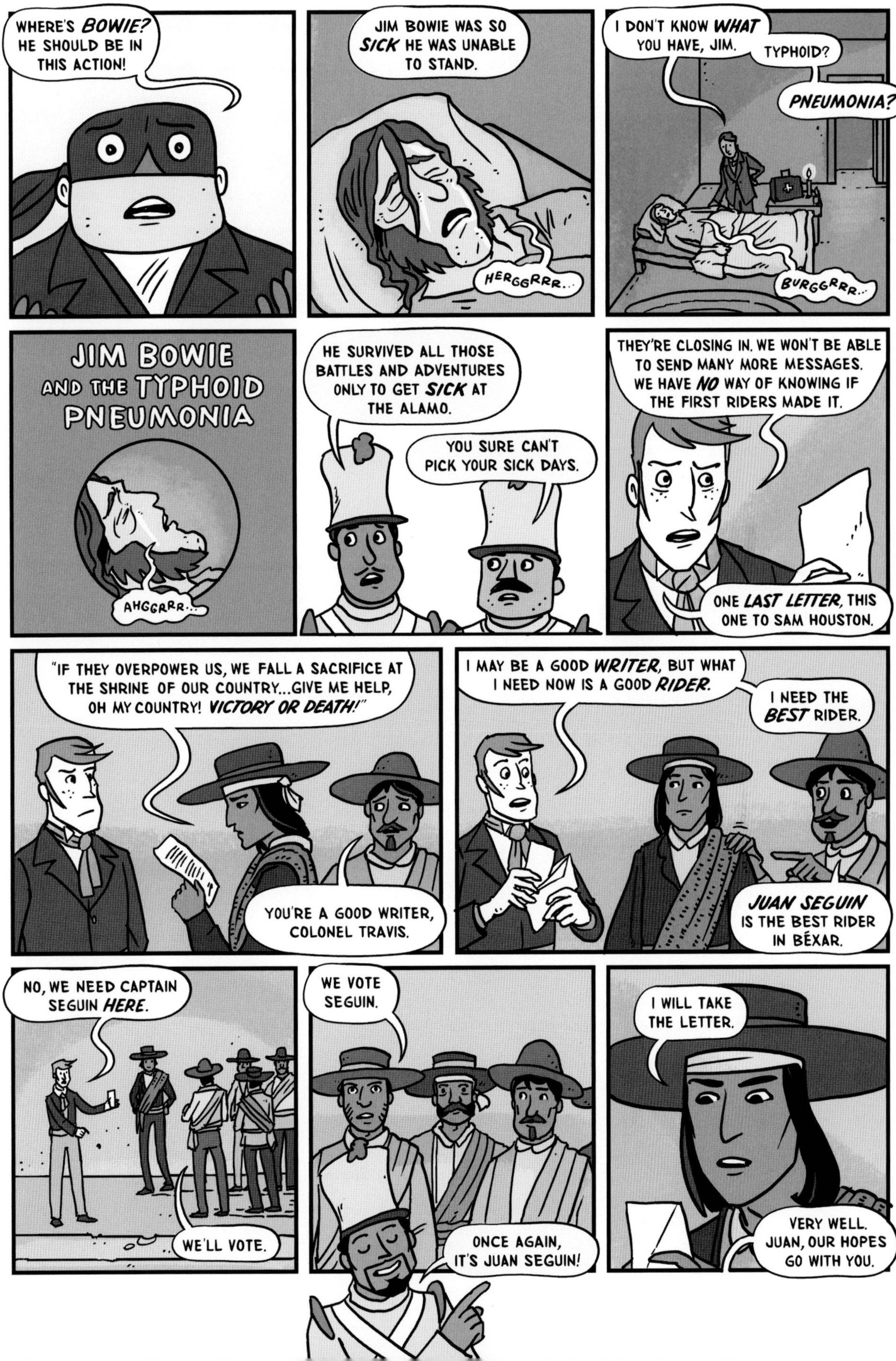
WHERE'S *BOWIE?* HE SHOULD BE IN THIS ACTION!
JIM BOWIE WAS SO *SICK* HE WAS UNABLE TO STAND.
HERGGRRR...
I DON'T KNOW *WHAT* YOU HAVE, JIM.
TYPHOID?
PNEUMONIA?
BURGGRRR...
JIM BOWIE AND THE TYPHOID PNEUMONIA
AHGGRRR...
HE SURVIVED ALL THOSE BATTLES AND ADVENTURES ONLY TO GET *SICK* AT THE ALAMO.
YOU SURE CAN'T PICK YOUR SICK DAYS.
THEY'RE CLOSING IN. WE WON'T BE ABLE TO SEND MANY MORE MESSAGES. WE HAVE *NO* WAY OF KNOWING IF THE FIRST RIDERS MADE IT.
ONE *LAST LETTER*, THIS ONE TO SAM HOUSTON.
"IF THEY OVERPOWER US, WE FALL A SACRIFICE AT THE SHRINE OF OUR COUNTRY...GIVE ME HELP, OH MY COUNTRY! *VICTORY OR DEATH!*"
YOU'RE A GOOD WRITER, COLONEL TRAVIS.
I MAY BE A GOOD *WRITER*, BUT WHAT I NEED NOW IS A GOOD *RIDER*.
I NEED THE *BEST* RIDER.
JUAN SEGUIN IS THE BEST RIDER IN BÉXAR.
NO, WE NEED CAPTAIN SEGUIN *HERE*.
WE'LL VOTE.
WE VOTE SEGUIN.
ONCE AGAIN, IT'S JUAN SEGUIN!
I WILL TAKE THE LETTER.
VERY WELL. JUAN, OUR HOPES GO WITH YOU.

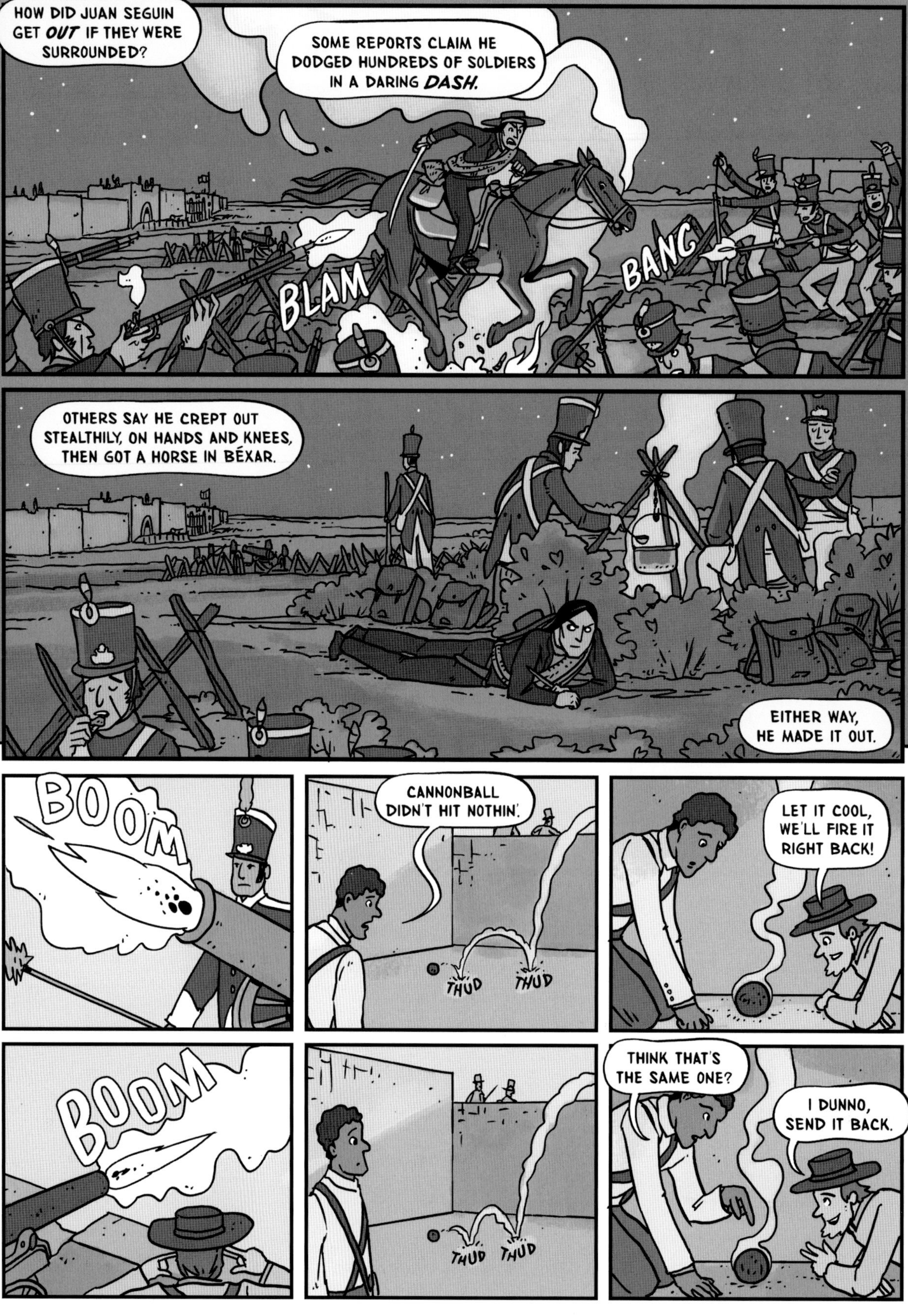
HOW DID JUAN SEGUIN GET *OUT* IF THEY WERE SURROUNDED?
SOME REPORTS CLAIM HE DODGED HUNDREDS OF SOLDIERS IN A DARING *DASH.*
BLAM
BANG
OTHERS SAY HE CREPT OUT STEALTHILY, ON HANDS AND KNEES, THEN GOT A HORSE IN BÉXAR.
EITHER WAY, HE MADE IT OUT.
BOOM
CANNONBALL DIDN'T HIT NOTHIN'.
THUD
THUD
LET IT COOL, WE'LL FIRE IT RIGHT BACK!
BOOM
THUD
THUD
THINK THAT'S THE SAME ONE?
I DUNNO, SEND IT BACK.

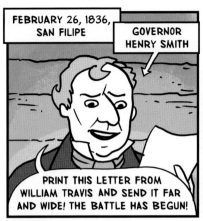

FEBRUARY 26, 1836, SAN FILIPE

GOVERNOR HENRY SMITH

PRINT THIS LETTER FROM WILLIAM TRAVIS AND SEND IT FAR AND WIDE! THE BATTLE HAS BEGUN!

TRAVIS AND BOWIE ARE HOLDING OFF SANTA ANNA'S ENTIRE ARMY WITH A HANDFUL OF MEN AT AN OLD FORT OUTSIDE OF BÉXAR.

THE ALAMO?

THEY WON'T LAST LONG ALONE. THEY NEED EVERY VOLUNTEER WE CAN SEND!

TELL THEM, "HOLD ON. WE'RE COMING!"

FEBRUARY 27, 1836, GOLIAD

COLONEL JAMES FANNIN

ONE HUNDRED WILL STAY TO MAN THE FORT HERE IN GOLIAD.

THREE HUNDRED WILL MARCH WITH ME.

TO BÉXAR! HO!

SPLORT

HOLD UP. THE SUPPLY WAGON'S BROKE.

SPLAT

THERE'S NO TIME TO LOSE!

DOUBLE THE OXEN ON THE ARTILLERY WAGON! WE'LL COME BACK FOR THE SUPPLIES AFTER WE GET THE BIG GUNS ACROSS THE RIVER.

THAT TOOK ALL DAY.

SHOULD WE SLEEP HERE WITH THE GUNS, OR BACK AT THE FORT?

WELL, THE FORT IS RIGHT HERE.

FEBRUARY 28, 1836, GOLIAD

TIME TO HITCH UP THE OXEN!

TO BÉXAR!

WHERE ARE THE OXEN, SIR?

I DON'T KNOW.

WHO WAS IN CHARGE OF THE OXEN!?

WE CAN'T GO TO BÉXAR WITHOUT SUPPLIES!

FIND THOSE OXEN!

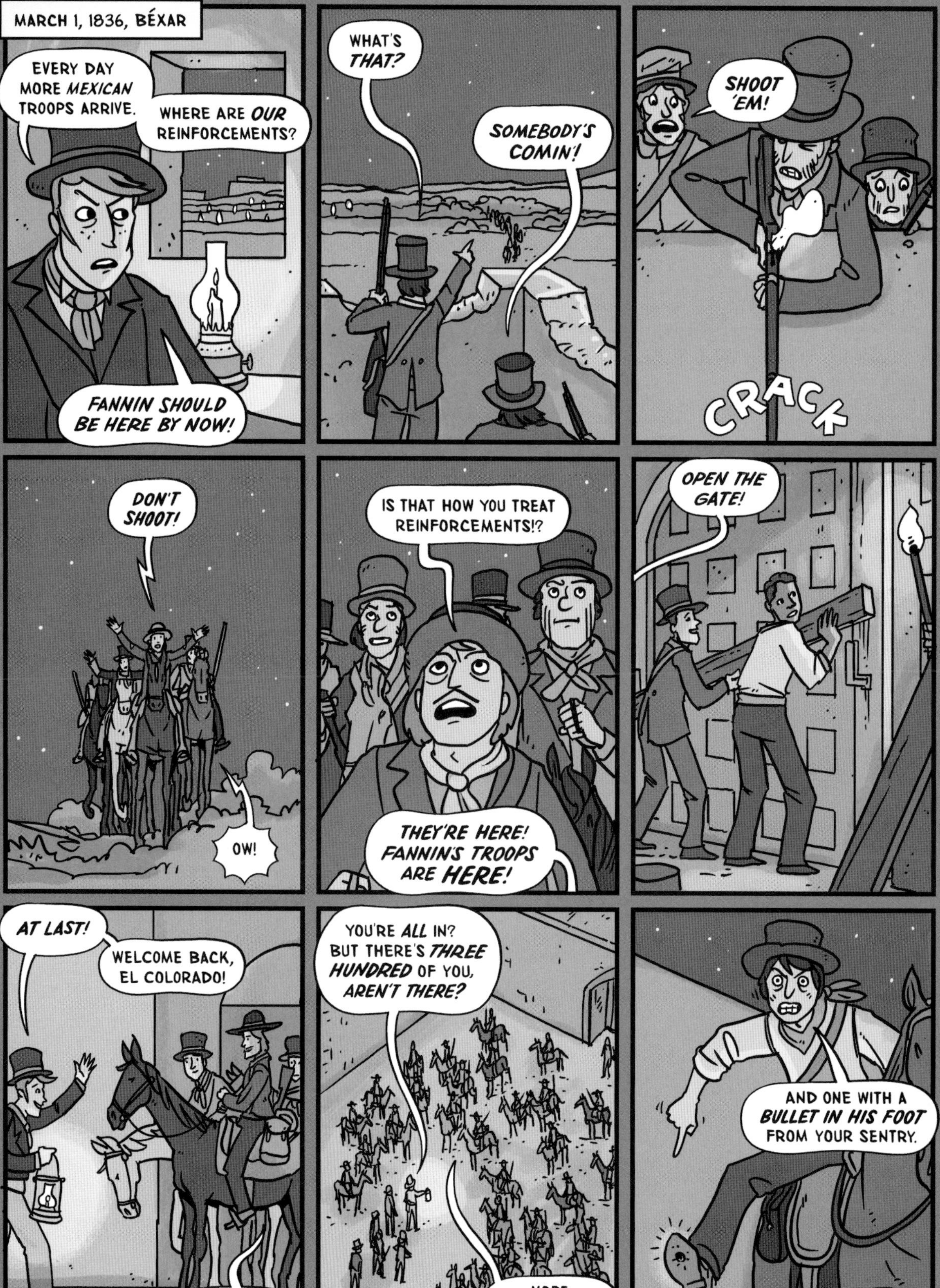

MARCH 1, 1836, BÉXAR
EVERY DAY MORE *MEXICAN* TROOPS ARRIVE.
WHERE ARE *OUR* REINFORCEMENTS?
FANNIN SHOULD BE HERE BY NOW!
WHAT'S *THAT?*
SOMEBODY'S COMIN'!
SHOOT 'EM!
CRACK
DON'T SHOOT!
OW!
IS THAT HOW YOU TREAT REINFORCEMENTS!?
THEY'RE HERE! FANNIN'S TROOPS ARE *HERE!*
OPEN THE GATE!
AT LAST!
WELCOME BACK, EL COLORADO!
CLOSE THE GATE, WE'RE IN.
YOU'RE *ALL* IN? BUT THERE'S *THREE HUNDRED* OF YOU, *AREN'T THERE?*
NOPE. THERE'S THIRTY-TWO OF US.
AND ONE WITH A *BULLET IN HIS FOOT* FROM YOUR SENTRY.
WHOOPS.

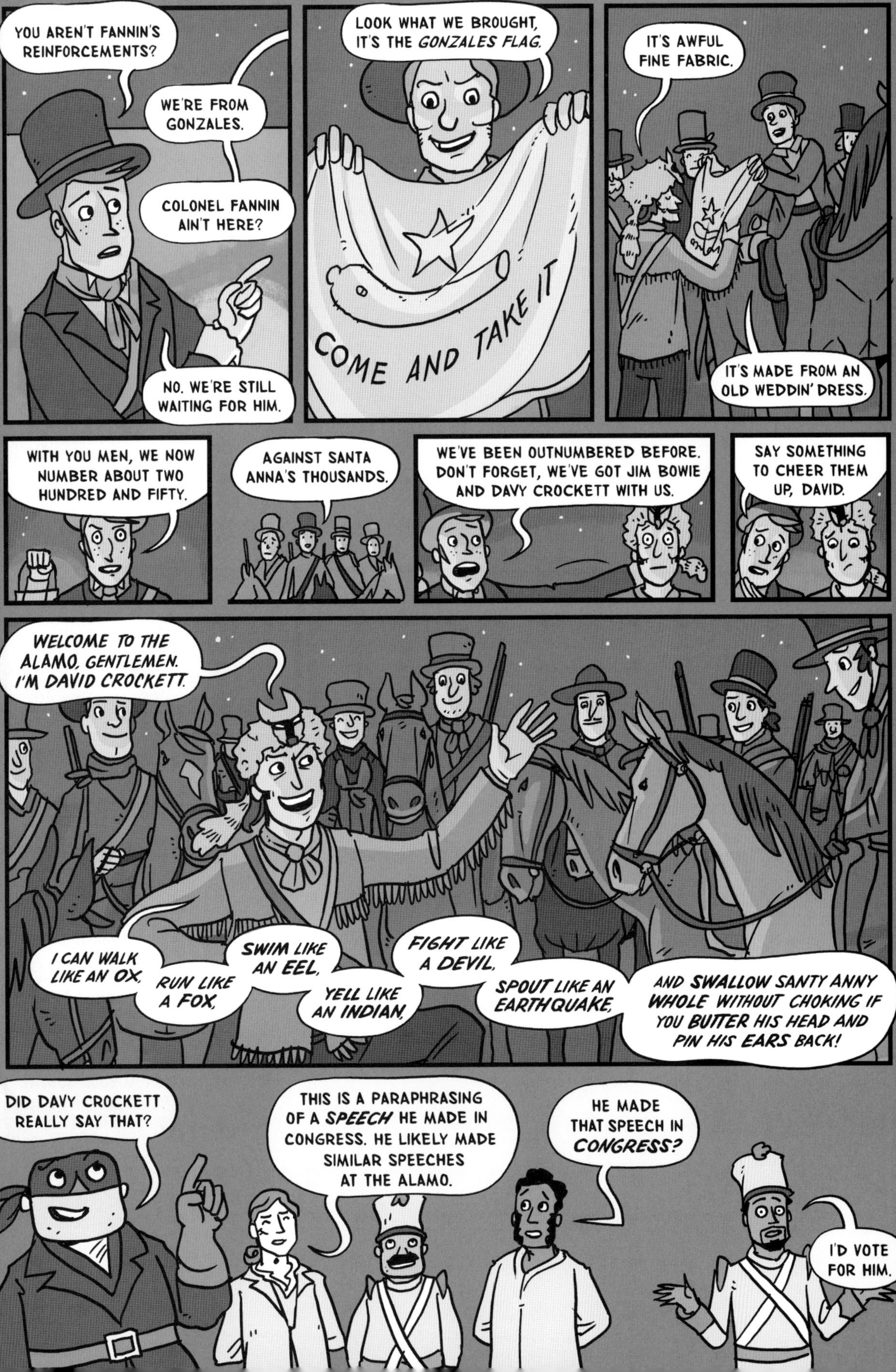
YOU AREN'T FANNIN'S REINFORCEMENTS?
WE'RE FROM GONZALES.
COLONEL FANNIN AIN'T HERE?
NO. WE'RE STILL WAITING FOR HIM.
LOOK WHAT WE BROUGHT, IT'S THE GONZALES FLAG.
COME AND TAKE IT
IT'S AWFUL FINE FABRIC.
IT'S MADE FROM AN OLD WEDDIN' DRESS.
WITH YOU MEN, WE NOW NUMBER ABOUT TWO HUNDRED AND FIFTY.
AGAINST SANTA ANNA'S THOUSANDS.
WE'VE BEEN OUTNUMBERED BEFORE. DON'T FORGET, WE'VE GOT JIM BOWIE AND DAVY CROCKETT WITH US.
SAY SOMETHING TO CHEER THEM UP, DAVID.
WELCOME TO THE ALAMO, GENTLEMEN. I'M DAVID CROCKETT.
I CAN WALK LIKE AN OX,
RUN LIKE A FOX,
SWIM LIKE AN EEL,
YELL LIKE AN INDIAN,
FIGHT LIKE A DEVIL,
SPOUT LIKE AN EARTHQUAKE,
AND SWALLOW SANTY ANNY WHOLE WITHOUT CHOKING IF YOU BUTTER HIS HEAD AND PIN HIS EARS BACK!
DID DAVY CROCKETT REALLY SAY THAT?
THIS IS A PARAPHRASING OF A SPEECH HE MADE IN CONGRESS. HE LIKELY MADE SIMILAR SPEECHES AT THE ALAMO.
HE MADE THAT SPEECH IN CONGRESS?
I'D VOTE FOR HIM.

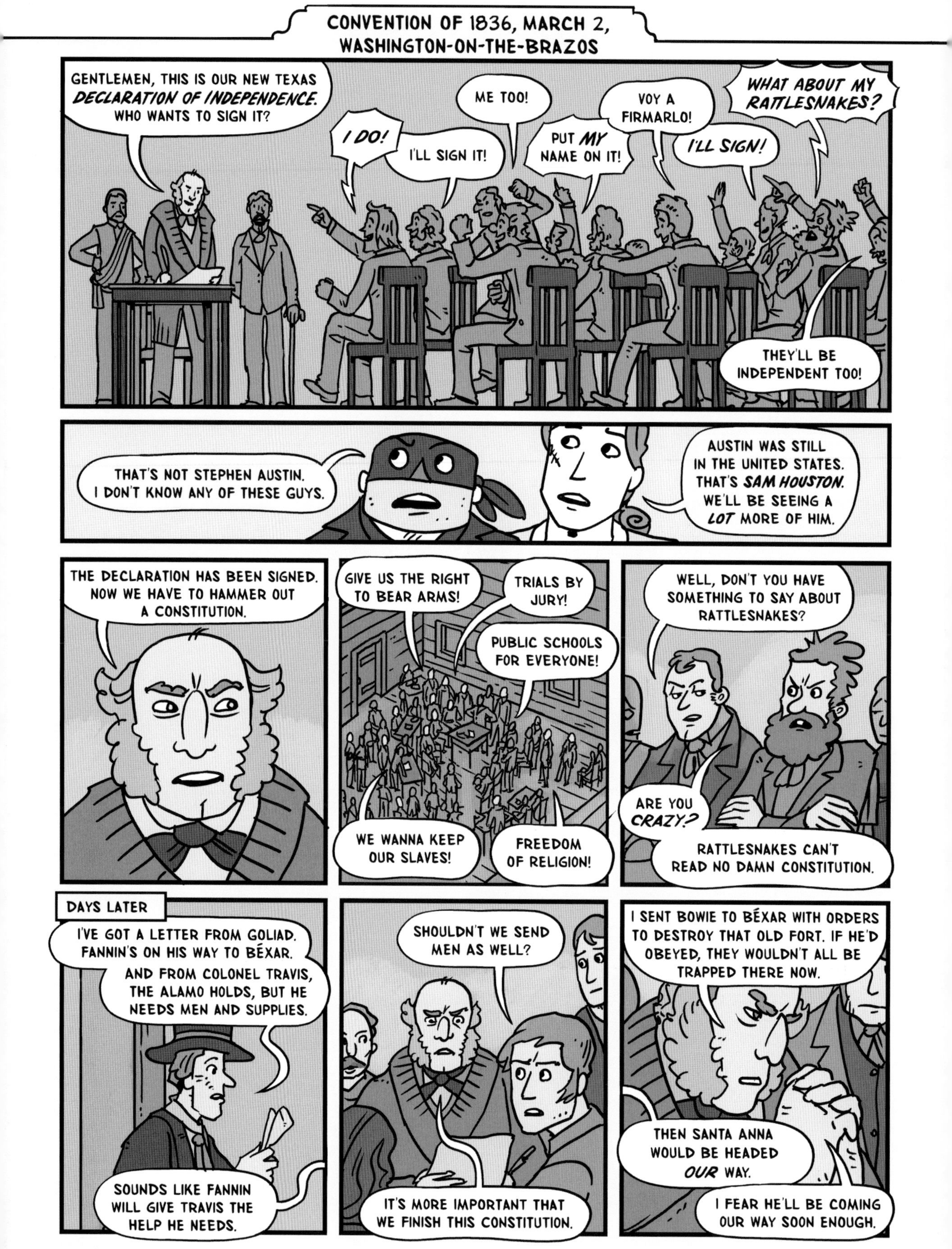
CONVENTION OF 1836, MARCH 2, WASHINGTON-ON-THE-BRAZOS
GENTLEMEN, THIS IS OUR NEW TEXAS *DECLARATION OF INDEPENDENCE.* WHO WANTS TO SIGN IT?
I DO!
I'LL SIGN IT!
ME TOO!
PUT *MY* NAME ON IT!
VOY A FIRMARLO!
I'LL SIGN!
WHAT ABOUT MY RATTLESNAKES?
THEY'LL BE INDEPENDENT TOO!
THAT'S NOT STEPHEN AUSTIN. I DON'T KNOW ANY OF THESE GUYS.
AUSTIN WAS STILL IN THE UNITED STATES. THAT'S *SAM HOUSTON.* WE'LL BE SEEING A *LOT* MORE OF HIM.
THE DECLARATION HAS BEEN SIGNED. NOW WE HAVE TO HAMMER OUT A CONSTITUTION.
GIVE US THE RIGHT TO BEAR ARMS!
TRIALS BY JURY!
PUBLIC SCHOOLS FOR EVERYONE!
WE WANNA KEEP OUR SLAVES!
FREEDOM OF RELIGION!
WELL, DON'T YOU HAVE SOMETHING TO SAY ABOUT RATTLESNAKES?
ARE YOU *CRAZY?*
RATTLESNAKES CAN'T READ NO DAMN CONSTITUTION.
DAYS LATER
I'VE GOT A LETTER FROM GOLIAD. FANNIN'S ON HIS WAY TO BÉXAR.
AND FROM COLONEL TRAVIS, THE ALAMO HOLDS, BUT HE NEEDS MEN AND SUPPLIES.
SOUNDS LIKE FANNIN WILL GIVE TRAVIS THE HELP HE NEEDS.
SHOULDN'T WE SEND MEN AS WELL?
IT'S MORE IMPORTANT THAT WE FINISH THIS CONSTITUTION.
I SENT BOWIE TO BÉXAR WITH ORDERS TO DESTROY THAT OLD FORT. IF HE'D OBEYED, THEY WOULDN'T ALL BE TRAPPED THERE NOW.
THEN SANTA ANNA WOULD BE HEADED *OUR* WAY.
I FEAR HE'LL BE COMING OUR WAY SOON ENOUGH.

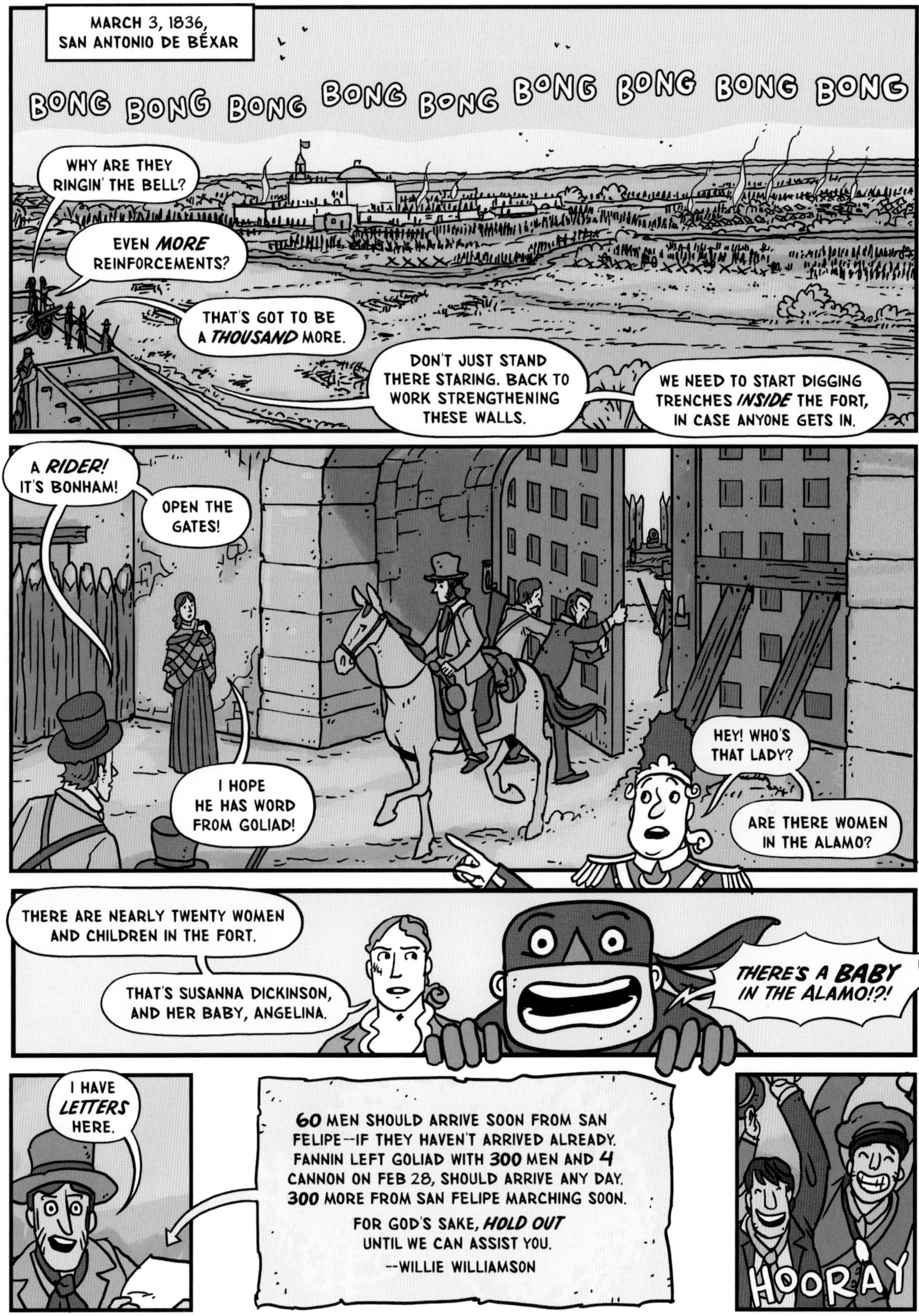
MARCH 3, 1836, SAN ANTONIO DE BÉXAR
BONG BONG BONG BONG BONG BONG BONG BONG BONG
WHY ARE THEY RINGIN' THE BELL?
EVEN MORE REINFORCEMENTS?
THAT'S GOT TO BE A THOUSAND MORE.
DON'T JUST STAND THERE STARING. BACK TO WORK STRENGTHENING THESE WALLS.
WE NEED TO START DIGGING TRENCHES INSIDE THE FORT, IN CASE ANYONE GETS IN.
A RIDER! IT'S BONHAM!
OPEN THE GATES!
I HOPE HE HAS WORD FROM GOLIAD!
HEY! WHO'S THAT LADY?
ARE THERE WOMEN IN THE ALAMO?
THERE ARE NEARLY TWENTY WOMEN AND CHILDREN IN THE FORT.
THAT'S SUSANNA DICKINSON, AND HER BABY, ANGELINA.
THERE'S A BABY IN THE ALAMO!?!
I HAVE LETTERS HERE.
60 MEN SHOULD ARRIVE SOON FROM SAN FELIPE--IF THEY HAVEN'T ARRIVED ALREADY. FANNIN LEFT GOLIAD WITH 300 MEN AND 4 CANNON ON FEB 28, SHOULD ARRIVE ANY DAY. 300 MORE FROM SAN FELIPE MARCHING SOON.
FOR GOD'S SAKE, HOLD OUT UNTIL WE CAN ASSIST YOU.
--WILLIE WILLIAMSON
HOORAY

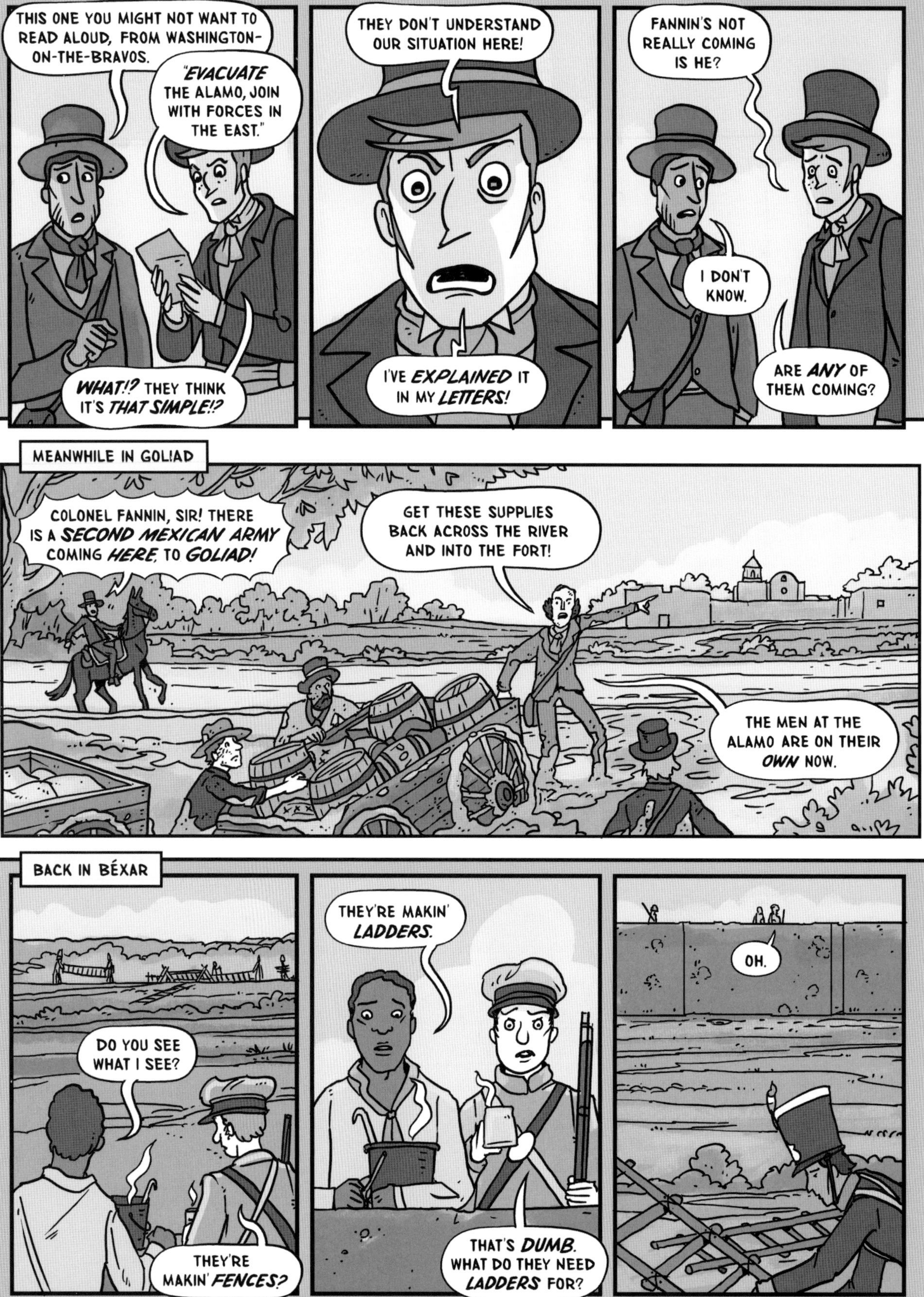
THIS ONE YOU MIGHT NOT WANT TO READ ALOUD, FROM WASHINGTON-ON-THE-BRAVOS.
"EVACUATE THE ALAMO, JOIN WITH FORCES IN THE EAST."
WHAT!? THEY THINK IT'S THAT SIMPLE!?
THEY DON'T UNDERSTAND OUR SITUATION HERE!
I'VE EXPLAINED IT IN MY LETTERS!
FANNIN'S NOT REALLY COMING IS HE?
I DON'T KNOW.
ARE ANY OF THEM COMING?
MEANWHILE IN GOLIAD
COLONEL FANNIN, SIR! THERE IS A SECOND MEXICAN ARMY COMING HERE, TO GOLIAD!
GET THESE SUPPLIES BACK ACROSS THE RIVER AND INTO THE FORT!
THE MEN AT THE ALAMO ARE ON THEIR OWN NOW.
BACK IN BÉXAR
DO YOU SEE WHAT I SEE?
THEY'RE MAKIN' FENCES?
THEY'RE MAKIN' LADDERS.
THAT'S DUMB. WHAT DO THEY NEED LADDERS FOR?
OH.

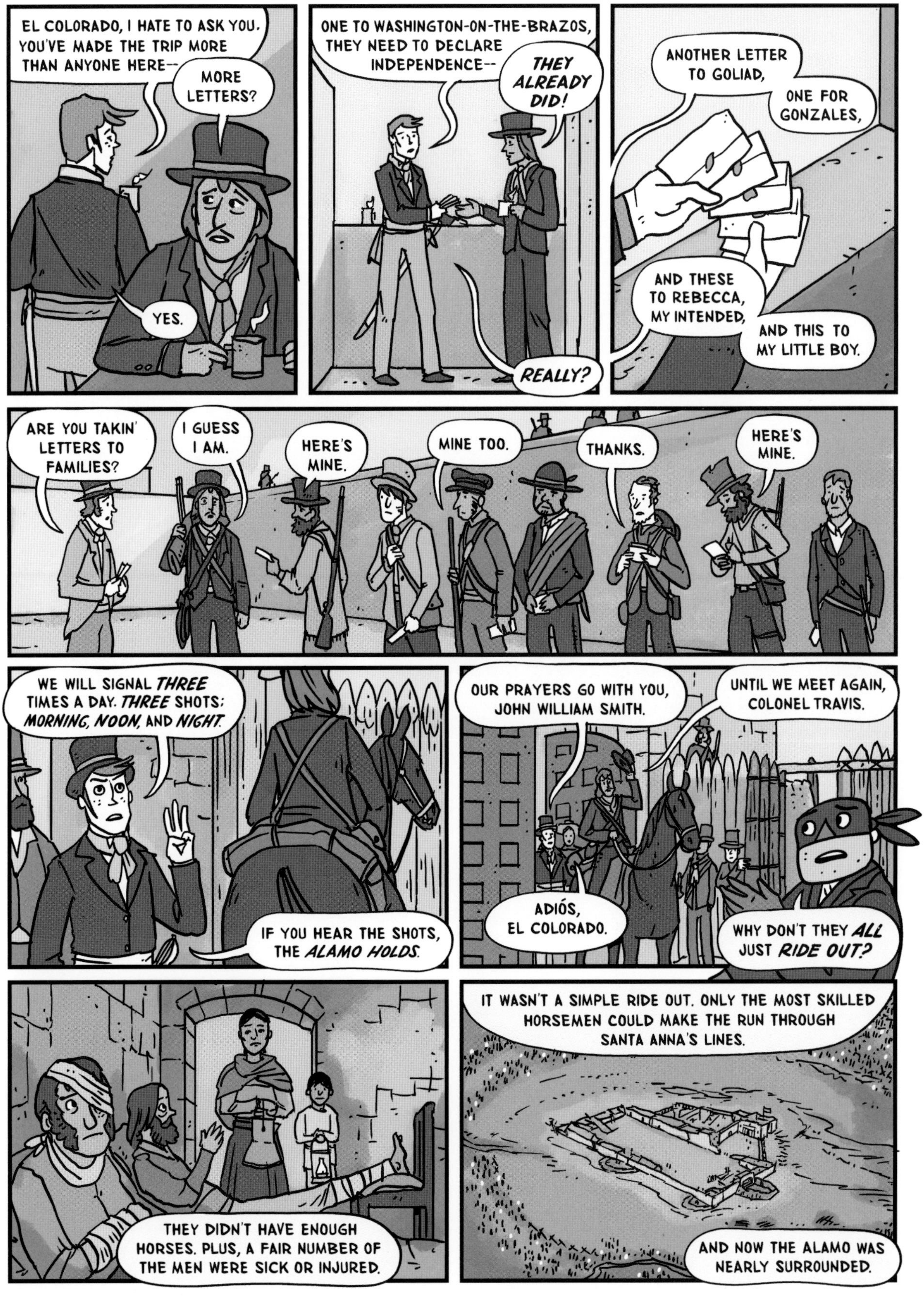
EL COLORADO, I HATE TO ASK YOU. YOU'VE MADE THE TRIP MORE THAN ANYONE HERE--
MORE LETTERS?
YES.
ONE TO WASHINGTON-ON-THE-BRAZOS, THEY NEED TO DECLARE INDEPENDENCE--
THEY ALREADY DID!
REALLY?
ANOTHER LETTER TO GOLIAD,
ONE FOR GONZALES,
AND THESE TO REBECCA, MY INTENDED,
AND THIS TO MY LITTLE BOY.
ARE YOU TAKIN' LETTERS TO FAMILIES?
I GUESS I AM.
HERE'S MINE.
MINE TOO.
THANKS.
HERE'S MINE.
WE WILL SIGNAL THREE TIMES A DAY. THREE SHOTS: MORNING, NOON, AND NIGHT.
IF YOU HEAR THE SHOTS, THE ALAMO HOLDS.
OUR PRAYERS GO WITH YOU, JOHN WILLIAM SMITH.
UNTIL WE MEET AGAIN, COLONEL TRAVIS.
ADIÓS, EL COLORADO.
WHY DON'T THEY ALL JUST RIDE OUT?
THEY DIDN'T HAVE ENOUGH HORSES. PLUS, A FAIR NUMBER OF THE MEN WERE SICK OR INJURED.
IT WASN'T A SIMPLE RIDE OUT. ONLY THE MOST SKILLED HORSEMEN COULD MAKE THE RUN THROUGH SANTA ANNA'S LINES.
AND NOW THE ALAMO WAS NEARLY SURROUNDED.

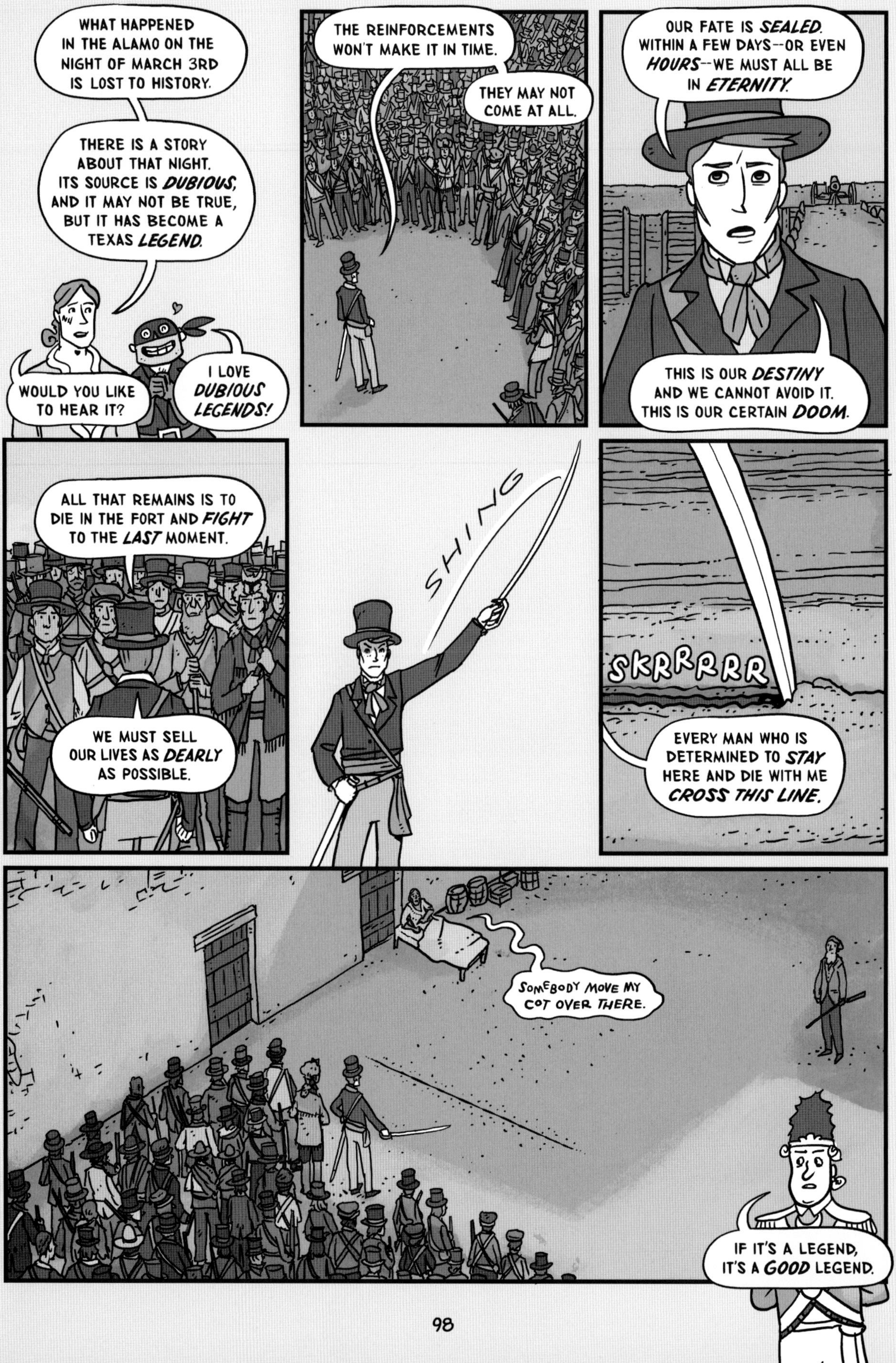
WHAT HAPPENED IN THE ALAMO ON THE NIGHT OF MARCH 3RD IS LOST TO HISTORY.
THERE IS A STORY ABOUT THAT NIGHT. ITS SOURCE IS DUBIOUS, AND IT MAY NOT BE TRUE, BUT IT HAS BECOME A TEXAS LEGEND.
WOULD YOU LIKE TO HEAR IT?
I LOVE DUBIOUS LEGENDS!
THE REINFORCEMENTS WON'T MAKE IT IN TIME.
THEY MAY NOT COME AT ALL.
OUR FATE IS SEALED. WITHIN A FEW DAYS--OR EVEN HOURS--WE MUST ALL BE IN ETERNITY.
THIS IS OUR DESTINY AND WE CANNOT AVOID IT. THIS IS OUR CERTAIN DOOM.
ALL THAT REMAINS IS TO DIE IN THE FORT AND FIGHT TO THE LAST MOMENT.
WE MUST SELL OUR LIVES AS DEARLY AS POSSIBLE.
SHING
SKRRRRR
EVERY MAN WHO IS DETERMINED TO STAY HERE AND DIE WITH ME CROSS THIS LINE.
SOMEBODY MOVE MY COT OVER THERE.
IF IT'S A LEGEND, IT'S A GOOD LEGEND.

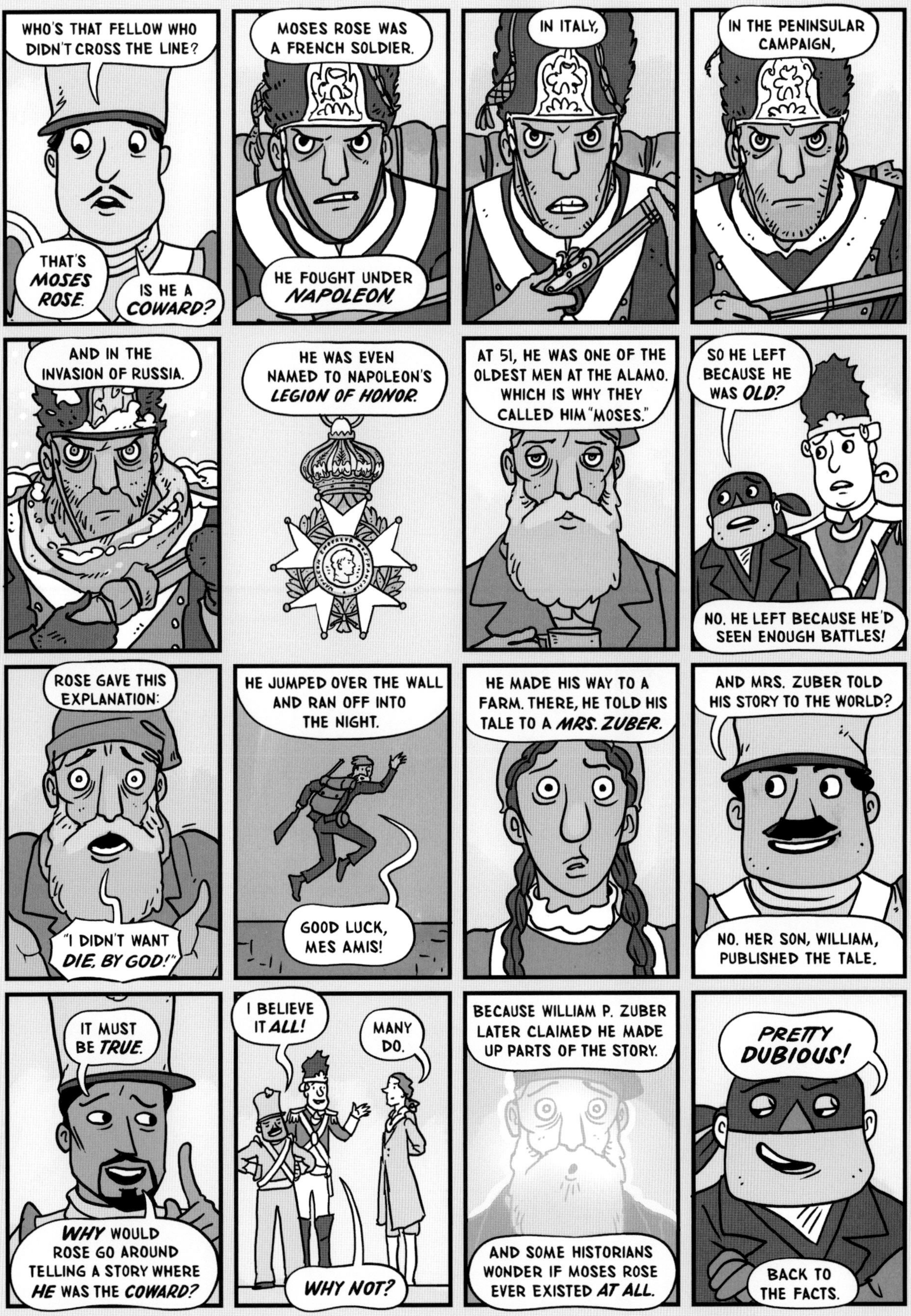
WHO'S THAT FELLOW WHO DIDN'T CROSS THE LINE?
THAT'S MOSES ROSE.
IS HE A COWARD?
MOSES ROSE WAS A FRENCH SOLDIER.
HE FOUGHT UNDER NAPOLEON,
IN ITALY,
IN THE PENINSULAR CAMPAIGN,
AND IN THE INVASION OF RUSSIA.
HE WAS EVEN NAMED TO NAPOLEON'S LEGION OF HONOR.
AT 51, HE WAS ONE OF THE OLDEST MEN AT THE ALAMO. WHICH IS WHY THEY CALLED HIM "MOSES."
SO HE LEFT BECAUSE HE WAS OLD?
NO. HE LEFT BECAUSE HE'D SEEN ENOUGH BATTLES!
ROSE GAVE THIS EXPLANATION:
"I DIDN'T WANT DIE, BY GOD!"
HE JUMPED OVER THE WALL AND RAN OFF INTO THE NIGHT.
GOOD LUCK, MES AMIS!
HE MADE HIS WAY TO A FARM. THERE, HE TOLD HIS TALE TO A MRS. ZUBER.
AND MRS. ZUBER TOLD HIS STORY TO THE WORLD?
NO. HER SON, WILLIAM, PUBLISHED THE TALE.
IT MUST BE TRUE.
WHY WOULD ROSE GO AROUND TELLING A STORY WHERE HE WAS THE COWARD?
I BELIEVE IT ALL!
MANY DO.
WHY NOT?
BECAUSE WILLIAM P. ZUBER LATER CLAIMED HE MADE UP PARTS OF THE STORY.
AND SOME HISTORIANS WONDER IF MOSES ROSE EVER EXISTED AT ALL.
PRETTY DUBIOUS!
BACK TO THE FACTS.

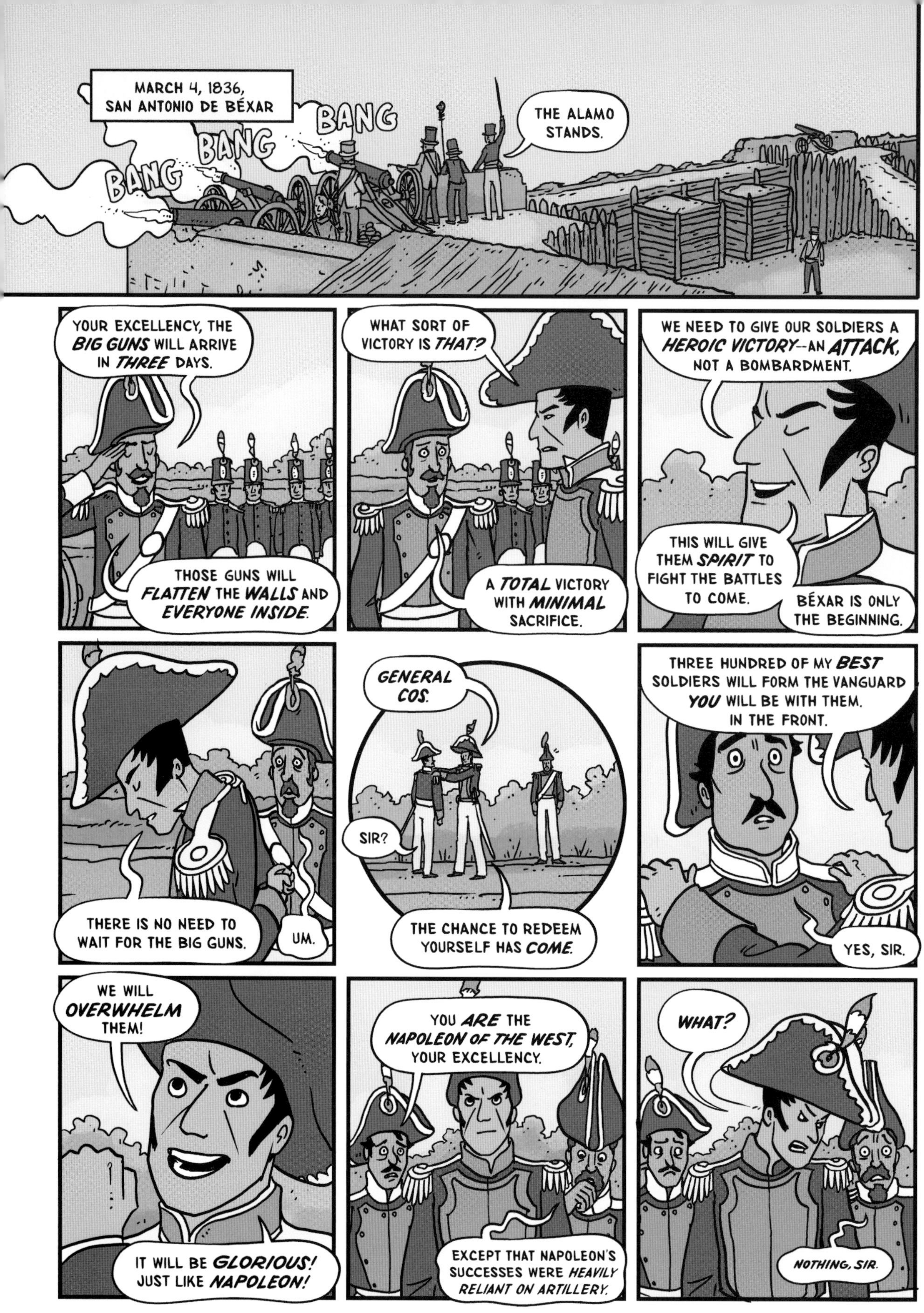

MARCH 4, 1836,
SAN ANTONIO DE BÉXAR
BANG
BANG
BANG
THE ALAMO STANDS.
YOUR EXCELLENCY, THE BIG GUNS WILL ARRIVE IN THREE DAYS.
THOSE GUNS WILL FLATTEN THE WALLS AND EVERYONE INSIDE.
WHAT SORT OF VICTORY IS THAT?
A TOTAL VICTORY WITH MINIMAL SACRIFICE.
WE NEED TO GIVE OUR SOLDIERS A HEROIC VICTORY--AN ATTACK, NOT A BOMBARDMENT.
THIS WILL GIVE THEM SPIRIT TO FIGHT THE BATTLES TO COME.
BÉXAR IS ONLY THE BEGINNING.
THERE IS NO NEED TO WAIT FOR THE BIG GUNS.
UM.
GENERAL COS.
SIR?
THE CHANCE TO REDEEM YOURSELF HAS COME.
THREE HUNDRED OF MY BEST SOLDIERS WILL FORM THE VANGUARD. YOU WILL BE WITH THEM. IN THE FRONT.
YES, SIR.
WE WILL OVERWHELM THEM!
IT WILL BE GLORIOUS! JUST LIKE NAPOLEON!
YOU ARE THE NAPOLEON OF THE WEST, YOUR EXCELLENCY.
EXCEPT THAT NAPOLEON'S SUCCESSES WERE HEAVILY RELIANT ON ARTILLERY.
WHAT?
NOTHING, SIR.

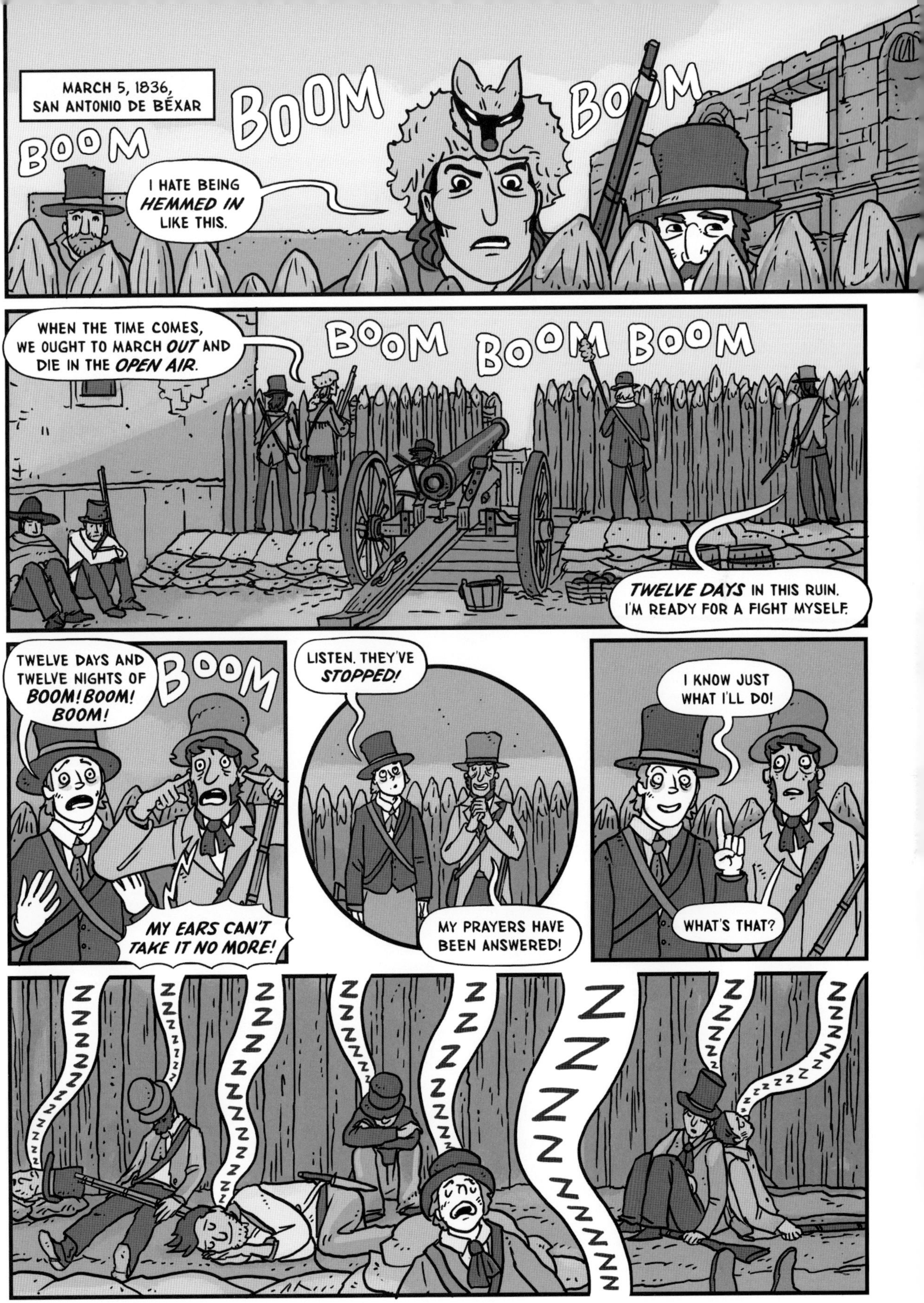
MARCH 5, 1836, SAN ANTONIO DE BÉXAR
BOOM
BOOM
BOOM
I HATE BEING *HEMMED IN* LIKE THIS.
WHEN THE TIME COMES, WE OUGHT TO MARCH *OUT* AND DIE IN THE *OPEN AIR*.
BOOM BOOM BOOM
TWELVE DAYS IN THIS RUIN. I'M READY FOR A FIGHT MYSELF.
TWELVE DAYS AND TWELVE NIGHTS OF *BOOM! BOOM! BOOM!*
BOOM
MY EARS CAN'T TAKE IT NO MORE!
LISTEN. THEY'VE *STOPPED!*
MY PRAYERS HAVE BEEN ANSWERED!
I KNOW JUST WHAT I'LL DO!
WHAT'S THAT?
ZZZZZZZZ

CHAPTER 18

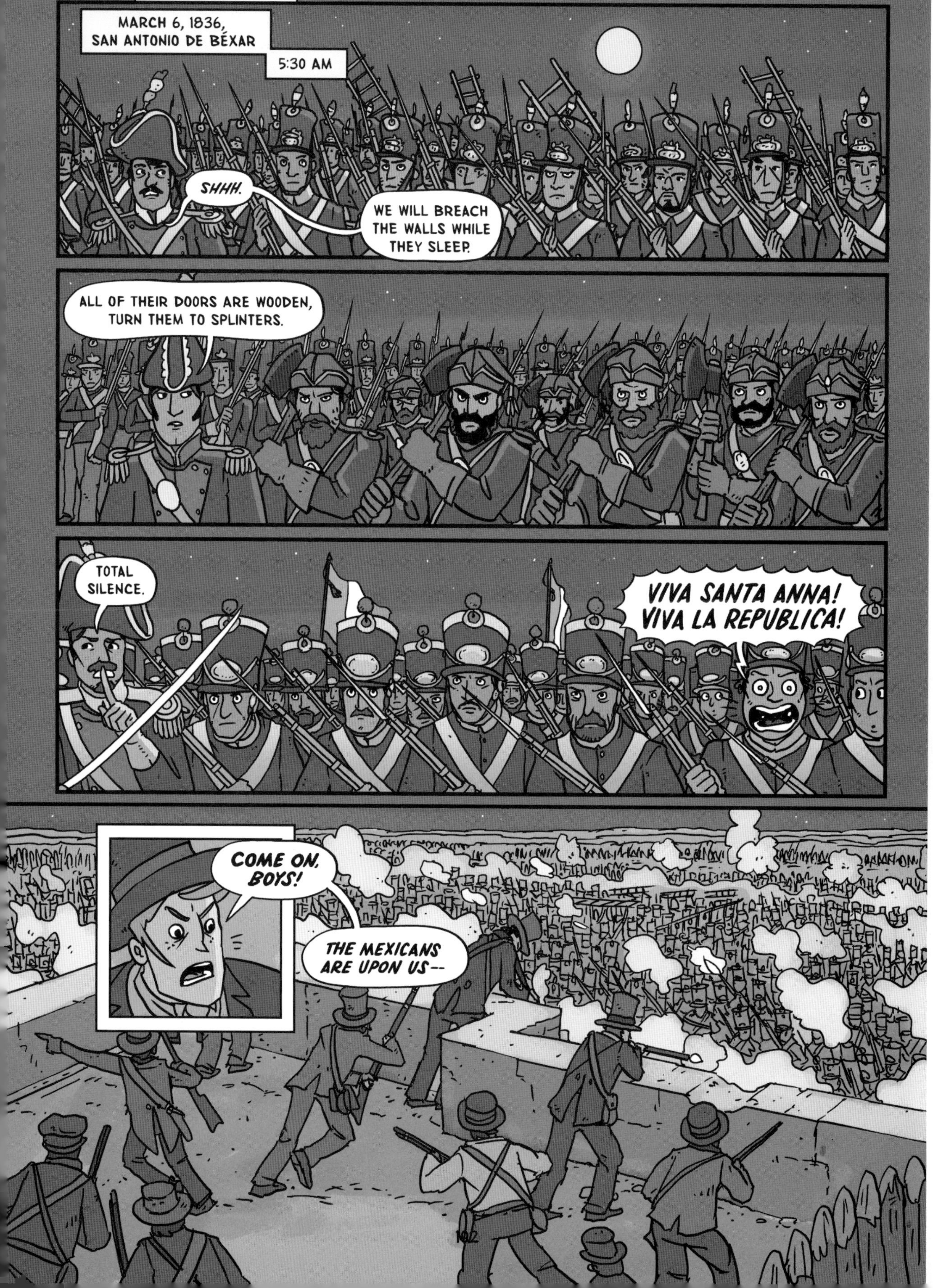

MARCH 6, 1836,
SAN ANTONIO DE BÉXAR
5:30 AM
SHHH.
WE WILL BREACH THE WALLS WHILE THEY SLEEP.
ALL OF THEIR DOORS ARE WOODEN, TURN THEM TO SPLINTERS.
TOTAL SILENCE.
VIVA SANTA ANNA! VIVA LA REPUBLICA!
COME ON, BOYS!
THE MEXICANS ARE UPON US--

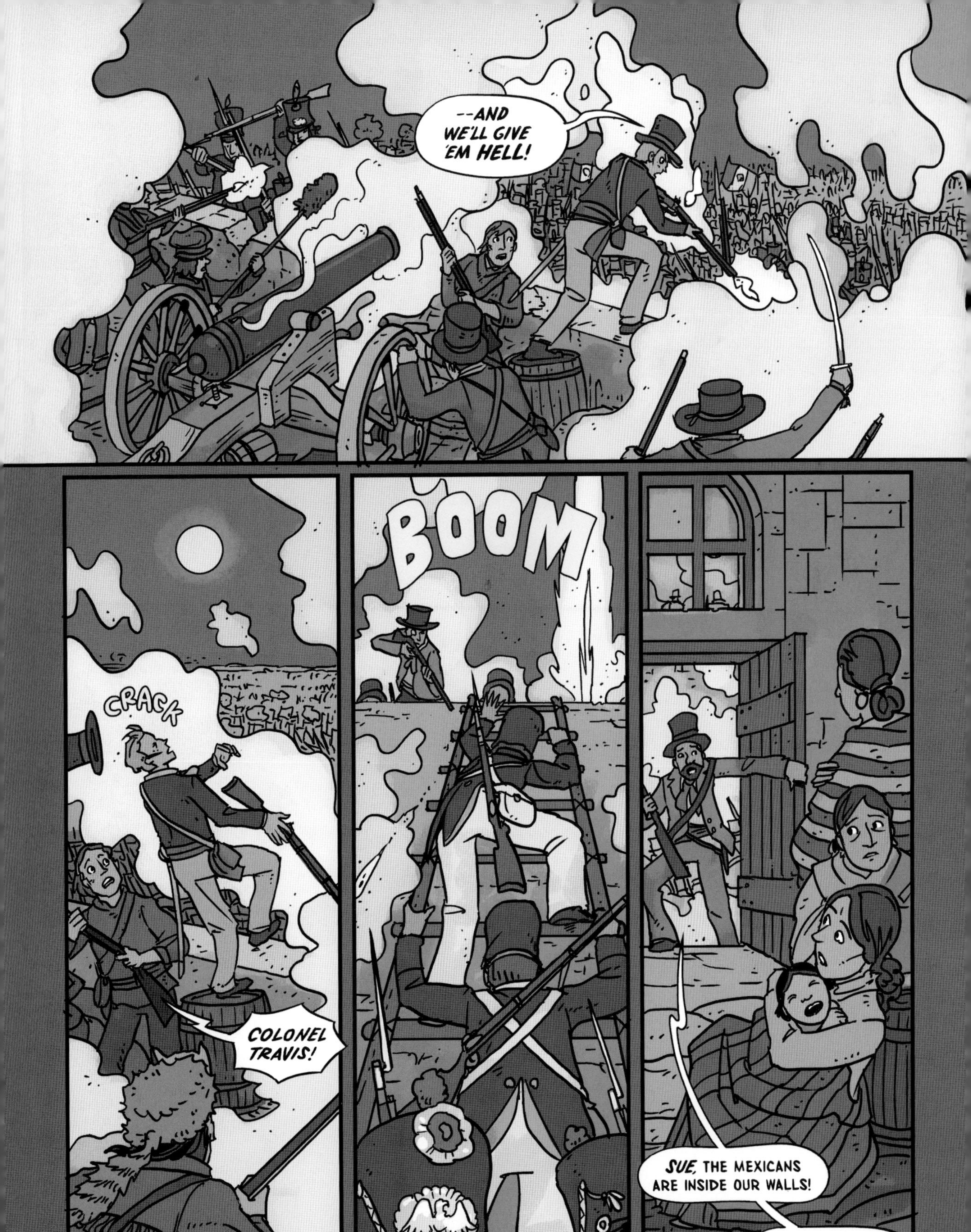
--AND WE'LL GIVE 'EM HELL!
CRACK
COLONEL TRAVIS!
BOOM
SUE, THE MEXICANS ARE INSIDE OUR WALLS!
IF THEY SPARE YOU, SAVE MY CHILD!

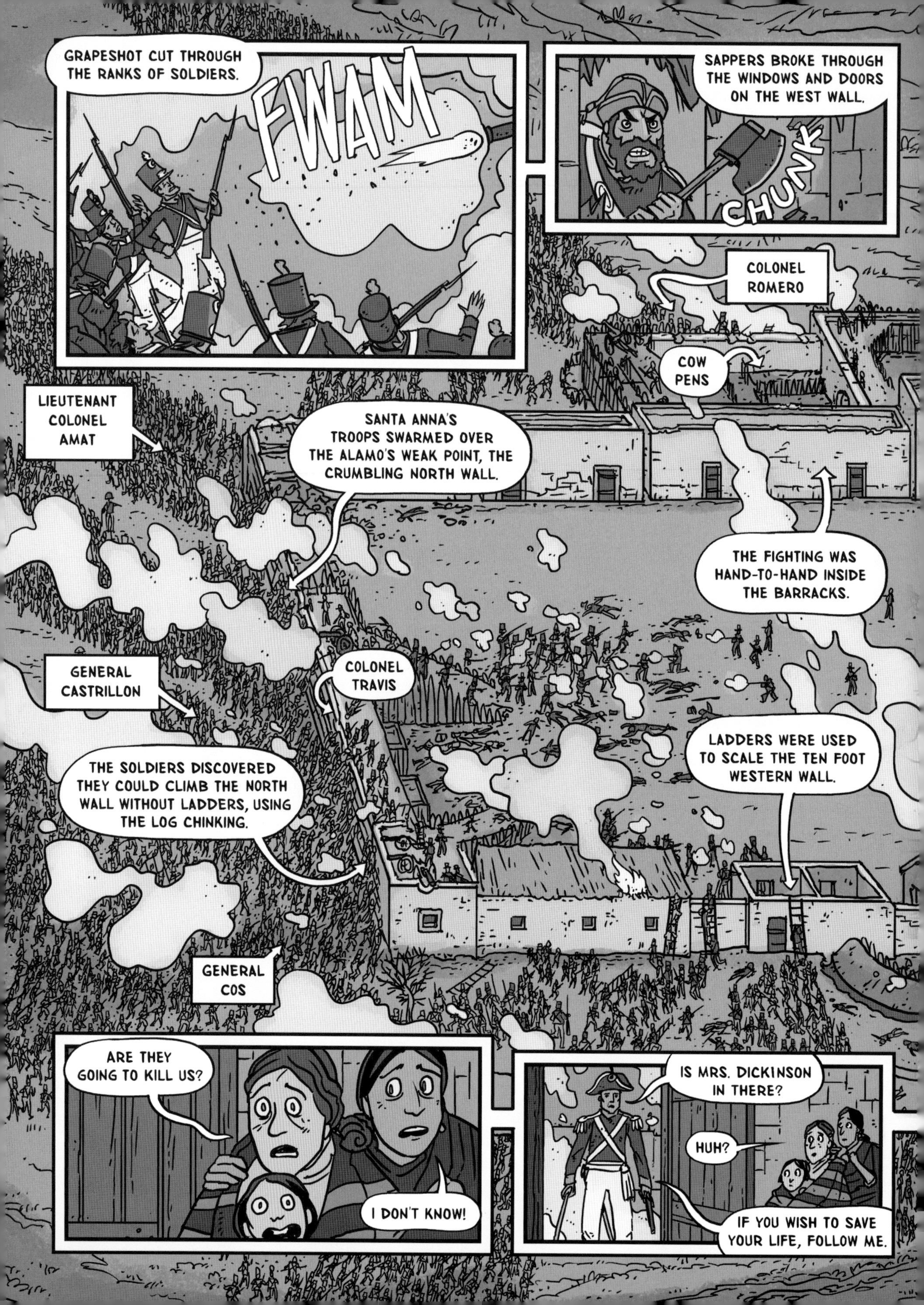
GRAPESHOT CUT THROUGH THE RANKS OF SOLDIERS.
FWAM
SAPPERS BROKE THROUGH THE WINDOWS AND DOORS ON THE WEST WALL.
CHUNK
COLONEL ROMERO
COW PENS
LIEUTENANT COLONEL AMAT
SANTA ANNA'S TROOPS SWARMED OVER THE ALAMO'S WEAK POINT, THE CRUMBLING NORTH WALL.
THE FIGHTING WAS HAND-TO-HAND INSIDE THE BARRACKS.
GENERAL CASTRILLON
COLONEL TRAVIS
LADDERS WERE USED TO SCALE THE TEN FOOT WESTERN WALL.
THE SOLDIERS DISCOVERED THEY COULD CLIMB THE NORTH WALL WITHOUT LADDERS, USING THE LOG CHINKING.
GENERAL COS
ARE THEY GOING TO KILL US?
I DON'T KNOW!
IS MRS. DICKINSON IN THERE?
HUH?
IF YOU WISH TO SAVE YOUR LIFE, FOLLOW ME.

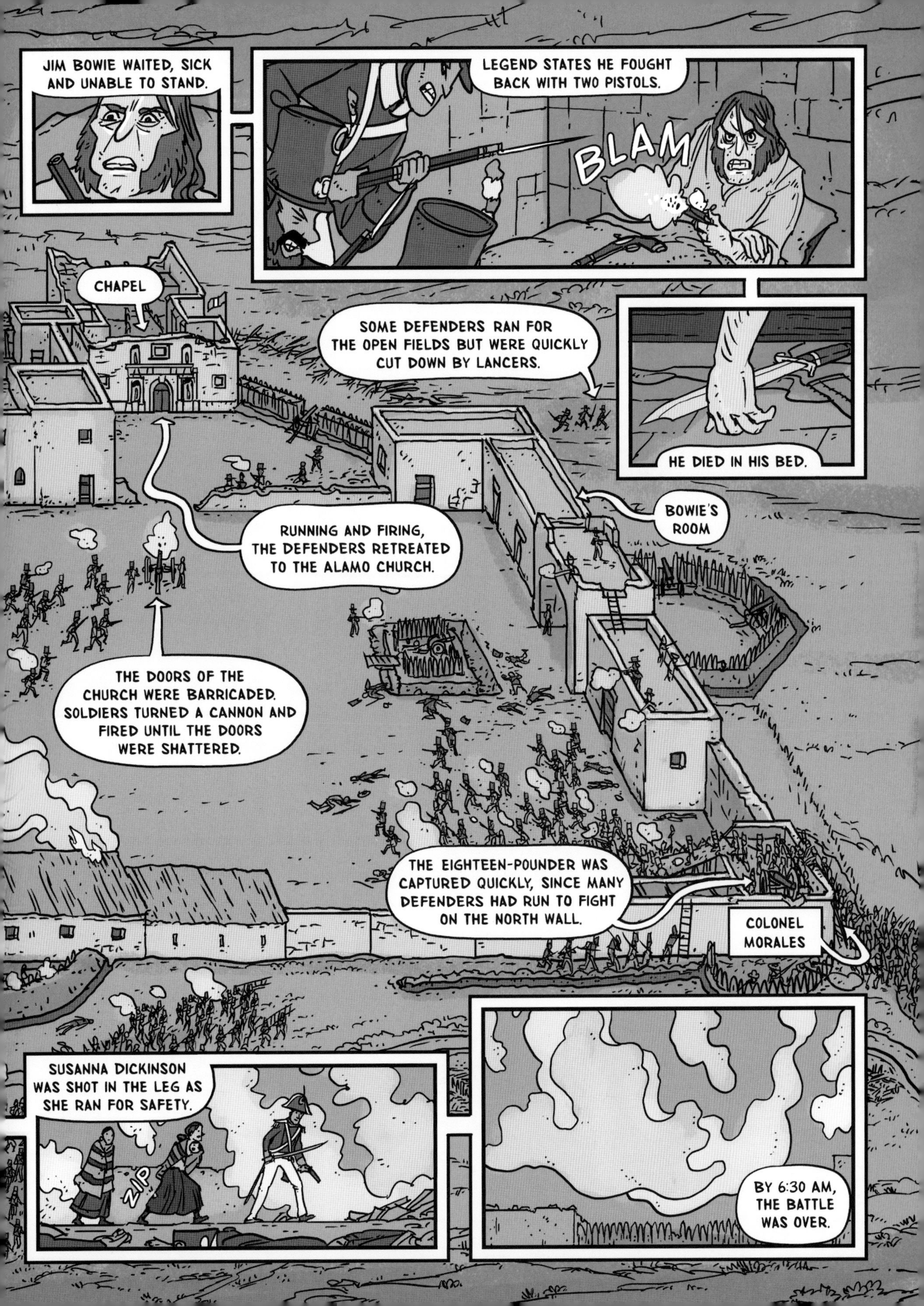
JIM BOWIE WAITED, SICK AND UNABLE TO STAND.
LEGEND STATES HE FOUGHT BACK WITH TWO PISTOLS.
BLAM
HE DIED IN HIS BED.
CHAPEL
SOME DEFENDERS RAN FOR THE OPEN FIELDS BUT WERE QUICKLY CUT DOWN BY LANCERS.
BOWIE'S ROOM
RUNNING AND FIRING, THE DEFENDERS RETREATED TO THE ALAMO CHURCH.
THE DOORS OF THE CHURCH WERE BARRICADED. SOLDIERS TURNED A CANNON AND FIRED UNTIL THE DOORS WERE SHATTERED.
THE EIGHTEEN-POUNDER WAS CAPTURED QUICKLY, SINCE MANY DEFENDERS HAD RUN TO FIGHT ON THE NORTH WALL.
COLONEL MORALES
SUSANNA DICKINSON WAS SHOT IN THE LEG AS SHE RAN FOR SAFETY.
ZIP
BY 6:30 AM, THE BATTLE WAS OVER.

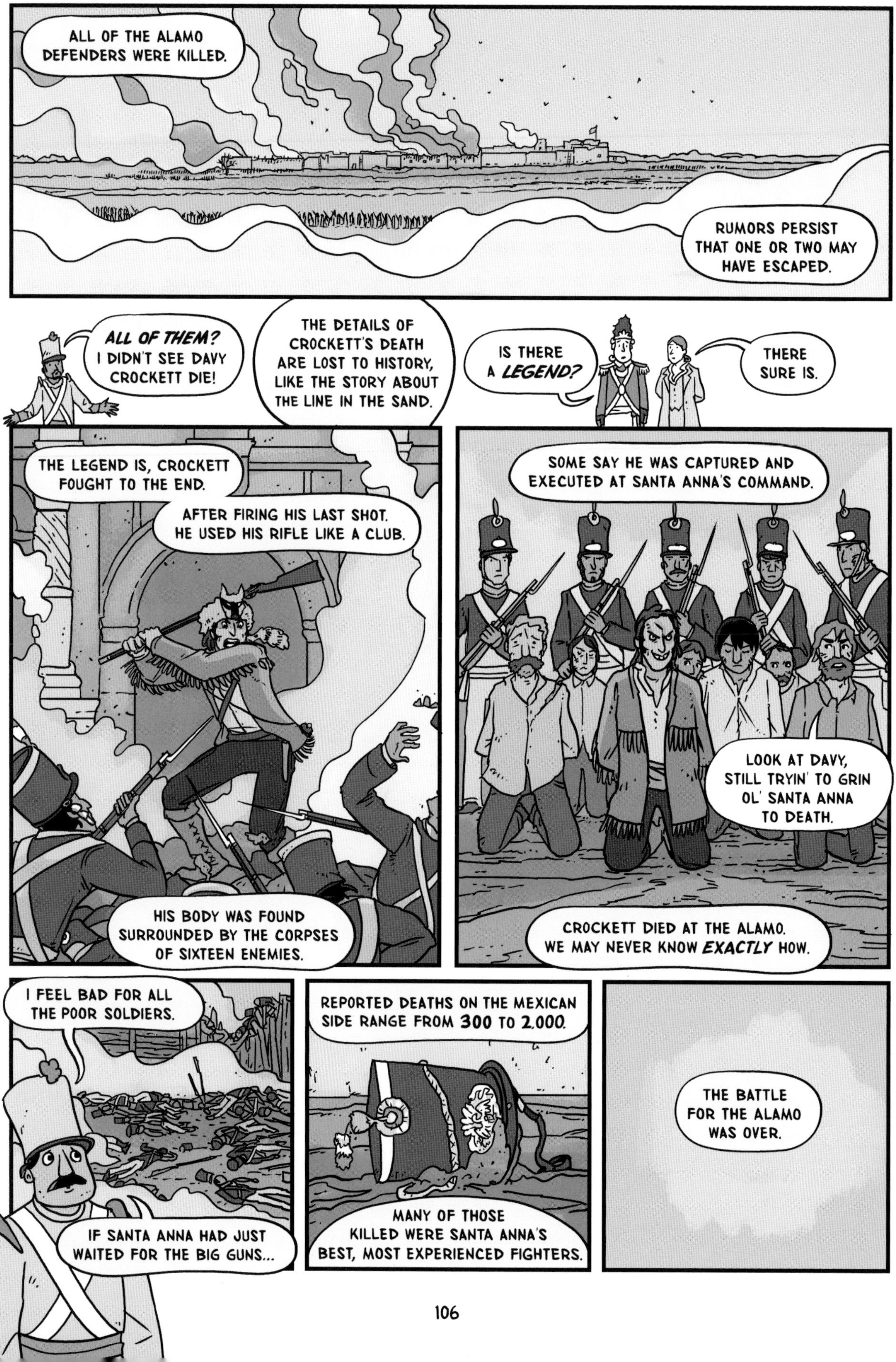
ALL OF THE ALAMO DEFENDERS WERE KILLED.
RUMORS PERSIST THAT ONE OR TWO MAY HAVE ESCAPED.
ALL OF THEM? I DIDN'T SEE DAVY CROCKETT DIE!
THE DETAILS OF CROCKETT'S DEATH ARE LOST TO HISTORY, LIKE THE STORY ABOUT THE LINE IN THE SAND.
IS THERE A LEGEND?
THERE SURE IS.
THE LEGEND IS, CROCKETT FOUGHT TO THE END.
AFTER FIRING HIS LAST SHOT, HE USED HIS RIFLE LIKE A CLUB.
HIS BODY WAS FOUND SURROUNDED BY THE CORPSES OF SIXTEEN ENEMIES.
SOME SAY HE WAS CAPTURED AND EXECUTED AT SANTA ANNA'S COMMAND.
LOOK AT DAVY, STILL TRYIN' TO GRIN OL' SANTA ANNA TO DEATH.
CROCKETT DIED AT THE ALAMO. WE MAY NEVER KNOW EXACTLY HOW.
I FEEL BAD FOR ALL THE POOR SOLDIERS.
IF SANTA ANNA HAD JUST WAITED FOR THE BIG GUNS...
REPORTED DEATHS ON THE MEXICAN SIDE RANGE FROM 300 TO 2,000.
MANY OF THOSE KILLED WERE SANTA ANNA'S BEST, MOST EXPERIENCED FIGHTERS.
THE BATTLE FOR THE ALAMO WAS OVER.

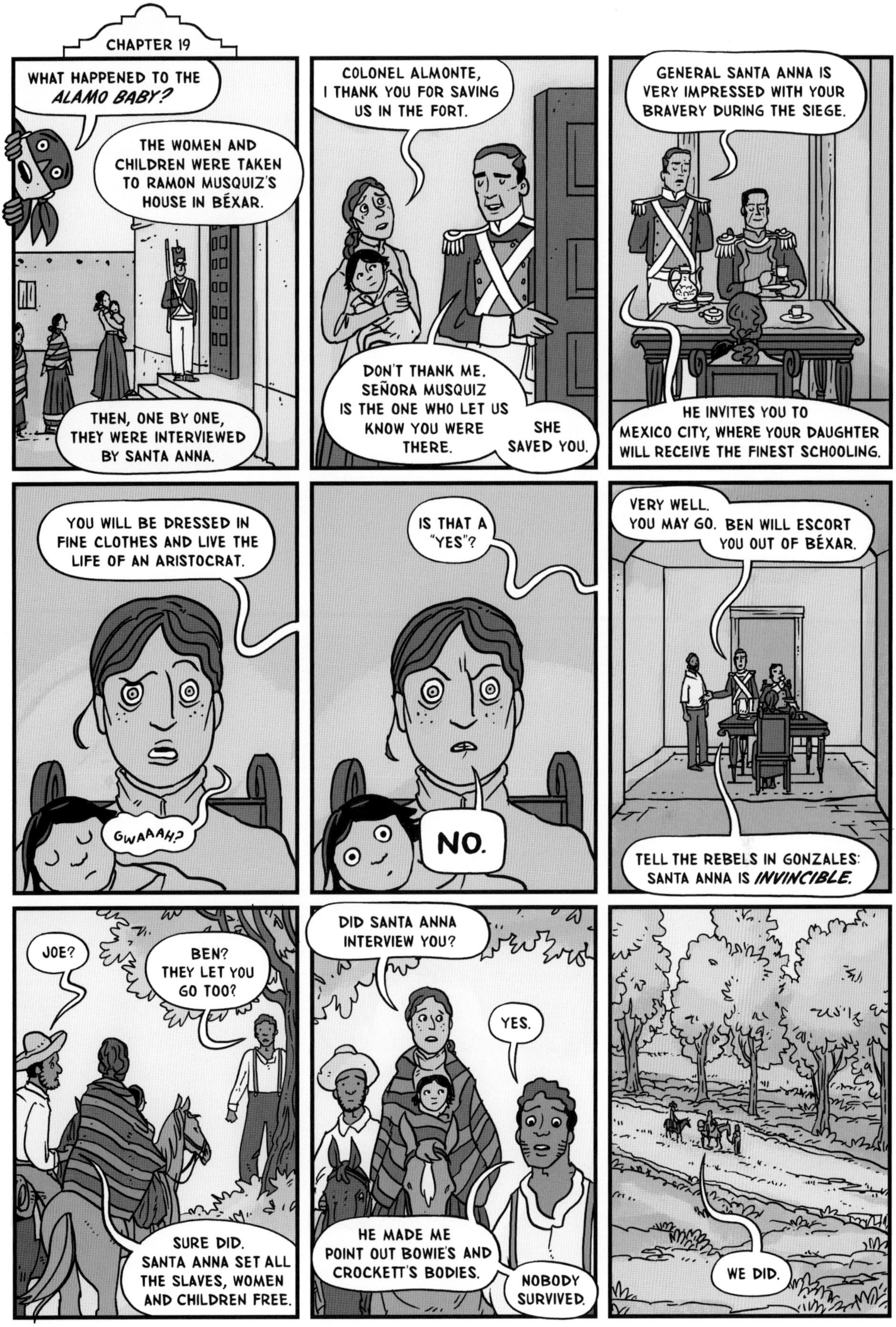
CHAPTER 19
WHAT HAPPENED TO THE *ALAMO BABY?*
THE WOMEN AND CHILDREN WERE TAKEN TO RAMON MUSQUIZ'S HOUSE IN BÉXAR.
THEN, ONE BY ONE, THEY WERE INTERVIEWED BY SANTA ANNA.
COLONEL ALMONTE, I THANK YOU FOR SAVING US IN THE FORT.
DON'T THANK ME. SEÑORA MUSQUIZ IS THE ONE WHO LET US KNOW YOU WERE THERE.
SHE SAVED YOU.
GENERAL SANTA ANNA IS VERY IMPRESSED WITH YOUR BRAVERY DURING THE SIEGE.
HE INVITES YOU TO MEXICO CITY, WHERE YOUR DAUGHTER WILL RECEIVE THE FINEST SCHOOLING.
YOU WILL BE DRESSED IN FINE CLOTHES AND LIVE THE LIFE OF AN ARISTOCRAT.
GWAAAH?
IS THAT A "YES"?
NO.
VERY WELL. YOU MAY GO. BEN WILL ESCORT YOU OUT OF BÉXAR.
TELL THE REBELS IN GONZALES: SANTA ANNA IS *INVINCIBLE.*
JOE?
BEN? THEY LET YOU GO TOO?
SURE DID. SANTA ANNA SET ALL THE SLAVES, WOMEN AND CHILDREN FREE.
DID SANTA ANNA INTERVIEW YOU?
YES.
HE MADE ME POINT OUT BOWIE'S AND CROCKETT'S BODIES.
NOBODY SURVIVED.
WE DID.

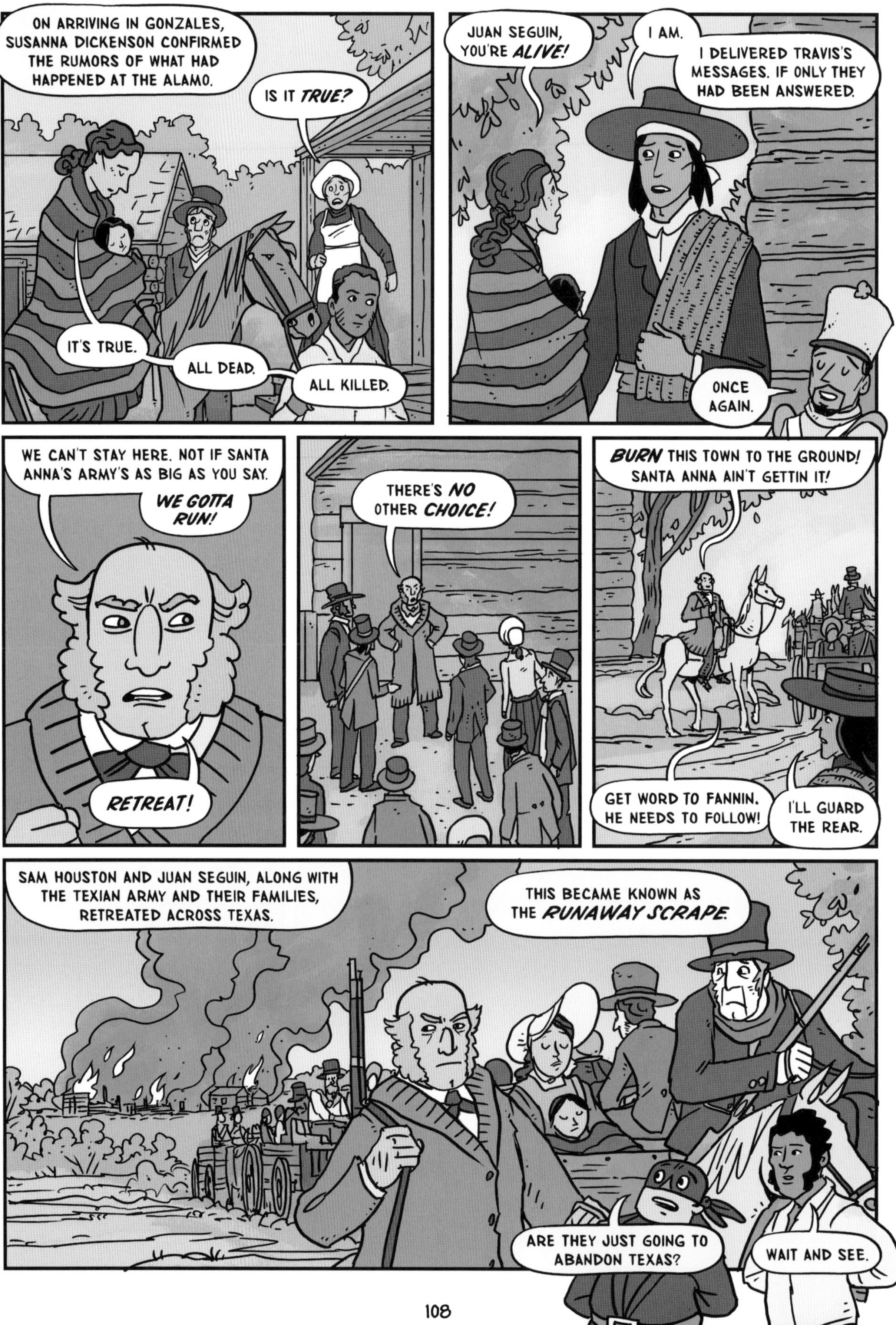
ON ARRIVING IN GONZALES, SUSANNA DICKENSON CONFIRMED THE RUMORS OF WHAT HAD HAPPENED AT THE ALAMO.
IS IT TRUE?
IT'S TRUE.
ALL DEAD.
ALL KILLED.
JUAN SEGUIN, YOU'RE ALIVE!
I AM.
I DELIVERED TRAVIS'S MESSAGES. IF ONLY THEY HAD BEEN ANSWERED.
ONCE AGAIN.
WE CAN'T STAY HERE. NOT IF SANTA ANNA'S ARMY'S AS BIG AS YOU SAY.
WE GOTTA RUN!
RETREAT!
THERE'S NO OTHER CHOICE!
BURN THIS TOWN TO THE GROUND! SANTA ANNA AIN'T GETTIN IT!
GET WORD TO FANNIN. HE NEEDS TO FOLLOW!
I'LL GUARD THE REAR.
SAM HOUSTON AND JUAN SEGUIN, ALONG WITH THE TEXIAN ARMY AND THEIR FAMILIES, RETREATED ACROSS TEXAS.
THIS BECAME KNOWN AS THE RUNAWAY SCRAPE.
ARE THEY JUST GOING TO ABANDON TEXAS?
WAIT AND SEE.

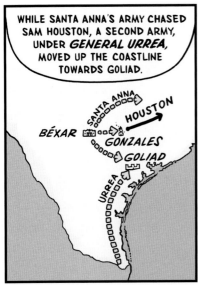

WHILE SANTA ANNA'S ARMY CHASED SAM HOUSTON, A SECOND ARMY, UNDER *GENERAL URREA,* MOVED UP THE COASTLINE TOWARDS GOLIAD.

SANTA ANNA
HOUSTON
BÉXAR
GONZALES
GOLIAD
URREA

I FORGOT ABOUT *GOLIAD!*

DON'T FEEL BAD. EVERYONE FORGETS ABOUT GOLIAD.

THEY REMEMBER THE ALAMO. THEY FORGET ABOUT GOLIAD.

COLONEL FANNIN, IF WE DON'T FOLLOW HOUSTON SOON, THEY'LL SURROUND THE FORT AND KILL US!

BUT WE'VE SPENT SO MUCH TIME FORTIFYING GOLIAD FOR BATTLE.

THEY FORTIFIED THE ALAMO, TOO.

WE'LL LEAVE WHEN *KING* AND *WARD* GET BACK WITH THEIR MEN.

SIR, CAPTAIN FRAZER BRINGS NEWS!

KING AND WARD'S MEN ARE DEAD--OR CAPTURED BY GENERAL URREA.

IT'S TIME TO *RETREAT!* *BURN* EVERYTHING THAT WON'T FIT INTO OUR WAGONS.

WHAT A WASTE.

MARCH 19, GOLIAD

TIME TO CROSS THE RIVER.

SPLORT

HERE WE GO AGAIN.

ONCE THE WAGONS ARE ACROSS UNHITCH THE OXEN AND LET THEM FEED.

IT'S GOING TO BE A LONG, HARD PULL.

WE DON'T HAVE TIME TO FEED THE OXEN!

BUT GENERAL URREA--

HE'LL STOP WHEN HE REACHES THE FORT. HE WON'T FOLLOW US.

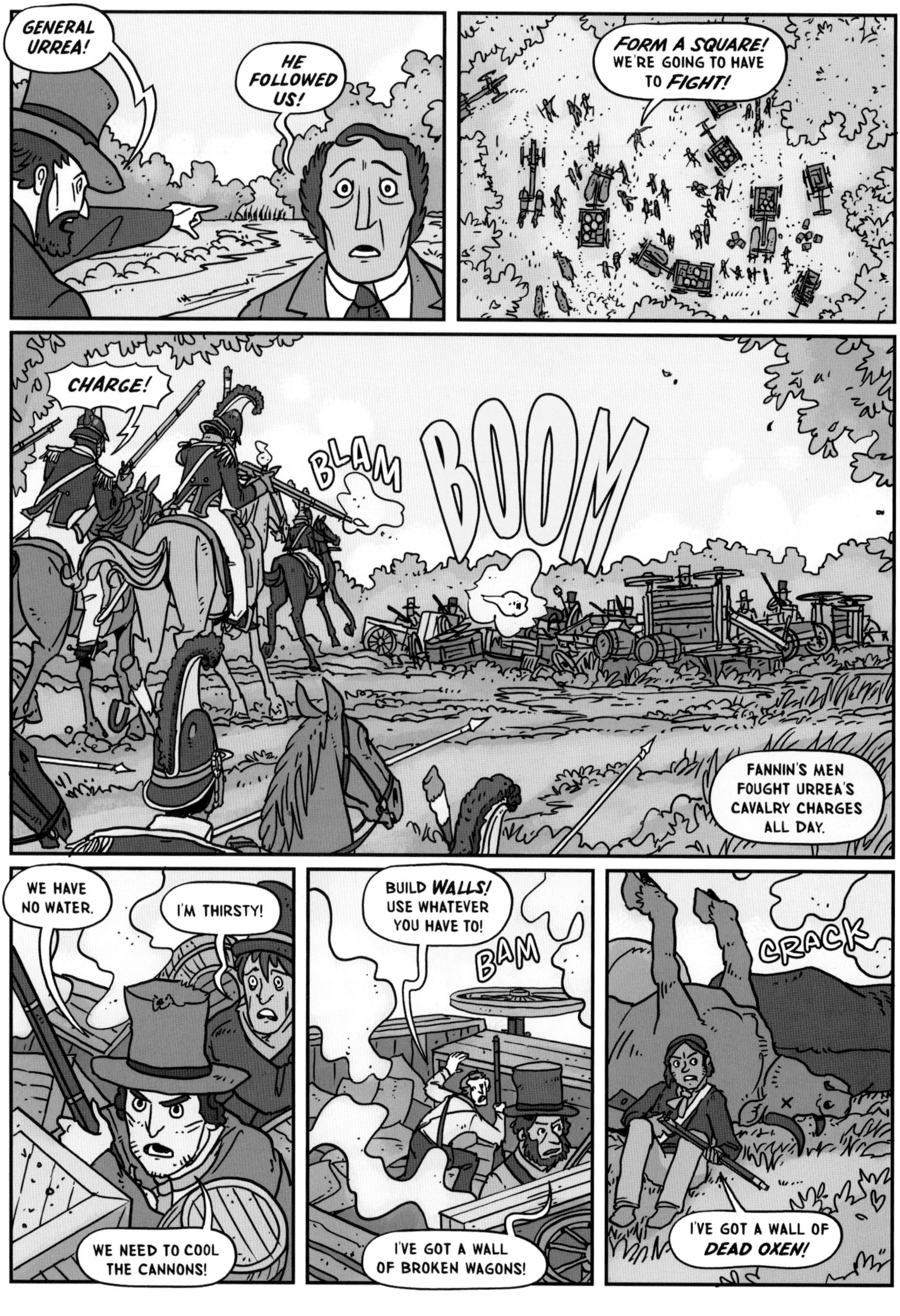
GENERAL URREA!
HE FOLLOWED US!
FORM A SQUARE! WE'RE GOING TO HAVE TO FIGHT!
CHARGE!
BLAM
BOOM
FANNIN'S MEN FOUGHT URREA'S CAVALRY CHARGES ALL DAY.
WE HAVE NO WATER.
I'M THIRSTY!
WE NEED TO COOL THE CANNONS!
BUILD WALLS! USE WHATEVER YOU HAVE TO!
BAM
I'VE GOT A WALL OF BROKEN WAGONS!
CRACK
I'VE GOT A WALL OF DEAD OXEN!

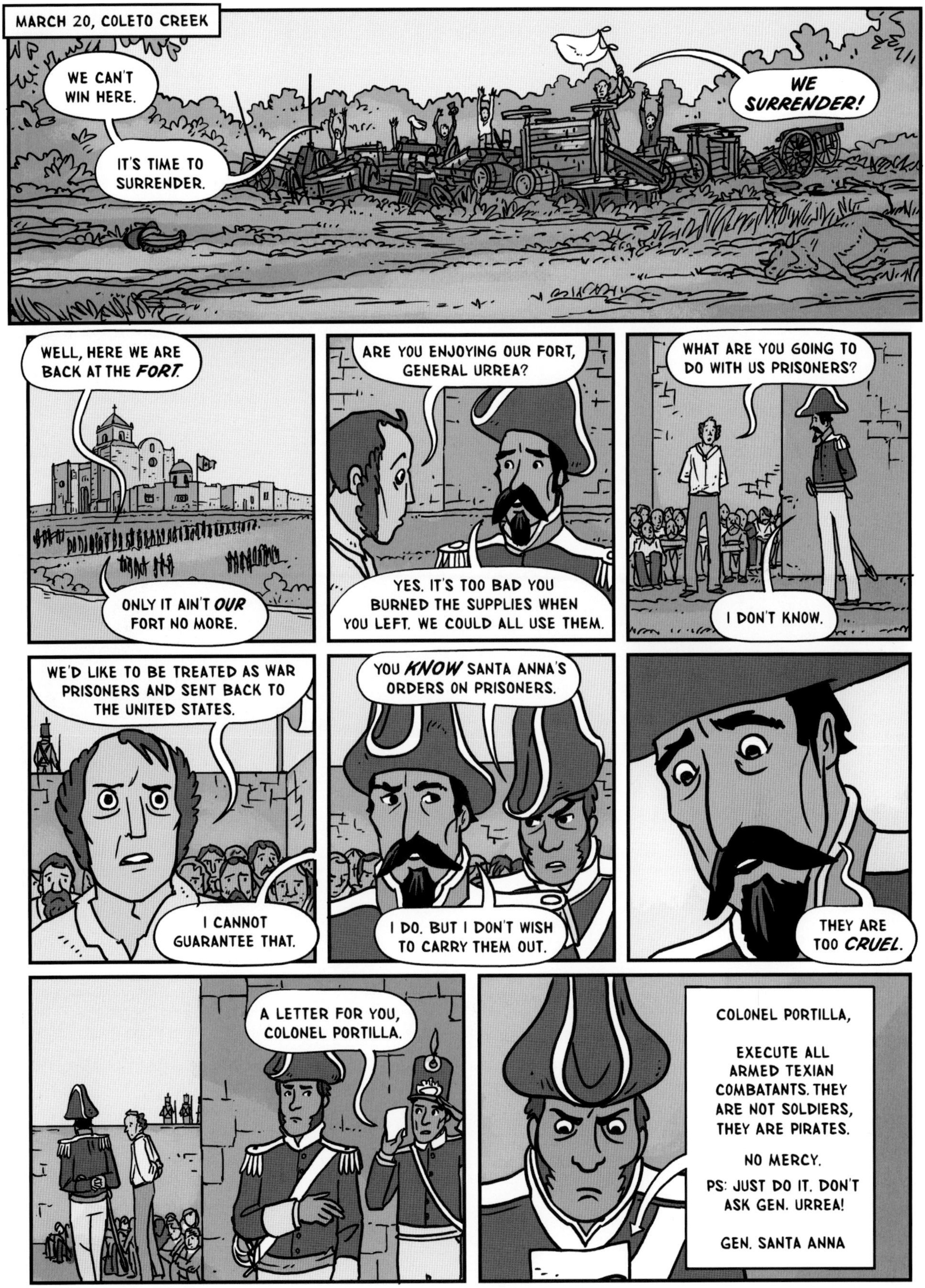
MARCH 20, COLETO CREEK
WE CAN'T WIN HERE.
IT'S TIME TO SURRENDER.
WE SURRENDER!
WELL, HERE WE ARE BACK AT THE FORT.
ONLY IT AIN'T OUR FORT NO MORE.
ARE YOU ENJOYING OUR FORT, GENERAL URREA?
YES. IT'S TOO BAD YOU BURNED THE SUPPLIES WHEN YOU LEFT. WE COULD ALL USE THEM.
WHAT ARE YOU GOING TO DO WITH US PRISONERS?
I DON'T KNOW.
WE'D LIKE TO BE TREATED AS WAR PRISONERS AND SENT BACK TO THE UNITED STATES.
I CANNOT GUARANTEE THAT.
YOU KNOW SANTA ANNA'S ORDERS ON PRISONERS.
I DO. BUT I DON'T WISH TO CARRY THEM OUT.
THEY ARE TOO CRUEL.
A LETTER FOR YOU, COLONEL PORTILLA.
COLONEL PORTILLA,
EXECUTE ALL ARMED TEXIAN COMBATANTS. THEY ARE NOT SOLDIERS, THEY ARE PIRATES.
NO MERCY.
PS: JUST DO IT. DON'T ASK GEN. URREA!
GEN. SANTA ANNA

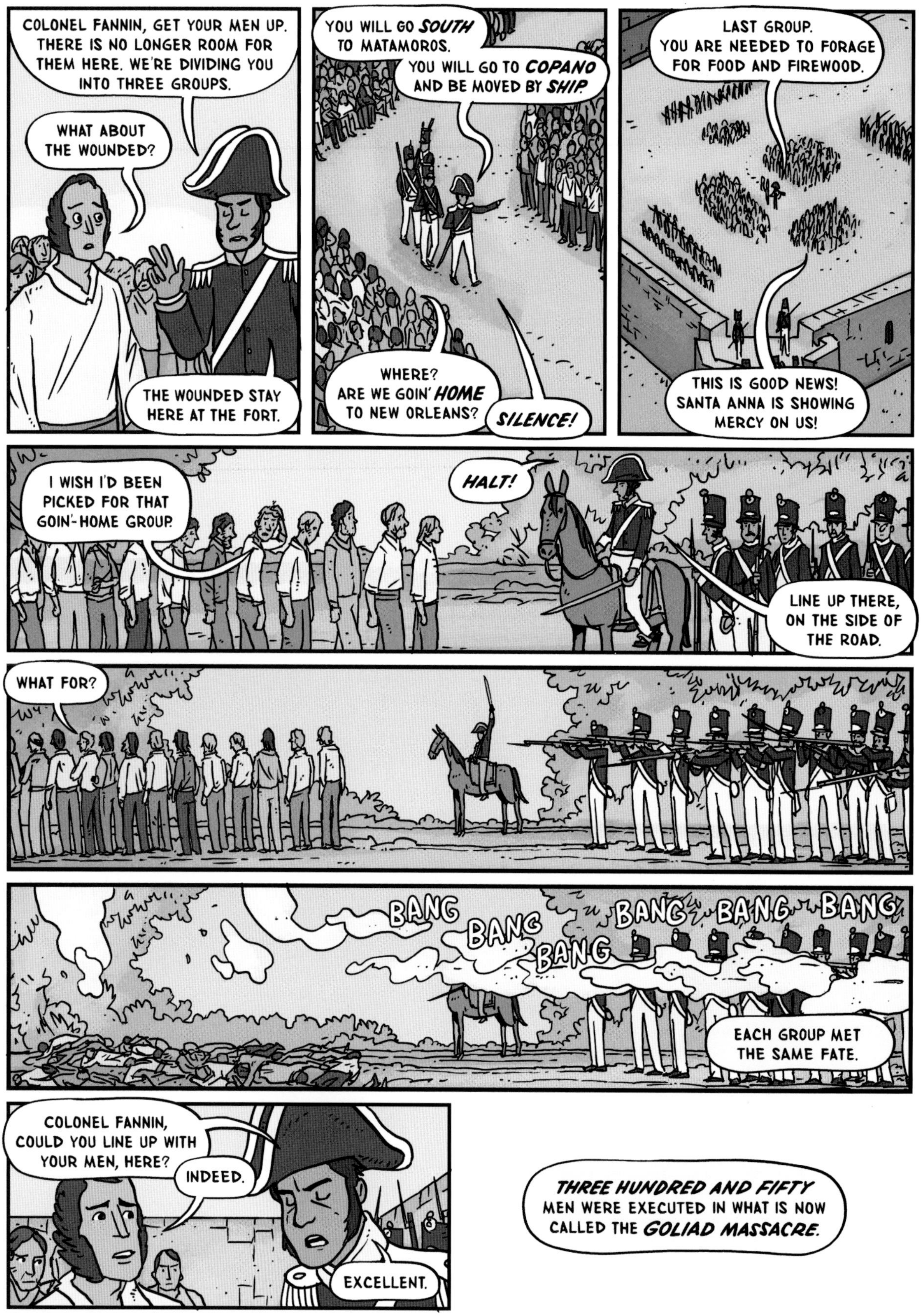
COLONEL FANNIN, GET YOUR MEN UP. THERE IS NO LONGER ROOM FOR THEM HERE. WE'RE DIVIDING YOU INTO THREE GROUPS.
WHAT ABOUT THE WOUNDED?
THE WOUNDED STAY HERE AT THE FORT.
YOU WILL GO SOUTH TO MATAMOROS.
YOU WILL GO TO COPANO AND BE MOVED BY SHIP.
WHERE? ARE WE GOIN' HOME TO NEW ORLEANS?
SILENCE!
LAST GROUP. YOU ARE NEEDED TO FORAGE FOR FOOD AND FIREWOOD.
THIS IS GOOD NEWS! SANTA ANNA IS SHOWING MERCY ON US!
I WISH I'D BEEN PICKED FOR THAT GOIN'-HOME GROUP.
HALT!
LINE UP THERE, ON THE SIDE OF THE ROAD.
WHAT FOR?
BANG
BANG
BANG
BANG
BANG
BANG
EACH GROUP MET THE SAME FATE.
COLONEL FANNIN, COULD YOU LINE UP WITH YOUR MEN, HERE?
INDEED.
EXCELLENT.
THREE HUNDRED AND FIFTY MEN WERE EXECUTED IN WHAT IS NOW CALLED THE GOLIAD MASSACRE.

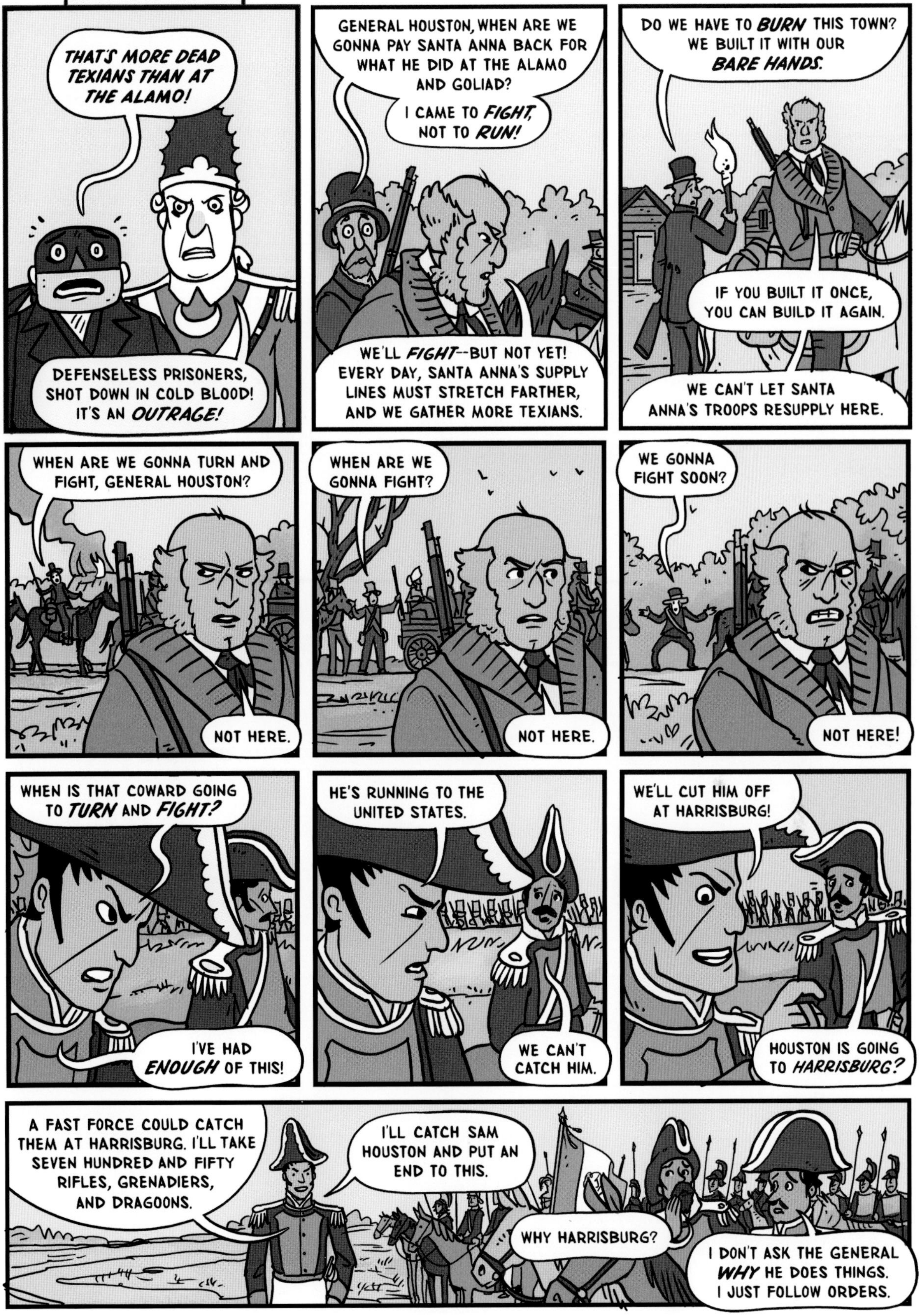
THAT'S MORE DEAD TEXIANS THAN AT THE ALAMO!
DEFENSELESS PRISONERS, SHOT DOWN IN COLD BLOOD! IT'S AN OUTRAGE!
GENERAL HOUSTON, WHEN ARE WE GONNA PAY SANTA ANNA BACK FOR WHAT HE DID AT THE ALAMO AND GOLIAD?
I CAME TO FIGHT, NOT TO RUN!
WE'LL FIGHT--BUT NOT YET! EVERY DAY, SANTA ANNA'S SUPPLY LINES MUST STRETCH FARTHER, AND WE GATHER MORE TEXIANS.
DO WE HAVE TO BURN THIS TOWN? WE BUILT IT WITH OUR BARE HANDS.
IF YOU BUILT IT ONCE, YOU CAN BUILD IT AGAIN.
WE CAN'T LET SANTA ANNA'S TROOPS RESUPPLY HERE.
WHEN ARE WE GONNA TURN AND FIGHT, GENERAL HOUSTON?
NOT HERE.
WHEN ARE WE GONNA FIGHT?
NOT HERE.
WE GONNA FIGHT SOON?
NOT HERE!
WHEN IS THAT COWARD GOING TO TURN AND FIGHT?
I'VE HAD ENOUGH OF THIS!
HE'S RUNNING TO THE UNITED STATES.
WE CAN'T CATCH HIM.
WE'LL CUT HIM OFF AT HARRISBURG!
HOUSTON IS GOING TO HARRISBURG?
A FAST FORCE COULD CATCH THEM AT HARRISBURG. I'LL TAKE SEVEN HUNDRED AND FIFTY RIFLES, GRENADIERS, AND DRAGOONS.
I'LL CATCH SAM HOUSTON AND PUT AN END TO THIS.
WHY HARRISBURG?
I DON'T ASK THE GENERAL WHY HE DOES THINGS. I JUST FOLLOW ORDERS.

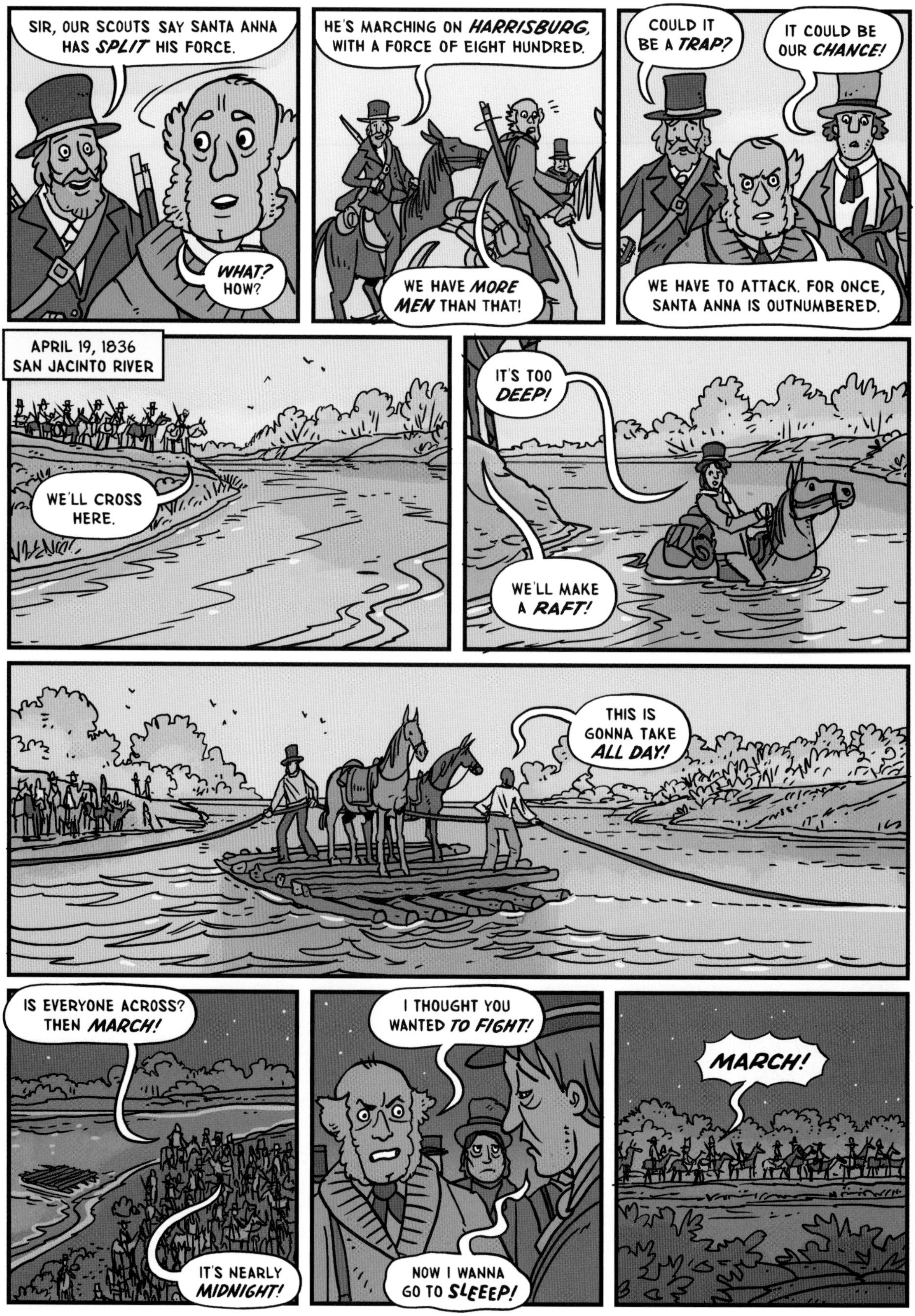
SIR, OUR SCOUTS SAY SANTA ANNA HAS SPLIT HIS FORCE.
WHAT? HOW?
HE'S MARCHING ON HARRISBURG, WITH A FORCE OF EIGHT HUNDRED.
WE HAVE MORE MEN THAN THAT!
COULD IT BE A TRAP?
IT COULD BE OUR CHANCE!
WE HAVE TO ATTACK. FOR ONCE, SANTA ANNA IS OUTNUMBERED.
APRIL 19, 1836 SAN JACINTO RIVER
WE'LL CROSS HERE.
IT'S TOO DEEP!
WE'LL MAKE A RAFT!
THIS IS GONNA TAKE ALL DAY!
IS EVERYONE ACROSS? THEN MARCH!
IT'S NEARLY MIDNIGHT!
I THOUGHT YOU WANTED TO FIGHT!
NOW I WANNA GO TO SLEEEP!
MARCH!

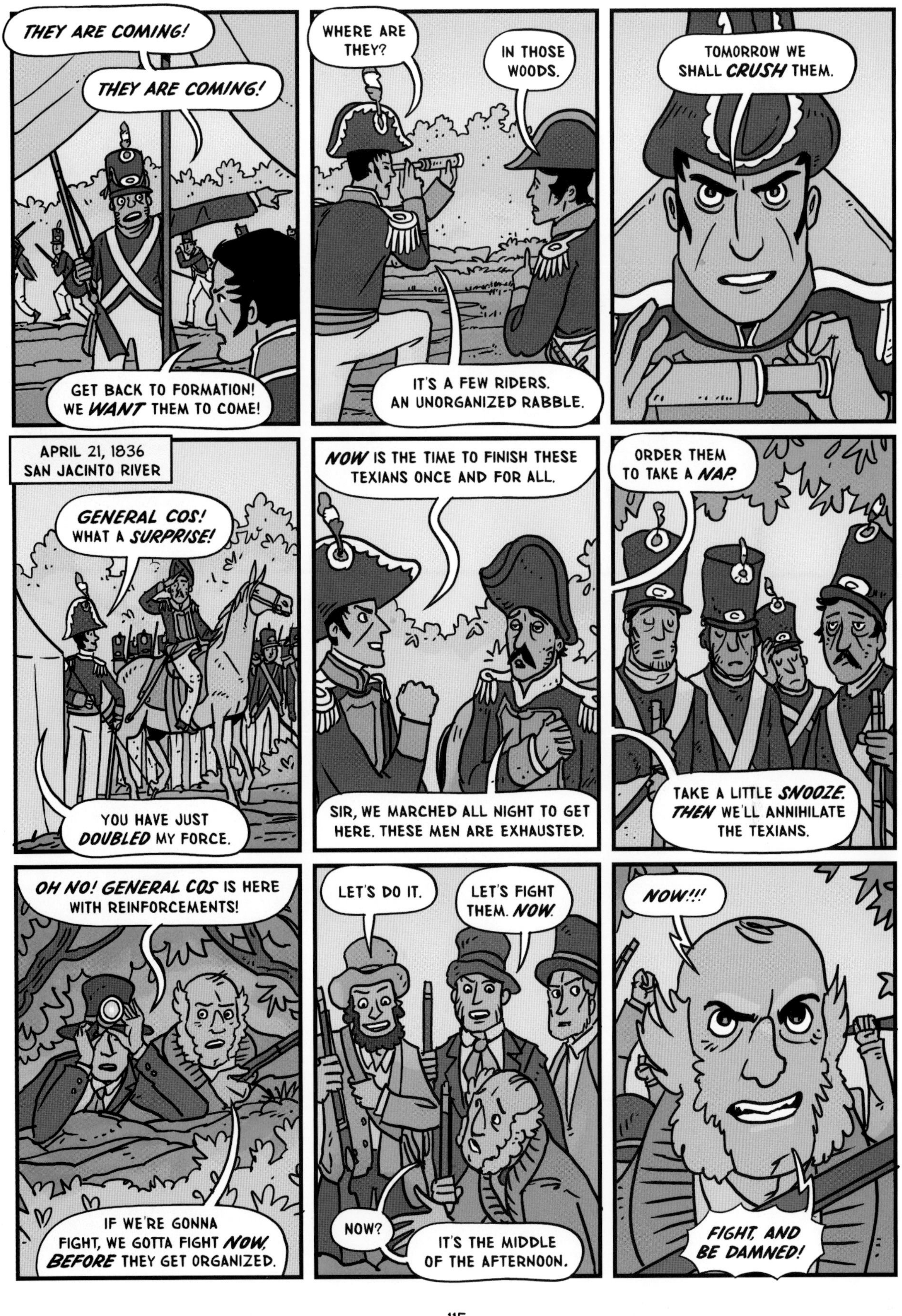

THEY ARE COMING!
THEY ARE COMING!
GET BACK TO FORMATION! WE WANT THEM TO COME!
WHERE ARE THEY?
IN THOSE WOODS.
IT'S A FEW RIDERS. AN UNORGANIZED RABBLE.
TOMORROW WE SHALL CRUSH THEM.
APRIL 21, 1836 SAN JACINTO RIVER
GENERAL COS! WHAT A SURPRISE!
YOU HAVE JUST DOUBLED MY FORCE.
NOW IS THE TIME TO FINISH THESE TEXIANS ONCE AND FOR ALL.
SIR, WE MARCHED ALL NIGHT TO GET HERE. THESE MEN ARE EXHAUSTED.
ORDER THEM TO TAKE A NAP.
TAKE A LITTLE SNOOZE. THEN WE'LL ANNIHILATE THE TEXIANS.
OH NO! GENERAL COS IS HERE WITH REINFORCEMENTS!
IF WE'RE GONNA FIGHT, WE GOTTA FIGHT NOW, BEFORE THEY GET ORGANIZED.
LET'S DO IT.
LET'S FIGHT THEM. NOW.
NOW?
IT'S THE MIDDLE OF THE AFTERNOON.
NOW!!!
FIGHT, AND BE DAMNED!

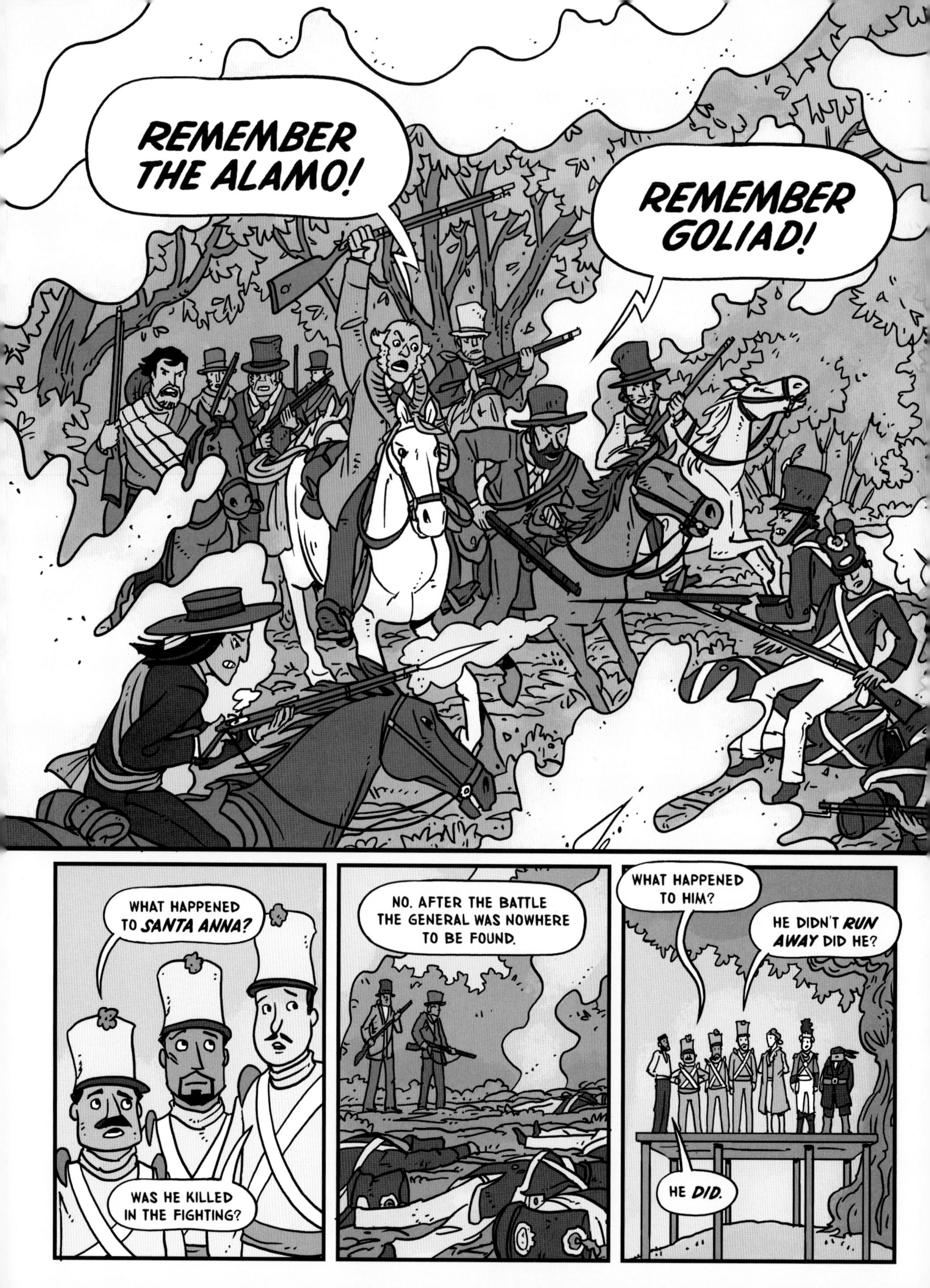
REMEMBER THE ALAMO!
REMEMBER GOLIAD!
WHAT HAPPENED TO *SANTA ANNA?*
WAS HE KILLED IN THE FIGHTING?
NO. AFTER THE BATTLE THE GENERAL WAS NOWHERE TO BE FOUND.
WHAT HAPPENED TO HIM?
HE DIDN'T *RUN AWAY* DID HE?
HE *DID.*

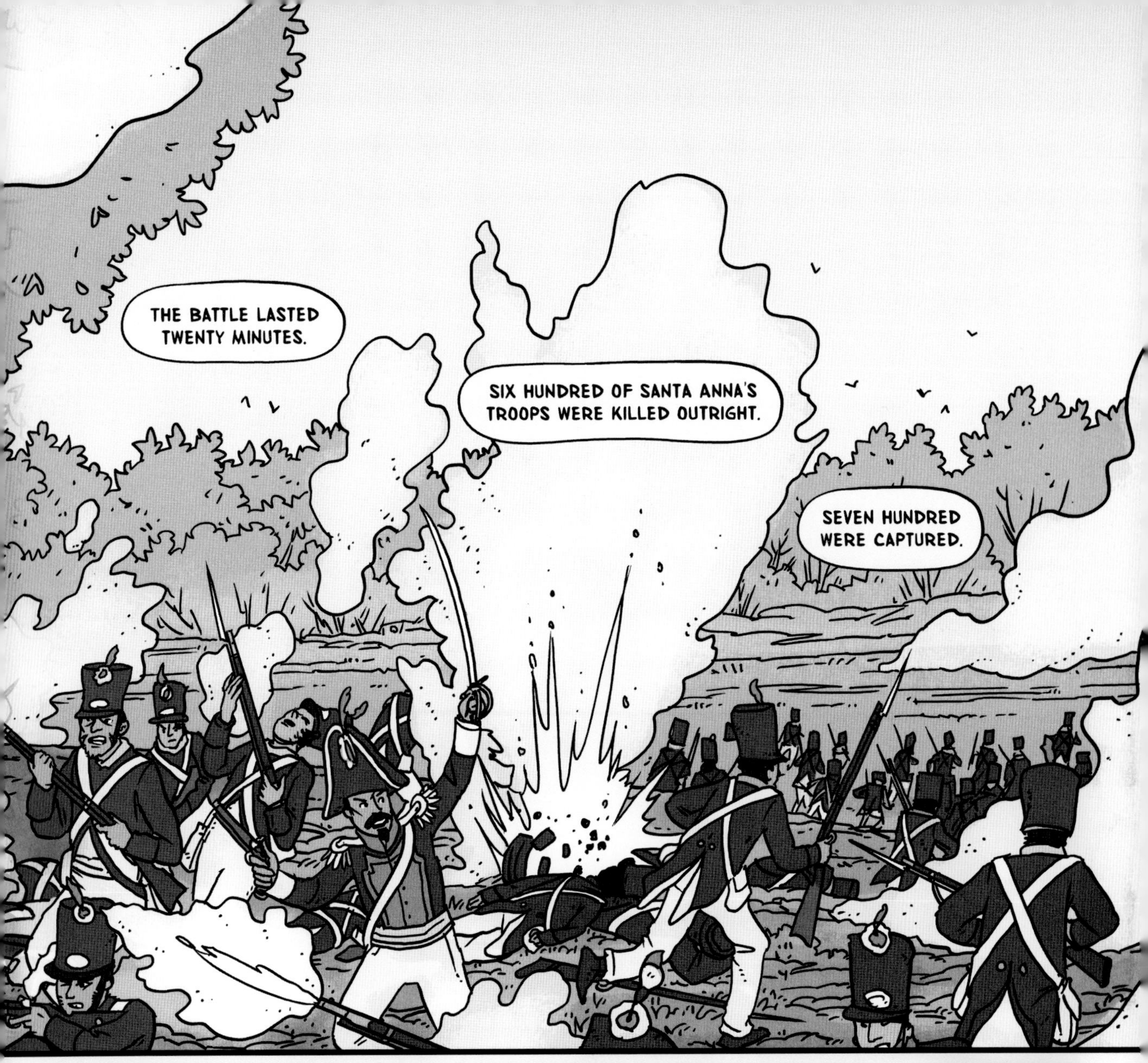
THE BATTLE LASTED TWENTY MINUTES.
SIX HUNDRED OF SANTA ANNA'S TROOPS WERE KILLED OUTRIGHT.
SEVEN HUNDRED WERE CAPTURED.

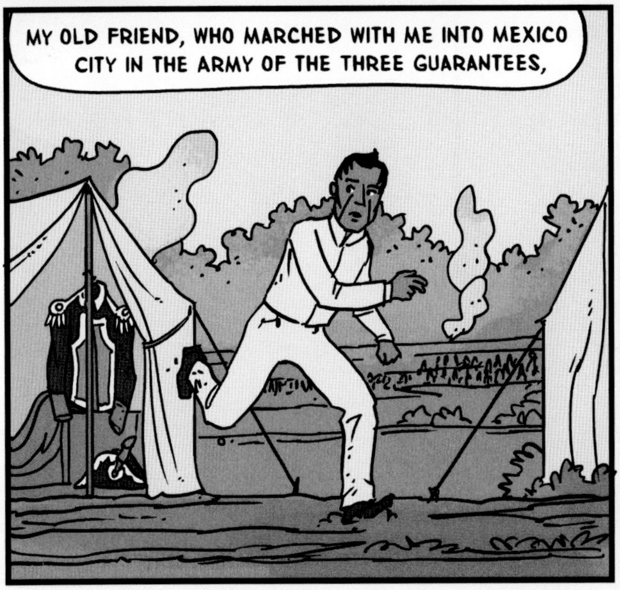
MY OLD FRIEND, WHO MARCHED WITH ME INTO MEXICO CITY IN THE ARMY OF THE THREE GUARANTEES,

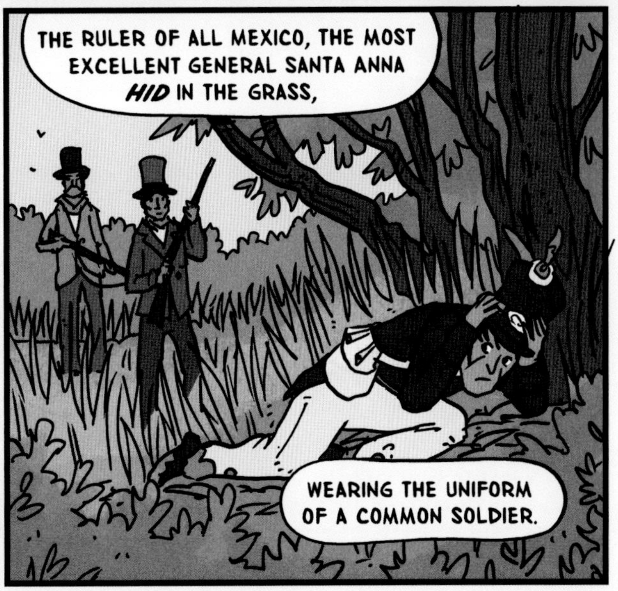
THE RULER OF ALL MEXICO, THE MOST EXCELLENT GENERAL SANTA ANNA *HID* IN THE GRASS,
WEARING THE UNIFORM OF A COMMON SOLDIER.

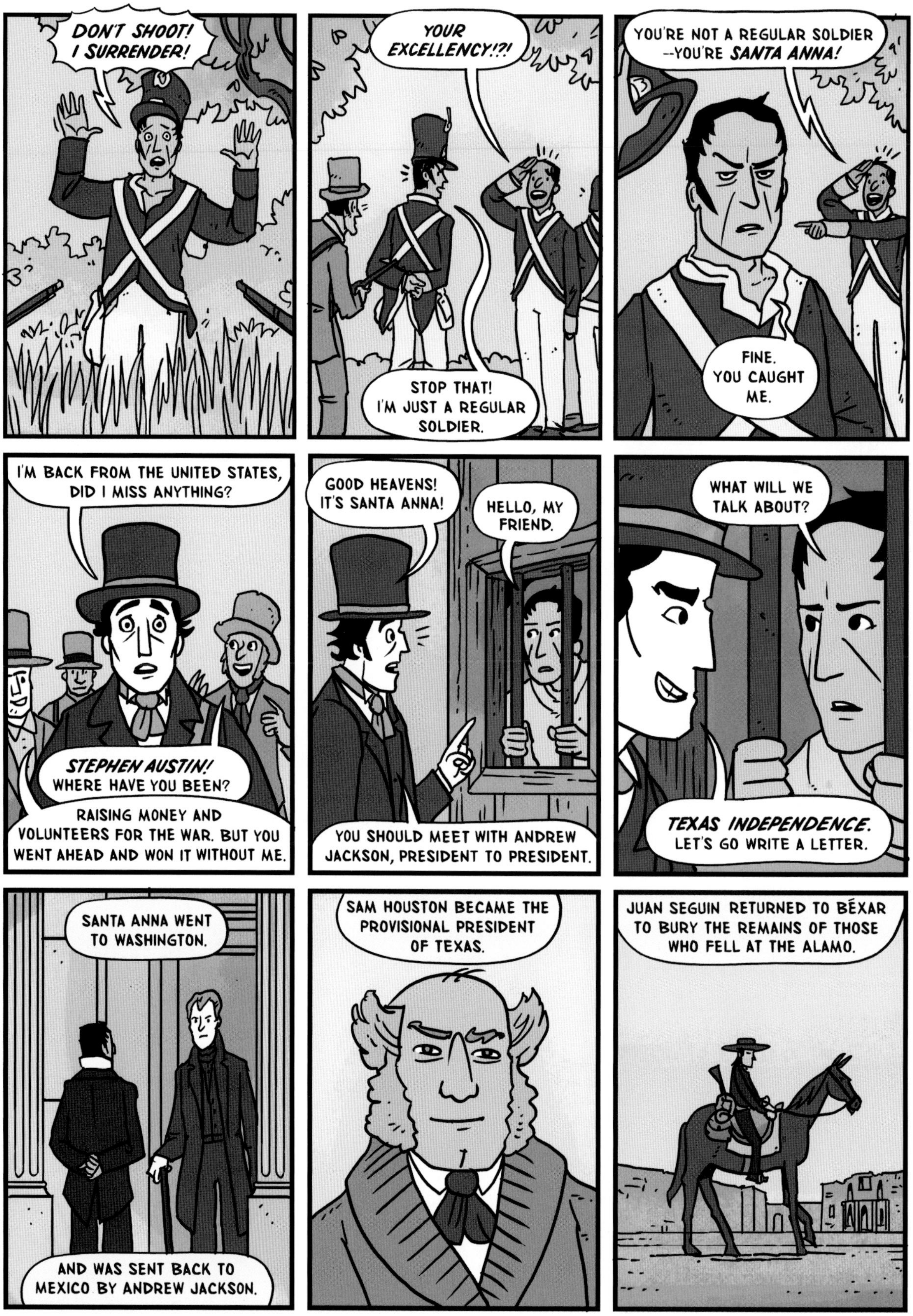
DON'T SHOOT! I SURRENDER!
YOUR EXCELLENCY!?!
STOP THAT! I'M JUST A REGULAR SOLDIER.
YOU'RE NOT A REGULAR SOLDIER --YOU'RE SANTA ANNA!
FINE. YOU CAUGHT ME.
I'M BACK FROM THE UNITED STATES, DID I MISS ANYTHING?
STEPHEN AUSTIN! WHERE HAVE YOU BEEN?
RAISING MONEY AND VOLUNTEERS FOR THE WAR. BUT YOU WENT AHEAD AND WON IT WITHOUT ME.
GOOD HEAVENS! IT'S SANTA ANNA!
HELLO, MY FRIEND.
YOU SHOULD MEET WITH ANDREW JACKSON, PRESIDENT TO PRESIDENT.
WHAT WILL WE TALK ABOUT?
TEXAS INDEPENDENCE. LET'S GO WRITE A LETTER.
SANTA ANNA WENT TO WASHINGTON.
AND WAS SENT BACK TO MEXICO BY ANDREW JACKSON.
SAM HOUSTON BECAME THE PROVISIONAL PRESIDENT OF TEXAS.
JUAN SEGUIN RETURNED TO BÉXAR TO BURY THE REMAINS OF THOSE WHO FELL AT THE ALAMO.

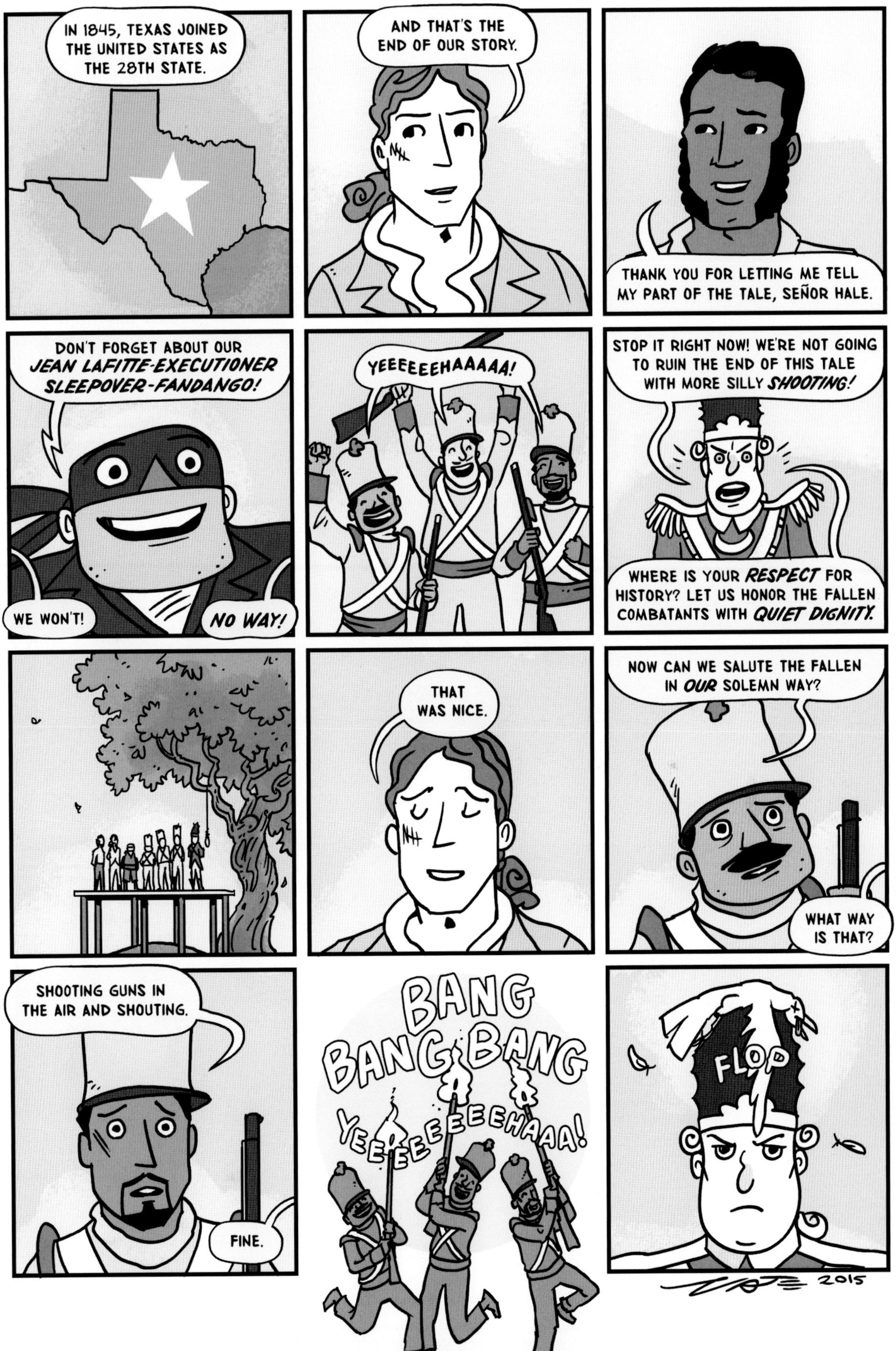
IN 1845, TEXAS JOINED THE UNITED STATES AS THE 28TH STATE.
AND THAT'S THE END OF OUR STORY.
THANK YOU FOR LETTING ME TELL MY PART OF THE TALE, SEÑOR HALE.
DON'T FORGET ABOUT OUR *JEAN LAFITTE-EXECUTIONER SLEEPOVER-FANDANGO!*
WE WON'T!
NO WAY!
YEEEEEEHAAAAA!
STOP IT RIGHT NOW! WE'RE NOT GOING TO RUIN THE END OF THIS TALE WITH MORE SILLY *SHOOTING!*
WHERE IS YOUR *RESPECT* FOR HISTORY? LET US HONOR THE FALLEN COMBATANTS WITH *QUIET DIGNITY.*
THAT WAS NICE.
NOW CAN WE SALUTE THE FALLEN IN *OUR* SOLEMN WAY?
WHAT WAY IS THAT?
SHOOTING GUNS IN THE AIR AND SHOUTING.
FINE.
BANG
BANG BANG BANG
YEEEEEEEEHAAAA!
FLOP
2015

NH
HT
NATHAN HALE'S HAZARDOUS TALES

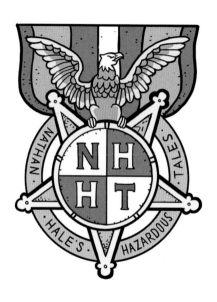

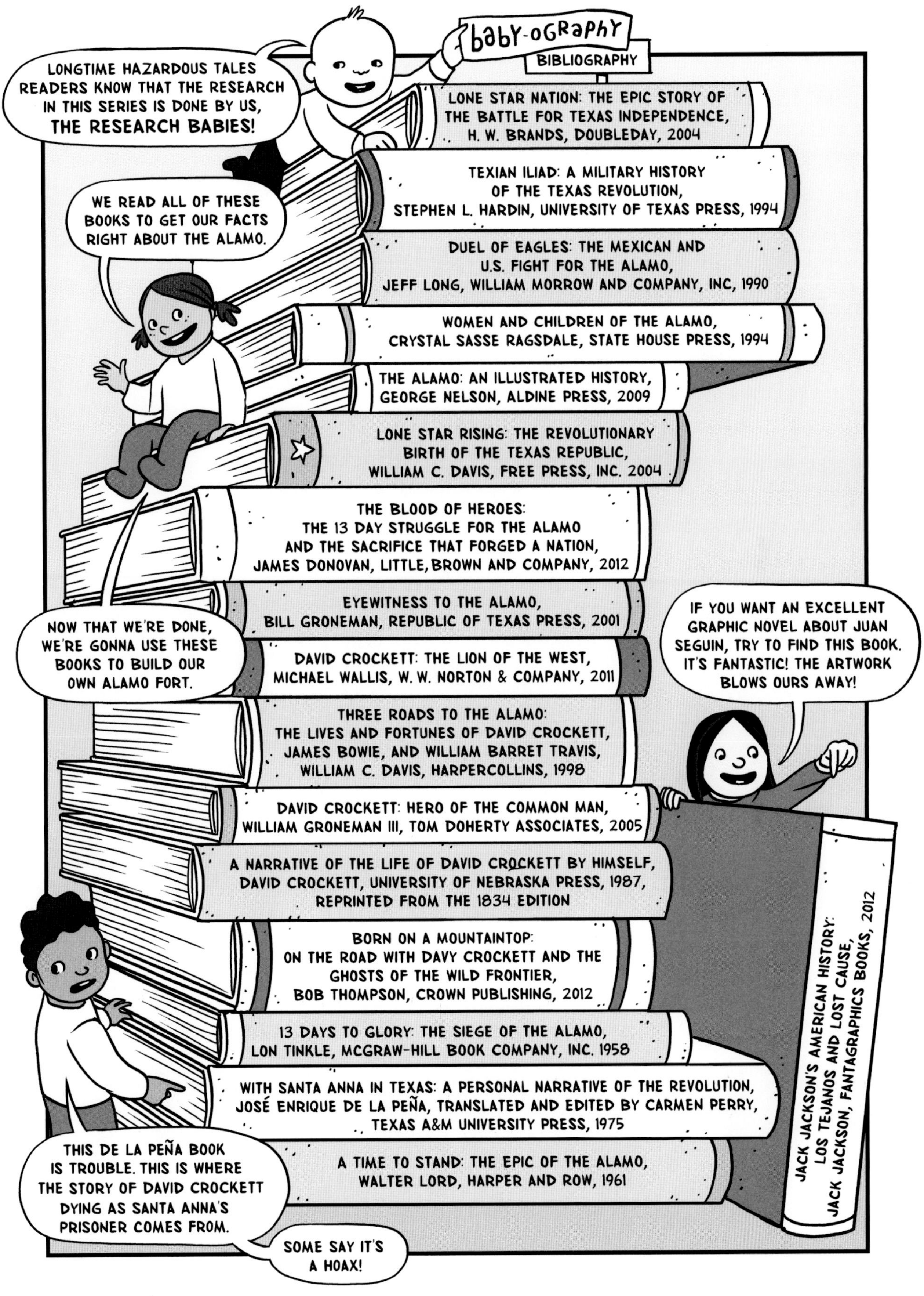

baby-ography
BIBLIOGRAPHY
LONGTIME HAZARDOUS TALES READERS KNOW THAT THE RESEARCH IN THIS SERIES IS DONE BY US, THE RESEARCH BABIES!
WE READ ALL OF THESE BOOKS TO GET OUR FACTS RIGHT ABOUT THE ALAMO.
NOW THAT WE'RE DONE, WE'RE GONNA USE THESE BOOKS TO BUILD OUR OWN ALAMO FORT.
IF YOU WANT AN EXCELLENT GRAPHIC NOVEL ABOUT JUAN SEGUIN, TRY TO FIND THIS BOOK. IT'S FANTASTIC! THE ARTWORK BLOWS OURS AWAY!
LONE STAR NATION: THE EPIC STORY OF THE BATTLE FOR TEXAS INDEPENDENCE, H. W. BRANDS, DOUBLEDAY, 2004
TEXIAN ILIAD: A MILITARY HISTORY OF THE TEXAS REVOLUTION, STEPHEN L. HARDIN, UNIVERSITY OF TEXAS PRESS, 1994
DUEL OF EAGLES: THE MEXICAN AND U.S. FIGHT FOR THE ALAMO, JEFF LONG, WILLIAM MORROW AND COMPANY, INC, 1990
WOMEN AND CHILDREN OF THE ALAMO, CRYSTAL SASSE RAGSDALE, STATE HOUSE PRESS, 1994
THE ALAMO: AN ILLUSTRATED HISTORY, GEORGE NELSON, ALDINE PRESS, 2009
LONE STAR RISING: THE REVOLUTIONARY BIRTH OF THE TEXAS REPUBLIC, WILLIAM C. DAVIS, FREE PRESS, INC. 2004
THE BLOOD OF HEROES: THE 13 DAY STRUGGLE FOR THE ALAMO AND THE SACRIFICE THAT FORGED A NATION, JAMES DONOVAN, LITTLE, BROWN AND COMPANY, 2012
EYEWITNESS TO THE ALAMO, BILL GRONEMAN, REPUBLIC OF TEXAS PRESS, 2001
DAVID CROCKETT: THE LION OF THE WEST, MICHAEL WALLIS, W. W. NORTON & COMPANY, 2011
THREE ROADS TO THE ALAMO: THE LIVES AND FORTUNES OF DAVID CROCKETT, JAMES BOWIE, AND WILLIAM BARRET TRAVIS, WILLIAM C. DAVIS, HARPERCOLLINS, 1998
DAVID CROCKETT: HERO OF THE COMMON MAN, WILLIAM GRONEMAN III, TOM DOHERTY ASSOCIATES, 2005
A NARRATIVE OF THE LIFE OF DAVID CROCKETT BY HIMSELF, DAVID CROCKETT, UNIVERSITY OF NEBRASKA PRESS, 1987, REPRINTED FROM THE 1834 EDITION
BORN ON A MOUNTAINTOP: ON THE ROAD WITH DAVY CROCKETT AND THE GHOSTS OF THE WILD FRONTIER, BOB THOMPSON, CROWN PUBLISHING, 2012
13 DAYS TO GLORY: THE SIEGE OF THE ALAMO, LON TINKLE, MCGRAW-HILL BOOK COMPANY, INC. 1958
WITH SANTA ANNA IN TEXAS: A PERSONAL NARRATIVE OF THE REVOLUTION, JOSÉ ENRIQUE DE LA PEÑA, TRANSLATED AND EDITED BY CARMEN PERRY, TEXAS A&M UNIVERSITY PRESS, 1975
A TIME TO STAND: THE EPIC OF THE ALAMO, WALTER LORD, HARPER AND ROW, 1961
JACK JACKSON'S AMERICAN HISTORY: LOS TEJANOS AND LOST CAUSE, JACK JACKSON, FANTAGRAPHICS BOOKS, 2012
THIS DE LA PEÑA BOOK IS TROUBLE. THIS IS WHERE THE STORY OF DAVID CROCKETT DYING AS SANTA ANNA'S PRISONER COMES FROM.
SOME SAY IT'S A HOAX!

CARTOONS ABOUT THE ALAMO AND ITS HEROES APPEARED AS EARLY AS 1836.

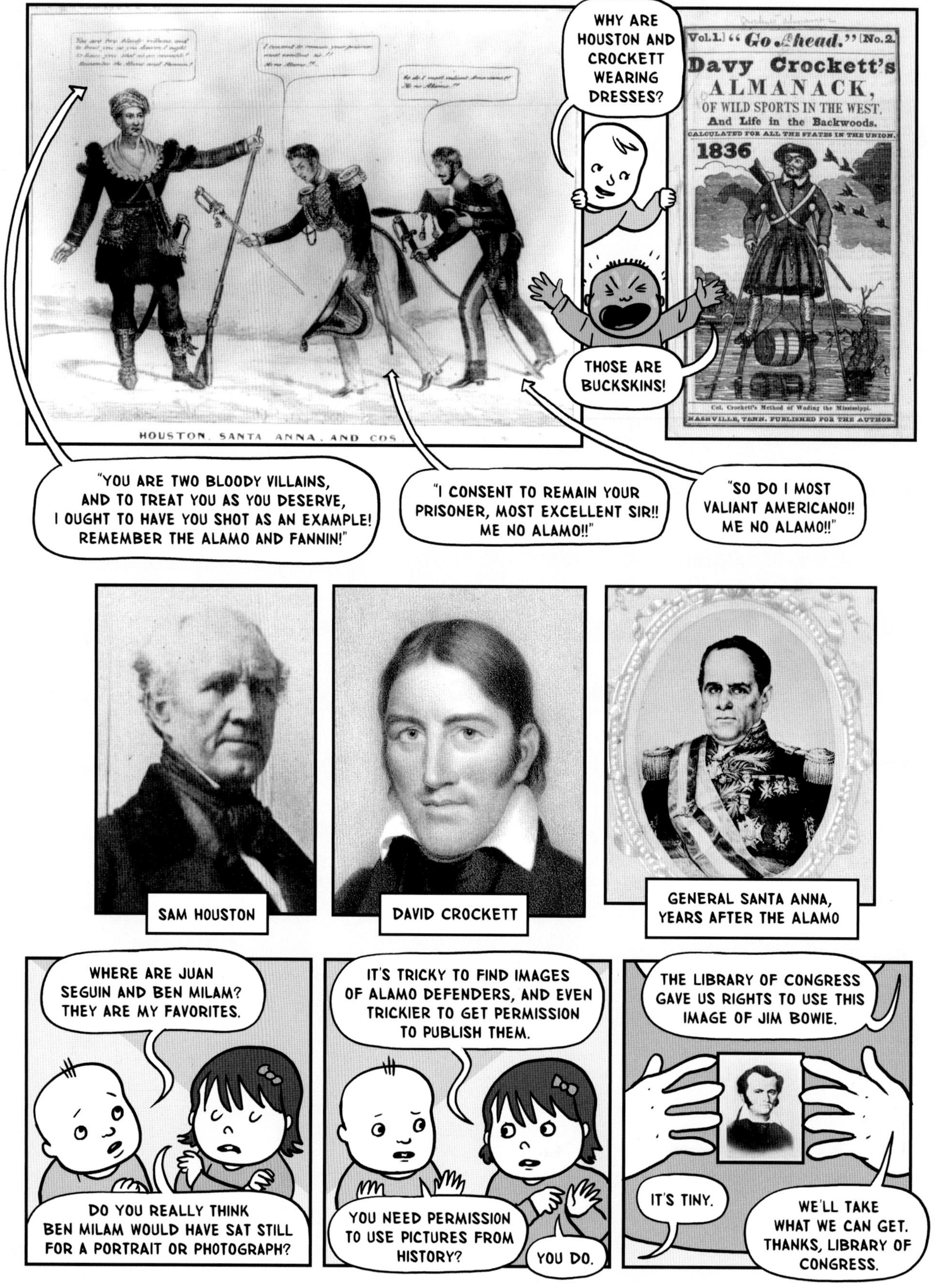
HOUSTON, SANTA ANNA, AND COS.
WHY ARE HOUSTON AND CROCKETT WEARING DRESSES?
THOSE ARE BUCKSKINS!
Vol.1.] "Go Ahead." [No.2.
Davy Crockett's ALMANACK, OF WILD SPORTS IN THE WEST, And Life in the Backwoods.
CALCULATED FOR ALL THE STATES IN THE UNION.
1836
Col. Crockett's Method of Wading the Mississippi.
NASHVILLE, TENN. PUBLISHED FOR THE AUTHOR.
"YOU ARE TWO BLOODY VILLAINS, AND TO TREAT YOU AS YOU DESERVE, I OUGHT TO HAVE YOU SHOT AS AN EXAMPLE! REMEMBER THE ALAMO AND FANNIN!"
"I CONSENT TO REMAIN YOUR PRISONER, MOST EXCELLENT SIR!! ME NO ALAMO!!"
"SO DO I MOST VALIANT AMERICANO!! ME NO ALAMO!!"
SAM HOUSTON
DAVID CROCKETT
GENERAL SANTA ANNA, YEARS AFTER THE ALAMO
WHERE ARE JUAN SEGUIN AND BEN MILAM? THEY ARE MY FAVORITES.
DO YOU REALLY THINK BEN MILAM WOULD HAVE SAT STILL FOR A PORTRAIT OR PHOTOGRAPH?
IT'S TRICKY TO FIND IMAGES OF ALAMO DEFENDERS, AND EVEN TRICKIER TO GET PERMISSION TO PUBLISH THEM.
YOU NEED PERMISSION TO USE PICTURES FROM HISTORY?
YOU DO.
THE LIBRARY OF CONGRESS GAVE US RIGHTS TO USE THIS IMAGE OF JIM BOWIE.
IT'S TINY.
WE'LL TAKE WHAT WE CAN GET. THANKS, LIBRARY OF CONGRESS.

THE SURRENDER OF SANTA ANNA, BY WILLIAM HENRY HUDDLE

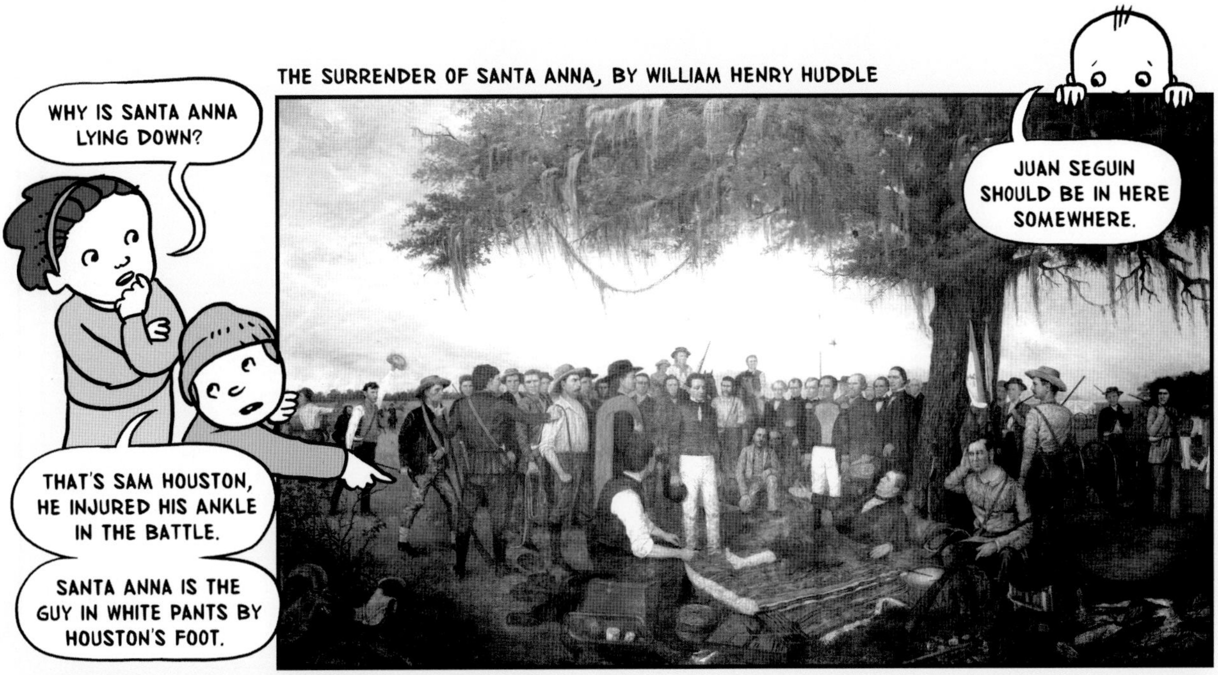
WHY IS SANTA ANNA LYING DOWN?
JUAN SEGUIN SHOULD BE IN HERE SOMEWHERE.
THAT'S SAM HOUSTON, HE INJURED HIS ANKLE IN THE BATTLE.
SANTA ANNA IS THE GUY IN WHITE PANTS BY HOUSTON'S FOOT.

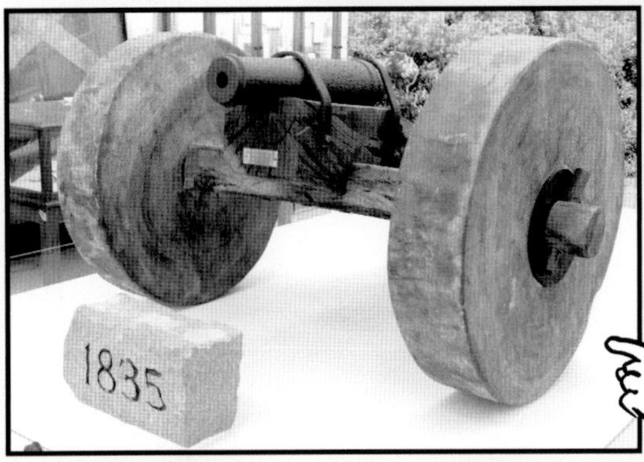
1835

THE "COME AND TAKE IT" CANNON, ON DISPLAY AT THE GONZALES MEMORIAL MUSEUM IN GONZALES, TEXAS

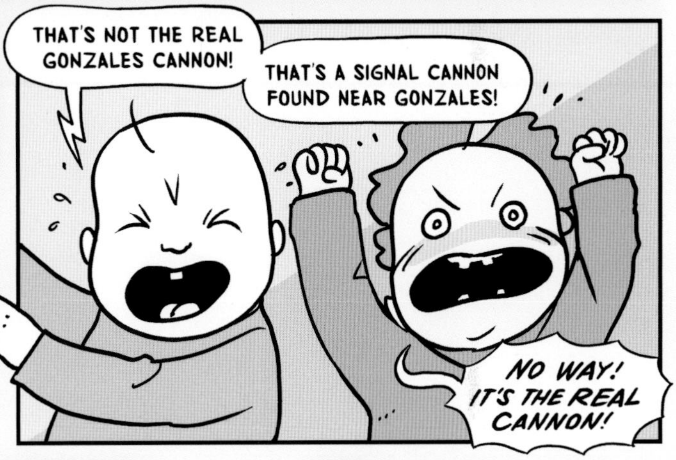
THAT'S NOT THE REAL GONZALES CANNON!
THAT'S A SIGNAL CANNON FOUND NEAR GONZALES!
NO WAY! IT'S THE REAL CANNON!

SEND YOUR COMMENTS, QUESTIONS, AND CORRECTIONS TO CORRECTIONBABY@HAZARDOUSTALES.COM

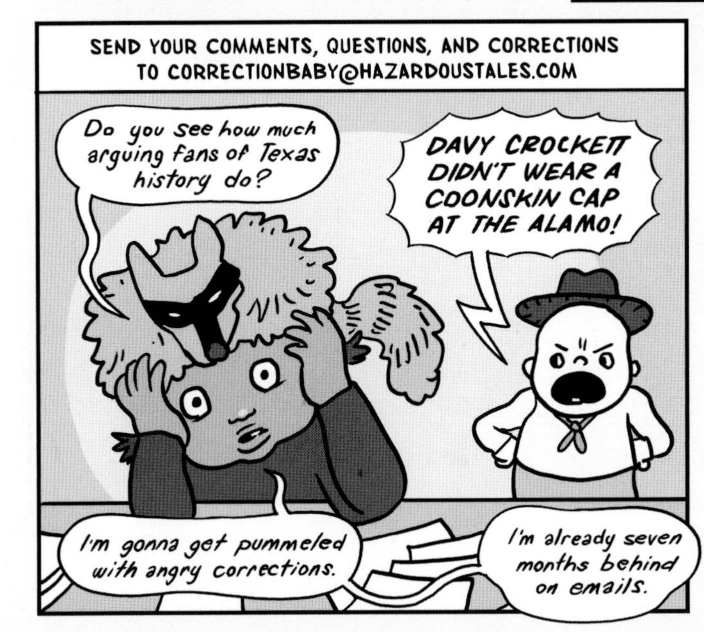
Do you see how much arguing fans of Texas history do?
DAVY CROCKETT DIDN'T WEAR A COONSKIN CAP AT THE ALAMO!
I'm gonna get pummeled with angry corrections.
I'm already seven months behind on emails.

THANKS—

SPECIAL THANKS TO CHRIS SCHWEIZER FOR THE ONCE AGAIN/JUAN SEGUIN JOKE. IF YOU DON'T KNOW MR. SCHWEIZER'S HISTORICAL FICTION COMIC, THE CROGAN ADVENTURES, YOU SHOULD. SUPER FUN SWASHBUCKLING BOOKS FOR READERS OF ALL AGES.

BIG THANKS TO THE MANY TEXAS LIBRARIANS WHO HOSTED ME AT THEIR SCHOOLS DURING THE WRITING AND RESEARCHING OF THIS BOOK, AND TO THE MANY STUDENTS WHO EXPRESSED THIER ENTHUSIASM FOR HISTORY AND SUGGESTED NEW SUBJECTS FOR FUTURE HAZARDOUS TALES BOOKS.

I CAN EASILY SAY I'VE VISITED MORE SCHOOLS IN TEXAS THAN ANY OTHER STATE!

AND THANK *YOU* FOR BEING A HISTORY READER, A COMICS READER, AND THE TYPE OF READER WHO READS THIS KIND OF INFORMATION IN THE BACK OF BOOKS. YOU ARE SERIOUSLY AN OUTSTANDING READER.

—NATHAN HALE, 2015

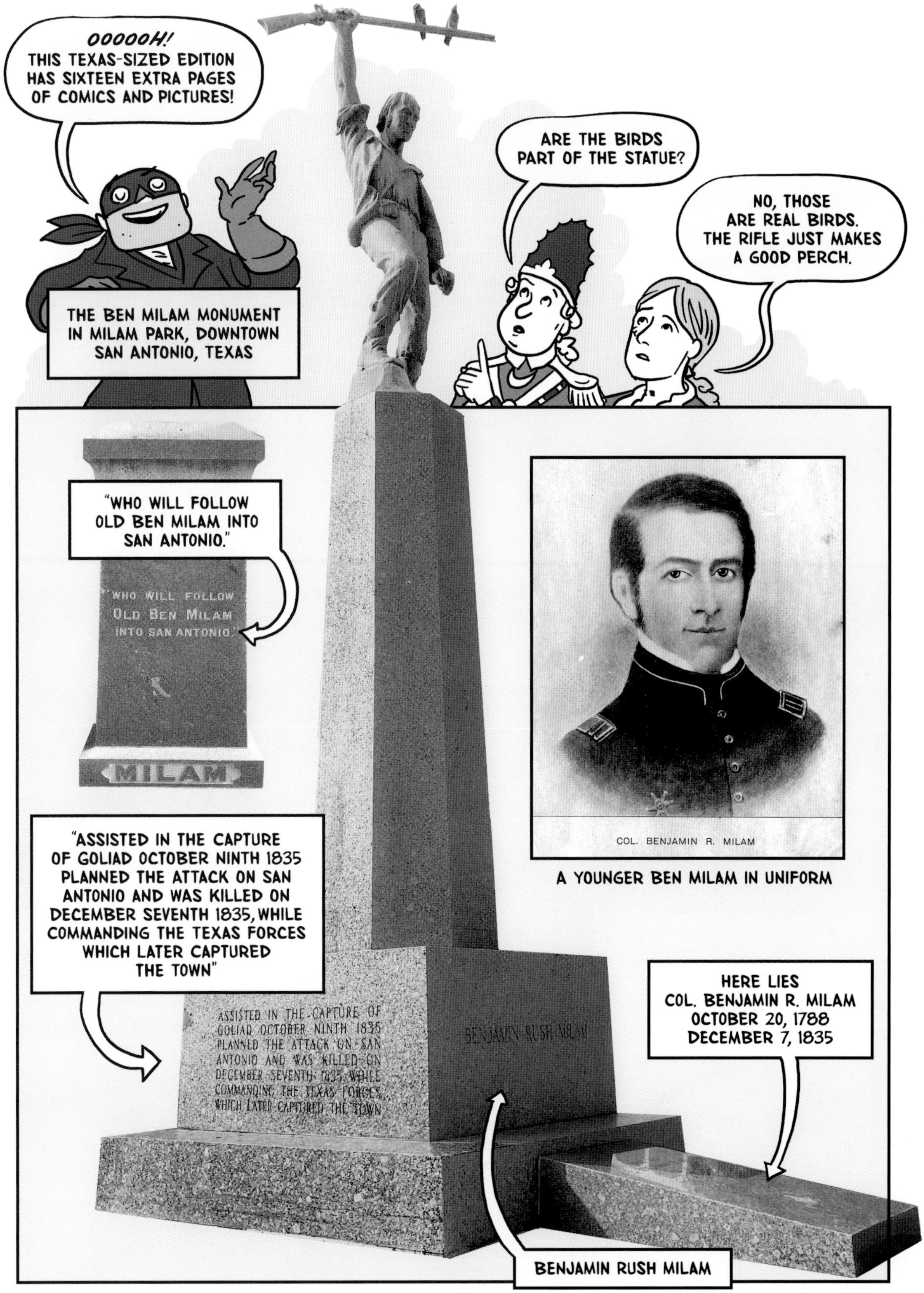
OOOOOH!
THIS TEXAS-SIZED EDITION HAS SIXTEEN EXTRA PAGES OF COMICS AND PICTURES!
THE BEN MILAM MONUMENT IN MILAM PARK, DOWNTOWN SAN ANTONIO, TEXAS
ARE THE BIRDS PART OF THE STATUE?
NO, THOSE ARE REAL BIRDS. THE RIFLE JUST MAKES A GOOD PERCH.
"WHO WILL FOLLOW OLD BEN MILAM INTO SAN ANTONIO."
"WHO WILL FOLLOW OLD BEN MILAM INTO SAN ANTONIO."
MILAM
COL. BENJAMIN R. MILAM
A YOUNGER BEN MILAM IN UNIFORM
"ASSISTED IN THE CAPTURE OF GOLIAD OCTOBER NINTH 1835 PLANNED THE ATTACK ON SAN ANTONIO AND WAS KILLED ON DECEMBER SEVENTH 1835, WHILE COMMANDING THE TEXAS FORCES WHICH LATER CAPTURED THE TOWN"
ASSISTED IN THE CAPTURE OF GOLIAD OCTOBER NINTH 1835 PLANNED THE ATTACK ON SAN ANTONIO AND WAS KILLED ON DECEMBER SEVENTH 1835 WHILE COMMANDING THE TEXAS FORCES WHICH LATER CAPTURED THE TOWN
BENJAMIN RUSH MILAM
HERE LIES COL. BENJAMIN R. MILAM OCTOBER 20, 1788 DECEMBER 7, 1835
BENJAMIN RUSH MILAM

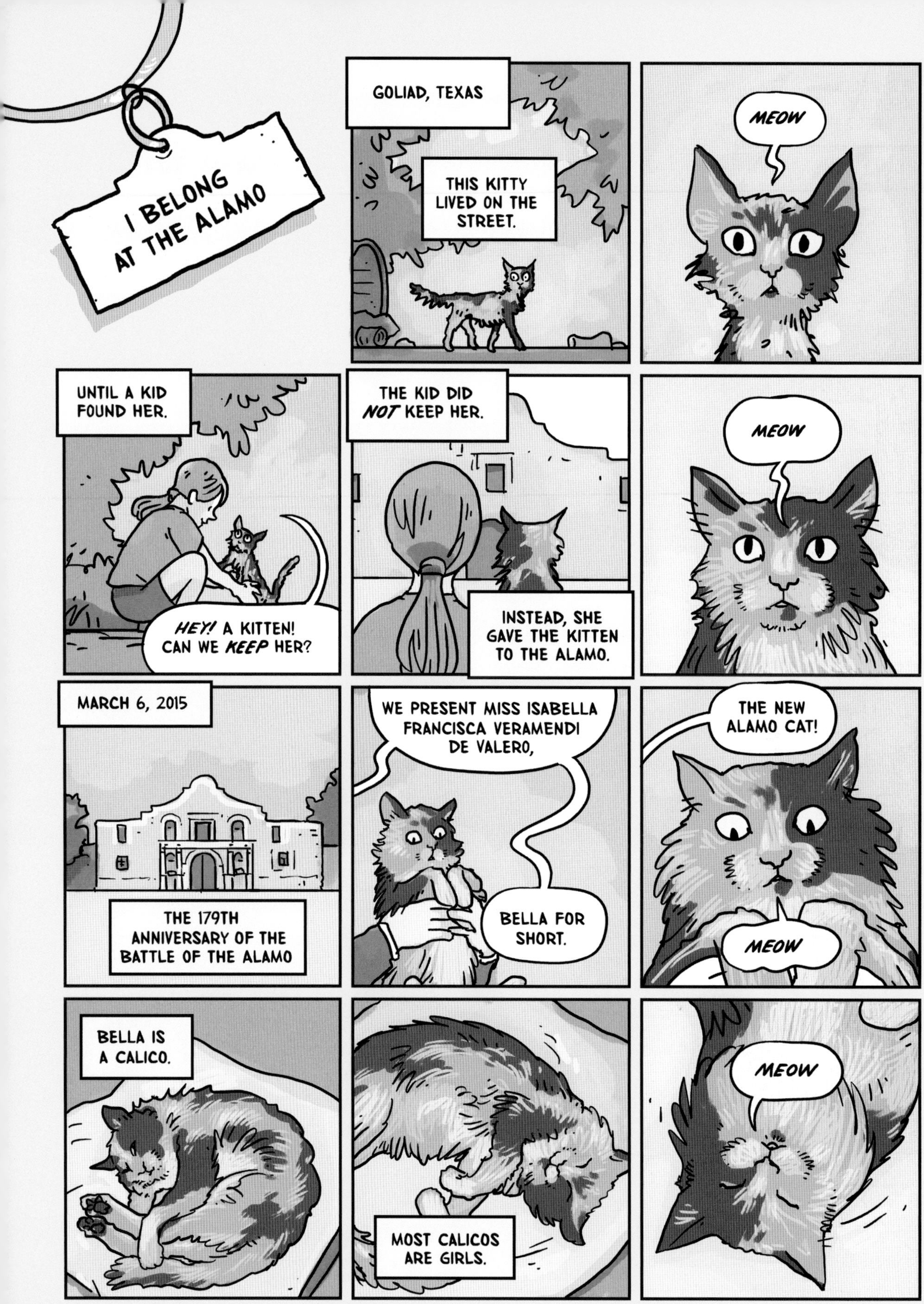
I BELONG AT THE ALAMO
GOLIAD, TEXAS
THIS KITTY LIVED ON THE STREET.
MEOW
UNTIL A KID FOUND HER.
HEY! A KITTEN! CAN WE KEEP HER?
THE KID DID NOT KEEP HER.
INSTEAD, SHE GAVE THE KITTEN TO THE ALAMO.
MEOW
MARCH 6, 2015
THE 179TH ANNIVERSARY OF THE BATTLE OF THE ALAMO
WE PRESENT MISS ISABELLA FRANCISCA VERAMENDI DE VALERO,
BELLA FOR SHORT.
THE NEW ALAMO CAT!
MEOW
BELLA IS A CALICO.
MOST CALICOS ARE GIRLS.
MEOW

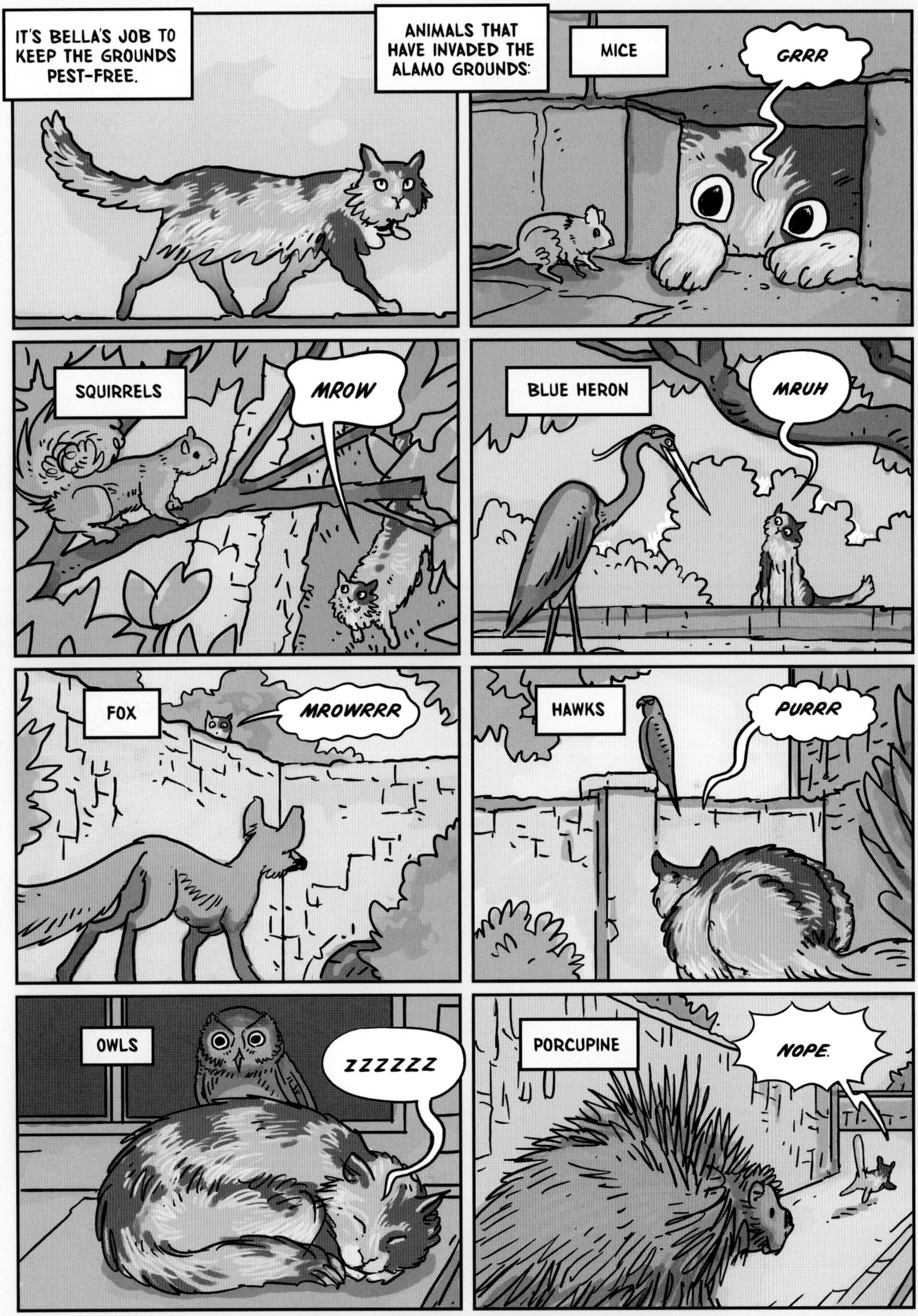
IT'S BELLA'S JOB TO KEEP THE GROUNDS PEST-FREE.
ANIMALS THAT HAVE INVADED THE ALAMO GROUNDS:
MICE
GRRR
SQUIRRELS
MROW
BLUE HERON
MRUH
FOX
MROWRRR
HAWKS
PURRR
OWLS
ZZZZZZ
PORCUPINE
NOPE.

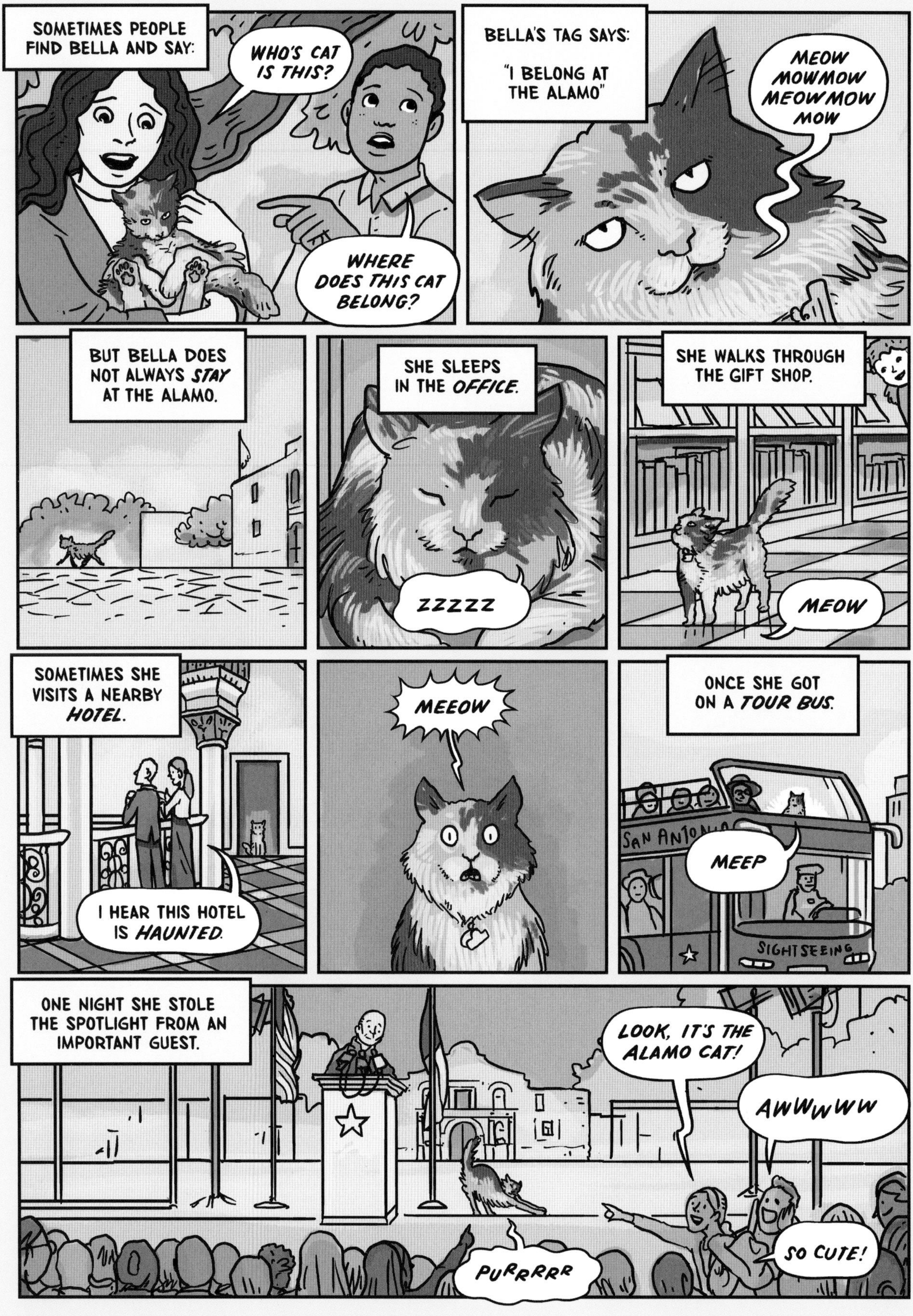
SOMETIMES PEOPLE FIND BELLA AND SAY:
WHO'S CAT IS THIS?
WHERE DOES THIS CAT BELONG?
BELLA'S TAG SAYS: "I BELONG AT THE ALAMO"
MEOW MOWMOW MEOWMOW MOW
BUT BELLA DOES NOT ALWAYS STAY AT THE ALAMO.
SHE SLEEPS IN THE OFFICE.
ZZZZZ
SHE WALKS THROUGH THE GIFT SHOP.
MEOW
SOMETIMES SHE VISITS A NEARBY HOTEL.
I HEAR THIS HOTEL IS HAUNTED.
MEEOW
ONCE SHE GOT ON A TOUR BUS.
SAN ANTONIO
MEEP
SIGHTSEEING
ONE NIGHT SHE STOLE THE SPOTLIGHT FROM AN IMPORTANT GUEST.
LOOK, IT'S THE ALAMO CAT!
AWWWWW
SO CUTE!
PURRRRR

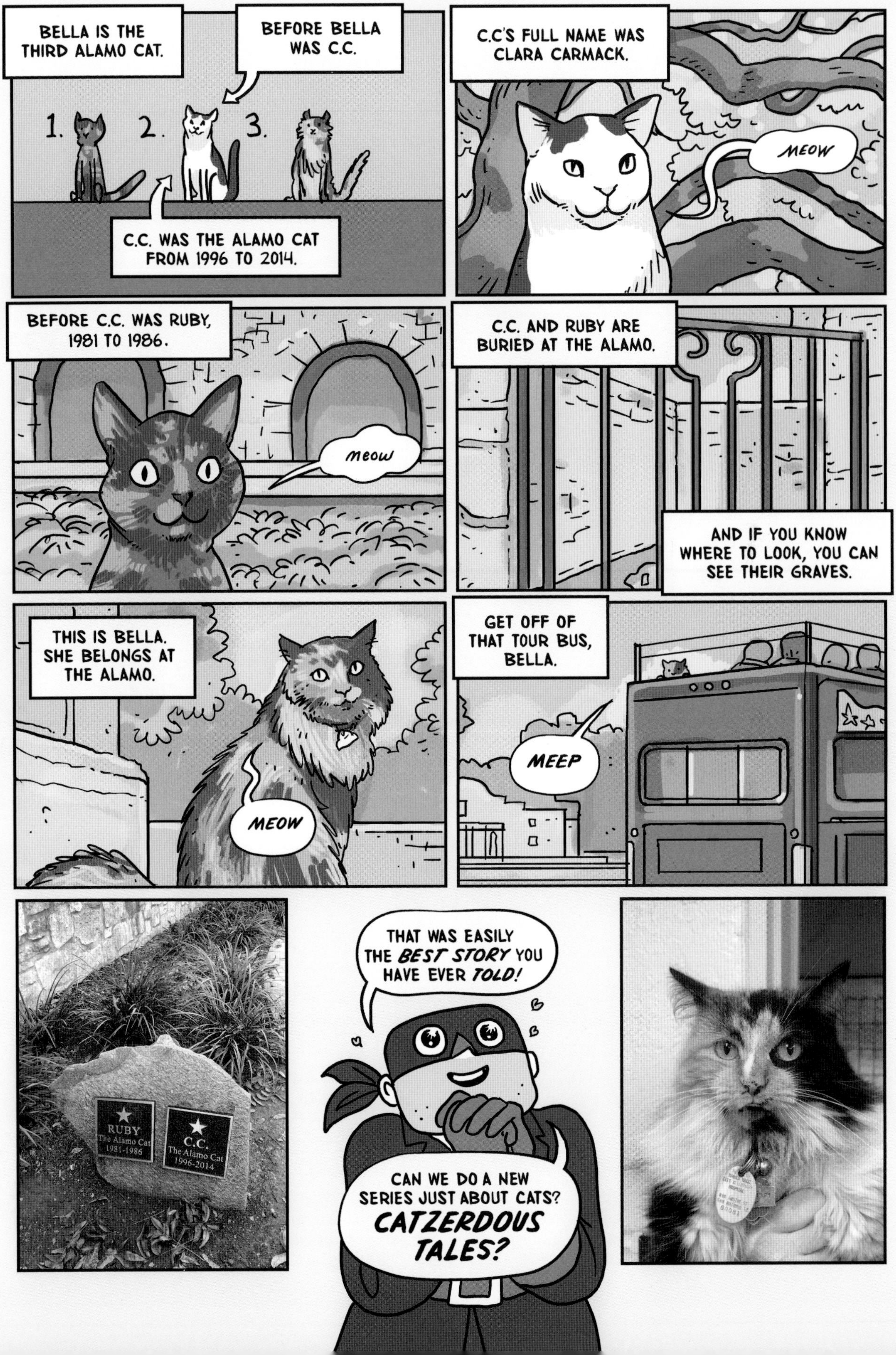
BELLA IS THE THIRD ALAMO CAT.
BEFORE BELLA WAS C.C.
1.
2.
3.
C.C. WAS THE ALAMO CAT FROM 1996 TO 2014.
C.C'S FULL NAME WAS CLARA CARMACK.
MEOW
BEFORE C.C. WAS RUBY, 1981 TO 1986.
meow
C.C. AND RUBY ARE BURIED AT THE ALAMO.
AND IF YOU KNOW WHERE TO LOOK, YOU CAN SEE THEIR GRAVES.
THIS IS BELLA. SHE BELONGS AT THE ALAMO.
MEOW
GET OFF OF THAT TOUR BUS, BELLA.
MEEP
RUBY
The Alamo Cat
1981-1986
C.C.
The Alamo Cat
1996-2014
THAT WAS EASILY THE *BEST STORY* YOU HAVE EVER *TOLD!*
CAN WE DO A NEW SERIES JUST ABOUT CATS? ***CATZERDOUS TALES?***

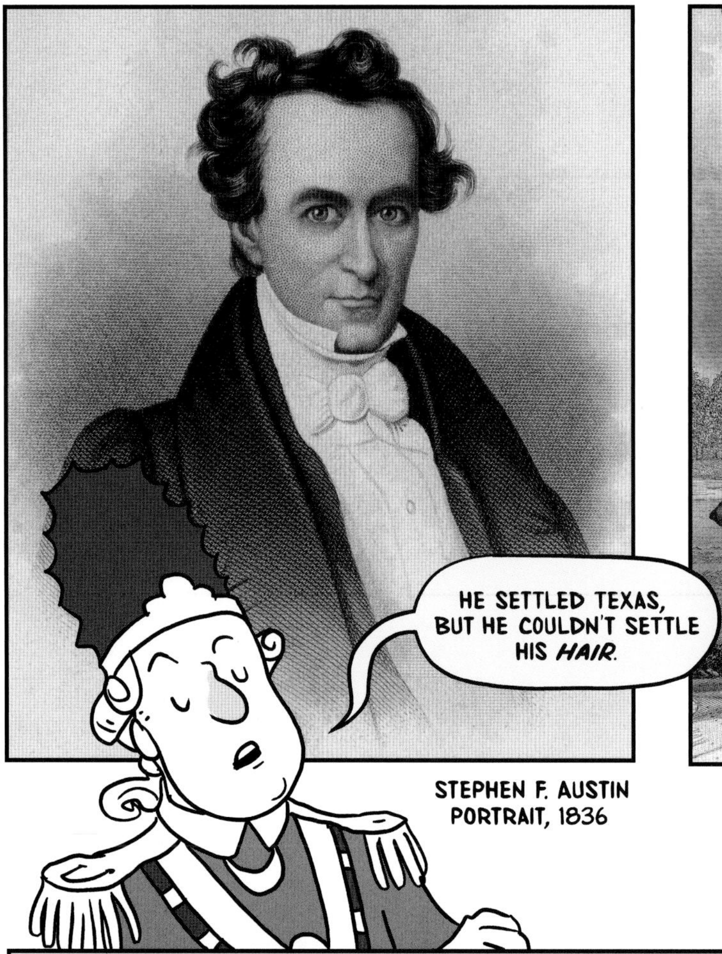
HE SETTLED TEXAS, BUT HE COULDN'T SETTLE HIS *HAIR*.

STEPHEN F. AUSTIN PORTRAIT, 1836

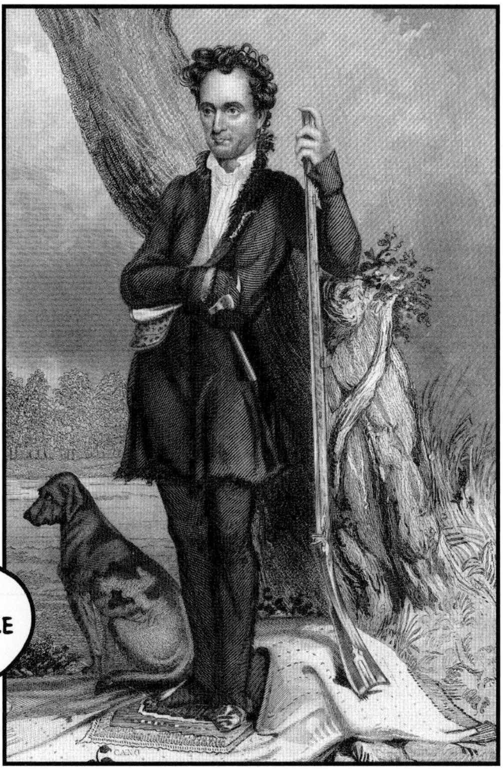

STEPHEN F. AUSTIN PRINT BASED ON MINIATURE PAINTING

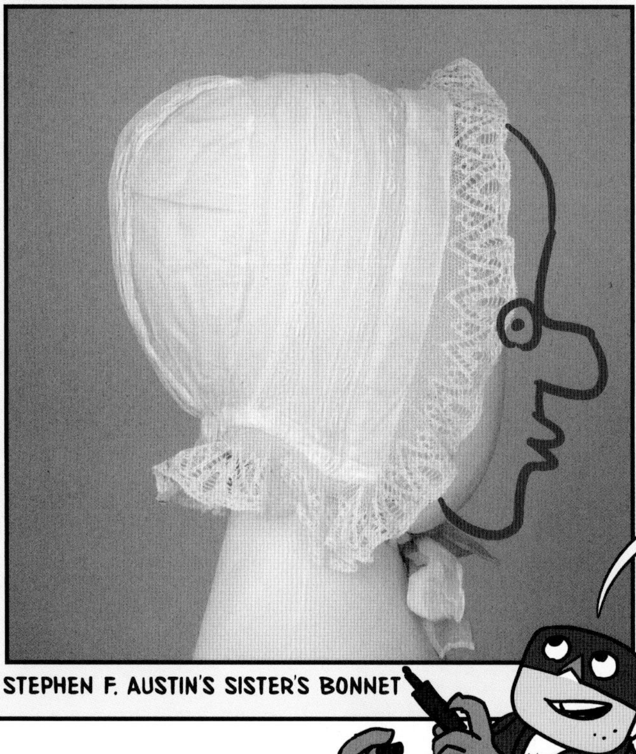

STEPHEN F. AUSTIN'S SISTER'S BONNET

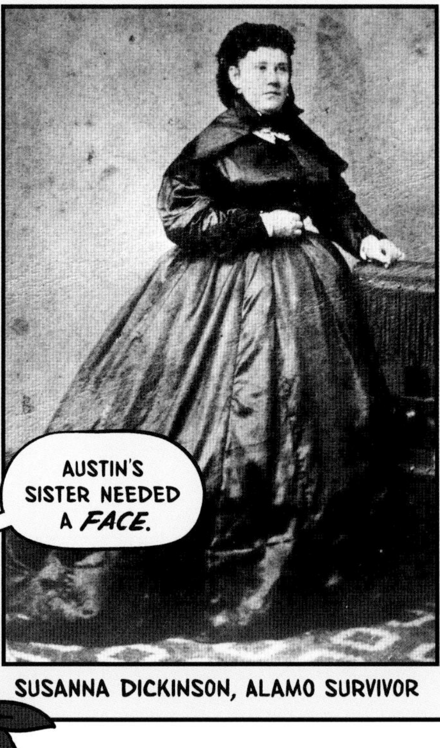
AUSTIN'S SISTER NEEDED A *FACE*.

SUSANNA DICKINSON, ALAMO SURVIVOR

THE GRAVES
OF ALAMO HEROES,
INCLUDING

WILLIAM B. TRAVIS,
DAVID CROCKETT,
AND JAMES BOWIE

IN THE CATHEDRAL
OF SAN FERNANDO,
SAN ANTONIO, TEXAS

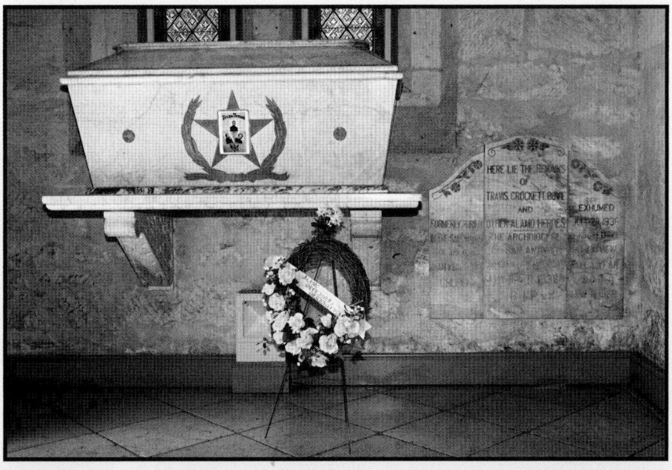
HERE LIE THE REMAINS
OF
TRAVIS CROCKETT BOWIE
AND
OTHER ALAMO HEROES

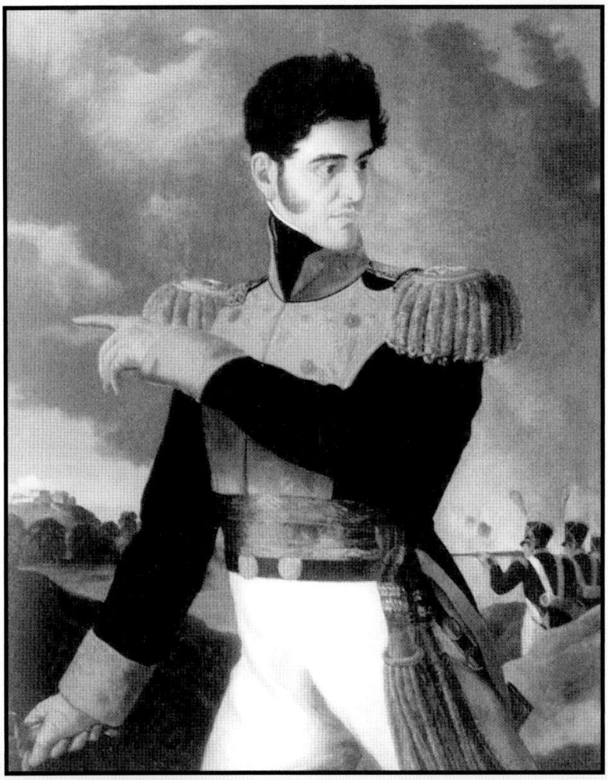

ANTONIO LÓPEZ DE SANTA ANNA

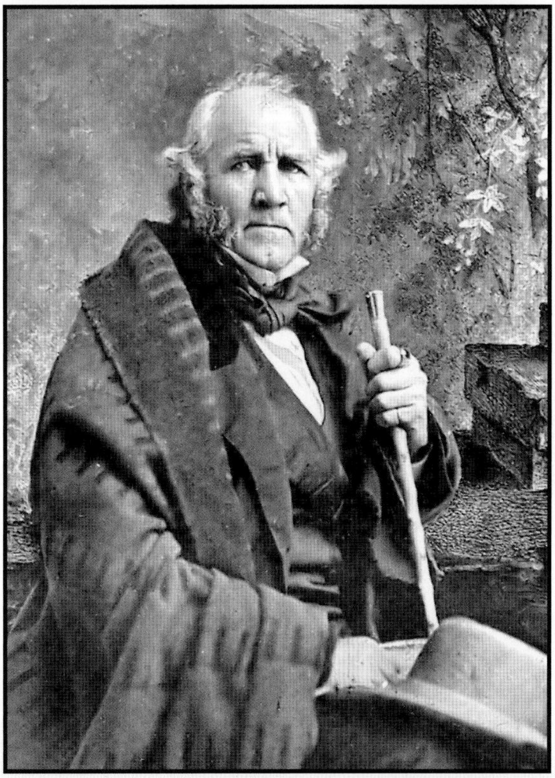

SAM HOUSTON

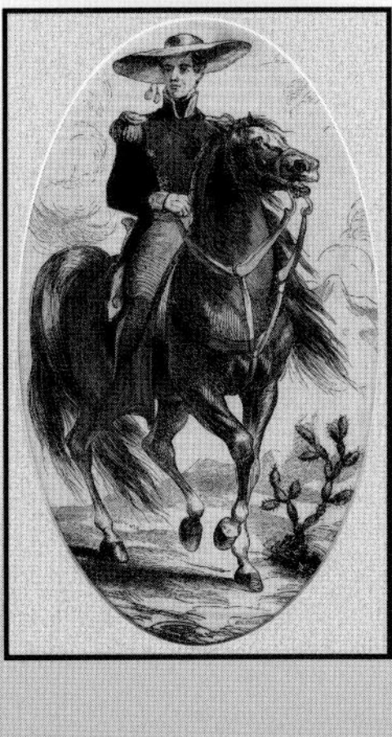

SANTA ANNA
ON HORSE
PRINT

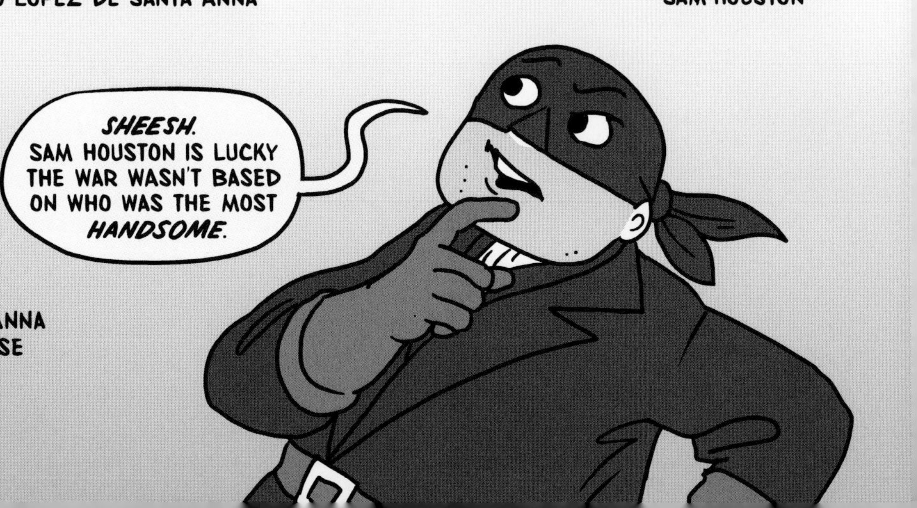
SHEESH. SAM HOUSTON IS LUCKY THE WAR WASN'T BASED ON WHO WAS THE MOST *HANDSOME*.

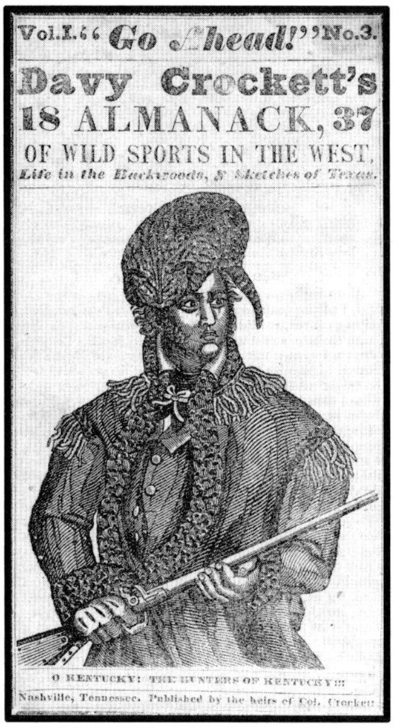
Vol.I. "Go Ahead!" No.3.
Davy Crockett's
18 ALMANACK, 37
OF WILD SPORTS IN THE WEST,
Life in the Backwoods, & Sketches of Texas.
O KENTUCKY: THE HUNTERS OF KENTUCKY!!!
Nashville, Tennessee. Published by the heirs of Col. Crockett.

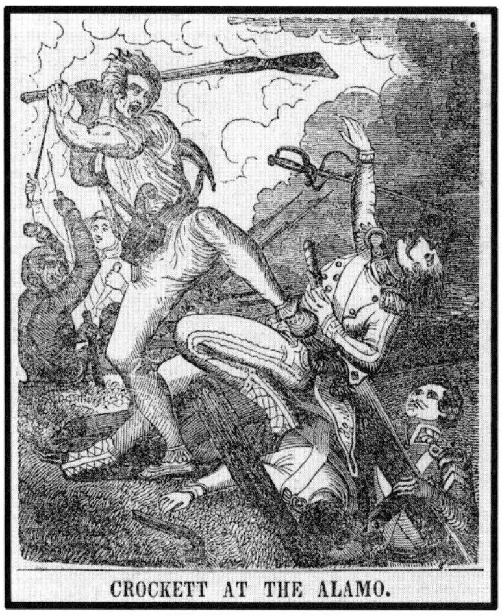
CROCKETT AT THE ALAMO.

CROCKETT AT THE ALAMO CARTOON

DAVY CROCKETT ALMANACK, 1837

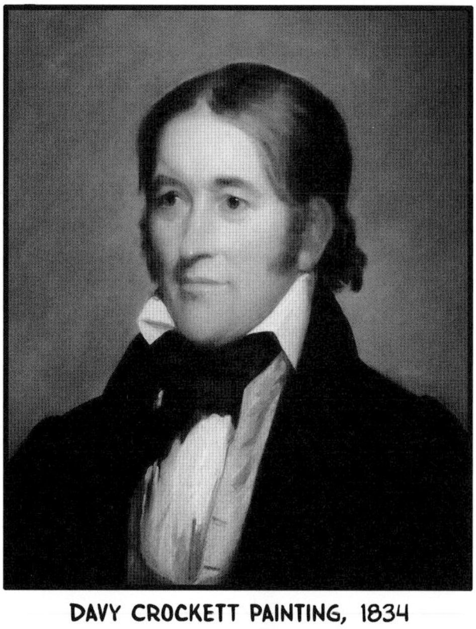

DAVY CROCKETT PAINTING, 1834

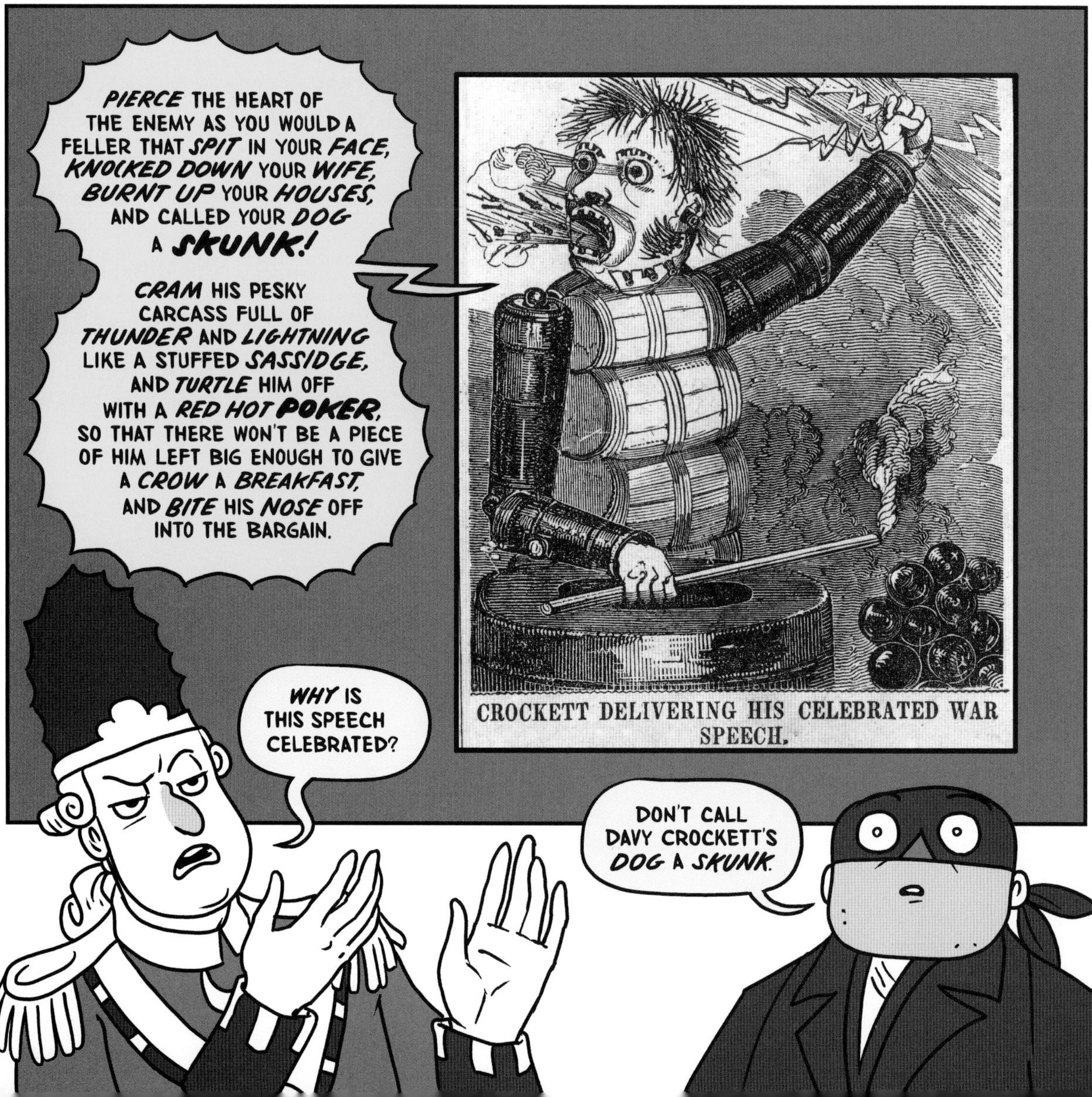
PIERCE THE HEART OF THE ENEMY AS YOU WOULD A FELLER THAT SPIT IN YOUR FACE, KNOCKED DOWN YOUR WIFE, BURNT UP YOUR HOUSES, AND CALLED YOUR DOG A SKUNK!
CRAM HIS PESKY CARCASS FULL OF THUNDER AND LIGHTNING LIKE A STUFFED SASSIDGE, AND TURTLE HIM OFF WITH A RED HOT POKER, SO THAT THERE WON'T BE A PIECE OF HIM LEFT BIG ENOUGH TO GIVE A CROW A BREAKFAST, AND BITE HIS NOSE OFF INTO THE BARGAIN.
CROCKETT DELIVERING HIS CELEBRATED WAR SPEECH.
WHY IS THIS SPEECH CELEBRATED?
DON'T CALL DAVY CROCKETT'S DOG A SKUNK.

VERY OLD BOWIE KNIFE

ONE OF THESE PORTRAITS IS A COPY CAT OF THE OTHER.

JIM BOWIE PORTRAITS

HOLY SMOKES! JIM BOWIE HAS A *TINY BABY EAGLE* FOR A *PET!*

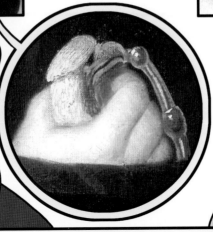

THAT'S NOT A PET EAGLE. IT'S A DECORATIVE SWORD POMMEL.

JOSÉ ANTONIO NAVARRO PHOTO

NAVARRO'S PRAYERBOOK

ADINA EMILIA DE ZAVALA AT VERAMENDI PALACE

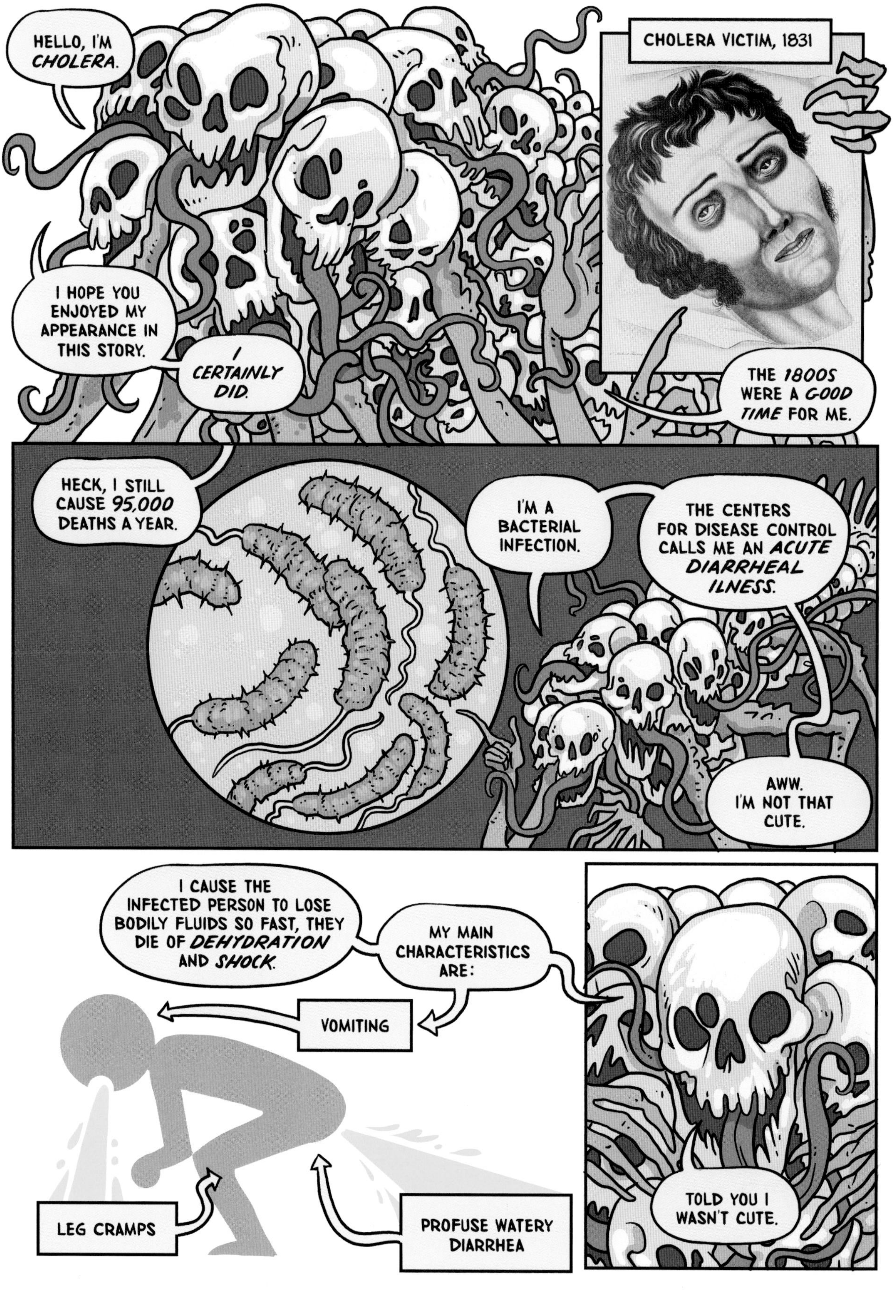

HELLO, I'M CHOLERA.
CHOLERA VICTIM, 1831
I HOPE YOU ENJOYED MY APPEARANCE IN THIS STORY.
I CERTAINLY DID.
THE 1800S WERE A GOOD TIME FOR ME.
HECK, I STILL CAUSE 95,000 DEATHS A YEAR.
I'M A BACTERIAL INFECTION.
THE CENTERS FOR DISEASE CONTROL CALLS ME AN ACUTE DIARRHEAL ILNESS.
AWW. I'M NOT THAT CUTE.
I CAUSE THE INFECTED PERSON TO LOSE BODILY FLUIDS SO FAST, THEY DIE OF DEHYDRATION AND SHOCK.
MY MAIN CHARACTERISTICS ARE:
VOMITING
LEG CRAMPS
PROFUSE WATERY DIARRHEA
TOLD YOU I WASN'T CUTE.

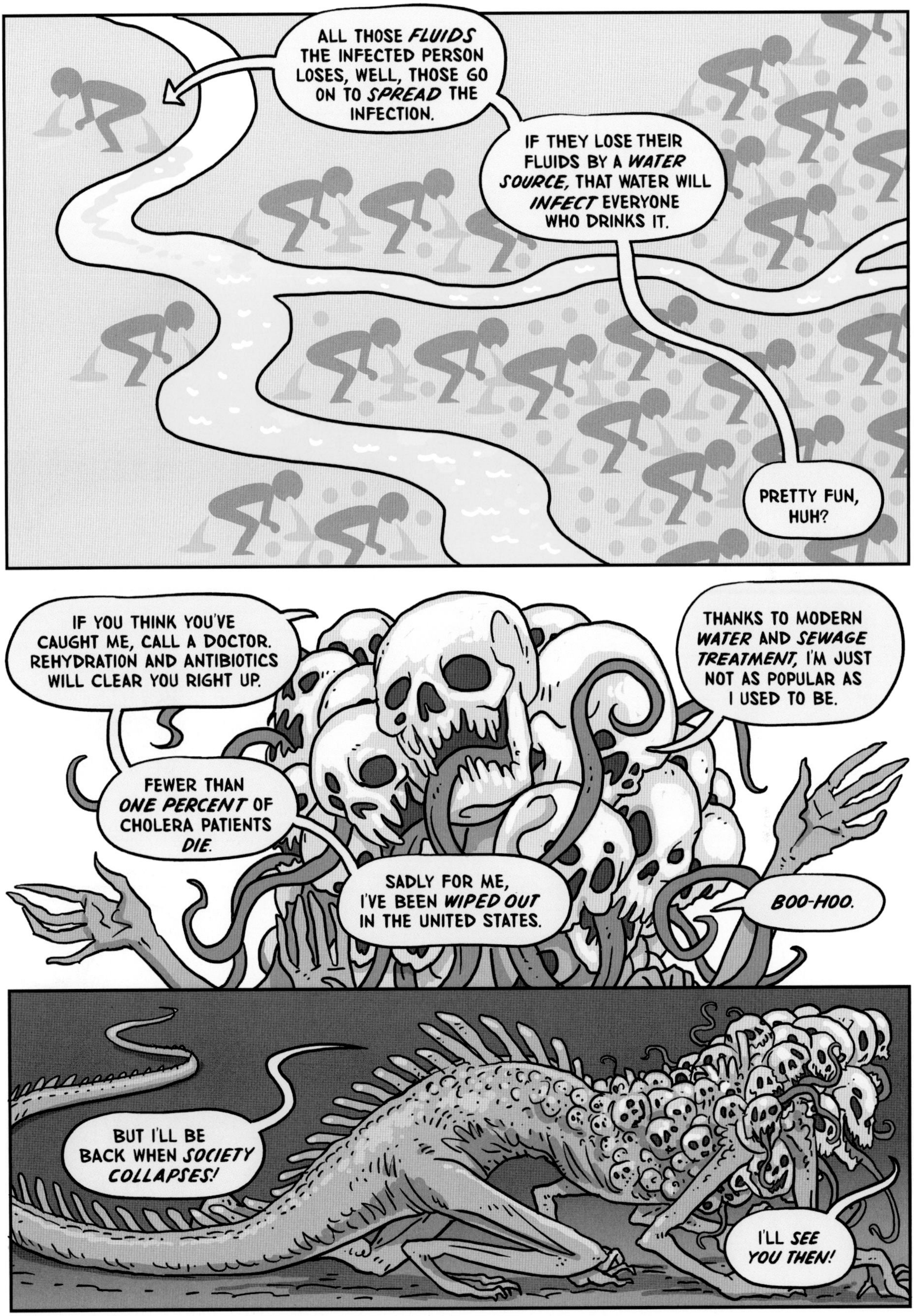
ALL THOSE FLUIDS THE INFECTED PERSON LOSES, WELL, THOSE GO ON TO SPREAD THE INFECTION.
IF THEY LOSE THEIR FLUIDS BY A WATER SOURCE, THAT WATER WILL INFECT EVERYONE WHO DRINKS IT.
PRETTY FUN, HUH?
IF YOU THINK YOU'VE CAUGHT ME, CALL A DOCTOR. REHYDRATION AND ANTIBIOTICS WILL CLEAR YOU RIGHT UP.
FEWER THAN ONE PERCENT OF CHOLERA PATIENTS DIE.
THANKS TO MODERN WATER AND SEWAGE TREATMENT, I'M JUST NOT AS POPULAR AS I USED TO BE.
SADLY FOR ME, I'VE BEEN WIPED OUT IN THE UNITED STATES.
BOO-HOO.
BUT I'LL BE BACK WHEN SOCIETY COLLAPSES!
I'LL SEE YOU THEN!

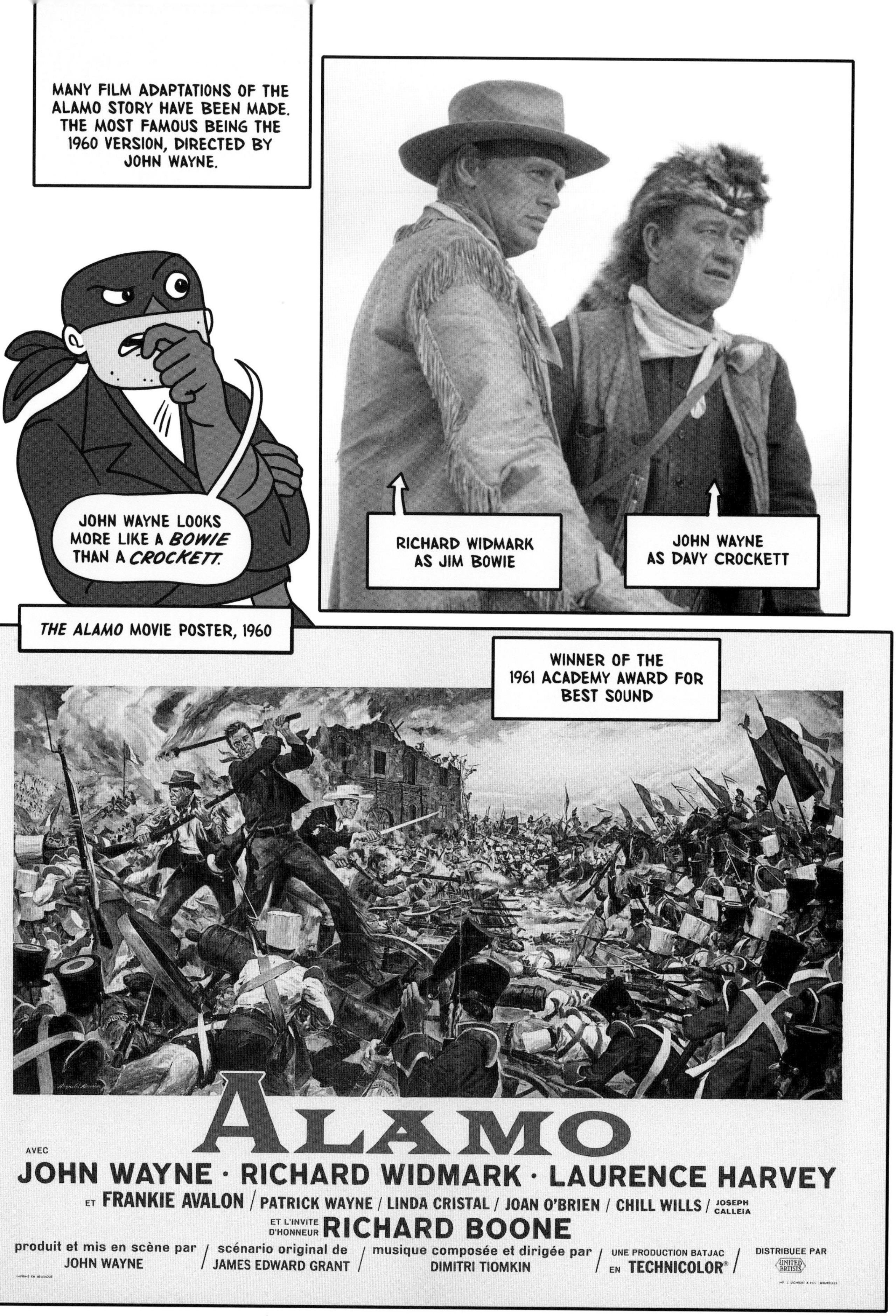
MANY FILM ADAPTATIONS OF THE ALAMO STORY HAVE BEEN MADE. THE MOST FAMOUS BEING THE 1960 VERSION, DIRECTED BY JOHN WAYNE.
RICHARD WIDMARK AS JIM BOWIE
JOHN WAYNE AS DAVY CROCKETT
JOHN WAYNE LOOKS MORE LIKE A *BOWIE* THAN A *CROCKETT*.
THE ALAMO MOVIE POSTER, 1960
WINNER OF THE 1961 ACADEMY AWARD FOR BEST SOUND
ALAMO
AVEC
JOHN WAYNE · RICHARD WIDMARK · LAURENCE HARVEY
ET FRANKIE AVALON / PATRICK WAYNE / LINDA CRISTAL / JOAN O'BRIEN / CHILL WILLS / JOSEPH CALLEIA
ET L'INVITE D'HONNEUR RICHARD BOONE
produit et mis en scène par JOHN WAYNE / scénario original de JAMES EDWARD GRANT / musique composée et dirigée par DIMITRI TIOMKIN / UNE PRODUCTION BATJAC EN TECHNICOLOR® / DISTRIBUEE PAR UNITED ARTISTS

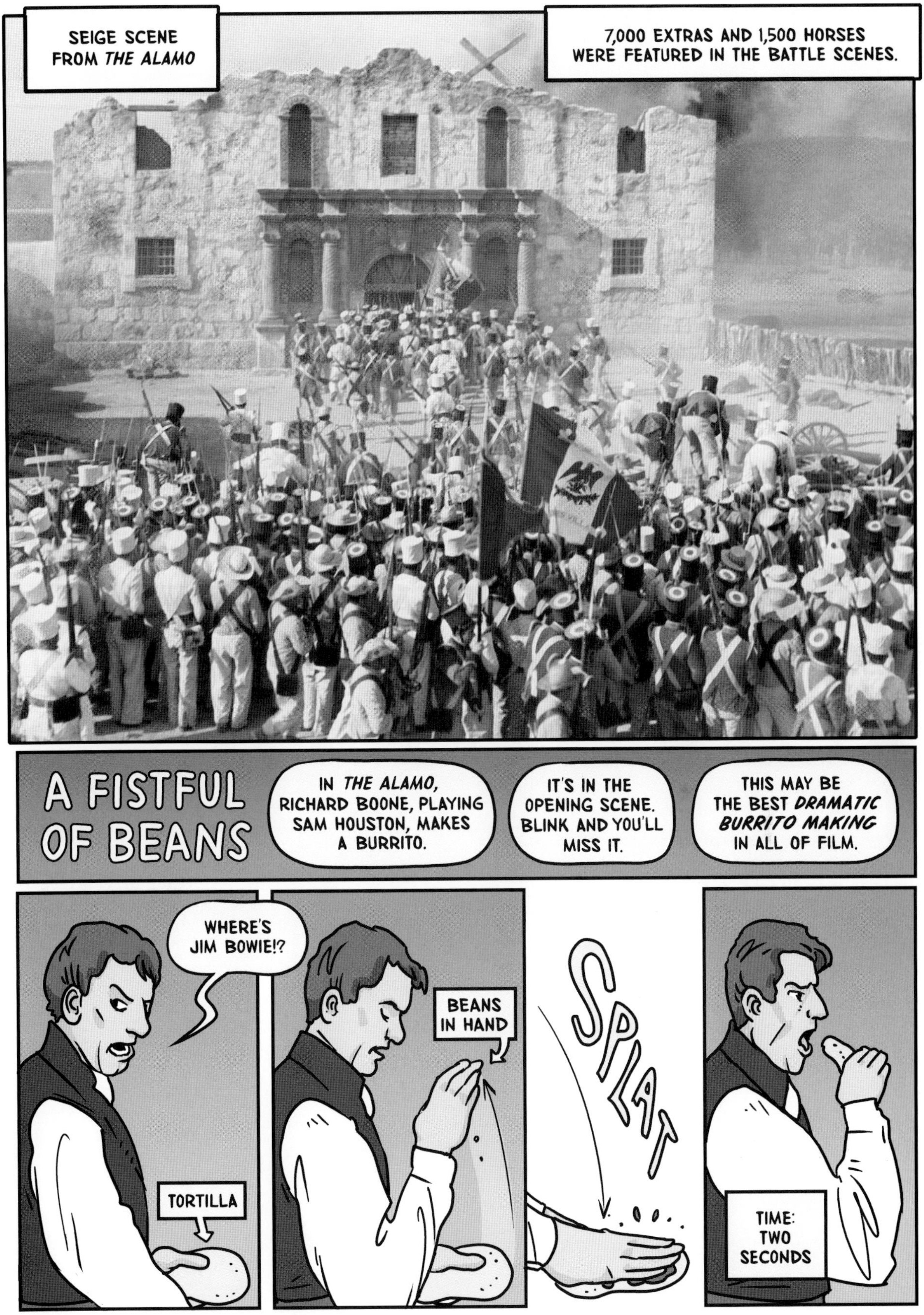
SEIGE SCENE FROM *THE ALAMO*
7,000 EXTRAS AND 1,500 HORSES WERE FEATURED IN THE BATTLE SCENES.
A FISTFUL OF BEANS
IN *THE ALAMO*, RICHARD BOONE, PLAYING SAM HOUSTON, MAKES A BURRITO.
IT'S IN THE OPENING SCENE. BLINK AND YOU'LL MISS IT.
THIS MAY BE THE BEST *DRAMATIC BURRITO MAKING* IN ALL OF FILM.
WHERE'S JIM BOWIE!?
TORTILLA
BEANS IN HAND
SPLAT
TIME: TWO SECONDS

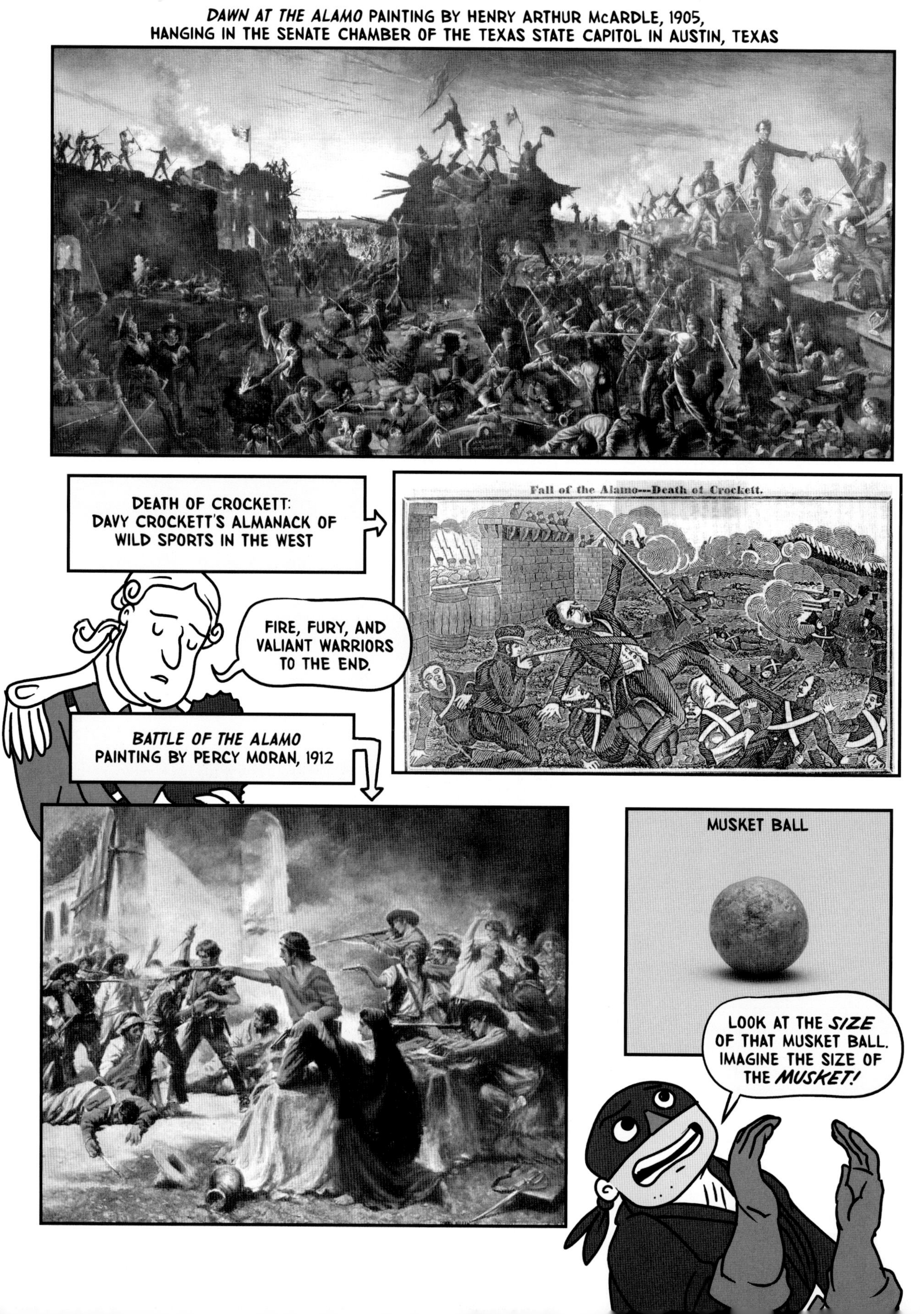
DAWN AT THE ALAMO PAINTING BY HENRY ARTHUR McARDLE, 1905,
HANGING IN THE SENATE CHAMBER OF THE TEXAS STATE CAPITOL IN AUSTIN, TEXAS
DEATH OF CROCKETT: DAVY CROCKETT'S ALMANACK OF WILD SPORTS IN THE WEST
Fall of the Alamo---Death of Crockett.
FIRE, FURY, AND VALIANT WARRIORS TO THE END.
BATTLE OF THE ALAMO PAINTING BY PERCY MORAN, 1912
MUSKET BALL
LOOK AT THE *SIZE* OF THAT MUSKET BALL. IMAGINE THE SIZE OF THE *MUSKET!*

PHIL COLLINS AND THE ALAMO

YOUNG PHIL COLLINS LIKED TWO THINGS: *DAVY CROCKETT*, AND PLAYING *DRUMS*.

HIS GRANDMOTHER CUT UP A FUR COAT TO MAKE HIM A COONSKIN CAP.

NOW YOU ARE A *PROPER* CROCKETT.

HE SAW THE JOHN WAYNE ALAMO MOVIE IN 1960.

WOO!

TEN YEARS LATER HE JOINED A BAND CALLED GENESIS.

HE WAS THE DRUMMER.

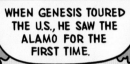

WHEN GENESIS TOURED THE U.S., HE SAW THE ALAMO FOR THE FIRST TIME.

OOOOH.

CAN WE *GO* NOW, PHIL?

PETER GABRIEL, LEAD SINGER

IN 1975 PHIL BECAME THE *LEAD SINGER* OF GENESIS.

CAN I *GO* NOW, PHIL?

PETER GABRIEL, SOLO ARTIST

GENESIS SOLD *150 MILLION* RECORDS.

PHIL COLLINS STARTED COLLECTING ALAMO ARTIFACTS.

PHIL BECAME A SOLO ARTIST.

HE SOLD *150 MILLION* RECORDS BY HIMSELF.

HE KEPT BUYING ALAMO ITEMS.

OVER THE YEARS, HE GATHERED POSSIBLY THE WORLD'S *LARGEST PRIVATE COLLECTION* OF ALAMO RELICS.

HE THEN *DONATED* HIS ENTIRE COLLECTION TO THE ALAMO.

PHIL'S ALAMO STUFF

HE GAVE RIFLES FROM CROCKETT, A BELT FROM TRAVIS, AND EVEN A JIM BOWIE KNIFE.

SOME PEOPLE WOULD BUY FERRARIS, SOME PEOPLE WOULD BUY HOUSES.

I BOUGHT OLD BITS OF METAL AND OLD BITS OF PAPER.

--QUOTE FROM AN ARTICLE ON HISTORY.COM

IN 2015 HE WAS MADE AN *HONORARY TEXAN*.

CROCKETT'S BULLET POUCH C1836

SHOT POUCH USED BY JESSE ROBINSON

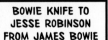

BOWIE KNIFE TO JESSE ROBINSON FROM JAMES BOWIE

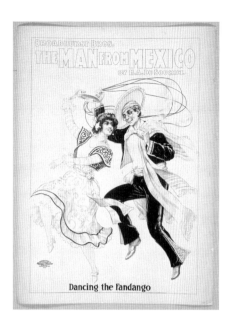

BROADHURST BROS.
THE MAN FROM MEXICO
BY H.A. DU SOUCHET
Dancing the Fandango

IMAGE CREDITS

PAGE 125: *LEFT AND CENTER:* COURTESY OF THE AUTHOR. *RIGHT:* © THE DOLPH BRISCOE CENTER FOR AMERICAN HISTORY, THE UNIVERSITY OF TEXAS AT AUSTIN.

PAGE 129: *BOTTOM LEFT AND BOTTOM RIGHT:* COURTESY OF THE AUTHOR.

PAGE 130: *TOP LEFT:* © PRINTS AND PHOTOGRAPHS COLLECTION, THE DOLPH BRISCOE CENTER FOR AMERICAN HISTORY. *TOP RIGHT:* © UT TEXAS MEMORIAL MUSEUM COLLECTION, DOLPH BRISCOE CENTER. *BOTTOM LEFT:* © DOLPH BRISCOE CENTER. *BOTTOM RIGHT:* © ADINA EMILIA DE ZAVALA PAPERS, DOLPH BRISCOE CENTER.

PAGE 131: *TOP:* CHRIS HOWES/WILD PLACES PHOTOGRAPHY/ALAMY STOCK PHOTO. *CENTER LEFT:* MUSEUM OF THE CITY OF MEXICO. *CENTER RIGHT:* MATHEW BRADY. *BOTTOM:* © BY W. H. DODD, PRINTS AND PHOTOGRAPHS COLLECTION, THE DOLPH BRISCOE CENTER FOR AMERICAN HISTORY.

PAGE 132: *TOP LEFT:* © DAVY CROCKETT'S ALMANACK, 1837, THE DOLPH BRISCOE CENTER FOR AMERICAN HISTORY. *TOP CENTER:* © THE IDLE HOUR BOOK OR SCRAPIANA, DOLPH BRISCOE CENTER. *TOP RIGHT:* NIDAY PICTURE LIBRARY/ALAMY STOCK PHOTO. *BOTTOM:* FOTOSEARCH/GETTY IMAGES.

PAGE 133: *TOP:* MICHA KLOOTWIJK/ALAMY STOCK PHOTO. *CENTER LEFT:* JAMES BOWIE, ACCESSION ID: CHA 2001.004; COURTESY STATE PRESERVATION BOARD, AUSTIN, TEXAS; ORIGINAL ARTIST UNKNOWN; PHOTOGRAPHER: ERIC BEGGS, JUNE 25, 2004, POST CONSERVATION. *CENTER RIGHT:* © SAMUEL B. HILL, PRINTS AND PHOTOGRAPHS COLLECTION, THE DOLPH BRISCOE CENTER FOR AMERICAN HISTORY. *BOTTOM LEFT:* © PRINTS AND PHOTOGRAPHS COLLECTION, DOLPH BRISCOE CENTER. *BOTTOM CENTER:* © C. BURT, UNIVERSITY OF TEXAS MEMORIAL MUSEUM COLLECTION CREATOR, DOLPH BRISCOE CENTER. *BOTTOM RIGHT:* © ADINA EMILIA DE ZAVALA PAPERS, DOLPH BRISCOE CENTER.

PAGE 134: SCIENCE HISTORY IMAGES/ALAMY STOCK PHOTO.

PAGE 136: *TOP:* SCREENPROD/PHOTONONSTOP/ALAMY STOCK PHOTO. *BOTTOM:* SILVERSCREEN/ALAMY STOCK PHOTO.

PAGE 137: AF ARCHIVE/ALAMY STOCK PHOTO.

PAGE 138: *TOP AND BOTTOM LEFT:* LIBRARY OF CONGRESS. *CENTER:* © THE DOLPH BRISCOE CENTER FOR AMERICAN HISTORY. *BOTTOM RIGHT:* © SAN JACINTO MUSEUM.

PAGE 139: *BOTTOM, ALL IMAGES:* ROBERT DAEMMRICH PHOTOGRAPHY INC/CORBIS/GETTY IMAGES.

PAGE 140: LIBRARY OF CONGRESS.

SPECIAL THANKS TO:

SHERRI DRISCOLL,
DIRECTOR OF EDUCATION,
THE ALAMO

ERNESTO RODRIGUEZ III,
ASSOCIATE CURATOR,
THE ALAMO

MACHAIA MCCLENNY,
EDUCATION SPECIALIST,
THE ALAMO

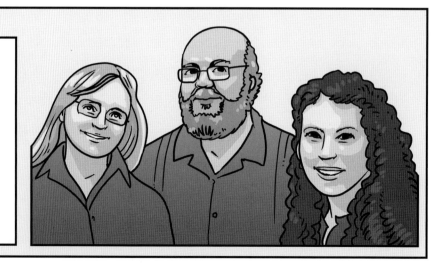

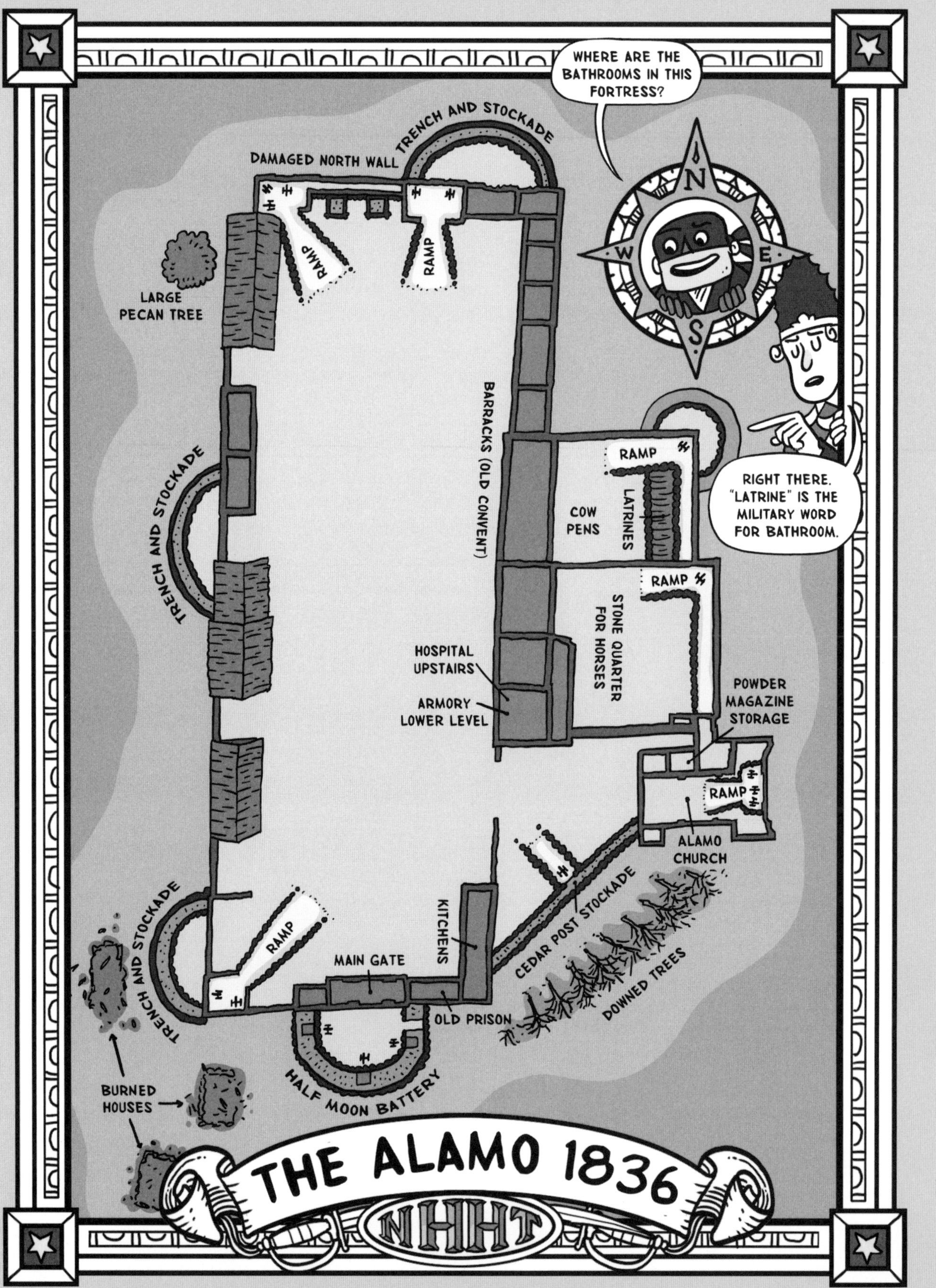
WHERE ARE THE BATHROOMS IN THIS FORTRESS?
RIGHT THERE. "LATRINE" IS THE MILITARY WORD FOR BATHROOM.
N
E
S
W
TRENCH AND STOCKADE
DAMAGED NORTH WALL
RAMP
RAMP
LARGE PECAN TREE
BARRACKS (OLD CONVENT)
TRENCH AND STOCKADE
RAMP
COW PENS
LATRINES
RAMP
STONE QUARTER FOR HORSES
HOSPITAL UPSTAIRS
ARMORY LOWER LEVEL
POWDER MAGAZINE STORAGE
RAMP
ALAMO CHURCH
CEDAR POST STOCKADE
DOWNED TREES
KITCHENS
RAMP
MAIN GATE
OLD PRISON
TRENCH AND STOCKADE
HALF MOON BATTERY
BURNED HOUSES
THE ALAMO 1836
NHHT